*The La Salle Expedition to Texas*

The unfortunate Adventures of the Sieur de la Salle.

# The La Salle Expedition to Texas

## THE JOURNAL OF HENRI JOUTEL
## 1684–1687

EDITED AND WITH AN INTRODUCTION BY WILLIAM C. FOSTER

TRANSLATED BY JOHANNA S. WARREN

Texas State Historical Association

Austin

First paperback printing, November 2014

*Library of Congress Cataloging-in-Publication Data:*
Joutel, Henri, 1640?–1735
    The La Salle expedition to Texas : the journal of Henri Joutel, 1684–1687 / edited and with an introduction by William C. Foster ; translated by Johanna S. Warren.
    p.        cm.
    Translation of the version of Henri Joutel's journal found in v. 3 of Pierre Margry's compilation, Découvertes et établissements des Français dans l'ouest et dans le sud de l'Amérique septentrionale, 1614–1754.
    Includes bibliographical references and index.
    ISBN 0-87611-165-7 (alk. paper)
    1. La Salle, Robert Cavelier, Sieur de, 1643–1687.  2. Joutel, Henri, 1640?–1735—Diaries.  3. Mississippi River Valley—Discovery and exploration.  4. Texas—History—To 1846.  5. Texas—Discovery and exploration.  6. Gulf Region (Tex.)—Discovery and exploration.  7. Indians of North America—Texas—History—17th century.
    I. Foster, William C., 1928–  .  II. Title.
F352.J68         1998
977' .01' 092—dc21                                                98-6924
                                                                   CIP

5    4    3    2                                                 00    01    02

Published by the Texas State Historical Association in cooperation with the Center for Studies in Texas History at the University of Texas at Austin. Publication of this book is partially supported by a grant from the Summerfield G. Roberts Foundation, Dallas.

∞ The paper used in this book meets the minimum requirements of the American National Standard for Permanence of Paper for Printed Library Materials, z39.48—1984.

Designed by David Timmons

*Frontispiece:* "The unfortunate Adventures of the Sieur de la Salle" is an imaginative engraving of La Salle's 1685 landing on the Texas coast. From L. Hennepin, *A New Discovery of a Vast Country. . . .(1698) Courtesy Center for American History, The University of Texas at Austin, CN 09719.*

To my Norman Grandfather
William Guy Crozier

# Contents

∞

*Appendices*

# ILLUSTRATIONS

# Preface

n preparing the manuscript *Spanish Expeditions into Texas, 1689–1768*, I discovered that several very significant seventeenth- and eighteenth-century diaries, journals, and histories relating to Texas had not been translated from French or Spanish into English, and I found that many contemporary historians, anthropologists, archeologists, and geographers were reluctant to use or cite these important untranslated documents. With the support of the Texas State Historical Association, the University of Texas Press, and a number of scholars including Jack Jackson and several professional translators, I have advanced the English translation and annotation of the diaries of Alonso de León's 1686 and 1690 expeditions, Governor Gregorio de Salinas Varona's 1693 expedition, Brigadier Pedro de Rivera's 1727 inspection tour, Marqués de Rubí's 1767 expedition, and Juan Bautista Chapa's history of Texas and Northeastern Mexico from 1630 to 1690. This translation continues that effort by making available in English a widely acclaimed French classic, Henri Joutel's journal of La Salle's expedition to Texas.

The work covers La Salle's voyage from France in late 1684 to his landing on the Texas coast in early 1685, his journeys southwest toward Mexico and northeast toward the Mississippi in 1685 and 1686, and his final trip in 1687. On the last journey, La Salle was assassinated, and Joutel and a small French party led by a succession of Indian guides continued across modern-day Texas to the Red River and across Arkansas to the Mississippi River, where this account closes. Joutel and his party proceeded up the Mississippi to Canada and returned to France, arriving there in 1688.

The book is a translation of Henri Joutel's journal found in Volume III of Pierre Margry's *Découvertes et établissements des Français dans l'ouest et dans le sud de l'Amérique Septentrionale, 1614–1754*. A transcript copy of Joutel's unedited manuscript (with passages missing) is held in the Manuscript Division of the Library of Congress, which graciously provided a photostatic copy of the document for use in this study.

Joutel's journal gives the most complete and accurate account of La Salle's expedition to Texas and thereby helps answer a number of unresolved geographical questions regarding the venture, such as where La Salle landed on the Texas coast, where he was killed, the current names of rivers given French names by La Salle, and the line of march from the Texas coast to the Mississippi taken by La Salle and his surviving party. The projection of La Salle's 1687 overland route is made in this study with a high degree of confidence because Joutel records daily the distance traveled in 1687 in French leagues and the direction by compass. Confidence is enhanced as La Salle's route follows in large part the same clearly identified Indian trade routes that numerous Spanish expeditions followed from present-day Mexico to East Texas soon after La Salle's death.

The translation of Joutel's journal was prepared by Johanna S. Warren, a linguist who presently resides in the Washington, D.C., area and in Marathon, Texas. The meticulous care and attention to detail that Warren devoted to our translation fully matches Joutel's own commitment to accuracy. Diana Carr and Richard Carr, professors of French at Indiana University, clarified numerous archaic French words or passages. Cynthia Kaul, author/sailor, was very helpful in translating passages in the first three chapters involving sailing vessel movements and French nautical terms. Ned P. Brierley and Adela Pacheco Cobb of Washington, D.C., provided valuable assistance in translating the important interrogation of Pierre Meunier from Spanish into English (Appendix A).

Jack and Christina Jackson again provided exceptional service in reviewing the manuscript and suggesting improvements and maps and documents to be consulted. The preparation of the manuscript was blessed with having an anonymous reader who was eminently knowledgable with respect to La Salle's venture and extremely helpful in seeking an accurate and balanced story. The numerous maps included in the study were prepared by John V. Cotter, the highly skilled cartographer who was responsible for the excellent maps included in my earlier Spanish expedition route studies.

*The La Salle Expedition to Texas*

A portrait of René-Robert Cavelier, Sieur de La Salle, used as a frontispiece of Paul
Chesnel's *History of Cavalier de La Salle* (Paris, 1901). *Courtesy Center for American History, The
University of Texas at Austin, CN 09718.*

# Introduction

n the early hours of March 19, 1687, the great French explorer René-Robert Cavelier, Sieur de La Salle, was camped with his entourage deep in the Texas wilderness. There was a sense of uneasiness in the camp as La Salle approached his trusted aide Henri Joutel with a change in plans. Joutel explained the situation in his journal entry for that day: "La Salle had first decided that I should go with him, [but] he changed his mind in the morning because there would be no one to remain on watch at that camp. . . . After that he told me to give him my musket because it was the best one of our party; I gave it to him with my pistol. Thus, three of them left: La Salle, Father Anastase, and the Indian guide. In leaving the gentleman ordered me to take care of everything and to be sure, from time to time, to make smoke signals on a small rise near our camp, so that if they were lost, that would serve to set them straight and direct them toward the smoke. So they departed. Only five of us remained there which was not much defense. . . .

"As La Salle, on leaving, had directed me to make smoke signals from hour to hour by setting fire to the small area of dry grass on a rise that would flare for a while, I carried out this maneuver during the day. But toward evening I was greatly surprised . . . to see one of the men approaching. . . . When we met, I saw that he was quite stupified and rather wandering. On approaching me, he began to tell me that there was much news and that a mishap had occurred. I asked him what. He told me that La Salle was dead. . . .

"At this news I stopped, completely disconcerted, not knowing what to say. . . . The person who brought me this ugly news added that the murderers had at first sworn my death as well. I had no trouble believing that because, as I said before, I had always acted in the interests of La Salle. Having command, it is difficult to satisfy everyone and to prevent there being a few malcontents. At this juncture, I was greatly confounded as to what part I should take, if I should go off into the forest where Providence and God would lead me. . . . In no matter what direction I should turn, my life was at great risk."

4

What strange currents of history had brought the great explorer to the distant forests of Spanish Texas, only to be murdered by his own men? What forces would be unleashed by the presence of the Frenchmen in territory that was claimed by Spain? What did they seek in the New World, and what did they find? Ultimately what were the legacies of La Salle's adventures in Texas—besides his death? La Salle's faithful lieutenant Henri Joutel, who accompanied his leader and wrote about these events at great length in his journal, provides many of the keys to this significant French expedition to the New World. It was both a grand, tragic adventure, and an event with international implications; the French presence resulted in significant new Spanish exploration and settlement in Texas. With great care and humor, and with great intelligence and insight, Henri Joutel left a superb written record that has the power of a great adventure story and the gravity of the truth.

In 1685 La Salle landed at Matagorda Bay, on the coast of Texas between present-day Galveston and Corpus Christi. He had left France in July 1684 with four ships and nearly three hundred people, intent upon gathering further glory for himself and the French crown by establishing a military colony on the Mississippi River. The expedition encountered trouble from the beginning. En route La Salle lost one ship to Spanish privateers and later, nearly one third of his settlers and men to disease. Overshooting the Mississippi with La Salle's fleet, the supply ship, *L'Aimable*, ran aground and broke apart at the entrance to Matagorda Bay, and her disenchanted crew and several would-be colonists returned to France on a third ship. The remaining 180 people took their limited supplies farther inland and established Fort Saint Louis, while La Salle explored westward, perhaps far up the Rio Grande. The settlers suffered another blow when their remaining link to the outside world, the bark *La Belle*, grounded and was wrecked during a winter storm in 1686. Convinced now that he had landed too far west, La Salle led a small party eastward the following year, hoping to reach a French settlement in the Illinois Territory. He was killed by one of his own men during the journey. The rest of the party made their way through the wilderness to the Mississippi, then upriver to Canada. Only six of them returned to France. One was Henri Joutel, and his journal is the most complete and accurate account of this ill-fated but historic French incursion into Spanish Texas.

Joutel had been La Salle's neighbor in France, and La Salle had confidence in him. He served for two years as post commander of Fort Saint Louis and, finally, was a member, and sometimes leader, of the small band of soldiers, deserters, priests, and murderers who crossed central and northeast Texas and southern Arkansas en route to the Mississippi and home. Both French and American scholars recognize his account of the La Salle expedition as the most comprehensive and authoritative, and this book constitutes the first published and fully annotated English translation of Pierre Margry's version of the journal.[1]

---

[1] Pierre Margry (ed.), *Découvertes et établissements des Francais dans l'ouest et dans le sud de l'Amérique Septentrionale, 1614–1754* (6 vols.; Paris: D. Jouaust, 1876–1886), III, 91–534. In his comments on Margry's version of Joutel's journal, John H. Jenkins notes that "Ironically, no edition in English has ever appeared." See *Basic Texas Books: An Annotated Bibliography of Selected Works for a Research Library*, rev. ed. (Austin: Texas State Historical Association, 1988), 301.

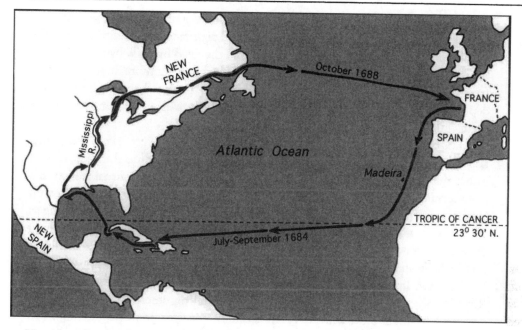

Henri Joutel's route from France to the New World and back, 1684–1688

Joutel's journal is a true French-American classic. Using careful notes taken over a four-year period, this engaging author and precise military man produced a true adventure story set in a Texas coastal wilderness occupied by dangerous wild animals and exotic plants and populated by strange, unknown, and sometimes hostile natives. With a passion for detail and accuracy, he identifies more than eighty Indian tribes and describes more than eighty species of wild animals and native and domesticated plants, more than any subsequent seventeenth-century Spanish expedition diarist in Texas. With a flair for the dramatic, Joutel tells a suspenseful and sometimes humorous story in such an intimate fashion that the reader finds a comfortable place in the narrative. Joutel, for example, tells and retells the riveting story of La Salle's assassination, giving first his own account and then that given him by the priest Anastase Douay, who was at La Salle's side when his leader was murdered. Joutel later provides an account by Jean L'Archevêque, an accomplice to the murder. And, in Appendix A, one of Joutel's soldier-companions, Pierre Meunier, who was also at the scene when La Salle was shot, offers his version.

Joutel reveals an unexpected humorous side as he relates some of the lighter and more comical episodes of the expedition. With perhaps a twinkle in his eye, he recounts the tale of an Indian chasing on foot a seriously wounded and maddened bison that would, at times, turn on the Indian. The two wound up wildly chasing each other in circles, accompanied by the howls and cheers of the nearby Indians and Frenchmen. He also tells of an incident in which he accidently kicked the priest Douay hard in the stomach as the two were desperately trying to swim across a large, raging creek holding on to a floating log.

Nor do the rich details of Indian life—ceremonies, dress, huts, and methods of hunting, planting crops, and preparing food—escape Joutel's attention. His

6 respect for Indian ways is evident in the care and detail he uses to describe the exact gestures the natives used in greetings and sign language and to portray the deeply spiritual manner in which they honored the dead by daily bringing food to the grave sites. His portrayal of them evolves as he becomes more aware of the differences among the various cultures, and as the French become increasingly dependent on the natives to guide them toward the Mississippi, and to furnish them with food and supplies along the way.

The entire French party faced overwhelming hardships such as disease, injury, and the death of all too many friends and companions as well as their leader, but, rather than being a dull recitation of facts and figures, Joutel's journal is instead a page-turning adventure story that draws the reader in and makes the seventeenth century come alive. The translation is fashioned to be easily readable, expressing as clearly as possible the author's thoughts. Annotations will help clarify the meaning of certain terms Joutel uses; identify and locate the rivers, Indian camps and villages that La Salle and Joutel visited; delineate, as precisely as possible, the line of march La Salle and Joutel's party followed from the Gulf of Mexico to the Mississippi River in 1687; and identify the flora and fauna the author described. Texas botanists Scooter Cheatham and Lynn Marshall carefully reviewed Joutel's descriptions of both native and domesticated plants; their professional comments are in the annotations. Accompanying Joutel's account are maps prepared by John V. Cotter, and, in the appendices, the table of the names of Indian tribes reported on La Salle's expedition, Joutel's 1687 itinerary from Matagorda Bay to the middle Mississippi, and the translation of Pierre Meunier's account of La Salle's expedition.

A number of recent archeological studies conducted near La Salle's post and his 1687 expedition route across Texas and Arkansas have provided significant information that supplements Joutel's account. These studies, which are referenced in the notes, help confirm where events Joutel mentions occurred and help determine the more precise location of the French post on Garcitas Creek and the Indian villages Joutel identifies on the Red River and the Arkansas River.

In addition, the discovery of La Salle's ship *La Belle* in 1995, and its subsequent recovery, which has yielded hundreds of thousands of artifacts, will further expand our understanding of many facets of the La Salle saga, as will the assessment the Texas Historical Commission is conducting of cannon found near the site of Fort Saint Louis. In March 1998 the Texas Historical Commission and the National Underwater and Marine Agency announced the discovery of the wreck of a ship believed to be *L'Aimable*, the largest of La Salle's ships and the one that contained many of his personal belongings. Subsequent tests proved that the wreck was not La Salle's ship, but the speculation and publicity about the possibility that it was *L'Aimable* have indicated continuing public interest in La Salle's expedition to Texas. If *L'Aimable*, which was perhaps six times larger than *La Belle*, is eventually discovered, the recovery of its artifacts will add another chapter to this exciting story.

La Salle's expedition was a journey of epic proportions that had global consequences. Joutel's narrative of the French party's adventures and misadventures is set historically in the center of a violent continental struggle for control of the New World. Spain's discovery of the Americas in the late fifteenth century

Eight French cannon discovered in 1996 at the site of Fort Saint Louis on Garcitas Creek. This project, as well as the wreck of La Salle's *La Belle*, discovered in 1995, has provided archeologists and historians with thousands of tangible artifacts from La Salle's remarkable expedition to Texas. *Courtesy Texas Historical Commission.*

signaled not only the commencement of a fierce rivalry among the dominant western European nations but also a broader conflict between Europeans and the indigenous Americans who, according to some contemporary scholars, had a population in 1492 of over 70 million, roughly equivalent to that of western Europe. By the late seventeenth century when La Salle sailed to the Gulf of Mexico, however, the Native American population in parts of Northern Mexico and Texas had been seriously reduced by perhaps over fifty percent because of highly contagious and deadly European diseases. By 1684, the three principal European powers (Spain, France, and England) were well established on the North American mainland and in the Caribbean. The northern Gulf of Mexico, from present-day Florida to Texas, was one of the battlegrounds of the rivalry between Spain and France.[2]

An understanding of the natural environment and ecology of the Texas Gulf region, including the climatic changes that were occurring in the seventeenth century, is necessary to follow Joutel's account. Equally important is an appreciation of the geographical areas occupied by the major Indian tribes La Salle and his people

[2] One of the finest histories of this rivalry is William Edward Dunn, *Spanish and French Rivalry in the Gulf Region of the United States, 1678–1702, The Beginnings of Texas and Pensacola* (Austin: University of Texas, 1917). For a more recent account of the rivalry, see Henry Folmer, *Franco-Spanish Rivalry in North America, 1524–1763* (Glendale, Calif.: A. H. Clark, 1953).

encountered as well as knowledge of which principal European powers controlled which areas of the North American mainland and Caribbean islands in the 1680s. Following this ecological and geographical overview, the introduction briefly reviews La Salle's life up to the time of his 1684 embarkation from France and then examines in more detail the perplexing geographical questions surrounding La Salle's expedition route and the areas in which native tribes were encountered in Texas and Arkansas. Finally, a review of Joutel's ethnographic contribution to the understanding of the native population between the central Texas coast and the middle Mississippi in the late seventeenth century is given before presenting Joutel's account of the La Salle expedition.

## TEXAS NATURAL ENVIRONMENT AND HUMAN ECOLOGY

An understanding of the major Texas river systems and the natural topography and escarpment patterns of Central Texas are critical to our interpretation of Joutel's account. Most major Texas rivers flow from the northwest to southeast, and the Balcones and Oakville escarpments and the Post Oak Belt intersect the river systems by running southwest to northeast. This geologic and botanical mosaic is fashioned upon a rather flat terrain that rises only a few hundred feet from the Gulf prairies inland for several hundred miles. Annual precipitation increases today from under ten inches in the west to over sixty inches in the eastern parts of Texas. La Salle's 1687 expedition, like many seventeenth- and eighteenth-century Spanish expeditions, originated in the southwest or coastal area and moved northeast. Joutel's account reports crossing major rivers every fifty to one hundred miles, events that serve as natural benchmarks in making accurate projections of expedition routes. From the Colorado crossing, Joutel's party followed the southern edge of the Oakville Escarpment northeastward, with the thirty- to fifty-mile-wide dense Post Oak Belt to the north serving as a natural barrier.

Significant global climatic changes were occurring in North America before and during the period of French exploration in the Gulf.[3] Climatologists agree that the broad warming climatic trend that developed about twelve millennia ago (10,000 B.C.) melted the ice cap and snow pack that covered parts of North America, including the Great Lakes region and the Northern Plains (but not Texas). The runoff from this meltdown helped shape the contours of present-day Texas rivers, and the glacial water and melted snow contributed to the worldwide

[3] For an overview of the climatic changes that have occurred generally in North America and more specifically in the Plains States and Texas, see W. Raymond Wood and Michael J. O'Brien's 1995 assessment of the Late Holocene climatic changes in the Midwest and their conclusion that between 1550 and 1850 the climate in the general area was relatively cool and moist and that glaciers in the Rocky Mountains advanced. The authors add: "This episode, sometimes known as the Little Ice Age, was a long, cool, moist period that witnessed a resurgence in mountain glaciation worldwide. Bitter cold was registered in Europe, and the temperature and cold led to crop failure and widespread starvation there. It is not as well documented in North America. Global warming began about A.D. 1850." W. Raymond Wood and Michael J. O'Brien, "Environmental Setting," in W. Raymond Wood, et al., *Holocene Human Adaptations in the Missouri Prairie-Timberlands* Arkansas Archeological Research Series no. 45 (Fayetteville: Arkansas Archeological Survey, 1995), 44–45.

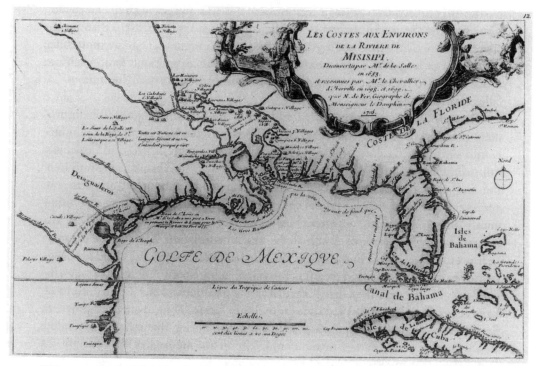

This 1705 map by Nicholas de Fer contains a cartouche that illustrates the assassination of La Salle. Numerous details of the French expedition's experiences in Texas are included in the map. *Courtesy F. Carrington Weems, Houston.*

replenishment of the oceans and the corresponding rise in the sea level. The Texas coastline stabilized to its present form in approximately 2000 B.C., which allows the latitude citings Joutel reported along the coast to be transposed and followed on contemporary maps. Although the configuration of the barrier islands and many major riverbeds were basically stabilized four millennia ago, climatic changes continued, oscillating from a warmer and drier (xeric) period that continued for several hundred years (ca. A.D. 850 to 1350) before turning to a cooler and sometimes wetter (mesic) cycle (1350 to 1850), and then returning to the warmer period we know today.

The climatologists H. H. Lamb and Jean Grove have sketched the climatic changes that occurred from about A.D. 850 to 1850 and have documented events between the years 1000 and 1400, when the ice pack in the Arctic remained far to the north and permitted the first North American discovery voyages by the Norse to Iceland, Greenland, and then on to the present-day Canadian province of Newfoundland.[4] By 1300, Grove continues, vineyards flourished on the European continent three hundred miles north of their present limits. By the close of the

---

[4] Jean M. Grove, *The Little Ice Age* (New York: Methuen, 1988), 1–12; H. H. Lamb, *Climate, History, and the Modern World,* 2nd ed. (New York: Routledge, 1995), 170–240. See also Gwyn Jones, *The Norse Atlantic Saga: Being the Norse Voyages of Discovery and Settlement to Iceland, Greenland, and North America,* 2nd ed. (New York: Oxford University Press, 1986), 1–115.

fourteenth century, the climate in Europe and North America began to cool again, becoming damper and initiating the Little Ice Age (ca. 1550 to 1850). Lamb concludes that the Little Ice Age represents "the coldest regime . . . at any time since the last major ice age that ended ten thousand years or so ago" and that the climax of the Little Ice Age occurred in the late seventeenth century, at the time of La Salle's expedition to Texas.[5]

Texas archeologists have studied evidence of the Little Ice Age and the movement toward a cooler and wetter period in Texas between the fourteenth and nineteenth centuries. The archeologists agree that the climate in parts of Texas was noticeably wetter and cooler during the time of French and Spanish exploration of the Gulf than it is today.[6] As higher levels of precipitation altered patterns and species of plant growth and animal concentrations, the climatic change also influenced Native American subsistence patterns and migration, particularly in the marginal growing areas of South Texas and northeastern Mexico. Rich grassy prairies stretched across South Texas into northeastern Mexico and acted as a magnet for herds of thousands of bison that roamed below the Rio Grande into northern Coahuila. In turn these herds acted as a magnet that attracted Indian hunting bands from both East and West Texas into South Texas. Thus, the mesic climate in South Texas, favorable for prairie grasses and bison during the period of La Salle's visit, may have contributed to the complexity of the intertribal relationships in South Texas that the French expedition encountered.

Although the native population in South Texas and northeastern Mexico at the time of first European contact is acknowledged to be one of the least understood on the North American continent,[7] some general observations can be made about the native tribes La Salle and his party encountered. The local tribes in the Matagorda Bay area with whom La Salle remained at war during most of his stay are today known collectively as the Karankawa, although neither the French nor the Spanish referred to the tribe by that name. According to Jean-Baptiste Talon, who lived as a captive with the coastal group he called the Clamcoehs for about two and a half years (1689–1691), his hosts did not plant crops and normally remained near the bay areas. Although the Karankawa hunted bison near the bay, they lived principally on small game (deer, turkey, and water fowl), fish (including dolphin from the bay), other coastal aquatic resources, and products of local flora such as pecans, cactus fruit, and berries. The Karankawa were the only known

[5] Lamb, *Climate, History, and the Modern World*, 85–89, 212.

[6] LeRoy Johnson and Glenn T. Goode have studied climatic changes that occurred during the past nine thousand years in the Eastern Edwards Plateau, an area about 150 miles northwest of Matagorda Bay. In the 1995 study, the authors concluded that the relatively dry climate experienced in their study during the period approximately A.D. 800 to 1400 was followed by a wetter (mesic) period, from about 1400 to 1900. See figure 35, chart of Holocene precipitation fluctuations, in LeRoy Johnson and Glenn T. Goode, *Past Cultures and Climates at the Jonas Terrace 41ME29, Medina County, Texas*, Office of the State Archeologist Report no. 40 (Austin: Texas Historical Commission, 1995), 72.

[7] The area is identified as "Poorly Known Groups of the Gulf Coastal Plain and Interior" on the map "Key to Tribal Territory" in Alfonso Ortiz (ed.), *Southwest*, vol. 10 of William C. Sturtevant (ed.), *Handbook of North American Indians* (Washington, D.C.: Smithsonian Institution, 1983), ix. All other areas of North America on the map are identified with the name of the dominant Indian tribe that resided in the region.

South Texas tribe that considered the Caddo Indians as enemies. Talon tells that the Karankawa with whom he was living raided the East Texas Caddo, "the ancient enemies" of the Karankawa. The raiding party returned to the coast with horses and between thirty and forty slaves taken from the Ayennis, a western Caddoan band.[8] The Karankawa consumed several Caddo captives during a three-day cele-bration, but, as Joutel tells, the Caddo consumed enemy captives after a similarly successful raid.

The Karankawa's relationship with linguistically unaffiliated neighboring tribes appears guarded and distant as the Karankawa (usually identified to include not only the Karankawa band but also the Cujane, Coapite, Copano, and perhaps the Coco) were seldom reported mixing and meeting at shared encampments of tribes living twenty to fifty miles to the north.[9] The Coco are a distinct exception to this as they were found meeting with neighboring tribes fifty or more miles from the coast, perhaps suggesting that the Coco were not a typical Karankawa band.[10]

A recent study by Robert A. Ricklis helps identify the narrow coastal habitat range of the Karankawa, which ran from Matagorda to the Corpus Christi and Baffin bay areas.[11] Ricklis employs comparative information on the composition and style of Karankawan ceramic pottery to set residential boundaries. Ricklis's study of the Karankawa is supplemented with information from several recent independent archeological surveys and site-specific studies conducted on the lower Guadalupe and Lavaca rivers.[12]

The tribes living from twenty to one hundred miles or so north of the bay, between the lower Guadalupe and Colorado rivers, moved frequently among local subsistence camp areas in relatively small bands with populations of several hun-dred to several thousand. Of course, the population of these tribes (as well as other native Texas tribes) was probably substantially larger, perhaps twice the reported population in the 1680s, or even larger, before their number was thinned by suc-cessive waves of epidemic European diseases.[13]

[8] See R. T. Huntington (trans.), "The Interrogation of the Talon Brothers, 1698," *The Iowa Review*, 15, no. 2 (1985), 121–122. Two years after the Huntington translation was published, Robert S. Weddle annotated a new translation. See Pierre and Jean-Baptiste Talon, "Voyage to the Mississippi through the Gulf of Mexico," trans. Ann Linda Bell, in Robert S. Weddle (ed.), *La Salle, the Mississippi, and the Gulf: Three Primary Documents* (College Station: Texas A&M University Press, 1987), 248, 249.

[9] See recorded meetings of different South Texas tribes described in entries "Cantona," "Cava," "Emet," "Sana," "Tohaha," and "Toho" in William C. Foster, *Spanish Expeditions into Texas, 1689–1768* (Austin: University of Texas Press, 1995), 270, 271, 274, 285, 287, 288. W. W. Newcomb Jr. describes the traditional identification of the Karankawa bands or tribes in his entry "Karankawa," in Ortiz (ed.), *Southwest*, vol. 10 of Sturtevant (ed.), *Handbook of North American Indians*, 359–367.

[10] See entry "Coco" in Foster, *Spanish Expeditions into Texas*, 272–273.

[11] Robert A. Ricklis, *The Karankawa Indians of Texas: An Ecological Study of Cultural Tradition and Change* (Austin: University of Texas Press, 1996), 5–12.

[12] See Jeffrey A. Huebner and Anthony G. Comuzzie, *The Archeology and Bioarcheology of Blue Bayou: A Late Archaic and Late Prehistoric Mortuary Locality in Victoria County, Texas* (Austin: Texas Archeological Research Laboratory, University of Texas at Austin, 1992); Richard A. Weinstein, *Archaeology and Paelogeography of the Lower Guadalupe River/San Antonio Bay Region* (Baton Rouge, La.: Coastal Environments, Inc., 1992); Richard A. Weinstein, *Archaeological Investigations Along the Lower Lavaca River, Jackson County, Texas* (Baton Rouge, La.: Coastal Environments, Inc., 1994).

[13] For a table listing some major epidemic disease episodes in Texas and Northeastern Mexico from

Although no collective name has been given to the Indian bands living in this area, a recent study suggests that several of the tribes spoke Sanan, a language distinct from that spoken by the Karankawa and from the natives living to the west and east of the bay.[14] La Salle visited several of these tribes, who Joutel reports were closely aligned with both the western Caddo in East Texas and the Trans-Pecos Jumano and Cibola. The Caddo frequently visited the Indian trade grounds and centers west of the customary crossing area on the Colorado River in Fayette County. The Trans-Pecos tribes annually came to the same trade centers, but they arrived mounted and prepared to hunt bison on the fertile central prairies west of the lower Colorado. Joutel lists nineteen tribes that lived in the general area and reports that the natives considered the Colorado a boundary river, which they crossed only to go to war against a common enemy to the east.

A number of seventeenth-century Spanish sources identify by name other tribes who lived between the lower Guadalupe and Colorado rivers in the late 1600s. These sources include the expedition diary accounts of Governor Alonso de León, Governor Salinas Varona, and the padre Damián Massanet, prepared on the 1689, 1690, and 1693 Spanish expeditions into Texas.[15] Joutel and the Talon brothers listed the Toho and the Tohaha as living west of the lower Colorado, and De León, Salinas Varona, and Massanet also identified the two tribes by name in the same area.

In the area between the lower Colorado and the Brazos, French and Spanish sources reported encountering only a few named tribes (principally Caddoan affiliated), perhaps because the expedition routes crossed only a narrow part of the region that ran east-to-west a few miles below and parallel to the Post Oak Belt. No Spanish or French expedition party crossed the lower and more open prairie lands farther south near the coast. Joutel gives a list of twenty-two tribes that lived east of the lower Colorado (which the French called the Maligne) and writes of encountering another two—the Teao and Palaquechare; the second tribe La Salle linguistically associated with the Caddo. Both tribes kept horses and enjoyed good relations with the West Texas Jumano and East Texas Caddo. The Palaquechare were not only bison hunters but also horticulturists who occasionally planted corn and beans. One of the tribes Joutel listed as living between the lower Colorado and the Brazos was the Mayeye, a tribe Spanish expedition diarists later identified in the same area.[16]

About 150 miles to the southwest and west of the bay area was the lower Rio Grande, which ran through Coahuiltecan Indian country. According to historians Alonso de León (the elder) and Juan Bautista Chapa, the area in the seventeenth century included a conglomerate of indigenous local tribes plus other bands that

1577 to 1768, see "Appendix III: Documented Epidemic Disease Episodes in Northeastern New Spain, 1577–1768" in Foster, *Spanish Expeditions into Texas*, 261–264.

[14] See LeRoy Johnson and T. N. Campbell, "Sanan: Traces of a Previously Unknown Aboriginal Language in Colonial Coahuila and Texas," *Plains Anthropologist*, 37 (Aug., 1992), 185–212.

[15] See Foster, *Spanish Expeditions into Texas*, 17–51, 77–95.

[16] See discussion of Mayeye in William W. Newcomb Jr., "Historic Indians of Central Texas," *Bulletin of the Texas Archeological Society*, 64 (1993), 24–25.

had been driven north as the Spanish occupied Indian lands in the south. The Spanish mine operators near Zacatecas also used indigenous peoples for slave labor. These tribes, like their neighbors in South Texas, survived in part by hunting small game with bow and arrow, fishing, and picking and gathering local wild nuts and berries, cactus fruit, and other plant products. Although horticulture was practiced in nearby southern Tamaulipas along the upper Mexican Gulf Coast, where corn was grown, the natives along the lower Rio Grande apparently did not cultivate crops. The French reportedly visited the middle Rio Grande as far upstream as possibly the Pecos, and the Frenchman Jean Géry was captured by Spaniards between the middle Rio Grande and the Nueces.

Juan Bautista Chapa, writing in 1690, described in detail the Coahuiltecan tribes of northeastern Mexico and South Texas, identifying several hundred by name, and Thomas N. Campbell has expanded the list.[17] A survey of the archeological record of the South Texas area, including a brief summary of the historic Indians in the area, is found in a 1989 overview Thomas N. Hester and his associates, principally Stephen L. Black, prepared for the United States Army Corps of Engineers.[18] Along the western Gulf coast and inland south of the Rio Grande lived the Chichimeca Indians, who Capt. Alonso de León (the elder) described as rebellious and feisty in the 1640s,[19] and farther south between the present-day Soto de Marina and Tampico were the Huastec, who spoke a Mayan-related language; cultivated corn, beans, and cotton in large cleared fields; raised domesticated ducks and turkeys; and, like their neighbors on the lower Mississippi and in East Texas, flattened the heads of their children.[20]

Farther west in the Big Bend area near the junction of the Rio Grande and the Mexican Conchos River, natives cultivated corn, beans, squash, and cotton. Some tribes local to the area (such as the Jumano and Cibola) were also highly migratory bison hunters and traders. As mentioned earlier, the Jumano, Cibola, and other West Texas tribes, some mounted on Spanish horses, annually moved east from their mountainous country to the open prairies of Central Texas and the Gulf Coast to hunt bison and to trade with friendly Central and East Texas tribes. The Cibola visited the site of the Fort Saint Louis massacre in the winter of 1688–1689 and before De León arrived at the decimated French post, the Cibola had reported the destruction of the French settlement to Spanish authorities at Parral in modern-day Chihuahua.[21]

[17] See William C. Foster (ed.), *Texas and Northeastern Mexico, 1630–1690* (Austin: University of Texas Press, 1997); Thomas N. Campbell, "Coahuiltecans and Their Neighbors," in Ortiz (ed.), *Southwest*, vol. 10 of Sturtevant (ed.), *Handbook of North American Indians*, 343–359.

[18] The study focuses on the prehistoric record of much of the area covered by La Salle and his men, including the Central Texas Plateau Prairie and the South Texas Plains. Thomas R. Hester, et al., *From the Gulf to the Rio Grande: Human Adaptation in Central, South, and Lower Pecos Texas* Arkansas Archeological Survey Research Series no. 33 (Fayetteville, Ark.: Arkansas Archeological Survey, 1989).

[19] See Foster (ed.), *Texas and Northeastern Mexico*, 69, 91, 179.

[20] Donald E. Chipman, *Nuno de Guzman and the Province of Panuco in New Spain, 1518–1533* (Glendale, Calif.: A. H. Clark Co., 1967), 27–33.

[21] Statements made by the Jumano and Cibola leaders were recorded in Parral. See Charles Wilson Hackett (ed.), *Historical Documents Relating to New Mexico, Nueva Vizcaya, and Approaches Thereto, to 1773* (3 vols.; Washington, D.C.: The Carnegie Institution of Washington, 1923-1937), II, 251-281.

One hundred and fifty miles northwest of Matagorda Bay was hostile Apache country in the late seventeenth century; Apache occupied the Hill Country north and west of Austin and San Antonio. These Plains Indians were bison hunters who only planted crops occasionally. The Post Oak Belt separated the Apache from the Central Texas coastal tribes. Comanche at that time lived even farther to the north and west. These tribes and their Plains Indian friends were enemies of the Caddo and enemies of many West and Central Texas tribes as well. It appears that La Salle's people had no direct contact with the Apache.[22]

One hundred and fifty miles northeast of the bay and farther east and northeast along the Red River were the Caddo Indians, a confederacy of agrarian woodland mound builders. The Caddo probably exhibited a culture with which the French and the Spanish could most easily identify. The Caddo were expert horticulturists who grew corn, sunflowers, beans, squash, tobacco, and watermelons, but Joutel does not mention cotton.[23] Their plant diet was supplemented with game animals, including bison killed principally on the plains east of the lower Colorado. The Caddo lived in settled but scattered communities or hamlets associated with local small family or community farms. Members of the tribe had traded for horses with the West Texas Jumano and perhaps other sources, so they were able to provide La Salle with several pack horses. The Caddo were religious: they symbolically maintained a continuous fire in their large thatched huts and buried their dead with goods appropriate to use in an afterlife. The Caddo horticultural and mound-building traditions are probably traceable to earlier Mississippian cultures, but the seeds they planted (except for the sunflower and watermelon) probably originated in the west and southwest into Mexico. Both the French and the Spaniards were drawn to these people whom they considered physically attractive, intelligent, and friendly. Several Frenchmen deserted La Salle to live with the Western Caddo.

Most current authorities describe the western range of Caddoan Indians in the late 1600s to include an area that stretched only a few miles west of the middle Trinity.[24] However, Joutel's account, and the accounts of subsequent Spanish diarists, verify that the Western Caddo regularly used and occupied a larger area west of the Trinity. According to these reports, Caddo hunting parties and linguistically associated bands maintained what appears to be a continuous presence and occupation of the area near the lower Brazos and the territory between the lower

---

[22] For a brief summary of the location and activity of the Apache Indians in Texas in the late 1600s, see Donald E. Chipman, "Apache Indians" in Ron Tyler, et al. (eds.), *New Handbook of Texas* (6 vols.; Austin: Texas State Historical Association, 1996), I, 210–211. Two recent studies on the Plains Indians in Texas are Karl H. Schlesier (ed.), *Plains Indians, A.D. 500–1500, the Archaeological Past of Historic Groups* (Norman: University of Oklahoma Press, 1994) and Vance T. Holliday, *Paleoindian Geoarchaeology of the Southern High Plains* (Austin: University of Texas Press, 1997).

[23] In East Texas Moscoso found natives with cotton blankets and turquoise, but these goods were said to be imports from the West, not locally produced. See "The Account by a Gentleman from Elvas," trans. and ed. James Alexander Robertson, in Lawrence A. Clayton, Vernon J. Knight Jr., and Edward C. Moore (eds.), *The De Soto Chronicles: The Expedition of Hernando de Soto to North America in 1539–1543* (2 vols.; Tuscaloosa: University of Alabama Press, 1993), I, 148.

[24] See the tented Caddoan area in Timothy K. Perttula, *The Caddo Nation: Archaeological and Ethnohistoric Perspectives* (Austin: University of Texas Press, 1992), 8, fig. 1.

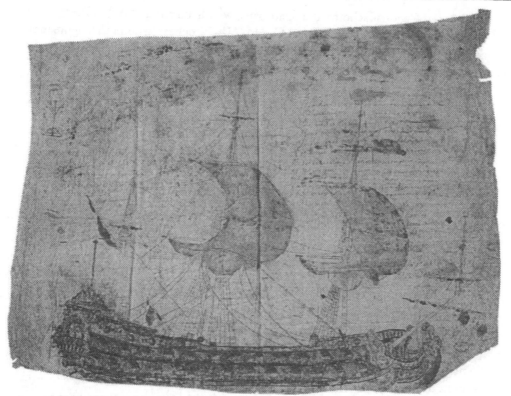

Jean L'Archevêque and Jacques Grollet, survivors of La Salle's disastrous expedition who were living with the Cenis (Tejas) Indians in Texas, gave this painting of a European frigate on parchment to Choumay (Jumano) and Cibola Indians to deliver to the Spaniards in Nueva Vizcaya. A note was written on the parchment that they were Frenchmen who wished to return to civilization. Eventually they gave themselves up to Alonso de León's expedition in 1689. *Courtesy Archivo General de Indias, Seville.*

Brazos and the Colorado. The Western Caddo did not exclusively occupy this country but shared it with other tribes.

Three excellent books on the Caddo Indians and an extensive study of the archeology and bioarcheology of the region and the Gulf coastal plain have been published recently.[25] These works describe the three principal tribal groups in the Caddo confederacy in the late seventeenth century—the Western (or Southern) Caddo (called the Tejas by the Spanish and Cenis by the French), who lived principally along the middle Neches and Angelina rivers but had continuous hunting parties and closely affiliated neighboring bands extending westward to the lower Colorado and middle Brazos; the Northern Caddo (called Cadodaquis by the

[25] See Perttula, *The Caddo Nation*; Cecile E. Carter, *Caddo Indians: Where We Come From* (Norman: University of Oklahoma Press, 1995); F. Todd Smith, *The Caddo Indians: Tribes at the Convergence of Empires, 1542–1854* (College Station: Texas A&M University Press, 1995); and Dee Ann Story, et al., *The Archeology and Bioarcheology of the Gulf Coastal Plain*, Arkansas Archeological Survey and Research Series no. 38 (Fayetteville, Ark.: Arkansas Archeological Survey, 1990).

French and Cadohadacho by the Spaniards), who lived along the Red River, west of the Great Bend; and the Eastern Caddo (Natchitoches), who in the eighteenth century resided near the Red River in present-day northern Louisiana. La Salle and Joutel's party in 1687 visited, traded, and relied heavily on the Cenis. Later Joutel's party visited the Cadodaquis and perhaps the Natchitoches on the upper Red River. Joutel did not consider the Cahaynohoua (or Cahinno) in Arkansas as Caddoan for the explicit reasons he gave after spending time visiting each.

To the immediate west of the Northern Caddo near the Red River lived the Wichita tribes. These tribes, who lived on the cusp between the eastern woodlands and the western plains, hunted bison and other game and were horticulturists as well. La Salle's people were not in direct contact with the Wichita, but several decades after La Salle's post at Matagorda Bay fell, French explorers and traders out of Louisiana, building on the Indian relationships La Salle initiated, developed close trading ties with the Wichita and their neighbors, some of whom, such as the Tonkawa, later moved south into Central Texas.[26]

To the east of the Northern Caddo, the Cahinno (or Cahaynihoua) lived on the middle Ouachita River in southern Arkansas; the Tanico were on the Ouachita and Saline rivers in southern Arkansas; and the Cappa lived near the mouth of the Arkansas River. Across the Mississippi lived the Chickasaw and other tribes La Salle had met on his 1682 exploration of the lower Mississippi River. Although Joutel did not consider the Cahinno to be a Caddoan tribe, most authorities from John R. Swanton forward have suggested that they were. The Tanico were identified as salt traders when Joutel visited the area, which they may have been when De Soto and his men passed through Arkansas about 150 years before Joutel. The Cappa (Quapaw) lived along the fertile lower Arkansas River and cultivated corn, watermelon, sunflower, pumpkin, and bean fields and orchards of peach and plum trees, which Joutel reported stretched for over four miles and were two and one-half miles wide.

Unlike the Caddo, who lived in scattered villages with small farming plots, the Cappa cultivated more in the Mississippian tradition, which employed large fields spread along fertile riverbed areas with associated orchards. The Cappa were friends of the Caddo; their enemies were the Machigamea to the north and upriver and the Chickasaw across the river. The Chickasaw, as well as numerous other tribes along the lower Mississippi, were horticulturists and mound builders. Texas tribes frequently referred to some lower Mississippi tribes as Flatheads, a name given to the natives who by tradition flattened the heads of infants, apparently to make their appearance more attractive.[27] Several Central Texas tribes refer to having fought the Flatheads living to the east, suggesting an overland trek of perhaps several hundred miles.

[26] See the discussion of the Wichita tribes in Newcomb, "Historic Indians of Central Texas," 32–45. See also a summary of the prehistoric record of the Wichita confederation in Schlesier, *Plains Indians*, 221–223, 346.

[27] See John D. Stubbs, "The Chickasaw Contact with the La Salle Expedition in 1682" in Patricia K. Galloway (ed.), *La Salle and His Legacy: Frenchmen and Indians in the Lower Mississippi Valley* (Jackson: University Press of Mississippi, 1982), 41–48.

The tribes living near the coast east of Matagorda Bay, whom La Salle enticed to swim out into the Gulf waters to board his ship in January 1685 (but most likely never saw again) were probably either the Coco or the Atakapa. Unlike the coastal natives in northern California and on Hispaniola, the Atakapa and other Texas coastal natives apparently had only inland shallow-draft dugout canoes that they propelled with poles and that were not serviceable in open deep water.[28] The Atakapa and the Bidai farther north along the Trinity occupied areas rich in deer, ducks, turkey, other small game, and marine food resources as well as an assortment of nuts, berries, and products from other flora. During the mid-eighteenth century (and probably hundreds of years before), an Indian trade route connected the Western Caddo in East Texas and the Trinity Bay Orcoquisa, a subgroup of the Atakapa.

Although these general comments on the location of the tribes that La Salle and his men encountered or that lived in the larger expedition area are reasonably accurate, it must be noted that most of these tribes were cosmopolitan and comfortably traveled distances of several hundred miles to hunt, trade, or raid. Several resident tribes that Joutel met in Lavaca and Fayette counties had visited distant tribes who lived several hundred miles west along the middle Rio Grande and in West Texas. Tribes from the middle Rio Grande, Coahuila, Chihuahua, and West Texas annually traveled hundreds of miles to hunt and trade in Central Texas. These same native groups from Central and West Texas visited the distant East Texas Caddo, who had farming settlements and hunting camps that spread from East Texas to the middle Brazos and lower Colorado. The northern Caddo on the Red River had cultural and trade connections that ran west to the Wichita along the Red and eastward to the Mississippi Cappa, who with their neighbors in turn had trade and cultural ties up the Mississippi and Ohio rivers to New England, and downriver to the Gulf and possibly farther south to the Huatecan and Mayan people. In summary, it appears that most of the prominent Texas Indian tribes La Salle and his men visited from the Rio Grande to the Red River were directly or indirectly in contact with their neighbors. In addition, many tribes were acquainted by territorial hunting arrangements and by long distance trade and cultural exchanges, as well as through intermediate contacts from Mesoamerica to New England.

## European Occupation

By the early 1680s the Spaniards had occupied parts of northern Mexico and Florida for over a century and continued to hold a number of prominent Caribbean islands, including Puerto Rico and Cuba.[29] The Gulf of Mexico was

[28] Samuel M. Wilson describes the use of large canoes in the open coastal waters by the Taíno Indians of Hispaniola in *Hispaniola: Caribbean Chiefdoms in the Age of Columbus* (Tuscaloosa: University of Alabama Press, 1990), 62–64. Father Miguel de la Campa describes in more detail the size and design of canoes used in the offshore Pacific waters by Pacific West Coast natives in *A Journal of Explorations Northward along the Coast from Monterey in the Year 1775* (San Francisco: John Howell, 1964), 34–35, 44–45.

[29] David J. Weber has written a comprehensive account of the Spanish expansion in North America in the sixteenth and seventeenth centuries, *The Spanish Frontier in North America* (New Haven: Yale University Press, 1992). See also Samuel E. Morison, *The European Discovery of America, The Southern*

Spanish water, at least by Spanish claim, a maritime assertion French, English, and Dutch buccaneers repeatedly ignored. At that time, Spain had discovery expeditions and temporary outposts as far upstream on the Rio Grande as New Mexico[30] and near the lower Rio Grande as far as Cerralvo.[31] The expanse between Florida and Texas, although largely unknown, was subject to Spanish claims based primarily on papal pronouncements[32] and on several Spanish overland explorations.

The first Spanish discovery expeditions along the coast of present-day Texas and northeastern Mexico were those of Alonso Alvarez de Pineda in 1519, Francisco de Garay in 1523, and Pánfilo de Narváez in 1527.[33] Alvar Núñez Cabeza de Vaca's party (survivors of the de Narváez expedition) landed near Galveston Island, traveled inland from the coast before entering northeastern Mexico, moved west to the Pacific coast, and eventually were escorted to Mexico City (1528–1536). During his visit to Texas, Cabeza de Vaca lived for three years as a trader, medicine man, and sometimes a slave, among some of the same Indian tribes that La Salle encountered on the Central Texas coast. Along his route through northern Mexico, Cabeza de Vaca reported silver near the lower Rio Grande and to the west. The Spanish silver mines in Chihuahua were an attraction to the French government in the 1680s and figured in the planning of La Salle's venture.

Cabeza de Vaca's journey was quickly followed by Francisco Vázquez de Coronado's trek from western Mexico to present-day Arizona, New Mexico, and

---

*Voyages, A.D. 1492–1616* (New York: Oxford University Press, 1974), 3–312. Philip W. Powell, *Soldiers, Indians, and Silver* (Berkeley: University of California Press, 1952) summarizes the Spaniards' advance from Central Mexico into northern New Spain between 1550 and 1600.

[30] For a translation of Gaspar Castaño de Sosa's journal account of his 1590–1591 expedition to New Mexico, see Albert H. Schroeder (annot.) and Dan S. Matson (trans.), *A Colony on the Move: Gaspar Castaño de Sosa's Journal, 1590–1591* (Santa Fe: School of American Research, 1965). For an overview of the exploration of New Mexico, see Marc Simmons, *The Last Conquistador: Juan de Oñate and the Settling of the Far Southwest* (Norman: University of Oklahoma Press, 1991), and George P. Hammond and Agapito Rey, *The Rediscovery of New Mexico, 1580–1594; the Explorations of Chamuscado, Espejo, Castaño de Sosa, Morlete, and Leyva de Bonilla and Humana* (Albuquerque: University of New Mexico Press, 1966).

[31] For a review of early Spanish occupation of the lower Rio Grande in the late 1500s and 1600s, see Vito Alessio Robles, *Coahuila y Texas en la época colonial* (Mexico: Editorial Porrua, 1978), 1–175; Eugenio del Hoyo, *Historia del Nuevo Reino de León (1577–1723)* (Monterrey: Instituto Tecnologico y de estudios superiores de Monterrey, 1972), 1–334; and Foster (ed.), *Texas and Northeastern Mexico*.

[32] A review of papal action confirming Spain's conquest of the Indies, including the issuance of the significant 1493 papal bull *Inter caetera* is covered in Folmer, *Franco-Spanish Rivalry*, 19–24.

[33] A brief discussion of the Pineda and Garay expeditions is found in Morison, *The European Discovery of America*, 516–525; Carlos E. Castañeda, *Our Catholic Heritage in Texas*, (7 vols., 1936–1958; reprint, New York: Arno Press, 1976), I, 1–28; Robert S. Weddle, *Spanish Sea, the Gulf of Mexico in North American Discovery, 1500–1685* (College Station: Texas A&M University Press, 1985), 95–146. For a translation of Cabeza de Vaca's account, see Alvar Núñez Cabeza de Vaca, "The Narrative of Alvar Núñez Cabeza de Vaca," ed. Frederick W. Hodge, in Frederick W. Hodge and Theodore H. Lewis (eds.), *Spanish Explorers in the Southern United States, 1528–1543* (1907; reprint, Austin: Texas State Historical Association, 1984), 1–126. For an assessment of the three accounts of the Narváez expedition, see the analysis by Paul E. Hoffman, "Narváez and Cabeza de Vaca in Florida," in Charles Hudson and Carmen C. Tesser (eds.), *The Forgotten Centuries: Indians and Europeans in the American South, 1521–1704* (Athens: University of Georgia Press, 1994), 67–69.

eastward into the Texas Panhandle country and beyond (1540–1542),[34] and the Hernando de Soto-Luis de Moscoso expedition from Cuba that landed on the Gulf Coast of Florida, crossed the South and the Mississippi River, and marched into Arkansas and the Caddo Indian country of present-day Texas.[35] In East Texas the Spaniards discovered that no large stores of maize (needed to sustain the mounted expedition) could be found in the arid Southwest below the Colorado river. Moscoso's party, after remaining west of the Mississippi for about two years, turned around in Texas and ultimately reached the Gulf Coast of Central Mexico via the lower Mississippi and the coastal waters of Texas and Tamaulipas (1539–1543). Thus, La Salle was not the first European to travel downstream on the Mississippi to the Gulf of Mexico, but he was the first to travel the full length of the river downstream from the Great Lakes region.

At the time of La Salle's voyage, the English had settled communities and posts at locations along the Atlantic coast, including those in Virginia and the Carolinas, and were well positioned in the Caribbean.[36] Starting from an initial base on St. Kitts in 1625, England occupied Nevis and Antigua, and in 1655 British troops captured the large island of Jamaica from the Spaniards. By 1680, however, this scrap was forgotten; Spain formally recognized the British claim to Jamaica in 1656, and the Spanish ambassador had negotiated with the British Catholic monarch, James II, regarding future action in North America. The

[34] The location of Coronado's route through Arizona, New Mexico, Texas, and points beyond continues to be argued as indicated in three recent publications: Jefferson Reid and Stephanie Whittlesey, *The Archaeology of Ancient Arizona* (Tucson: University of Arizona Press, 1997), 259–273; Richard Flint and Shirley Cushing Flint (eds.), *The Coronado Expedition to Tierra Nueva: The 1540–1542 Route Across the Southwest* (Niwot, Colo.: University of Colorado Press, 1997); John Miller Morris, *El Llano Estacado: Exploration and Imagination on the High Plains of Texas and New Mexico, 1536–1860* (Austin: Texas State Historical Association, 1997), 9–131. For purposes of identifying expedition routes, a principal difference between the sixteenth-century journal accounts of Coronado and De Soto and the late seventeenth-century accounts of Joutel and the subsequent Spanish expedition diarists in Texas is that the seventeenth-century diarists note systematically in the journals the direction and distance in leagues traveled each day but the sixteenth-century accounts of Coronado and De Soto do not. This added route information in itinenary accounts of late seventeenth-century French and Spanish diarists permits a consistent methodology to be applied to expedition route projections and a correspondingly high degree of confidence to be placed in the projections.

[35] The basic documents recording the De Soto expedition with some new translations and annotations have recently been published in Clayton, Knight, and Moore (eds.), *The De Soto Chronicles*. For a recent review of the extensive literature on Hernando de Soto's expedition, see David Sloan, "The Expedition of Hernando de Soto, a Post-mortem Report," in Jeannie Whayne (comp.), *Cultural Encounters in the Early South: Indians and Europeans in Arkansas* (Fayetteville: University of Arkansas Press, 1995), 3–37. A more precise description of the De Soto-Moscoso route west of the Mississippi is in Charles Hudson, "The Hernando de Soto Expedition, 1539–1543," in Hudson and Tesser (eds.), *The Forgotten Centuries*, 91–99.

[36] For an assessment of the English colonization of the Atlantic coast, see D. W. Meinig, *The Shaping of America: A Geographical Perspective on 500 Years of History* (2 vols.; New Haven: Yale University Press, 1986), I, 28–191 and Alden T. Vaughan, *New England Frontier; Puritans and Indians, 1620–1675*, 3rd ed. (Norman: University of Oklahoma Press, 1995). A more recent and broader account that emphasizes the influences of Holland and Sweden and uses little-known Jesuit sources has recently been translated from French; see Denys Delâge, *Bitter Feast: Amerindians and Europeans in Northeastern North America, 1600–64*, trans. Jane Brierley (Vancouver: UBC Press, 1993). The history of English settlements and trade in the Southeast is covered in Joel W. Martin, "Southeastern Indians and the English Trade in Skins and Slaves," in Hudson and Tesser (eds.), *The Forgotten Centuries*, 304–324.

British were as concerned as the Spaniards with any further expansion in North America by the energetic French king, Louis XIV. On the return trip to France in the summer of 1684, the French naval escort vessel that accompanied La Salle on the voyage west was resupplied at the English port on the Atlantic.

During the 1620s France initiated its expansion into the Spanish West Indies and occupied all or a part of a number of strategic islands, including Martinique, Guadalupe, Tortuga, and Hispaniola, Spain's former and oldest colony. By the 1680s, Hispaniola was divided, with the Spaniards holding the eastern part (the present-day Dominican Republic) and the French occupying the western side (modern Haiti), which the French called Saint Domingue. La Salle stopped there before sailing on to the Louisiana-Texas Gulf coastal area. As will be noted, the relationship between France and Spain continued to shift significantly during La Salle's explorations.

Before initiating efforts to occupy island points in the West Indies, the French had explored and claimed parts of eastern Canada, including the Saint Lawrence River basin, the maritime province of Newfoundland, the Hudson Bay region, and the area to the west called New France.[37] French explorers, churchmen, and trappers continued to expand the occupation of Canada westward; in 1673 the adventurer-trader Louis Jolliet and the Jesuit priest Jacques Marquette explored the Mississippi downriver from the Great Lakes region to the middle Mississippi but did not examine the great river (which La Salle and Joutel sometimes called the Colbert[38]) below the mouth of the Arkansas.[39] In 1682 La Salle initiated the exploration of the full stretch of the lower Mississippi, which culminated in the French claim of the entire river basin.

The fascinating story of La Salle's search for the mouth of the Mississippi in 1682 and his subsequent voyage to Texas was written in elegant prose by Francis Parkman, a leading late-nineteenth-century American historian.[40]

[37] A full account of the French expansion on the North American continent to 1744 is Pierre-François-Xavier de Charlevoix, *History and General Description of New France*, trans. and ed. John G. Shea (6 vols.; New York: John Gilmary Shea, 1870). The Englishman John Cabot explored the Newfoundland region as early as 1497, but in 1535 the Frenchman Jacques Cartier entered the St. Lawrence in search of a sea-level strait or the Northwest Passage to Asia. For a recent brief review of the French exploration of Canada in the early sixteenth century, see John L. Allen, "From Cabot to Cartier: the Early Exploration of Eastern North America 1497–1543" in *Annals of the Association of American Geographers*, 82 (Sept., 1992), 500–521. In his review of the early exploration of the North American coast, Allen is careful to mention that Norse discoveries of the tenth and eleventh centuries preceded French exploration and that the Norse settlement has been fully documented by historic records and archeological evidence in Newfoundland.

[38] For Frenchmen, it was appropriate to use the name Colbert for the Mississippi because Jean-Baptiste Colbert was the French minister to whom Governor Frontenac in Canada reported Marquette and Jolliet's discovery of the Mississippi. Francis Parkman, *La Salle and the Discovery of the Great West*, 11th ed. (Boston: Little, Brown, and Company, 1992), 33–34. Marquette refers to the Mississippi as *R. de la Concepción* in his map of his 1673 journey. See map in Joseph P. Donnelly, *Jacques Marquette, S. J., 1637–1675* (Chicago: Loyola University Press, 1968), 333.

[39] At or near the mouth of the Arkansas River in 1673, Jolliet and Marquette turned around after meeting and describing the friendly "Akansea," apparently the same tribe that favorably received La Salle in 1682 and Joutel's party in 1687. Donnelly, *Jacques Marquette*, 223–226.

[40] Parkman, *La Salle and the Discovery of the Great West*. It should be noted that the historian Fray Juan Agustín de Morfí included an assessment of La Salle's expedition in his *History of Texas, 1673–1779*, trans.

Parkman carefully recorded the details of René-Robert Cavelier's life from his birth at Rouen in northern France in 1643 to his death in Central Texas in 1687. La Salle's father was Jean Cavelier, a wealthy merchant of Rouen. The Caveliers held an estate named La Salle, and to Robert's name was added the title "Sieur de La Salle," his customary designation and the one used most frequently in this study. As a young man, La Salle had been immersed in the rigorous intellectual training and discipline of the French Jesuits, but he later abandoned the order to pursue his personal ambitions. At the age of twenty-three, La Salle sailed to Canada to seek adventure and fortune in the new country where his older brother, the Abbé Jean Cavelier, resided.

Soon after arriving in New France, La Salle began his exploration of the Great Lakes region; as a fur trader and explorer he learned to survive in the wilderness and studied the languages and customs of local Indian tribes. After he had navigated the Ohio River, received reports of Jolliet and Marquette's explorations, and heard Indian stories of the Mississippi, La Salle requested and finally received formal government approval to explore the lower Mississippi.

In late December 1681, La Salle's party crossed the frozen little Chicago River to reach the upper Illinois, which also was covered with solid ice. La Salle's group, which included the priest Père Zénobe Membré (who later followed La Salle to Texas), twenty-three other Frenchmen, and thirty-one Indians, including ten wives and three children, transported their canoes and baggage on sleds down the ice-packed river corridor, and reached the more open Mississippi in early February 1682. As the party continued downstream, La Salle paddled past the muddy Missouri River on his right and a few days later found the relatively clear Ohio on his left. In mid-March the party arrived near the mouth of the Arkansas River at the village of the Cappa (or Quapaw) that Jolliet and Marquette had visited earlier[41] and that Joutel's party would visit later. These natives impressed the Frenchmen, particularly Father Membré, who wrote about the civility and kindness their party received from the tribe.[42] Guided by two Cappas, La Salle proceeded from the Indian settlement downriver, past the Taensas and the Natchez Indian settlements to the point where the Mississippi divided into broad channels. La Salle and his men explored the channels of the river to the Gulf, and on April 9, 1682, La Salle formally announced his claim of the Mississippi for France.

---

and annot. Carlos E. Casteñeda (2 vols.; Albuquerque: The Quivira Society, 1935), I, 114–184. In addition, the French historian Paul Chesnel wrote a history of La Salle, in which the author gave credit for La Salle's adventurous spirit to the Normans' Viking ancestors. *History of Cavelier de La Salle, 1643–1687, Explorations in the Valleys of the Ohio, Illinois, and Mississippi Taken from Letters* (New York: G. P. Putnam's Sons, 1932), 222.

[41] Parkman describes both the Jolliet-Marquette expedition and La Salle's 1682 exploration of the Mississippi in *La Salle and the Discovery of the Great West*, 64–74; 295–327. La Salle's 1682 exploration is also detailed in Minet, "Voyage Made from Canada Inland Going Southward During the Year 1682," trans. Ann Linda Bell, annot. Patricia K. Galloway, in Weddle (ed.), *La Salle, the Mississippi, and the Gulf*, 29–68; and Patricia K. Galloway, "Sources for the La Salle Expedition of 1682," in Galloway (ed.), *La Salle and His Legacy*, 3–10.

[42] Isaac J. Cox (ed.), *Journeys of René Robert Cavelier, Sieur de La Salle* (2 vols; New York: A. S. Barnes and Company, 1905), I, 138.

As the first European to discover that the Mississippi flowed from the Great Lakes region into the Gulf of Mexico (some had thought that it drained into Pacific waters[43]), La Salle claimed for France not only the Mississippi but also all lands drained by the big river. According to Parkman, La Salle claimed even more, including "the fertile plains of Texas" to the Rio Grande.[44] In 1683 La Salle returned to Paris to report the details of his expedition and to seek support for his new venture to the Gulf of Mexico.

King Louis XIV was impressed not only with La Salle's exploits for France but also with his plan to establish a French fort near the mouth of the Mississippi. Fortunately, La Salle's proposal for French occupation of the lower Mississippi was not novel. The influential marine and colonial minister, the Marquis de Seignelay, had urged earlier that a French post be established on the Gulf Coast,[45] and the two proposals meshed. La Salle's proposal was even more attractive because Spain and France were again at war. According to a memoranda prepared to finalize the venture, one of the purposes of La Salle's fort was to establish a base from which French forces, supported by local Indian tribes, could seize the silver-rich Spanish northern province of New Biscay (called Nueva Vizcaya by the Spaniards). But for La Salle, the expedition undoubtedly held possibilities in addition to fame and military conquest, namely the economic opportunity to expand his extensive fur trading operation by using an ice-free southern port.

The French government was particularly interested in the highly profitable silver mining operations that had been initiated in the 1570s and 1580s in Parral and Santa Bárbara in northern New Spain. The former Spanish governor of New Mexico, Diego de Peñalosa, who had suffered under the Spanish Inquisition and moved to Paris, presented a series of detailed reports on these successful mining operations and provided plans to secure the mines of Nueva Vizcaya, or New Biscay, for France.[46] During this same period, Santa Bárbara, Parral, and other Spanish communities in northern Mexico were subject to numerous Indian raids by widely roving tribes to secure horses, arms, and supplies. In turn, the tribes traded their Spanish ponies directly or through further exchanges with other tribes in South and East Texas and perhaps as far north as Arkansas.[47]

---

[43] Count Frontenac believed in 1672 that the Mississippi flowed into the Gulf of California. Parkman, *La Salle and the Discovery of the Great West*, 33–34. However, Marquette thought it flowed into the Gulf, according to his 1673 expedition journal. Donnelly, *Jacques Marquette*, 221.

[44] Parkman, *La Salle and the Discovery of the Great West*, 308.

[45] Ibid., 344.

[46] Ibid., 348, n. 1. The relationship between Peñalosa and La Salle and a comparison of their proposals for the exploration and conquest of the Gulf region are found in Folmer, *Franco-Spanish Rivalry*, 137–154; Robert S. Weddle, *The French Thorn: Rival Explorers in the Spanish Sea, 1682–1762* (College Station: Texas A&M University Press, 1991), 13–14.

[47] In 1691 Governor Terán and Fray Massanet both recorded a several-day peaceful encounter in Central Texas near the San Marcos River with over three thousand Jumano, Cibola, and several other tribes who were well mounted. The Indian leaders had recently visited their friends the Caddo Indians, who had acquired a substantial number of horses by trade or raids. For a review of this historic encounter and the location of the meeting, see Foster, *Spanish Expeditions into Texas*, 57, 58.

Although authorities disagree as to the seriousness and the timing of France's intent to conquer the Spanish mining operations in northern New Spain, the composition of La Salle's party suggests that the French authorities planned more of a military expedition than a colonization effort. According to Joutel, of the 280 men (including crew) who sailed from France with La Salle, approximately one hundred were trained soldiers, and the balance were sailors, male enlistees and laborers, and volunteers, including entrepreneurs, priests, members of La Salle's family, and his personal servants and surgeons.[48] Several young women were added or lured on board near the time of departure, but there were apparently only two family groups among the lot.[49] La Salle's closest confidants on the trip were his brother the Abbé Jean Cavelier (who prepared two accounts of the trip that have been published), his nephew Lt. Crevel Morenger, the priest Zénobe Membré, his Shawnee hunter Nika, and Henri Joutel, the self-appointed historian for the journey. Other members who emerge as important figures in the written record of La Salle's journey include the priest Anastase Douay, who prepared an account primarily from memory after he returned to France; the engineer Minet, who remained on the *Joly* to return to France in early 1685 and who prepared two published accounts of the ocean voyage; and the Talon boys, Pierre and Jean-Baptiste, and the young Parisian Pierre Meunier, who gave separate accounts under Spanish or French interrogation. To this list could be added communications and reports of the Abbé D'Esmanville, Captain Beaujeu, and La Salle himself.[50]

La Salle's four-ship fleet left La Rochelle on the west coast of France in late July 1684, which is when Joutel's journal begins. The vessels sailed to the French port of Petit Goave in the western part of Hispaniola. After a short rest and the replenishment of water, wood, and stores, La Salle's party sailed around the southern coast of Cuba into the Gulf of Mexico and headed north toward the mouth of the Mississippi. As the frequent readings of latitude Joutel gives while on board the *Joly* and later aboard the storeship *L'Aimable* are remarkably accurate (as verified in the notes to the text), La Salle's maritime route from his approach to the Caribbean in September 1684 to his landing at Matagorda Bay in January 1685 is depicted with considerable confidence.

During the next two years, La Salle and members of his party conducted several expeditions of a hundred miles or more into the interior, at least one west toward Mexico, the others toward the northeast in search of the Mississippi. On each trip the French leader left Joutel in command of the compound and settlement at Fort Saint Louis near Matagorda Bay, but on his last journey to find the Mississippi, which commenced in January 1687, La Salle took Joutel with him. After La Salle was killed by his own men in Central Texas, Joutel and a small party that included the Abbé Cavelier, the priest Douay, and Pierre Meunier, continued to the Cenis (Hasinai or Tejas) Indians in East Texas and obtained other pack

[48] See text, Chapter I.
[49] See text, Chapter VI.
[50] La Salle's *procès-verbal*, dated April 18, 1686, is found in Margry (ed.), *Découvertes*, III, 535–550.

24

horses and supplies to continue their march toward the Mississippi. Joutel and the band of survivors (without Meunier) moved northeast and found the small French post near the junction of the Arkansas and the Mississippi rivers and returned to France via Canada, arriving in late 1688.[51]

After he returned to France, Henri Joutel, relying on notes he took during the journey, completed his comprehensive journal of La Salle's expedition. We do not know when Joutel finished his work, but his critical remarks on Chrétien Le Clercq's *First Establishment of the Faith in New France* suggest a date later than 1691. In his favorable assessment of the accuracy of Joutel's account, the scholar Jean Delanglez described the meticulous care that Joutel gave in maintaining his daily account. Delanglez wrote: "The shrewd Norman [Joutel] did not cease keeping notes at any time. Joutel assuredly did not lose the notes taken during his trip from the Gulf to Canada when he embarked for France. His narrative of the last journey contains ample internal evidence that during this time he not only made notes but that he faithfully entered in his journal also day by day facts and occurrences on the way."[52] Delanglez cites, in support of his judgment that Joutel kept a written daily account, Joutel's own comment in March 1685 that he was keeping a written record of the expedition. Joutel wrote that since some of his notes made before Captain Beaujeu departed had been lost, he therefore would not give a specific date when the departure occurred. Joutel apparently continued to keep a daily record because thereafter, as during the voyage, he gave specific dates for occurrences and provided other specific information such as the names of over one hundred Indian tribes. I fully concur with Delanglez's assessment that Joutel's journal is based on notes that he kept during the expedition and carried back to France.

We know little about Joutel's life before or after the expedition; Parkman records that Joutel, like La Salle, was a native of Rouen and that his father had been a gardener for Henri Cavelier, La Salle's uncle.[53] Parkman adds that Joutel joined the expedition at the conclusion of a sixteen-year tour in the army and that Joutel must have been a young man at the time of the expedition since the historian Charlevoix saw him thirty-five years after he returned to France in 1688. Regarding Joutel's physical appearance, we know from his journal comments that he was about as robust a figure as La Salle since the two could comfortably

---

[51] Although La Salle's life ended in Central Texas on March 19, 1687, Parkman continues the story of the expedition to include events that occurred after La Salle's death, including Joutel and his party's journey across Texas and Arkansas, up the Mississippi to Canada, and back to France. *La Salle and the Discovery of the Great West*, 435–473.

[52] Jean Delanglez (trans. and annot.), *The Journal of Jean Cavelier, The Account of a Survivor of La Salle's Texas Expedition* (Chicago: Institute of Jesuit History, 1938), 10, 11.

[53] The material used in this brief account of Joutel is drawn principally from Pierre Margry's introductory remarks in Volume III of *Découvertes*, 3–15, in which the editor reviews the relationship between La Salle and Joutel; Parkman, *La Salle and the Discovery of the Great West*, 69, 314, 363–430, 462; Delanglez (ed.), *The Journal of Jean Cavelier*, 8–20; John C. Rule, "Jérôme Phélypeaux, Comte de Pontchartrain, and the Establishment of Louisiana, 1696–1715," in John F. McDermott (ed.), *Frenchmen and French Ways in the Mississippi Valley* (Urbana: University of Illinois Press, 1969), 179–198; and Jenkins, *Basic Texas Books*, 298–302.

*The Landing of Cavelier de la Salle in Texas* by Roger Casse, c. 1936. After the painting by
Theodore Gudin in the Musée National de Versailles. *Courtesy Dallas Historical Society.*

exchange clothes. Mason Wade, the editor of *The Journals of Francis Parkman,* suggests that Joutel may have been born in 1640 and that he died in 1735.[54]

Joutel was not an accomplished author, but his attention to detail, his discipline, and his ability to record events accurately are reflected in the observations found in his chronicle of the journey. Joutel may have developed his ability to make precise observations and the discipline to record them carefully, capabilities required of a good diarist or journalist, during his years in military service. But Joutel was far more than an alert military man—he was an intelligent and sensitive writer who respected the truth over church or temporal authority and who appreciated the significance of recording for the future with scientific precision the cultural details of native life and the natural history of the flora and fauna he observed. Some of these traits later became identified with the Age of Enlightenment. His account does not attempt to portray his respected leader La Salle as an unimpeachable French nobleman or to expound on the glories of such authorities as the French nation or the Catholic church. At times he is critical of each. He concentrated on the daily details of settlement life; on the itinerary and a close account of

[54] Mason Wade (ed.), *The Journals of Francis Parkman* (2 vols.; New York: Harper, 1947), II, 655, n. 4.

the final expedition march; on the emotions felt by the colonists and the natives; and on the customs of the many different Indian tribes between the Texas coast and the middle Mississippi. In summary, Joutel, and he alone, provides the specificity necessary to track with confidence his party's daily line of march across Texas to the Mississippi in 1687. In addition, Joutel adds a detailed account of Indian life that ethnographers will find useful in interpreting Native American ways at the time Europeans arrived.

A precise chronology of the preparation and circulation of Joutel's manuscript has not been documented, but some relevant information on the distribution and use of a few transcript copies of his manuscript is available.[55] When the French decided in the late 1690s to launch a second effort to colonize the lower Mississippi by sending the first Iberville expedition to the Gulf of Mexico, Louis Phélypeaux, Comte de Pontchartrain[56] wrote to the intendant of the Rouen district, where Joutel was residing, and requested that a copy of Joutel's manuscript account of the journey be sent to the marine ministry to help develop plans for the new expedition. Apparently in 1698, in response to the minister's request, Joutel made a copy of his journal available to Pontchartrain, who in turn provided a copy to Iberville, who then took the manuscript with him on the expedition. Later Iberville gave a copy to the noted French cartographers Claude and Guillaume Delisle (De l'Isle).[57] The copy given to the Delisles, however, had been altered by the extraction of a number of passages. The absence of the deleted material frustrated the geographers' effort to identify Joutel and La Salle's route, including the important 1687 trip from Matagorda Bay to the Mississippi. In 1703 Claude Delisle wrote to Joutel personally and requested a copy of the material that corresponded to the deleted sections, which Joutel provided.[58]

While Delisle was using one copy of Joutel's manuscript to prepare his maps, another copy was made available to the French editor Jean Michel. In 1713, Michel severely reduced, altered, and published a condensation of Joutel's manuscript, without Joutel's approval of the text.[59] In the introduction to his abbreviated version

[55]  Several brief accounts have been written on the history of Joutel's manuscript. See Rule, "Jérôme Phélypeaux," 182–184; Margry (ed.), *Découvertes*, III, 50–65; Henri Joutel, *A Journal of La Salle's Last Voyage*, ed. Darrett B. Rutman (New York: Corinth Books, 1962), v–ix; Delanglez (ed.), *The Journal of Jean Cavelier*, 3–26.

[56]  The Comte de Pontchartrain was secretary of state and finance for Louis XIV from 1690 to 1699 and chancellor of France to 1714. A review of the role of the family in the exploration of lower Mississippi is found in Rule, "Jérôme Phélypeaux," 179–197.

[57]  Guillaume was the son of the famous French cartographer Claude Delisle, with whom he and his brother Nicolas worked. For a review of the contribution of this family group to French mapmaking, see Jack Jackson, Robert S. Weddle, and Winston De Ville, *Mapping Texas and the Gulf Coast: The Contributions of Saint-Denis, Olivan, and Le Maire* (College Station: Texas A&M University Press, 1990), 28–32, 41–45.

[58]  A transcript of the manuscript copy of the correspondence between Claude Delisle and Joutel is in the Manuscript Division of the Library of Congress. See Archives du Service Hydrographique, Paris, ASH, Cartes et Plans, 115–9, n. 12.

[59]  Henri Joutel, *Journal Historique du Dernier Voyage que feu M. de La Salle fit dans le Golfe de Mexique, pour Trouver L'embouchere, & Le Cours de La Rivere de Missicipi, nommee a present La Rivere de Saint Louis, qui traverse la Louisiane: ou l'on voit l'histoire tragique de sa mort, & Plusiers choses Curieuses du nouveau monde . . .* , ed. Monsieur de Michel (Paris: Chez Estienne Robinot, 1713). A copy of this book is in the Rare Books Division of the Library of Congress, as is the 1714 English translation. Henri Joutel, *A Journal of*

of Joutel's journal, Michel wrote that he altered Joutel's full-length journal to put it in "a new dress" fit for the commercial public. In fact, the editor had deleted more than half of the manuscript, added materials outside Joutel's journal without so indicating, and changed the meaning of some of Joutel's account. In disappointment and perhaps rage, Joutel complained about Michel's abuse of his manuscript to the prominent French historian Pierre-François-Xavier de Charlevoix.[60] Although Joutel denounced Michel's condensation as seriously flawed and unacceptable, an English translation quickly followed the next year. The 1714 English translation was reprinted in 1846 in Benjamin F. French (ed.), *Historical Collections of Louisiana*, Volume I. More recently the work has been reprinted by others, including Isaac J. Cox (ed.), *The Journeys of René Robert Cavelier, Sieur de la Salle*, Volume II.[61]

Joutel's complete manuscript journal was not published for almost two hundred years. The highly respected French archivist and historian Pierre Margry[62] edited the first publication of Joutel's full-length journal as the principal work in the third volume of his six-volume *Découvertes et établissements des Français dans l'ouest et dan le sud de l'Amérique Septentrionale, 1614–1754*, the only printing to date of Joutel's complete account.[63] Margry explained that he had "found the original journal of Joutel which with other documents enables us to follow rather clearly this last part of the drama."[64] In addition to Joutel's journal, Margry included in his *Découvertes* a number of other previously unpublished French manuscript documents associated with the exploration of North America in the seventeenth and eighteenth centuries.

In the early 1870s, as Margry was at work preparing his compilation, several American historians, including Francis Parkman, persuaded Congress to appropriate funds to purchase five hundred volumes of *Découvertes*, thus making the United States government the sponsor of Margry's work. In his comments on the relationship of Parkman and Margry, Mason Wade explains that by 1872 their

---

the *Last Voyage Perform'd by Monsr. de la Salle, to the Gulph of Mexico, to Find out the Mouth of the Mississippi River; Containing, An Account of the Settlements He Endeavour'd to Make on the Coast of the Aforesaid Bay, His Unfortunate Death, and the Travels of His Companions for the Space of Eight Hundred Leagues across that Inland Country of America, Now Call'd Louisiana* . . . , ed. Monsieur de Michel (London: A. Bell, 1714). Both the French and English editions were consulted in preparing this work.

[60] Charlevoix, *History of New France*, IV, 63. See also the account of Joutel's negative reaction to Michel's condensation of his journal in Delanglez (ed.), *The Journal of Jean Cavelier*, 26, and in Margry (ed.), *Découvertes*, III, 1–88.

[61] For a listing of the reprints, see Jenkins, *Basic Texas Books*, 298–302.

[62] Pierre Margry held the official position of assistant custodian of the Archives of the Marine and Colonies at Paris at the time. Daniel C. Mearns, *The Story up to Now: The Library of Congress, 1800–1946* (Boston: Gregg Press, 1972), 109.

[63] Margry (ed.), *Découvertes*, III, 89–534. It should be noted that an unpublished, more literal translation of Joutel's journal is available in the Burton Historical Collection of the Detroit Public Library. This unpublished translation was consulted by the present editor, although it is not a translation of Margry's version of Joutel's journal account. A transcript of the manuscript of Joutel's journal and related correspondence are in the Manuscript Division of the Library of Congress. See Archives du Service Hydrographique, Paris, ASH, Cartes Plans, 67, n. 1. This transcript also was consulted when uncertainties arose in our translation of Margry's version of Joutel's diary.

[64] Margry (ed.), *Découvertes*, III, 43.

acquaintance had ripened into friendship, and thus Parkman lobbied for a Congressional appropriation for the publication of Margry's documents. According to Wade, the principal supporters were Sen. George F. Hoar, Gen. James Garfield, and William D. Howells.[65] In 1878, Parkman noted the assistance of the Honorable E. B. Washburne, Col. Charles Wittlesey, and O. H. Marshall, Esq. in securing the appropriation.[66] In his history of the Library of Congress, Daniel C. Mearns writes that the *Découvertes* was "the only purely historical publication sponsored by the Government of the United States" during the late nineteenth century.[67]

Clerical survivors who returned with Joutel to France prepared two other accounts of La Salle's journey. These were much shorter works, and also were subjected to serious alterations during their preparation for publication. The first clerical chronicler to have his account published was Father Anastase Douay, whose work was heavily edited or rewritten by Chrétien Le Clercq before being included in his *First Establishment of the Faith in New France.*[68] Joutel's journal includes bitter and derisive criticism of many of the statements included in Le Clercq's *First Establishment of the Faith*, but Joutel blames Le Clercq, not Douay, for the misleading parts.[69]

The second clerical chronicler was the Abbé Jean Cavelier, La Salle's brother, whose brief account (published in two versions) took the form of a report to the French minister, Seignelay. An English translation of the first version appeared in John Gilmary Shea's *Early Voyages Up and Down the Mississippi* and was reprinted in *Journeys of La Salle*, edited by Isaac Joslin Cox.[70] A more extensive, but no less questionable, version was translated into English by Jean Delanglez with an extensive introduction and notes identifying numerous deficiencies of the Abbé's narrative.[71] Several references to the misinformation in the Abbé's account are found in the notes.

Although Margry's compilation of Joutel's complete journal may be subject to some criticism, most authorities agree that this account is by any reasonable mea-

---

[65] Wade (ed.), *The Journals of Francis Parkman*, 558. A discussion of the relationship between Pierre Margry and Francis Parkman and their correspondence is found in Jean Delanglez (ed.), *Some La Salle Journeys* (Chicago: Institute of Jesuit History, 1938), 3–10.

[66] Francis Parkman, *The Discovery of the Great West: La Salle*, ed. William R. Taylor (New York: Rinehart and Company, Inc., 1956), xiv.

[67] Mearns, *The Story up to Now*, 109.

[68] The English translation of Douay's narrative reprinted in Cox (ed.), *Journeys of La Salle*, I, 222–267, is the same version that appeared in Chrétien LeClercq, *First Establishment of the Faith in New France*, ed. and trans. John Gilmary Shea (2 vols.; New York: John Shea, 1881), II, 229–261.

[69] See text, Chapter II. Although Cox identifies the narrative as "by Father Anastasius Douay," the narrative closes with a sentence indicating Le Clercq wrote it: "This, adds Le Clercq, is a faithful extract of what Father Anastasius could remember from his toilsome voyage." Cox (ed.), *Journeys of La Salle*, I, 267. Joutel's serious and apparently justified criticism of Le Clercq's rendition of some identified passages of Douay's account may raise questions about the credibility of other passages that conflict with Joutel's account. However, passages that Joutel did not question regarding the distances traveled may be presumed to be creditable.

[70] John Gilmary Shea (ed.), *Early Voyages Up and Down the Mississippi* (Albany: J. Munsell, 1861), 13–42. The reprint of Shea's translation is found in Cox (ed.), *Journeys of La Salle*, I, 268–298.

[71] Delanglez (ed.), *The Journal of Jean Cavelier*.

sure the most extensive, accurate, and impartial rendition of La Salle's expedition to Texas. The eighteenth-century French scholar and historian Charlevoix wrote, "[Joutel's] account is the only one of this expedition which can be relied upon."[72] Delanglez agrees and adds that Charlevoix's assessment "will be adopted by all who study critically the various versions of La Salle's last expedition, especially those events which took place from the time La Salle landed in Texas at the beginning of 1685, until Cavelier, Douay, and Joutel arrived in France in 1688."[73] It should be noted that Delanglez was praising Margry's complete version of Joutel's journal, not the English translation of Michel's abbreviated version, which is the rendition that most American scholars have used.

Margry published a copy of Joutel's journal obtained from the collector La Galissonnière in which sections of three copy books were missing. Margry filled in the missing record with a combination of corresponding materials from Michel's condensed 1713 version and selected extracts of Joutel's journal that had been provided by Claude Delisle, father of the noted French geographer Guillaume, who was France's premier cartographer of the period.[74] The two supplemented parts, which comprise only about three percent of the total volume of the text, are indicated in the notes to the translated text. In preparing this translation we also have consulted the transcript of the manuscript copy of Joutel's diary in the Manuscript Division of the Library of Congress to resolve questions regarding uncertain passages and the precise spelling of Indian tribal names. The original document is in the Archives du Service Hydrographique, Paris.

This translation commences at the beginning of Joutel's narrative as La Salle's party sailed from France in the summer of 1684. It closes three years later, in the summer of 1687, when Joutel and his small party departed the French post near the mouth of the Arkansas River to commence the trip up the Mississippi to the Great Lakes region and to continue on to Canada and France. The translation closes at this juncture because Joutel's daily account and richly descriptive narrative is discontinued at that point. Joutel explained that a continuation of their daily itinerary and a detailed descriptive account of the trip up the Mississippi was unnecessary because several other explorers and journalists, including La Salle, had written at length about the Indians and the country found along the Mississippi between the Arkansas River and the Great Lakes region. Joutel concluded: "As the Colbert or Mississippi River has been described by others, it seems to me almost useless to write anything about it . . . . Moreover, I had no time to examine it carefully."[75] The closing passages of Joutel's journal cover his party's trip with Indian guides up the Mississippi River to Fort Saint Louis on the Illinois in the fall of 1688, the group's winter delay at the fort until the party could continue to Montreal the following July, and the survivors' return to France in October 1688.

[72] Charlevoix, *History of New France*, IV, 63.
[73] Delanglez (ed.), *The Journal of Jean Cavelier*, 26.
[74] For a detailed analysis of how Margry filled the missing record, see his several explanations and comments in the introduction to *Découvertes*, III, 1–88.
[75] See Margry (ed.), *Découvertes*, III, 465.

## LA SALLE'S MARITIME AND OVERLAND ROUTE

Although La Salle and others had described in detail the route and the fauna and flora found on Joutel's trip up the Mississippi, the Indian communities, fauna, and flora from Matagorda Bay to East Texas and across Arkansas to the Mississippi had not been previously described. Only the sizable De Soto-Moscoso expedition in the early 1540s had crossed into the areas of southern Arkansas and East Texas Joutel's party visited. Unfortunately, the route De Soto and Moscoso followed is very uncertain because, unlike Joutel and Spanish expedition diarists who followed him, the chroniclers in Moscoso's party gave no systematic daily itinerary including the number of leagues traveled each day, and they did not have a compass.[76] As Charles Hudson and Carmen C. Tesser have recently explained, "lacking this [an accurate reconstructed route], one cannot even be certain where the major Indian societies were located."[77] The authors add: "Reconstructions of the routes followed by Spanish explorers are fundamental to any understanding of the two earliest centuries of the history of the southern United States."[78] I agree. The accurate reconstruction of the French and Spanish expedition routes is important to the understanding of sixteenth-, seventeenth-, and eighteenth-century history of Texas and the Southwest and to the ability to identify accurately the location and geographic range of native Texas Indian tribes during this period. Without this geographic route specificity, the historical and archeological records cannot be geographically correlated and compared.

Historians often have failed to provide reliable geographic information on the line of march, the location of river crossings, or even the correct present-day identification of rivers and creeks used by Spanish and French explorers. Until accurate geographical information is available and the confusion is cleared, archeologists, ethnohistorians, biogeographers, demographers, and other specialists will be unable to contribute fully to the multidisciplinary effort that is necessary to understand the native cultures found in Texas and the Southwest when Europeans arrived on this continent.

For almost a century, American historians have disagreed on the proper modern names for the rivers that La Salle and his chroniclers called the Maligne, Canoe, and Cenis. Consequently, there has been disagreement about the correct location of Indian villages and tribes listed as living near or on either side of these rivers. In addition, there is substantial uncertainty about the site where La Salle was killed.[79] All writers agree that La Salle was killed a few leagues east of the

---

[76] "The Account by a Gentlemen from Elvas," 139.

[77] Charles Hudson and Carmen C. Tesser, "Introduction," in Hudson and Tesser (eds.), *The Forgotten Centuries*, 3.

[78] Ibid.

[79] Paul Chesnel wrote in 1901 that La Salle was killed near the Red River in *History of Cavelier de La Salle*, 217. A recent example of the confusion and uncertainty of where La Salle was killed is found in articles published in early 1997 on La Salle's expedition in David Roberts, "Sieur de la Salle's Fateful Landfall," *Smithsonian Magazine*, 28 (Apr., 1997), 48, 52, which asserts that the site of La Salle's death "is difficult to pinpoint on a map," but is "somewhere between the Brazos and the Trinity rivers," and Lisa Moore LaRoe, "La Salle's Last Voyage," *National Geographic*, 191 (May, 1997), 79, which claims that La Salle was killed near the Trinity River.

Canoe River, as specifically reported in all accounts; the disagreement arises in determining whether the Canoe was the present-day Brazos or the Trinity. There are also widely conflicting projections on the maritime and overland route taken by La Salle's party from Santo Domingo to Matagorda Bay and from the bay to the Mississippi.

As Peter H. Wood noted in the *American Historical Review* in 1984: "After three hundred years we still do not know definitely the spot on the Texas coast where the [La Salle's] company disembarked in late February 1685."[80] This geographic uncertainty and confusion on where La Salle landed and was killed was compounded in a 1978 study prepared by H. Dickson Hoese (and cited by Wood) that suggested that the correct landfall of La Salle in Texas was Aransas Pass rather than Pass Cavallo and that La Salle established Fort Saint Louis near Aransas Bay, not Matagorda Bay, and that La Salle was killed east of the Trinity.[81] Geographic certainty was not advanced by Wood's unsupported statement agreeing that La Salle was killed near the Trinity.[82]

The translation and annotation of Joutel's diary may help resolve some of the persistent and perplexing geographical questions that long have been associated with La Salle's expedition to Texas. As indicated in Appendix C, I have devoted much attention to tracing as closely as possible Joutel's route, just as I have the expedition routes taken by Spanish diarists during the discovery period. A brief review of how this confusion arose in the literature may be helpful.

Some leading Texas historians, including Carlos E. Castañeda, have incorrectly described the route of La Salle's voyage across the Gulf as proceeding first to the west coast of Florida in the vicinity of Apalache Bay and moving westward to and beyond the mouth of the Mississippi, and then on westward to the Texas coast.[83] The numerous and remarkably accurate latitude readings[84] Joutel reported as he crossed the Gulf and proceeded west toward the Texas coast confirm the maritime route projections made by Robert S. Weddle, which suggests that La Salle's three ships first sighted land along the western Louisiana coast within about a hundred miles of the mouth of the Mississippi.[85]

---

[80] Peter H. Wood, "La Salle: Discovery of a Lost Explorer," *American Historical Review*, 89 (Apr., 1984), 317.

[81] H. Dickson Hoese, "On the Correct Landfall of La Salle in Texas, 1685," *Louisiana History*, 19 (1978), 5–31.

[82] Wood, "La Salle: Discovery of a Lost Explorer," 323.

[83] Castañeda, *Our Catholic Heritage in Texas*, III, 286.

[84] Although Joutel gives both the latitude and the longitude readings, only the latitude readings were accurate. By the late 1600s, French, Spanish, and English mariners could take sightings with the astrolabe to locate positions north and south (latitude) at sea with reasonable accuracy. But precisely determining a ship's longitude required an ability to record time at sea with an accuracy that was not technologically available until late in the eighteenth century. The British Parliament in 1714 established a Board of Longitude to award prizes to those who contributed to the discovery of a useful and accurate method of reading longitude at sea. The board continued its work until 1828 and paid out approximately $100,000 in the long and arduous effort. See Eric Bruton, *The History of Clocks and Watches* (New York: Rizzoli, 1979), 85–89. See also an excellent recent study of the history of the development of methods and devices used to determine longitude, Dava Sobel, *Longitude: The True Story of a Lone Genius Who Solved the Greatest Scientific Problem of His Time* (New York: Walker, 1995).

[85] Weddle, *The French Thorn*, 20.

La Salle's failure to find the Mississippi rested not with any serious misjudgment about the proper route across the Gulf but perhaps more on the misguided assumption made by La Salle and his escorting naval commander, Beaujeu, that the Gulf surface currents had carried the French vessels far to the east of the Mississippi. Unknown to the French at that time, the Gulf surface currents move westward, not eastward, during the winter months in the area the small French fleet crossed and in the coastal area La Salle first reached.[86] Rather than sailing east for several days and finding the Mississippi, La Salle sailed over three hundred miles to the west during the following three weeks searching for his river, finally landing at Matagorda Bay.

While some authorities have associated La Salle's failure to find the Mississippi as simply a misinterpretation of the Gulf maps of the period or a misunderstanding of the geography and surface currents of the Gulf, other writers have pointed out that La Salle may have intended to land west of the Mississippi in order to permit a more convenient reconnaissance of northern New Spain.[87] This explanation should not be discounted; Joutel acknowledges that La Salle's first overland search was, to Joutel's surprise, to the west and not to the northeast where the Mississippi was thought to be.

The confusion about La Salle's overland exploration efforts arose at the close of the last century when Francis Parkman completed his exhaustive work on La Salle's life. Parkman's study, *La Salle and the Discovery of the Great West*, was published in 1897 and is still cited in France as well as the United States as one of the most authoritative accounts of La Salle's life and his explorations of the Mississippi and Texas.[88] Although Parkman's account is impeccable in many respects, the author makes a number of mistakes in geography. These include his assessment that the site of La Salle's French fort was on the modern Lavaca River (rather than Garcitas Creek) and his projection that La Salle was killed near the Trinity River (rather than the Brazos).[89] Parkman simply was not interested in tracking La Salle's route: "It is impossible, as it would be needless, to follow the detail of their [the Joutel party's] daily march."[90] Parkman obviously disagreed with the recognized French cartographer Guillaume Delisle, who in the early 1700s diligently had sought Joutel's complete account so he could use the full itinerary account to chart, as accurately as possible, the location of the rivers, Indian tribes, and La Salle's route—which Joutel had reported in detail. These features began appearing on Delisle's maps as early as 1701 and continued to be used thereafter. I obviously disagree with Parkman; it is neither impossible nor needless to follow the detail of

---

[86] The report that surface currents in parts of the Central Gulf northwest of Cuba and along the Texas coast tend to move westward in winter and eastward in summer is based primarily on a map prepared by Nancy Place adapted from U. S. Department of Commerce, NOAA, Ocean Assessment Division (1985) found in Eric R. Swanson, *Geo-Texas, A Guide to the Earth Sciences* (College Station: Texas A&M University Press, 1995), 149, fig. 9.4.

[87] This possibility is discussed in Wood, "La Salle: Discovery of a Lost Explorer," 312–322.

[88] Anka Muhlstein, *La Salle, Explorer of the North American Frontier* (New York: Arcade Publishing, 1992), 221.

[89] Parkman, *La Salle and the Discovery of the Great West*, 392, 432–434, n. 1.

[90] Ibid., 421.

Joutel's daily march in 1687. On the contrary, it is possible and highly rewarding for ethnographers, geographers, biologists, botanists, demographers, and archeologists to track Joutel's daily march as closely as possible.

The confusion about the location of La Salle's 1687 route (including the site of his assassination) and the current names of the rivers that the French called the Maligne, Canoe, and the Cenis, has continued for over one hundred years, from Parkman's day to the present. In the early 1900s, one of the first American scholars to comment on La Salle's route was Isaac Joslin Cox, who in 1905 edited (with a few annotations) a collection of previously translated French works associated with La Salle's journeys, including the 1714 English translation of Michel's condensation of Joutel's diary. Rather than follow Parkman's interpretation of the modern names of rivers that had been given French names by La Salle, Cox offered his own assessment by suggesting, I think correctly, that the Canoe River, where La Salle was killed, was the Brazos, that the Cenis River was the Trinity, and that the Maligne was the Colorado.[91]

The identification of La Salle's route also attracted the attention of two of the most prominent early twentieth-century Texas historians, Herbert E. Bolton and William E. Dunn. In his definitive 1915 study establishing the location of La Salle's colony on Garcitas Creek in Victoria County, Bolton cited Margry's version of Joutel's journal to correct the record of where La Salle was killed and to identify the Brazos as the river that the French called the Canoe (*la Rivière aux Canots*): "Historians have supposed that this act [La Salle's murder] was committed near the Trinity or the Neches, but evidence now available makes it quite clear that the spot was between the Brazos and the Navasota."[92] In support of his argument, Bolton added: "The correctness of this conclusion is clear to any one who reads Joutel's journal [citing Margry's version] in the light of contemporary Spanish sources and of established ethnographic data regarding the Hasinai Indians. New light . . . is shed by the declaration made before the viceroy in Mexico City by Pedro Muni [Pierre Meunier], one of the Frenchmen picked up in Texas by De León in 1690. . . . He [Meunier] confirms by a positive statement the present writer's conclusion, reached some years ago, that La Salle's death occurred on the Brazos (Espíritu Santo) River."[93]

Bolton's conclusion was reached, as he suggests, during an earlier period, probably when he was engaged in the study of the Hasinai Indians, a work that was unpublished in 1915 when Bolton wrote about the location of Fort Saint Louis. In early 1906, Bolton began his ethnographic work on the Hasinai using Joutel's French account in Pierre Margry's *Découvertes* as a principal source. Bolton's study was not published until 1987, but it reveals that Bolton had concluded that La

[91] Cox (ed.), *Journeys of La Salle*, I, 224 and II, 122, 131. Adding uncertainty, Cox notes that Hennepin supposed that La Salle was murdered near a "southern branch of the Trinity" (I, 244, n. 12). Cox continued writing Texas history after editing and lightly annotating the works included in his *Journeys of La Salle*; see his three informative articles, "The Louisiana-Texas Frontier," *Quarterly of the Texas State Historical Association*, 10 (July, 1907), 1–75; 17 (July, 1913), 1–42; 17 (Oct., 1913), 140–175.

[92] Herbert E. Bolton, "The Location of La Salle's Colony on the Gulf of Mexico," *Southwestern Historical Quarterly*, 27 (Jan., 1924), 174, n. 8.

[93] Ibid.

34

Salle was killed on the Brazos, based in part on his knowledge of the range of bison. Bolton wrote in the early 1900s: "At the coming of the French these animals [bison] did not range, in the latitude of the Hasinai, much east of the Brazos and Navasota rivers. La Salle's party, in February and March, 1687, found them in plenty all of the way from the mouth of the La Vaca River northeastward to the Brazos, but east of that river there were few. Joutel specifically states that beyond the place where La Salle was murdered, only a short distance from the Brazos, there were none."[94]

In his *Spanish and French Rivalry in the Gulf Region of the United States*, published shortly after Bolton's study, William E. Dunn also corrected Parkman, pointing out that Bolton had established that the French settlement was on Garcitas Creek, not the Lavaca River, and that the scene of La Salle's assassination was near the Brazos River, not the Trinity.[95] Dunn concluded his assessment as follows: "The mistake of older writers in stating that La Salle was killed on the Trinity was first corrected by Professor Bolton, who has placed the scene of the tragedy near the Brazos River."[96] Dunn's own independent investigations had led him to the same conclusion.

Carlos E. Castañeda, who wrote in detail about La Salle's trip to Texas, agreed with Bolton and Dunn that the French fort was on Garcitas Creek and that La Salle was killed near the junction of the Brazos and the Navasota.[97] Thus Bolton, Dunn, and Castañeda concluded that the river that the French called the Canoe (where La Salle was killed) was the Brazos; and that the slightly smaller river (the Maligne) that La Salle's party had crossed several weeks earlier was the Colorado; and that the third river (the Cenis) that was small enough to be waded across, located north-northeast of the Canoe (or Brazos) about ten leagues west of the principal Cenis villages, was the upper Trinity. This is my judgment also, based upon Joutel's unabridged journal, and in particular, his statements of the directions and distances traveled on the final trip.

Bolton's 1915 study and Dunn and Castañeda's work confirming that the site of Fort Saint Louis was on Garcitas Creek and that La Salle was killed near the Brazos were not convincing to E. W. Cole, who in 1946 directly challenged the trio's findings. In his article published in the *Southwestern Historical Quarterly*, Cole concluded that Parkman was correct in projecting that Fort Saint Louis was on the Lavaca River and wrote that La Salle was killed even farther east of the Trinity than Parkman had suggested.[98] Because Cole's geographical projections are based on an incorrect initial premise of the location of the French fort and are otherwise seriously flawed, as indicated in the annotations to this study, Cole's journal article and misjudgments need not be reviewed here in detail. Nevertheless, knowledgeable scholars such as Peter H. Wood, after citing Cole's article and noting that

[94] Herbert E. Bolton, *The Hasinais, Southern Caddoans as Seen by the Earliest Europeans*, ed. Russell M. Magnaghi (Norman: University of Oklahoma Press, 1987), 102.

[95] Dunn, *Spanish and French Rivalry*, 35, n. 2.

[96] Ibid., 35, n. 3.

[97] Castañeda, *Our Catholic Heritage in Texas*, I, 196–198.

[98] See E.W. Cole, "La Salle in Texas," *Southwestern Historical Quarterly*, 49 (Apr., 1946), 473–500.

"skills associated with old-style geographical history . . . have fallen into relative disuse," also concluded in 1984 that La Salle was killed "near the Trinity River."[99]

Although most knowledgeable modern Texas scholars who have written about La Salle, such as Robert S. Weddle and Donald E. Chipman, agree with Bolton's assessment that Fort Saint Louis was located on Garcitas Creek, these two contemporary historians disagree with Cox, Bolton, Dunn, and Castañeda on the question of where La Salle was assassinated, as well as the proper corresponding modern names for the rivers identified by La Salle. Weddle projects that La Salle was killed east of the Trinity,[100] that the French Maligne was the Brazos,[101] not the Colorado, and that La Salle's route carried his party into Walker County,[102] east of the route projected by Bolton. Chipman generally concurs with Weddle's projections.[103]

Faced with these conflicting opinions, contemporary anthropologists, ethnohistorians, and archeologists frequently have agreed with and cited the more contemporary historians and have thereby mislocated (in my opinion) many of the Indian tribes or bands La Salle's party encountered. In his 1994 articles identifying the geographic location of the Central Texas Indian tribes Joutel listed, Professor W. W. Newcomb Jr. assumed that the river La Salle called the Maligne was the modern Brazos River rather than the Colorado and that La Salle's Canoe River was the Trinity rather than the Brazos, thus agreeing with Cole and Weddle and disagreeing with the assessment of Bolton, Dunn, and Castañeda.[104] Apparently, Thomas N. Campbell also agrees with some of Cole and Weddle's geographical assumptions, as reflected in his identification of the location of Central Texas Indian tribes in the *New Handbook of Texas*.[105] French chroniclers with La Salle identified by name and location more Indian tribes living between the Matagorda Bay area and the Brazos in the late seventeenth century than Spanish expedition

---

[99]  Wood, "La Salle: Discovery of a Lost Explorer," 323.

[100]  See Robert S. Weddle, "La Salle, René Robert Cavelier, Sieur de la Salle" in Tyler, et al. (eds.), *New Handbook of Texas*, IV, 82.

[101]  Weddle, *The French Thorn*, 37.

[102]  Ibid., 37, 38.

[103]  Donald E. Chipman, *Spanish Texas, 1519–1821* (Austin: University of Texas Press, 1992), 84.

[104]  See William W. Newcomb Jr., "Historic Indians of Central Texas," 13, 14. Newcomb agrees with Cole that the Teao Indians lived east of the Brazos River in Grimes and Montgomery counties, rather than near the Fayette-Washington county line west of the Brazos, as I project. Newcomb also agrees with Cole that the Maligne was the Brazos and the Canoe was the Trinity, thus distorting his projected location of the other Central Texas tribes Joutel and La Salle's other journalists identified.

[105]  According to Margry, Joutel reports that the Orcan, Petaro, and Tsepcoen lived west of the Maligne River, which I believe is the Colorado but other authorities, including Campbell, consider to be the Brazos River. In identifying the residential area of the three tribes, Campbell writes that each lived to the north or northeast of Matagorda Bay, probably near the Brazos or between the Brazos and Trinity. If the Maligne is the Colorado, the three tribes lived between the Guadalupe and the Colorado, northwest not northeast of the bay. See Thomas N. Campbell, "Orcan Indians," "Petaro Indians," "Tsepehoen Indians," and "Palaquesson Indians" in Tyler, et al. (eds.), *New Handbook of Texas*, IV, 1165; V, 166; VI, 581; V, 21. As noted in Chapter IX, Joutel spells the tribal name Palaquechare. Campbell's spelling of the tribal name is the same as that found in Douay's account. See Cox (ed.), *The Journeys of La Salle*, I, 241. Joutel reports that the tribe lived between the Maligne and Canoe rivers, which I interpret to mean between the Colorado and the Brazos. Campbell interprets the Maligne and Canoe rivers to be the Brazos and the Trinity, respectively, as he writes that the tribe probably lived between the Brazos and Trinity rivers in the general vicinity of present Grimes County.

36    diarists named. The subsequent failure of historians and anthropologists to interpret correctly French place-names and to give the correct contemporary names for
the French-named rivers has perpetuated the confusion and adversely affected
efforts to understand where specific Texas Indian tribes lived, where they hunted,
and where horticulture was a part of native subsistence.[106]

This study argues that the continuing geographic uncertainty of the correct
corresponding modern names of rivers given French names by La Salle, the location of the site of La Salle's assassination, and finally La Salle's 1687 route can be
overcome by closely studying Joutel's unabridged journal, in which he provides
extensive route information and other geographical details comparable to those
found in the most accurate seventeenth- and eighteenth-century Spanish expedition diaries. Joutel, like the later Spanish diarists, carried a compass that permitted accurate readings of the daily direction traveled.[107] Based on the recorded
number of leagues traveled each day (as found in the unabridged version used in
this translation, but deleted from Michel's 1713 condensed version), a reliable
route projection can be made.[108] The route projection can be checked against
other information such as Douay's account, the presently identified location and
comparative size of named rivers and creeks, contemporary terrain maps and aerial photographs that picture the density of vegetation growth, and the identified
location of Indian tribes, specific flora, and wildlife reported by Spanish expedition diarists who, in 1690, 1691, and 1693, followed parts of the La Salle-Joutel
route to East Texas. Cross-document analyses and on-site inspections have been
used to verify route projections, and recent studies of Spanish expedition routes
into Texas have shown that an expedition line of march can be projected with a
high degree of accuracy.[109]

My assessment that the river the French called the Maligne was the modern
Colorado River, the French Canoe River was the Brazos, and the French Cenis
River was the Trinity is further supported by the testimony Pierre Meunier gave to

[106] Joutel reports that the Palaquechare Indians, who lived between the lower Colorado and Brazos
rivers, planted corn when conditions permitted. Despite Joutel's and other similar reports, contemporary
geographers, including William E. Doolittle, describe only those tribes living near and east of the Trinity
as having an agricultural subsistence at the time of the first European contact. See William E. Doolittle,
"Agriculture in North America on the Eve of Contact: A Reassessment," in *Annals of the Association of
American Geographers*, 82 (Sept., 1992), 386–401. Joutel's report contradicts Doolittle's projections
because Joutel and Douay record meeting natives west of both the Trinity and the Brazos who reported
that they locally raised crops.

[107] See text, Chapter XIV.

[108] The customary French *lieue*, or league, was 2.4 miles, slightly shorter than the 2.6-mile Spanish
league. John F. McDermott, *A Glossary of Mississippi Valley French* (St. Louis: Washington University,
1941), 93. Based on a review of the number of French leagues Joutel recorded between two known locations with the measured distance on a United States Geological Survey map between the same two locations, it is apparent that Joutel was using the customary French league. For example, Joutel reports that the
distance from the settlement to the bay was about two leagues; the measured distance is about five miles.

It should be noted that some archeologists and other writers have used a 2.76-mile French league. See
Mildred M. Weddell, "La Harpe's Post on the Red River and Nearby Caddo Settlements," *Bulletin* 30
(1978), Texas Memorial Museum, University of Texas, Austin.

[109] The methodology used in this study to track Joutel's daily itinerary and to project the line of march
is the same as that described in Foster, *Spanish Expeditions into Texas*, 8–11.

Spanish officials in 1690, three years after La Salle's murder, which is found in Appendix A. Meunier testified that La Salle was killed near the "Río de Espíritu Santo" (or Brazos River), which the French called the Canoe.[110] Weddle acknowledges that his personal assessment of the location of La Salle's death conflicts with Meunier's account, but Weddle warns that "Meunier's reference to 'Río del Espíritu Santo' should not be taken as proof that La Salle was killed on the Brazos River, as Herbert Eugene Bolton . . . suggests that it should."[111] Actually, Bolton made a special effort to disclose that his conclusion that La Salle was killed on the Brazos was reached before, and independent of, his reading of Meunier's account.[112] This study concludes that Bolton's original designation, which is supported by Pierre Meunier's report, was basically accurate: La Salle was killed near the junction of the Brazos (or the French Canoe) and the Navasota rivers.

This study considers several other geographical questions regarding La Salle's expedition and concludes that La Salle first sighted land along the western Louisiana coast and that Joutel and his men landed on the southwest tip of Matagorda Island and marched northeast up the island to modern Pass Cavallo. Although it appears clear from Joutel that La Salle personally explored to the west of the settlement for a short time during the summer of 1685, it is also clear from Spanish documents that either La Salle or his men also explored west along the Rio Grande in the winter of 1685–1686.

According to Joutel, La Salle proceeded at some time in the fall of 1685 aboard the *Belle* eastward in search of the Mississippi and returned to the settlement from the east in the spring of 1686. Directly challenging Joutel's account, Henry Folmer wrote in 1953 that "La Salle continued his search for the Spaniards toward the west during the winter of 1685–86 as he had done in May and June, and did not look for the Mississippi, as Joutel claimed."[113] Folmer cites Spanish sources, particularly the testimony of Jumano and Cibola Indians who reported that they had met and entertained strangers, who were dressed in armor and had muskets, along the Rio Grande in West Texas in the fall of 1685.[114] Without offering any basis for his conclusion, Folmer states that La Salle personally must have been among the group of Frenchmen that the Indians met on the river. Castañeda noted these reports of Indian testimony when he concluded that La Salle had searched toward the west, not the east, in the winter of 1685 and the spring of 1686.[115] In his 1970 treatise on the Spanish borderlands, John F. Bannon (citing Folmer and Cole) writes that La Salle turned west in the fall of 1685 "ultimately reaching the lower Pecos and coming close enough to the junction of the Conchos with the Rio Grande that those along feared a possible encounter with the

---

[110] Pierre Meunier, *Declaration*, Archivo General de Indias, Seville, Mexico (cited hereafter as AGI), (61–6–21), Manuscript Division, Library of Congress, 196–197. See translation in Appendix A.

[111] Robert S. Weddle, *Wilderness Manhunt, the Spanish Search for La Salle* (Austin: University of Texas Press, 1973), 220, 221, n. 8.

[112] Bolton, "The Location of La Salle's Colony on the Gulf of Mexico," 174, n. 8.

[113] Folmer, *Franco-Spanish Rivalry*, 162, 163.

[114] Charles W. Hackett, *Historical Documents Relating to New Mexico, Nueva Vizcaya, and Approaches Thereto*, II, 269–279.

[115] Casteñeda, *Our Catholic Heritage in Texas*, I, 293.

Spaniards."[116] More recently, Weddle has written that La Salle traveled west in the autumn of 1685[117] not east as Joutel reported.

As there is no direct evidence to support the claim advanced by Castañeda, Folmer, Bannon, and Weddle that La Salle personally was present in the French party the Cibola reported, there is at best uncertainty regarding this conclusion. One reading of the reports and evidence suggests that while La Salle and his party were exploring to the east in the fall of 1685 and the spring of 1686 as Joutel suggests, some of La Salle's men, unknown to Joutel, conducted a reconnaissance up the Rio Grande. Although the named authorities do not mention it, Jean Géry's testimony regarding meetings on the Rio Grande with other soldiers from La Salle's camp (but not La Salle) supports this conclusion.[118] In addition, Spanish documents indicate that local Indians reported Frenchmen on the lower Rio Grande in 1685 and Indians on the Nueces had French muskets in 1690.[119] Regardless of whether La Salle personally was or was not on the Rio Grande with the small band of armed Frenchmen, it is significant that Géry was captured on the Rio Grande and that La Salle's soldiers scouted the route up the lower Rio Grande toward the Spanish silver mines in Nueva Vizcaya, confirming the seriousness with which La Salle accepted his royal directive to prepare to secure the silver mines in northern New Spain.

Joutel's journal translation not only helps clarify some of the major uncertainties of La Salle's itinerary but also confirms the location of Indian tribes and the traditional Indian crossing of the Colorado River as well as the existence of an old Indian trade route that ran northeast from the Colorado crossing in Fayette County to the junction of the Brazos and the Navasota rivers and north to the Trinity crossing in Houston County. La Salle's route north from the French fort on Garcitas Creek to the Colorado River crossing near modern La Grange was probably close, though certainly not identical to, the general route that Governor Alonso de León (in 1690) and Captain Francisco Martínez (in 1691) followed southward from the same Colorado crossing area to the destroyed French fort.[120]

---

[116] John Francis Bannon, *The Spanish Borderlands Frontier, 1513–1821* (New York: Holt, Rinehart and Winston, 1970), 95, 96.

[117] Weddle, *The French Thorn*, 29.

[118] Walter J. O'Donnell, "La Salle's Occupation of Texas," *Preliminary Studies of the Catholic Historical Society*, 3 (Apr., 1936), 5–6, 9–11.

[119] See Marqués de Aguayo to the viceroy, June 15, 1685, AGI, Mexico 616, in which Indian reports from the Rio Grande near Cerralvo in 1685 suggest the presence of French visitors in the area. See also Governor Alonso de León's 1690 report of finding a French musket among the Indians with whom Géry formerly lived. "Appendix A: Governor Alonso de León's Revised 1690 Expedition Diary" in Foster (ed.), *Texas and Northeastern Mexico*, 158.

[120] See the route map of De León's 1690 expedition and the Martínez trip in 1691 in Foster, *Spanish Expeditions into Texas*, 34, 52. Bolton incorrectly projects that La Salle crossed the Colorado (or Maligne) near Columbus, about twenty-five miles below La Grange. See Bolton, "The Location of La Salle's Colony on the Gulf of Mexico," 173. However, Spanish expeditions from De León in 1689 to Rubí and Solís in 1767 and 1768 crossed the lower Colorado at the ford near the high hill that De León in 1690 named Jesús, María y Joseph Buena Vista (now Monument Hill) in Fayette County. The Anglo colonists continued to refer to the high bluff and hill as Mount María. In 1840, George W. Bonnell wrote: "Just below the mouth of this creek [Buckner's Creek] on the west side of the river is a high bluff known in the

It should be emphasized that there was no established Indian route from the Garcitas Creek site to the Colorado River crossing in modern Fayette County because the new French post on Garcitas Creek was not a significant location for native population movements. There was, however, an Indian trade route that ran from the Guadalupe crossing in DeWitt County north-northeast along the Oakville Escarpment to the crossing of the Colorado in Fayette County and east to the junction of the Navasota and Brazos. It was this Indian crossing and trail that La Salle used between the Colorado and the Brazos rivers.

Joutel makes several significant comments about the Indian tribes he encountered as La Salle's party moved along the lower Navidad River during the first two weeks of the trip and as they marched north-northeast from the upper Navidad to the Colorado crossing during the next two weeks. Although Douay reports by name several tribes that were encountered on the lower Navidad, Joutel identifies by name only the Ebahamo Indians, who the French met in northern Lavaca County. The Ebahamo, according to Joutel, were friends of the East Texas Cenis and one tribal member understood the Cenis (or Caddoan) language. These Indians had visited the Spaniards, who they said lived a ten-day journey to the west. The Ebahamo knew also that there were four large rivers to cross on the way west and that bison were available until the last few days of the trip. Joutel reported seeing or meeting with several other unnamed tribes or bands on the Navidad and encountered one abandoned Indian camp of two to three hundred hut pole frames that Joutel estimated could accommodate one thousand to twelve hundred inhabitants.

In Douay's account of the party's movements through the same area, he recorded meeting in 1686 a large party of mounted Indians riding with saddles, boots, and spurs, who, the priest wrote, traded extensively with the Spaniards. The Indian party may have been composed of some of the same tribes (Jumano and Cibola) that Terán and Massanet described in 1691 as West Texas Indian bison hunters and traders. According to the Spaniards, Indians who were mounted and rode in saddles with boots and spurs were near present San Marcos, about 120 miles from the bay.

About three leagues west of the Colorado crossing area, Joutel reports encountering an encampment of a band of about two hundred and fifty to three hundred unidentified Indians who said they were friends of the Cenis; this tribe had a few horses and kept dogs. Other Indians had told this tribe that La Salle was on his way to visit the Cenis and they, knowing the customary river crossing that La Salle would use, were camped near the Colorado ford waiting for the French party. They gave Joutel the names of twenty-two tribes that lived to the north or east of the lower Colorado and nineteen tribes that lived to the west of the river.

---

neighborhood as Mount María. It is about 500 feet in height and commands a magnificent prospect." George W. Bonnell, *Topographical Description of Texas* (1840; reprint, Austin: Texian Press, 1964), 59. This crossing area, known as the "Ripples" was used widely by the native population (and the bison population as well) and was employed by both French and Spanish explorers. It is the solid rock ledge that extends across the Colorado a few miles upstream from the mouth of Buckner's Creek according to Colorado River guide Gary E. McKee.

40

Many different bands or tribes visited La Salle's party while they were camped on the Colorado near modern La Grange and each, according to Joutel, had their own language or dialect. Joutel astutely comments that the Indian language variations may only have been dialects of the same Indian language, just as there were several dialects of the French language spoken in different parts of France.

After crossing the Colorado, La Salle's party picked up and began to follow the Indian trade route than ran from northeastern Mexico to the Colorado crossing and from the crossing northeast below the southern contour of the dense Post Oak Belt and along the Oakville Escarpment through present Fayette and Washington counties to the river crossing below the junction of the Brazos and the Navasota. According to Joutel, La Salle had used the same Indian trail the year before. The Oakville Escarpment runs through Central Texas generally parallel to, and about sixty to seventy miles to the southeast of the larger and more familiar Balcones Escarpment.[121] The smaller escarpment afforded long-distance travelers a slightly elevated, more open, well drained avenue that originates near the crossing of the San Antonio River in Karnes County and continues across the Guadalupe near Hochheim in the Hill Country, across the Colorado near La Grange in Fayette County, and extends to the Brazos in Washington County. Parts of the same Indian trade route from the San Antonio River crossing to the Brazos were used by Governor De León in 1690, Governor Terán in late 1691, and Governor Salinas Varona in 1693. The governors crossed the Brazos a few miles above the junction of the Navasota during the drier summer months,[122] but the constant rains and the flooded Brazos and Navasota at the point of their merger forced La Salle to cross below the junction in the winter of 1687.

Joutel recorded meeting two named Indian tribes on the trek from the Colorado to the Brazos. The first, called the Teao, were found in a village of more than forty huts on upper Cummins Creek. This tribe had dogs and had horses to trade; their huts were described as larger than those seen earlier near the coast. Like the Ebahamo, they knew that Spaniards were living to their southwest, and some of them had gone there with their Jumano friends. Surprisingly, one of the elders was able to inform La Salle about the location of three of his deserters.

Three days after visiting the Teao and about two to three leagues farther east, Joutel reported that their party met the Palaquechare Indians who La Salle thought were Cenis, based on the words and accent the natives used. Their chief also had visited the Jumano, presumably in West Texas. This tribe was preparing to go to war with a tribe that lived to the east, whose members had flat heads and planted corn (as did many tribes on the lower Mississippi). The Palaquechare said that although they themselves did not always live in a fixed place, they planted corn and beans when they were in a favorable location. But usually hunting and fishing

[121] See Erwin Raisz's map, "Landforms of the United States," reprinted for the *Historical Atlas of the United States* (Washington, D.C.: National Geographic Society, 1988). See also the map in Swanson, *Geo-Texas*, 24, fig. 2.1. The maps show the escarpment that runs from Live Oak County through Karnes County, along the county line between Gonzales and DeWitt counties and Gonzales and Lavaca counties, and through Fayette and Washington counties to the Brazos.

[122] Foster, *Spanish Expeditions Into Texas*, 35, 52, 53, 78, and 79.

"The Sieur de la Salle unhappily assassinated" portrays the death of La Salle. From L. Hennepin, *A New Discovery of a Vast Country. . . .*(1698) *Courtesy Center for American History, The University of Texas at Austin, CN 09720.*

42

were so good that there was no need to worry about planting corn and beans. Significantly, they added that they could not always defend their crops and fields from their enemies.

Four days later, at a location about two leagues east of Brenham, La Salle's party met a small group of Cenis hunters, one of whom La Salle and his Indian hunter Nika recognized as the former owner of one of the pack horses they had acquired in a trade at the principal Cenis village where La Salle had recovered from an illness the previous fall. The Cenis said that there were several other small groups of Cenis hunting bison and other game in the area. However, they agreed to escort the French party to their principal villages east of the Trinity.

After moving farther east and crossing the Brazos, La Salle followed for a few leagues the Indian pathway that ran north through a limited open area. At this point, La Salle dispatched Nika and a small party to locate and secure a cache of maize that La Salle had left the year before on the east bank of the river. The party found the cache, but the maize was spoiled. In the area, Nika killed two bison near a creek. On March 19, during La Salle's trip to locate his party's hunting camp, he was ambushed and shot by some of his own men. Joutel carefully offers a dramatic and composite account of La Salle's death by incorporating his own impression of the events and his feelings as well as relating the detailed reports Douay and L'Archevêque, both of whom witnessed the murder, gave him.

After regrouping, La Salle's remaining party led by the Abbé Cavelier and Joutel (with Cenis guides) proceeded northward to the Bedias Creek area of Madison County and on to the upper Trinity River, where the woods become too dense to attract large herds of bison. Joutel reported that their party crossed the Trinity River (*la Rivière des Cenis*) at the ford La Salle and his men had used the year before when they waded across, but high water forced Joutel and his party to ford the river in bison-skin boats. This customary low-water crossing of the Trinity was described by Nicolás de Lafora, who served as diarist and engineer on the Marqués de Rubí's tour of East Texas in 1767, and wrote that Rubí's party waded across the Trinity "on a stone ledge which extends across its entire width."[123] J. W. Williams carefully describes this same crossing area where one can wade across the Trinity and identifies it as the ford Ramón and other Spanish expedition leaders used as well.[124]

Joutel says that the large Cenis villages were ten to twelve leagues northeast of the Cenis or Trinity river crossing area. If the ford was located as I project, the straight-line measured distance between the Trinity crossing and the upper reaches of San Pedro Creek (the principal Cenis or Hasinai/Tejas village area) is approximately thirty miles (or about twelve leagues) east-northeast. This was about the same distance measured from the Trinity to the Cenis residential area that De León visited three years later (in the summer of 1690) where he met an Indian visitor (Tomás) from Nueva Vizcaya,[125] confirming the connecting link between the

[123] Lawrence Kinnaird (ed.), *The Frontiers of New Spain: Nicolás de Lafora's Description, 1766–1768* (Berkeley: The Quivira Society, 1958), 165.

[124] J. W. Williams, *Old Texas Trails* (Burnet, Tex.: Eakin Press, 1979), 159

[125] Herbert Eugene Bolton (ed.), *Spanish Exploration in the Southwest, 1542–1706* (New York: Charles Scribner's Sons, 1916), 381, 415.

Cenis Indians and the tribes in northern Mexico. Furthermore, Joutel described, all the Indian villages or encampments visited from the lower Navidad to the Trinity were either affiliated or were allied with the Cenis. Ethnohistorians in Texas have not universally appreciated the extent to which, in the late seventeenth century, the Cenis were the dominant tribe in the area from the upper Trinity to the lower Colorado. Their influence was felt even among tribes living between the Colorado and the Guadalupe, a fact scholars who have written about the western Caddoan people seldom acknowledge. The prairies in Grimes, Washington, and Fayette counties, and perhaps other areas to the south and west were open and available to Cenis hunters searching for bison and deer to supplement their horticultural production. As Joutel notes, some of these Central Texas tribes (who were perhaps Cenis) planted corn and beans, a fact usually ignored or misunderstood by geographers and other specialists writing about where Texas Indians practiced horticulture.

In summary, a comparison and cross-document analysis of Joutel's recorded number of leagues and directions traveled from the fort on Matagorda Bay to the Colorado River crossing and on to the Brazos and Trinity River crossings confirm his accuracy in recording the daily distance and direction traveled. Joutel's account is easily compared with Spanish expedition accounts through the same area that used the same river crossings areas two to six years later. Spanish diarists along the same route also took notice of many of the same terrain features, wildlife, and vegetation that Joutel recorded. This close cross-document analysis permits a high degree of confidence to be placed in the location of Joutel's 1687 route to the Cenis, and therefore in the identification of the rivers and the location of named tribes along the route.

From the Cenis villages along present San Pedro Creek, the local Indians guided Joutel and his party across the present-day Angelina River northeast to the Nasonis, another Caddoan tribe in northern Nacogdoches County. Nasoni guides led Joutel's party along the Caddo trail and trade route farther north-northeast to the four principal villages of the Cadodaquis near the Great Bend of the Red River[126] (perhaps the village that Governor Terán visited in the winter of 1691–1692[127]). Perttula reviews relevant archeological sites on the Red and Ouachita rivers in *The Caddo Nation*,[128] and I offer my comments in notes on recent archeological studies made in the area and on earlier studies of the Caddo.

---

[126] Cecile E. Carter describes Joutel's trip from the Neches River to the Cadohadachos (Cadodaquis) and on to the Quapaws in *Caddo Indians: Where We Come From*, 49–55, but Carter does not identify the line of march. In his assessment of the Caddos and their connecting trade routes, Timothy K. Perttula identifies the "Hasinai Trace," later known as "Trammell's Trace," which ran between the Red River and the Caddoan settlements near the Neches. Perttula, *The Caddo Nation*, 26.

[127] Perttula, *The Caddo Nation*, 159–161. A close review of the location of the village near the Red River that Governor Terán visited in the winter of 1691–1692 is in James E. Bruseth and Nancy A. Kenmotsu, "From Naguatex to the River Daycao: The Route of the Hernando de Soto Expedition Through Texas," *North American Archeologist*, 14, no. 3 (1993), 209–212. The authors also conclude, I think correctly, that Joutel's party also visited the village.

[128] Perttula, *The Caddo Nation*, 97–182.

Moving east toward the Mississippi, the French party visited the Cahaynohoua[129] (or Cahinno) near the middle Ouachita River and entered the land of the Cappa (Quapaw or Acansas).[130] As my notes indicate, Joutel's description of the Cahinno and my projected route are not consistent with the views of other traditional authorities, who consider the Cahinno to be an eastern Caddo affiliate. Joutel reports that the Cahinno guides spoke a language that included words used by the Shawnee Nika, words that were quite different from the Caddo language, which Joutel had spent time trying to learn. In describing the Cahinno, Joutel stressed other ways in which the tribe differed from the Caddoan tribes: first, their huts were all assembled together "unlike the Cenis, the Assonis, and others we had seen which were spread out in hamlets"; secondly, the Cahinno practiced an elaborate pipe-smoking calumet ceremony that Joutel witnessed; and finally, the Cahinno looked different: "neither the men nor the women of this tribe [Cahinno] are as handsome as those we had seen previously," Joutel wrote.

After leaving the Cahinno village, Joutel's party crossed the Ouachita River and moved east. The local guides informed the Frenchmen that a friendly Tanico village was only a day's travel downstream. Continuing the journey, Joutel wrote about reaching another large river (the Saline) where again the guides reported a nearby Tanico village. Joutel's party paused here for an afternoon to permit the Cahinno guides a brief visit with their Tanico friends, who were described as traders of salt blocks. Between the Ouachita and the Cappa village on the Arkansas River, Joutel and his guides killed several bison, the first they had seen since leaving the Brazos River area.

The Cappa were friends of the Caddo tribes and traded with them on a regular basis. They had an horticultural economy supported by extensive fields of corn and beans and large orchards. The Cappa or Quapaw lived in four separate villages, the first of which, Otsoté, was about five to six leagues northwest of the mouth of the Arkansas River, where La Salle's lieutenant Tonty earlier had established a small French post. Joutel's party rested at this site before visiting the other three villages on the Mississippi and moving upriver to Canada. Although Douay and the Abbé Cavelier both recorded the presence of "hermaphrodites" or homosexuals (called berdaches by modern scholars) among Texas Indian tribes, Joutel acknowledges the presence of a "hermaphrodite" only once, as his party prepared to depart the last Quapaw village on the Mississippi. Joutel notes that one of the natives who volunteered to guide the French party on the long journey upriver to the Great Lakes was a "hermaphrodite." It is interesting that although Joutel comments specifically on relying on a homosexual guide, he does not mention that La

[129] Joutel's trip but not his line of march through Arkansas and his visit to the Cahaynohoua (Cahinno) community along the Ouachita River is described in George Sabo III, "Rituals of Encounters: Interpreting Native American Views of European Explorers" in Whayne (comp.), *Cultural Encounters in the Early South*, 82. Joutel's line of march from the Caddo community near the Texas-Arkansas border to the Mississippi is depicted on a map and discussed in Gerald T. Hanson and Carl H. Moneyhon, *Historical Atlas of Arkansas* (Norman: University of Oklahoma Press, 1989), 14, 22.

[130] A recent review of Indian tribes found in Arkansas at the time of Joutel's visit, including the Caddo, Cahinno, and the Acansas or Quapaws, is found in Willard H. Rollings, "Living in a Graveyard: Native Americans in Colonial Arkansas," in Whayne (comp.), *Cultural Encounters in the Early South*, 38–60.

Salle (who never married after he left the Jesuit order) made his male servants sleep with him, as La Salle's engineer Minet observed.[131]

Having located the Indian trail and river crossings La Salle and Joutel used, one can more accurately identify the residential and camping areas of the Indian tribes Joutel and the other French journalists named. Joutel alone identifies by name more tribes residing in south-central Texas (between the lower Guadalupe and the lower Brazos rivers) in the late seventeenth century than any single seventeenth- or eighteenth-century Spanish expedition diarist, many of whom gave excellent accounts of the Texas native population. Father Douay and the Abbé Cavelier named other tribes that lived near the settlement or that the French encountered along the route. As the original work of these two French priests was subsequently modified by themselves or others, the ethnographic information found in their accounts must be used with appropriate care and reservation. In fact, Jean Delanglez, the Jesuit scholar and translator of the Abbé Cavelier's letter account, concludes that the Abbé invented the names of some Indian tribes.[132]

As Joutel's narrative moves from the Gulf Coast to the Mississippi River and from one tribe to another, attention is called in the notes to the contribution Joutel makes to the ethnography of the Native American tribes that he visited. Joutel's interest in the cultures of Native Americans seems to grow and mature as his journey progresses. An expanding respect for native life is noted as Joutel's comments become increasingly detailed and astute as he moves east. Joutel seems to accept as an obligation, and to view as an opportunity, his position as a narrator reporting on native cultures vastly different from his own.

Thus, Joutel identified the full length of the system of connecting Indian trade routes that ran from South Texas to the central Mississippi Valley, and he identified many of the tribes that lived along the way. The southern leg of the ancient trail from northeastern Mexico into Texas was identified in my earlier work[133] and in the studies that Jack Jackson and I prepared on the expeditions of Governor Salinas Varona (1693), Pedro de Rivera (1727), and the Marqués de Rubí (1767) through northeastern Mexico and Texas.[134]

A full consideration of the implications of identifying an ancient trade route connecting Mexico and the Mississippi is far beyond the scope of this study, but to ignore that La Salle and his men were the first Europeans to explore and record the northern segment of such a route would do a disservice to Joutel's historic account. It is clear that Joutel's French party followed the line of connecting Indian trade routes, which tracked the natural pathway skirting along the southern edge

---

[131] Minet, "Journal of Our Voyage to the Gulf of Mexico," trans. Ann Linda Bell, in Weddle (ed.), *La Salle, the Mississippi, and the Gulf*, 123.

[132] Delanglez (ed.), *The Journal of Jean Cavelier*, 147.

[133] See the map of connecting Indian trade routes out of Mexico across Texas to the Red River in Foster, *Spanish Expeditions into Texas*, 2. Also see the map showing Joutel's route from the Bay to the Mississippi in Foster (ed.), *Texas and Northeastern Mexico*, 2.

[134] William C. Foster and Jack Jackson (eds.) and Ned F. Brierley (trans.), "The 1693 Expedition of Gregorio de Salinas Varona," *Southwestern Historical Quarterly*, 97 (Oct., 1993), 265–312; Jack Jackson (ed.) and William C. Foster (annot.), *Imaginary Kingdom: Texas as Seen by the Rivera and Rubí Military Expeditions, 1727 and 1767* (Austin: Texas State Historical Association, 1995), 2, 70.

46    of the thick Post Oak Belt and following the slightly raised and open Oakville Escarpment, a geologic feature favorable for long-distance travel from the San Antonio River to the lower Brazos. The Indian route continued north-northeast through Caddo Indian country toward the Mississippi, following culturally connected trade routes that ran between Caddoan tribes and to their trading partners Joutel knew as the Cahaynohoua (Cahinno) on the Ouachita River and the Cappa (Quapaws) on the Mississippi. Joutel's French party alone, and no subsequent Spanish expedition, followed the entire route from the Colorado to the Mississippi. Joutel noted that the Cappa had their own trade network and cultural connections that extended up and down the Mississippi and to New England. To the southwest from the Colorado, as Governor Alonso de León and Juan Bautista Chapa in 1690 confirmed, the Cenis or Tejas also had trade routes that reached west to the Big Bend and deep into Mexico, as far as southern Coahuila, Nuevo León, and modern-day southern Chihuahua.

These natural and culturally-linked trade routes apparently had been in place several hundreds, perhaps thousands, of years when some form of commerce or trade moved overland (and perhaps through Gulf waters) between the advanced cultures of modern-day Mexico and the early North American native civilization along the Mississippi. As noted by Stuart J. Fiedel, the most graphic indications of the early cultural connection between the Mississippian culture (A.D. 700–1500) and Mesoamerica are that both were platform mound builders, both were supported by extensive maize cultivation, and both used similar symbols and artistic motifs.[135] The prominent Spanish engineer and diarist Nicolás de Lafora (in 1767) and later the naturalist William L. Kennedy (in 1844) described the Indian mounds in East Texas—handmade mounds the East Texas Caddo constructed, similar to those found in eastern Oklahoma, Ohio, Illinois, Missouri, Arkansas, Louisiana, and across the South.[136]

Recent archeological studies that suggest the native population along the Mississippi two thousand years ago may have adopted maize, beans, and even cultural patterns from cultures south of the Rio Grande often ignore the trade route from northern Mexico across Texas and Arkansas to the Mississippi. Most contemporary studies suggest that the products and influence from Mexico moved north up the Rio Grande to New Mexico and then across the Great Plains to the Mississippi and then downstream to the Ohio Valley and the lower Mississippi. As Bruce D. Smith conjectures, maize was carried northward from Central Mexico to the Southwest by about 1200 B.C., and from there, he argues, it was taken across the Great Plains and arrived in the eastern woodlands about A.D. 1 to 200.[137]

---

[135] Stuart J. Fiedel also notes that the end of the Mississippian period coincides with the onset of the Little Ice Age, which perhaps had an adverse effect on Mississippian agriculture as it did on agriculture in northern countries such as Greenland and Iceland. See Stuart J. Fiedel, *Prehistory of the Americas*, 2nd ed. (Cambridge: Press Syndicate of the University of Cambridge, 1992), 251–261.

[136] William L. Kennedy, *Texas: Its Geography, Natural History, and Topography* (New York: William Jackson, 1844), 70.

[137] Bruce D. Smith, *The Emergence of Agriculture* (New York: Scientific American Library, 1995), 136.

William H. MacLeich arrives at the same conclusion regarding the trade route over which maize and beans moved from Mexico to the lower Mississippi.[138]

This study suggests that maize seed stock may have traveled from Mexico to the lower Mississippi along a more direct trade route across Texas and Arkansas—the old Indian trade route that Joutel described from the Colorado crossing to the Mississippi and the connecting southern leg of the ancient Indian trail that Alonso de León followed out of northeastern Mexico to the same crossing of the Colorado in 1690.[139]

As mentioned earlier, a number of recent archeological studies have provided significant information to supplement Joutel's account. For too long Texas historians have ignored information in regional archeological overviews and site-specific studies that can help interpret and enrich the documentary record of the French and Spanish period of exploration. Understanding from recent archeological studies that people from West Texas living more than a thousand years ago hunted and processed large game animals on the lower Colorado while East Texas people regularly visited or traded with natives on the lower Brazos helps the reader understand and appreciate Joutel's description of the same long-distance movements by natives across Texas to hunt and trade. The ethnographic information in Joutel's work can clearly aid archeologists interested in native lifeways and patterns of long-distance exchange in the prehistoric Southwest and middle Mississippi.

Joutel contributes not only to ethnography and to our understanding of the trade route from South Texas to the Mississippi, but also adds significantly to our understanding of the natural history of the area. He identifies by name or description more than forty species of trees, bushes, and wildflowers, and more than forty wild animals. Joutel's list of wildlife and plants is comparable in number to that recorded by Spanish diarists on the eleven expeditions out of northeastern Mexico into Texas conducted between 1689 and 1768. Both Joutel and the Spanish chroniclers mention alligators, bears, deer, and wolves, and identify several large birds such as turkeys, vultures, eagles, cranes, Canada geese, and prairie chickens. Spanish diarists added a few species Joutel did not mention, such as pronghorn antelope, jaguar, and the wildcat, and Joutel lists dolphins and the roseate spoonbill, which the Spanish diarists missed. Joutel often compares or attempts to compare Texas plants and animals to those he had known in France, but he had never encountered anything like the lethal rattlesnake or deadly prickly pear. Joutel describes the painful suffering of a close companion who was bitten on the ankle by a rattlesnake, and of the man's death shortly after his leg was amputated. Joutel also tells about the slow choking death of a soldier who ate a ripe prickly pear tuna

---

[138] William H. MacLeich, *The Day Before America* (Boston: Houghton Mifflin, 1994), 136.

[139] The projection of a possible cultural trade route that involved a series of exchanges from Mesoamerica through Northeastern Mexico and Texas to the lower Mississippi over a thousand years ago has been postulated as the possible means by which Mayan cultural influences reached the Mississippian culture. See Charles H. McNutt, "The Central Mississippi Valley: A Summary," in Charles H. McNutt (ed.), *Prehistory of the Central Mississippi Valley* (Tuscaloosa: University of Alabama Press, 1996), 223.

48   without first removing the tiny stickers. Joutel's journal is a vivid testament to the dramatic and thriving ecosystems of what is now Texas.

The historical account is unusual in another way; the work is dramatic and captivating. It was composed as an historic journal but the text comes alive and becomes a diary that gives a thrilling day-to-day account. In focusing on all of the fascinating details one should not lose sight of the grand adventure the narrative encompasses. Joutel and the French party walked, using horses only to carry some of their supplies, from the Texas Gulf Coast to the Mississippi River, a journey of more than six hundred miles that took them seven months. On this journey they followed bison trails and the directions of Indians with whom they could communicate in only rudimentary sign language, not knowing if the Indians would send them directly into the hands of the Spaniards, confident only that every step east took them farther away from at least one known enemy. La Salle brought approximately two hundred and eighty people with him from France; Joutel was among the few to make it back to his homeland, four years after their departure. His journal of the La Salle expedition in Texas is a remarkable story of adventure and survival, a compelling account written by one who was tenaciously trying to get the story straight, for his own satisfaction, but for his reader's benefit as well.

# CHAPTER I

# *La Salle Sails to North America*[1]

n the 24th of July, 1684, after the Sieur de La Salle had concluded everything necessary for his journey and had overcome difficulties posed by several persons who were opposed to it, we departed the roadstead of Chefdebois at La Rochelle. We had four ships: one was a man-of-war named the *Joly* with 36 to 40 cannon, commanded by the Sieur de Beaujeu[2]; the others, a small frigate called the *Belle* of about 60 tons armed with six cannon and commanded by two masters (the ship had been given to La Salle by the King); a storeship of about 300 tons named the *Aimable*, belonging to a merchant of La Rochelle named Massiot and commanded by someone called Aygron, which carried the bulk of the cargo intended for the settlement; and the last ship was a ketch on which La Salle had loaded the cargo of about 30 tons of wine, meat, and vegetables that were to be transported to the island of Saint Domingue.[3] Aboard the ships there were about 280 men including the crews of the man-of-war and the storeship. The rest of the men were intended for the settlement, among whom were 100 soldiers who had been recruited at La Rochelle. Officers, volunteers, and other men engaged in several trades such as carpenters, masons, edge-tool makers, and others completed the number given. La Salle was aboard the *Joly* with his brother [the Abbé Jean

---

[1]  Joutel did not divide his journal manuscript into chapters, and thus he included no chapter titles. We have followed Margry's chapter divisions but have substituted brief chapter titles for Margry's more lengthy nineteenth-century styled titles.

[2]  Captain Beaujeu, who was in command of the *Joly*, was an "old and experienced" officer in the Royal French Navy, according to Francis Parkman, *La Salle and the Discovery of the Great West*, 353. Weddle identifies the captain with his full name, Taneguy le Gallios de Beaujeu, in *The French Thorn*, 15. The captain was charged to deliver René-Robert Cavelier, Sieur de La Salle, and his expedition party to a location La Salle would identify near the mouth of the Mississippi River and then Beaujeu would return to France.

[3]  Saint Domingue was the island of Hispaniola or Santo Domingo, specifically the western part of the island known today as Haiti. See Map 2, "The Spanish frontier, circa 1550–1600," in Weber, *The Spanish Frontier in North America*, 66. For a study of the sixteenth-century history of the island, see Wilson, *Hispaniola: Caribbean Chiefdoms in the Age of Columbus*.

Cavelier],[4] the Sieurs Chefdeville and d'Esmanville, priests, his nephew,[5] and two of the Recollet fathers[6] destined for the settlement mission. The third priest was on board the storeship with 30 others, officers as well as volunteers. This accounted for about 200 men. The rest were on the other two ships.

At the same time that we left, 20 other vessels bound for Canada and the Islands also departed. The *Joly* was to be the flagship until the latitude of Cape Finisterre[7] where each one would go her own way. We set our course, but, after four days of sailing, an accident occurred that forced us to change the bowsprit, which had broken in half, although it was not heavy weather. We had to lower our sails and furl them to cut all the riggings and cordage holding the mast for fear that it would damage the ship. After that, counsel was held about what should be done, whether to proceed ahead or put in to port. Some were of the opinion that we should go as far as Lisbon where we could get another mast; others considered it more prudent to put in to port near the mouth of the river at Rochefort where we were more certain to find a mast. The latter side prevailed. We were at that time at 40° 23' north latitude, about 50 leagues from La Rochelle. We left the other ships to pursue their course. A few of us conjectured that this was not an accident. Forthwith, the shallop[8] was sent to shore to obtain a mast. The intendant had one brought to us immediately, and he came on board the same day. He held a few meetings with La Salle, and afterward we were ready to leave. This dispatch dissipated all our suspicions.

On the first day of August, in the evening, the departure shot was fired and we weighed anchor heading west–¼-west [west-by-southwest] to recover our course. On the 8th, we passed the Cape of Finisterre at 43°. At La Rochelle, we had been warned about Dutch, English, and Spanish vessels which were waiting on our route under the appearance of privateers, although we were not at war with them, to rout La Salle's enterprise in whatever way possible. We did not encounter any of them. On the 12th, we reached the latitude of Lisbon at 39° and, on the 16th, we were at 36°, the latitude of the strait. On the 20th, we reached the latitude of Madeira at 32°. Beaujeu had his lieutenant, the Chevalier d'Hère, propose to La Salle to anchor there to take on fresh water and procure some provisions, but having departed from France only 21 days earlier, all the vessels had water and provisions for more than two months. La Salle had no thought of putting into port, given that

[4] Abbé Jean Cavelier was La Salle's older brother. He was born in Rouen in 1636, ordained a Catholic priest, and sent to Canada in 1666. Delanglez (ed.), *The Journal of Jean Cavelier*, 4, n. 3, citing *Bulletin des Recherches Historiques*, 33 (1927), 544. See also Robert S. Weddle, "Cavelier, Jean," in Tyler, et al. (eds.), *New Handbook of Texas*, I, 1048.

[5] La Salle had two nephews on the voyage: a lieutenant named Crevel Morenger and Colin Cavelier who, according to Parkman, was about seventeen years old at the time of the voyage. *La Salle and the Discovery of the Great West*, 420. Colin returned to France with his uncle, the Abbé, and according to Parkman's entry in his 1869 Paris notebook, Colin died a few years after his return, having served as an officer in the French army. Wade (ed.), *The Journals of Francis Parkman*, II, 530.

[6] A Recollet father (or *Père Recollect*) is a member of a branch of the Franciscan order. *Webster's Third New International Dictionary (Unabridged)* (Springfield, Mass.: Merriam-Webster, Inc., 1986), 1897.

[7] Cape de Finisterre is located on the northwest coast of Spain. *Webster's New Geographical Dictionary* (Springfield, Mass.: Merriam-Webster, 1988), 396.

[8] The French boat called *chaloupe* is translated as a shallop.

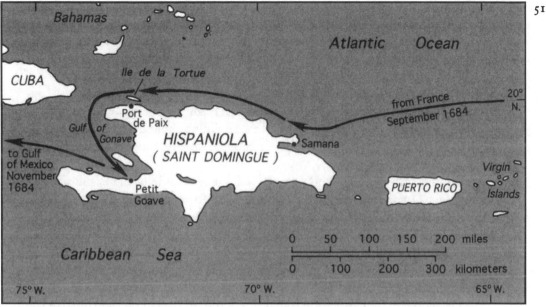

The La Salle expedition's route to the island of Hispaniola (Saint Domingue), 1684

would have been a loss of eight or ten days and could expose knowledge of our voyage; someone on the island could reveal it. This response did not please Beaujeu or several officers of his crew. The vehemence with which they insisted on anchoring at Madeira suggested that they might have some goods which they wished to trade. One passenger from La Rochelle spoke so loudly that La Salle was forced to silence him and to question Beaujeu if it was with his consent that a man without any authority spoke in such a way. This produced several disputes between La Salle and Beaujeu. Nevertheless, La Salle held firm and Beaujeu decided to proceed on course—which perhaps contributed to a less than happy conclusion. Thus, we continued and after we had rounded the Island of Madeira, we saw flying fish. Nature has given them wings to protect them from their enemies, other fish that pursue them. As is the usual, and the proverb is too true, big fish eat little fish. We had the pleasure of seeing these fish rise in schools which launch themselves out of the water and fly the range of a pistol shot. Some even fell on our decks. They are as large as medium-sized herring but the color of mackerel. The sailors make imitations of them with a rag that they attach to a fish-hook. Then they trail them along behind the ship in order to catch fish such as *dorado coryphene* and *germons*, which take them for fish, swallow them, and so find themselves caught on the hook. This is better than the usual, for seamen eat almost solely salted fish, and therefore they are very pleased when they can have some fresh fish.

On the 24th, we encountered the trade winds. On the 28th, we were at 27° 45'[9] latitude, 344° longitude. On the 30th, heavy weather arose which lasted two days

[9] In Margry, the literal translation is "twenty-seven and three quarters."

in force; but the wind was astern and only the ketch did not handle well, causing us to lose sight of her. However, she rejoined us a few days later.

On the 6th of September, we reached the Tropic of Cancer at 23° 30' latitude and 319° longitude. The sailors, as was their custom, prepared to "baptize" all those who had not crossed the line. To them, the exercise was worth plenty of money and brandy, which was the required offering for exemption from "baptism." They had filled their vats with water, just ready for this event, when La Salle learned of it and sent word to Beaujeu that he did not intend for his people to be exposed to this ceremony. The sailors, assuredly, would have gladly killed us all.[10] We continued on our course.

On the 11th of that month, we arrived at the latitude of the Island of Saint Domingue (20° latitude and 320° longitude), and from that point we set course to the west, the wind dead calm. This provided the Sieur d'Esmanville the opportunity to hear the confession of an old gunner, 65 years of age, who was aboard the *Belle* and who died a few days later. The next day, the ketch that we had lost rejoined us. La Salle ordered me to go aboard the storeship concerning some disputes among several individuals.

On the 16th, we cleared the Island of La Sombrere, and on the 18th, we had heavy weather that made us fear a hurricane. The bad weather lasted two days during which we hove to and lost sight of the other vessels. A conference was held to consider whether we should wait or continue on course. As fresh water was beginning to run short, and there were more than 50 sick people including La Salle and most of the surgeons (the crew's surgeons as well as his), it was decided to press on sail to arrive without delay at the first port on the Island of Saint Domingue, called Port de Paix.[11]

On the 22nd, we first sighted land on the Island of Saint Domingue, called Cape Samana,[12] situated at 19° latitude and 308° longitude. On the 25th, we were to have arrived at Port de Paix, according to what had been agreed; but, for some reason unknown to me, Beaujeu wanted to go farther that night rounding the Island of La Tortue,[13] some leagues distant from the coast of Saint Domingue. This was injurious for us not only because, as can be seen in what followed, provisions were more abundant at Port de Paix, but also that was the place where the

---

[10] In the account of this incident in his condensed version of Joutel's journal, Michel exaggerated to include new material from outside Joutel's journal. See Cox (ed.), *The Journeys of La Salle*, II, 8. This is noted as an example of one of many instances in which Michel's condensation distorted Joutel's work, and it illustrates the need for the publication of an accurate translation of Joutel's full account.

[11] Port de Paix was a port on the northwestern coast of Hispaniola identified on the U.S. Defense Mapping Agency map, JNCA-6.

[12] According to the U.S. Defense Mapping Agency map, JNCA-6, Cape Samana is on the east coast of Hispaniola, located at approximately 19°10' north latitude. This reading indicates that the latitude readings reported by Joutel aboard the *Joly* were reasonably accurate, this one being within about twelve miles of the reading on contemporary government maps. When Columbus was returning to Spain after his first discovery voyage in the late fall and early winter of 1492, he landed on the peninsula of Samana to trade for fresh supplies for the return trip. Wilson, *Hispaniola*, 72–73.

[13] The island is cited as Ile de la Tortue located about 20° north latitude on U.S. Defense Mapping Agency map, JNCA-6.

Sieur de Cussy,[14] governor for the King of the Island of Tortue and the coast of Saint Domingue, ordinarily resided. We continued ahead. The same day we rounded the cape or point of Saint Nicolas to enter into the Gulf of La Gonave, coasting along the Island of La Gonave which is in the middle. Finally, in the evening of the 27th of September, we arrived at Petit Goave[15] after a crossing of 58 days since our last departure.

If the other three ships had been as good sailers as the *Joly*, we would have arrived after a month of sailing a distance one calculates as about 1,500 leagues from France. Only two of our men died among the more than 50 who were sick. The ship's officers said that it had been a long time since they had had such a fortuitous crossing, but we had some sick people because the provisions were inadequate for our number.

After we had anchored, a pirogue with about 20 men aboard arrived to identify us. When they recognized us, they came aboard and informed us that the Sieur de Cussy was in Port de Paix where the Sieur de Saint Laurent, Governor General of the Islands, and the Sieur Begon, the intendant, had arrived. This greatly annoyed La Salle, who had business with these gentlemen. However, there was nothing to be done; patience was necessary.

The *Te Deum* was sung in thanksgiving for our fortunate crossing, and La Salle, feeling somewhat recovered from his indisposition, went ashore with some of his party to find some provisions to relieve the sick and to find a way to inform Saint Laurent and Begon of his arrival. He wrote personally to the Sieur de Cussy requesting him to come to Petit Goave and undertake together with him the measures necessary for the success of the enterprise. A few days later, as the sick were suffering from the heat in the ship where they were a bit crowded, La Salle ordered the soldiers put ashore on a small island that is near Petit Goave, where the people of the so-called reformist church are ordinarily buried when they die in this region. The soldiers and the sick men were given fresh meat and fresh bread, and La Salle asked me to find a house where they would not be an inconvenience to the residents. I found one at the end of the island where they were taken with the surgeons to treat them.

One day, when I was taking a walk with La Salle and we were returning, he suddenly felt weak; he was forced to lie down on the ground, unable to stand erect. After he had regained his strength a bit, I led him into a room in the house that the Duhaut brothers had rented. A bed was made for him there, and he lay down. The next day, he was attacked with a violent fever and a fit of delirium that lasted seven days. The fever abating on the seventh day, he began to put matters in order for the continuation of the voyage which was not easy for him as he, at that moment, had neither money nor credit. He had been told that it was not at all necessary to carry money and, for credit, he had satisfied himself with a letter of exchange of

[14] Jean Paul Tarin de Cussy, the French governor of La Tortue, was under orders to assist La Salle and provide supplies. Parkman, *La Salle and the Discovery of the Great West*, 367.

[15] Petit Goave was a port city on the southern coast of the Gulf of Gonave. It is about thirty miles west of modern Port-Au-Prince. See "Caribbean Region" map, *Britannica Atlas* (Chicago: Encyclopaedia Britannica, 1980), 238, 239.

54    2,000 *livres*[16] which was not accepted. With two or three hundred *pistoles*, he was at the end of all he had. His relatives accompanying him had little to lend him, and those who had been willing to follow him and expose their persons (on only his word) to the perils of an unknown settlement did not consider it appropriate to lend him the money they had at that time. His recourse was with the Sieurs Duhaut.[17] They had many pieces of lace, Indian cloth, clothing, and other things of that sort which would be of no use in the wild country where we were going. They could earn some money from them on this island where all commodities were very expensive. A hen was worth 30 to 40 *sous* and the rest proportionally expensive; a day's wages for a worker were three to four *francs*. The Duhauts believed La Salle credible when he explained these matters. From the sale of some of the goods they advanced some money to La Salle. He asked the Sieur Le Gros, who was a businessman, to take charge of all that was unloaded, and he asked me to help him, which we did. We were fortunate, with the excessive price of commodities, to have an adequate supply of bread and wine.

On the 2nd day of October, the storeship the *Aimable* and the frigate the *Belle* arrived. They had joined a buccaneer ship and another from La Rochelle called *Saint Joseph*; but, when we saw them arrive without the ketch, we suspected that she had been seized. We were only sure of this a few days later.

On the 9th, an annoying incident happened to one of our Recollet fathers, Father Zénobe, superior of the mission. During the voyage he had written about everything that happened on board the *Joly*, that is to say, all the disputes that had taken place between Beaujeu and La Salle during the entire crossing. He had written them nearly as they had occurred. The father left his chest open, or someone opened it; but somehow or other the memoirs were seen by someone who took them to Beaujeu. He was extremely angry with the priest and went so far as to say that, if he returned on board his ship, he would have him eat with the crew.

On the 20th of October, a ship and a small sailing frigate appeared and we decided these might be the gentlemen I mentioned before coming from Port de Paix. Between 9 and 10 o'clock in the evening they disembarked to avoid the reception that was due them upon such occasion, particularly the Sieur de Saint Laurent, the Commander, Governor General for the King of the Islands of America. When La Salle learned of their arrival, he sent his first captain, named the Sieur de Valigny, to greet them for him and to make his apologies to them that he could not pay his respects in person because he was still in the grip of fever.

We received confirmation of the loss of the ketch which we had only conjectured. We were told that she had set sail a good 15 days earlier to come to rejoin us and that she was seized by two Spanish pirogues of 60 men each. These pirogues conceal themselves in coves in the shelter of some rocks. When they climb up the

---

[16] For comparative information on French money used in the seventeenth century, see McDermott, *Mississippi Valley French*, 95, 119.

[17] The Duhaut brothers were Pierre (the older) and Dominique. Parkman describes Pierre as a man of respectable birth and education and a man of some property who had a "large pecuniary stake in the [La Salle's] enterprise." *La Salle and the Discovery of the Great West*, 420, 424. The French historian Paul Chesnel adds that the brothers, like Joutel, were from Rouen. *History of Cavelier de la Salle*, 187.

rocks and sight some ship that they believe they could easily capture, they bear down upon it with the full force of sails and oars, using oars more than sails. This loss was very severe for us; aboard the ketch were most of our provisions, those most necessary for such an enterprise. We lost also nearly all our cooking pots, very precious and very important household items for settlement in this country. At first this loss was kept from La Salle who was still not doing very well. A few days later, one of the Duhaut brothers told him of it. He could not resist declaring to Beaujeu that he had contributed partly to the loss of this ship because, if they had anchored at Port de Paix as had been agreed, this might not have happened. Moreover, they would have been spared the difficulty and the risk to which they exposed themselves in coming to Petit Goave. Furthermore, the arrangement of things would have proven much better at Port de Paix than in this place where we were.

The Sieurs Saint Laurent and Begon came to see La Salle, and the Sieur de Cussy came there privately several times to offer what was in his power to do. As his fever was diminishing, La Salle wanted to move his residency so he could revive his spirits. The Capuchin fathers, having heard this, offered him their place which was located near the church. La Salle accepted this and went there to lodge. The Capuchin fathers also had a house in the middle of Petit Goave where they had built a church.

La Salle, having at last fully recovered, had several meetings with these gentlemen with which he was most satisfied, having obtained their word that they would assist him in every way possible, which they certainly would do, being united among them and having no purpose other than to place all of French America in good order. As meal was not in abundance where we were, they ordered 15 to 20 casks of maize or Indian corn (what we call in France, *bled de Turquie* [Turkish corn]) delivered to La Salle to replace the meal that was lost on the ketch, as well as a few casks of wine and similar things. De Cussy offered to send La Salle a ship or two in the spring with provisions and food supplies in case he needed them and wanted to send his news. For that purpose, they agreed upon several unmistakable signals which should be given.

During the time we stayed in Petit Goave, we were at work making *biscuit* [hardtack] for the rest of the passage. La Salle had engaged workers in several trades, and among them a baker, and there happened to be another one among the soldiers. They were both put to work and someone else was occupied going to cut wood which was collected with the shallop or some borrowed pirogue. In that way, money was saved that would have been spent in labor wages. A day's wages were from one *escu* to four *francs*. Meanwhile, the residents or buccaneers led several of our men astray by persuading them that to believe that the country where we were intent on going was as fine as La Salle had described it was to believe a myth. Several buccaneers, who had been there, asserted that it was an arid, desert country where there was not even likelihood of game. The map depicted it, from what they had seen, as a region marked *Costa Deserta*. They added that there were a number of armadas awaiting us on our voyage. These armadas were Spanish vessels of war or privateers. So several of our people, who were otherwise not too willing and had come by force or by trickery, deserted. Discovering this, La Salle made all of his enlisted men go aboard again except for a few he still trusted. Next he had some goods put ashore in order to make some money to repay what the Duhauts had advanced.

That done, on the 7th of November, La Salle accompanied Saint Laurent and Begon aboard the *Joly* to reach an agreement with Beaujeu (who was indisposed) on the course that should be taken on leaving Petit Goave. A buccaneer pilot who was there at that time, and claimed to know the coast very well having navigated its length several times, was also called to this conference. The pilots of the *Joly* along with the one from the *Aimable* were there also. After each one had given his opinion, it was concluded that we should sail straight to the western point of the island of Cuba that is called the Cape of Saint Antoine,[18] about 300 leagues[19] from Petit Goave, and where there was no danger as the ships would be in the lee of the island of Cuba and protected from the north winds. Once we arrived there, we could set anchor and await a favorable wind to cross the gulf which the residents told us is very rough, especially during this season, because of the gusty winds which they call *anordies*. They said that, after enduring the wind there, we could enter and cross the gulf that may be about 200 leagues across.[20] If we were then, in crossing, seized by some wind that could not be weathered, we could put in to port at the Cape.

When the conference finished, Beaujeu asked La Salle, in the presence of these gentlemen, for a certificate that he was satisfied with him, which M. de La Salle promised him in the form he desired, stating therein that he desired only to be on good terms with him so as to arrive safely. These gentlemen, who were aware of some of the disputes there had been between Beaujeu and La Salle, declared their pleasure with the state of affairs that they witnessed between the two men. Saint Laurent and Begon had appointed several judicial officers at Port-au-Prince to bring a little more order among the residents who did largely as they pleased without anyone being able to remedy this. They were doing the same while they were in Petit Goave, and from there they were going about seven leagues to Léogane, and from there to other places where there were French settlements to establish the same order there. I neglected to say that Begon, the intendant, had offered La Salle a frigate, loaded with salt, that had been captured by the buccaneers, but as she ran a bit low in the water and we would have such rough seas in the gulf, La Salle was forced to politely decline. However, she would have served us well if we had had her. I must publicly note again the union that existed among these gentlemen and the devotion with which they worked for the welfare of the French colonies in this country.

After their departure, we thought only of preparations to put back to sea. Indian corn and hardtack were loaded on the *Joly* to supply the soldiers and those who had embarked aboard her for the rest of the crossing and other provisions

---

[18] Cape Saint Antoine is identified as Cabo San Antonio on contemporary maps. See "The West Indies" map in *Webster's New Geographical Dictionary*, 1332, 1333.

[19] According to U.S. Defense Mapping Agency map, JNCA-6, the measured straight-line distance is approximately eight hundred miles.

[20] The straight-line measured distance from Cape Saint Antoine to the mouth of the Mississippi River is approximately six hundred miles.

which were extremely costly. Beef was valued at seven *sous*, six *deniers* per pound and turkey hens some *ecus*. No one had any knowledge of La Salle's business affairs. He had trusted his merchant who had given him an extract of the bill, but he had not appointed anyone on the ship to take account and inventory of everything. True, the captain was in charge of everything. So, only Le Gros, whom I mentioned before, was taking care of these things until our arrival in the country.

All speed was taken for the embarkation. Then, at that point, many of the soldiers lost heart for they had been told of ill-intentioned people. Each one had a pretext for not embarking. Even a secretary, of sorts, who had been given to him [La Salle] at La Rochelle by his dealer, demanded to return. He was a cleric and was included among those who, it seemed, had been inopportunely chosen. Seeing this change, La Salle was obliged to make those people who were ashore re-embark, even several laborers to whom he had given privilege and permitted them to work for other individuals. He forbade anyone to let them disembark without his order. Also several of those who were still ill died, among them Chefdeville (the younger), a priest like his brother. I believe it would have been better had we stayed there for only two or three days, just to let our sick gain strength and to procure some provisions. The air was bad, the fruit the same, and there were a great many women worse than the air or the fruit.

As La Salle and Beaujeu had engaged in several disputes in the past, La Salle was afraid that some misfortune would befall the storeship the *Aimable* aboard which were most of his belongings. To prevent this, he believed he must embark aboard her. For that reason, he went to see Beaujeu and at the same time to settle with him on the course and the manner of navigation. As the storeship did not sail as fast as the *Joly*, it was concluded between them that during the night a signal lantern would be placed by which the others would steer themselves, and during the day they would follow each other in sight. La Salle embarked then on the *Aimable* with his brother, two Recollet fathers, namely: Father Zénobe and Father Anastase, and several volunteers. I also embarked on her. Everything thus arranged, we weighed anchor the 25th day of November, about one o'clock after midnight.

# CHAPTER II

#  Across the Gulf

At first we did not make great headway, a calm having overtaken us after sailing about four leagues. At daybreak, the wind changed and blew against us. We were compelled to tack back and forth until about 10 o'clock in the morning on the 27th when we had calm again. As we were near land at a place where there was a French settlement called Nippes, La Salle embarked with seven or eight men in the shallop and headed there intending to buy some poultry and similar things. The shallop from the *Joly* also went along with several officers. A few empty casks were taken along to fill with water for a cow and a few small pigs that we had taken on board. At 9 o'clock in the evening, a fresh wind from the northeast arose, the two shallops returned, and we set sail. We sailed northwest until the next day. As the *Belle* had stayed behind and the wind had freshened and the sea was heavier, she signaled with a flare which obliged us to furl our sails, even the foresail on the mast, to wait for her. When she joined us, we learned that she had been in danger from the heavy sea which had washed a great wave of water down the hatchways. They were forced to run before the wind, not being able to steer or hoist their mainsail.

Having reefed our sails, we lay at rest for the remainder of the night with our two *pacfis* [1] and at daybreak, the wind having calmed a bit, we hoisted sails and continued our course until about 10 o'clock in the morning when we sighted the island of Cuba to the northwest about eight or nine leagues. After that we changed course and steered to the west–¼–northwest [west by north] until the evening. I am not stating definitely all the leagues we may have sailed, nor the tacks we made to the right and the left.

On November 30, we had a calm, but the wind having freshened a bit, we continued our course to the west. In the morning [December 1], the weather was a little overcast, so that we could not see Cuba. We sailed to the west-northwest in order to keep it in sight. At noon, having taken a sight, we found ourselves at 19° 45' north latitude which suggested that the currents had made us drift away from

---

[1] This term has not been identified.

the island. In order to sail close to the shore of Cuba, we headed west–¼-north-west [west by north] until 5 o'clock in the evening when we sighted the island of the *Caymans* [Cayman Islands] which lay off from us to the southwest–¼-north-west [southwest by west]. The latitude was taken which proved to be 30° [20°?] 32'. About midnight we lay-to until three o'clock in the morning [December 3] when we sailed to the northwest and, at about noon, we sighted the *Ile de Pin*,[2] which is a small island near Cuba that lay off from us to the north about four leagues. We coasted until about 5 o'clock in the evening when we lay-to having no knowledge of the anchorage. The wind was favorable to us.

On the 4th, we cleared a point of the island; but, as we were too close to the wind, we had to anchor until evening when we again lay-to all night. In the morn-ing, although the wind was contrary, we tacked back and forth without cease until the evening when we anchored in a cove in 15 fathoms of water.

The next morning, La Salle went ashore with several men in his party to inspect this island. They shot a cayman or crocodile,[3] and after they had been there some time he returned on board. Two men who had accompanied La Salle wan-dered a bit too far in the woods, lost their way, and did not return with him. He ordered me to go aboard the *Joly* to take 30 soldiers and go sleep ashore to await them. Also, he told me to fire several gunshots during the night so they might hear us which we did. Above all, we were to keep a close watch to avoid any surprise, in case there were some men on this island, even though it was not inhabited.

This island is covered with trees of several species; some bear fruit. I did not eat any. It appeared to me that some of the fruit were similar to the acorn but much harder. There were various plants, it seemed to me, much more diverse, on which I saw several kinds of berries. There were a number of parrots,[4] much larger than those I had seen in Saint Domingue at Petit Goave. There were many turtledoves and other birds similar to those of Europe and some were different. We saw sever-al diggings[5] which suggested that there were pigs[6] on this island as there were on

---

[2] The Ile de Pin or Island of the Pines is designated on contemporary maps as Isla de la Juventud or Island of Youth. See "Map of Cuba" in *Webster's New Geographical Dictionary*, 303, and U.S. Defense Mapping Agency map, JNCA-6.

[3] The reptile cited as a cayman or crocodile was probably accurately identified as a crocodile. See entry "caiman," in McDermott, *Mississippi Valley French*, 40.

[4] Parrots were found on the islands in the Caribbean and reported by Gonzalo Fernández de Oviedo, who wrote that he had presented to the king thirty or more parrots from the West Indies, most of which could speak very well. Gonzalo Fernández de Oviedo y Valdés, *Natural History of the West Indies* [1526], ed. and trans. Sterling A. Soudemire (Chapel Hill: University of North Carolina Press, 1959), 29. Parrots were also reported by Spanish historians and diarists in northern Mexico. See entry "Parrots" in Foster, *Spanish Expeditions into Texas*, 242. Today parrots are found in the United States principally along the lower Rio Grande and in Florida. John H. Rappole and Gene W. Blacklock, *Birds of Texas: A Field Guide* (College Station: Texas A&M University Press, 1994), 10, 124, 125.

[5] The manuscript indicates Margry's text is in error—"foulures" should read "fouilleurs," which is translated as "diggings."

[6] Pigs were brought to North America by both the French and the Spaniards and were reported wild or feral on Cuba by the late 1500s by Oviedo, *Natural History of the West Indies*, 50. According to Charles Hudson, many pigs the Spaniards originally brought as domestic stock to Cuba escaped into the wild and multiplied quickly because there were no wolves, bears, or cougars on the island to prey on them. Charles Hudson, *Knights of Spain, Warriors of the Sea: Hernando de Soto and the South's Ancient Chiefdoms* (Athens:

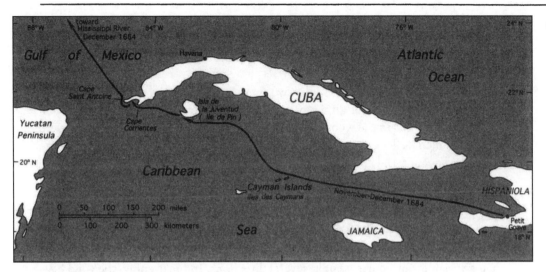

The La Salle expedition's route into the Gulf of Mexico, 1684

many others. In fact, one of our hunters wounded one; but as it was evening, he did not find it. He also killed several turtledoves and parrots. That evening, the soldiers ate the cayman or crocodile that La Salle had killed. The flesh is quite white and has a musk-like flavor. The night passed without any news of our two men although I had several gunshots fired.

The next day, the man who had shot the pig returned as soon as it was daylight to the place where he had fired. He found the animal still alive and fired at it again, killing it. He brought it to me, and I sent it to La Salle by the shallop which had come ashore. He shared half with Beaujeu. These pigs had been put on this island; they had multiplied just like those on the island of Saint Domingue. There are also on this island two species of animals which are as large as cats and resemble rats in the face but are a reddish color.[7] Our men killed and ate several of them and found them good. There were a number of shellfish on the seashore, like lobster and others, and an abundance of fish. At least we saw many on the shore. Also *passe pierre*[8] grew on the rocks; many kinds of sponges were found on the shore as well, but they were not large. That is what I observed on this island. We did not find much water.

As the soldiers had good appetites, they left nothing to waste: this was a refreshment point for them. On ship, only corn could be eaten so as to save the bread. Consequently, they found the crocodile good to eat and certain rats too. I

University of Georgia Press, 1997), 54. For a brief summary of the more recent distribution of wild hogs in Texas and throughout the United States, see David J. Schmidly, *Texas Mammals East of the Balcones Fault Zone* (College Station: Texas A&M University Press, 1983), 318–321.

[7] Minet describes the same wild rat-looking animal as large as a rabbit with the color of wolf fur. Minet, "Journal of Our Voyage to the Gulf of Mexico," 91. Weddle suggests muskrats as a possibility. Weddle (ed.), *La Salle, the Mississippi, and the Gulf*, 91, n. 14. Another guess would be the opossum, which has a long, slender snout like a rat. Oviedo describes the opossum (*churcha*) found in the West Indies as a small animal, about the size of a small rabbit, of tawny color with a pointed snout, a long tail, and ears like a rat's. Oviedo, *Natural History of the West Indies*, 58.

[8] This term was not identified by Margry, but we would translate it as "samphire" or "crithmene."

62　　was not overtaken by the desire to taste them. Besides I had a fever that night during which fresh water was taken from this island according to the author of a book published since our return to this country, entitled: *The Establishment of the Faith in New France*.[9]

To return to our discourse, our two men found us again. They told me that they would have had great difficulty rejoining us if they had not found the beach. As they had walked in the woods without noting the direction of the sun, they were going as much backward as forward. But the seashore guided them. They told me they had encountered almost the same country with the exception of a few savanna or pastures. They found no sign of men, which made me believe that they did not often come to this island which was about \_\_\_\_[10] leagues long, according to the charts. I informed La Salle of their return, and he ordered me to have everyone return aboard which was done. After this we weighed anchor for departure which was on Friday, December 8 at 10 o'clock in the morning. We set sail, and the wind being variable, our course went in several directions. In the evening, the wind having freshened, we steered to the west. We sailed all night, and Saturday, the 9th, in the evening we sighted the Cape of Corrientes[11] which lay to the west–¼-northwest [west by north] of us about four leagues. We had calm from evening until midnight when a wind arose from the west which made us drift four or five leagues and lasted until morning when it veered violently to the northwest. This compelled us to tack back and forth to coast along the shore for fear of an accident. In the evening of Sunday, December 10th, the wind having calmed a bit, we spent the night at anchor until Monday morning when the wind turned to the northwest. We rounded the Cape of Corrientes to reach the Cape of Saint Antoine.[12] At noon, the wind having freshened a bit, we had to tack back and forth until Tuesday, the 12th, when with the wind east-northwest [east-northeast?], we set our course at northwest because of the currents which seemed to be strong in these parts.

[9] The following quote is taken from Margry's footnote attributed to Joutel. "The author [Chrétien Le Clercq] claims to have taken his statements and allegations from the memoires of Father Anastase who was with us; but that would be very difficult to prove. Indeed, I did not observe that the priest had written down anything, at any rate not on his return with us; and with regard to what memory can supply him, I do not believe that he could say that water was taken from the island. Whatever the case may be, it is not about this matter that I intend to prove that the author made several errors, and I do not believe that Father Anastase told them to him, because I have always recognized him to be a very honest man and fine cleric, inacapable of wanting to advance anything false. However, he might have said something that the author exaggerated. That is why I address myself to the author of the book and not to Father Anastase." Margry (ed.), *Découvertes*, II, 110.

[10] Joutel omitted the number of leagues; according to U.S. Defense Mapping Agency map, JNCA-6, the distance is about forty miles.

[11] Cape of Corrientes is identified on contemporary maps of the Caribbean region as Cabo Corrientes. See "Caribbean Region" map in *Britannica Atlas*, 238–239. Cape Corrientes was identifed as a natural port of the western tip of Cuba and named by Spaniards over 150 years before La Salle rounded the cape. Francisco de Garay called the point by the same name when the governor landed in 1523 to resuppply his fleet headed for the northern gulf coast of modern-day Mexico. See Pietro Martire d'Anghiera, *De Orbe Novo, the Eight Decades of Peter Martyr D'Anghera*, trans. Francis A. MacNutt (2 vols.; New York: G. P. Putnam's Sons, 1912), II, 334.

[12] Cape San Antonio.

At 2 o'clock in the afternoon, when we were at the tip of Cape Saint Antoine, we had come too close to the wind to be able to enter the gulf. It was therefore decided, following the advice of Beaujeu, to put into a cove at the Cape, so we tacked about to head there. When we were abeam of the cove, the order was given to the *Belle* to go and sound to find out if there was good anchorage. She found out at the point of the[13] _____ that there was about 15 fathoms of water with a rocky bottom; but, toward the middle was found 15 or 16 fathoms of water and good bottom of coarse white sand. The sun had set a half hour earlier.

We remained there until Wednesday, the 13th, when we weighed anchor. At 9 o'clock in the morning, we set sail, steering to the northwest–¼-north [northwest by north], then west, and finally northwest to round the Cape and begin the course. We took a sight at that location of 22° latitude[14] and 288° 35' longitude. We were at that time about five leagues northwest of the Cape; but the wind having changed, we tacked about, not knowing the direction that the strong currents were moving. Therefore, we steered east–¼-northwest[15] and sailed thus until noon, Thursday, the 14th, when the latitude was taken and found to be 22° 2'. We continued to sail until about 3 o'clock after which the *Joly*, which was in front of us a good two or three leagues, tacked about and came to join us. La Salle asked Beaujeu the reason, and he told him that the wind was obstinate, that he did not consider it prudent to undertake the crossing, and that it was necessary to put in to shore again at the berth that we had left. La Salle complied with this. We steered to the east-southeast sailing until evening, one hour after sundown, when we anchored in the same depth as the previous day and we spent the night there. This precaution may have arisen from our not knowing these seas, but perhaps also it came from the lack of respect between Beaujeu and La Salle; each kept more on his guard and took measures to exonerate himself in case of an accident.

The following day, the 15th, as the wind was in the same quarter and there was no reason to leave, La Salle ordered some men to be put ashore to secure a few casks of fresh water. They found in the forest only a few ponds of stagnant water which, nevertheless, was not too bad. As there was no way to roll the casks, they put them on the beach and filled them using small galley kegs which were filled at

[13] This is one of the few instances in which there is a short lapse in Joutel's manuscript.

[14] The fact that Joutel reported the latitude reading of 22° at a point five leagues northwest of Cape San Antonio indicates that the latitude readings taken on the *Aimable* were remarkably accurate. Contemporary United States government maps show the Cape within one minute of 22°, indicating that Joutel' s reading was within a few miles of the current reading of the location.

The reading given by the Abbé D'Esmanville (who was on the *Joly*) was 21°48' near Cape Saint Antoine, a variation of only about twelve minutes or about fifteen miles. See "Journal de L'Abbé D'Esmanville," in Margry (ed.), *Découvertes*, II, 511. On Pierre LeMoyne d'Iberville's first expedition from France to the mouth of the Mississippi in 1699, he reported in his journal that on all his charts Cape San Antonio was marked 22° whereas he found it at 21°30' (a miscalculation by Iberville of over thirty miles). See Pierre LeMoyne d'Iberville, *Iberville's Gulf Journals*, ed. and trans. Richebourg Gaillard McWilliams (University, Ala.: University of Alabama Press, 1981), 27.

Based on the accuracy of the latitude readings given by Joutel at currently identifiable locations such as Cape Samana, Cape San Antonio, and later at the entrance to Galveston Bay and Matagorda Bay, this study projects with some confidence the maritime course of the *Aimable* along the Louisiana-Texas coast.

[15] The direction may have been east by north.

the ponds. Those who had gone ashore found a bottle with some wine remaining in it which gave the author, whom I mentioned, cause to say that a great many provisions were found there. This was Friday, the 16th. As the weather was calm, some men went ashore again to get some casks of water. I do not describe the country because I did not go ashore. The indisposition that I had at the Island of Pines had changed to a three-day fever, and I suffered five or six violent attacks which deprived me of seeing this land except from on board. From as much as I could determine, it must have been similar to that of the Island of Pines. On the shore there appeared many palm trees, a species of tree that is hardly fit to make anything but brooms. It is likely that the interior of the country is nicer than that of Saint Domingue, the climate being more temperate; but as I saw none of it, it is better not to say anything about it.

We saw some smoke trails farther inland. Some believed that it was a signal, because there were three smoke trails, the same as the number of ships. The following night, approaching the 17th, about 2 o'clock after midnight, the wind freshened, blowing rather strong from the northwest. The *Belle* dragged her anchor and proceeded to strike the bowsprit of our ship, splitting the yard of the bowsprit and the topgallant sail. If the cable had not been paid out quickly, she would have risked being lost. The frigate had a broken mizzen mast and lost a good 100 fathoms of hawser and the anchor. On the 18th, the wind blowing fresh from the northwest, we weighed anchor at 8 o'clock in the morning and set sail at 10 o'clock, steering north–¼-northwest [north by west]. We sailed until noon when the tip of Cape Saint Antoine was to the east of us, that is to say we were about five leagues to the west of the Cape at noon. We continued our course to the northwest until noon the next day, the 19th. We traveled some 30 leagues and the latitude was taken; it was determined to be 22° 58' which meant our course must have been approximately west-northwest, and we were at 287° 59' longitude. But I do not think it very necessary to specify the navigation in detail and will simply state the most essential details. We headed on several different courses, because the winds blew in several directions. What was advantageous for us was that we had good weather. Hardly a day passed that a sight was not taken.

On the 20th, a variation was observed on the compass; it was discovered to be 5° toward the northwest, and we were then at 26° 40' latitude and 285° 16' longitude. The 23rd, a heavy cloud gathered that threatened us with a strong gusts; preparations were made by lowering the sails of the topmast and the topgallant mast. But we had nothing worse to meet than fear. The cloud broke up, and by noon when it had dissipated, we were at a latitude of 27° 18' and 285° 15' longitude.

We continued to sail until the 27th when we took a sight by the sun and determined 28° 15' latitude and 283° 15' longitude. We continued on the same course. Thus, we made headway, and the latitudes indicated that we must not be too far from land. Orders were given to the *Belle* to go ahead and take a sounding and to signal in case she found land. About a half hour before sundown, she hoisted her flag which led us to think she must have discovered something, and she positioned herself broadside to await for us. When we joined her, we learned that she had taken a sounding of 30 fathoms of water with a muddy bottom. At 7 o'clock in the evening, we also sounded from our ship, finding 40 fathoms in the same bottom of grayish, muddy sand. Between 9 and 10 o'clock the same evening, we sounded again and found 25 fathoms; at midnight we had only 17 fathoms. That indicated that we must be near land, so we also lay broadside to await the *Joly* that was in the rear. Beaujeu also thought it was best to stay for the rest of the night to wait for daylight.

We set our course at west, and at 7 o'clock in the morning Beaujeu sent his canoe[16] with d'Hère, his lieutenant, and the two pilots to discuss with La Salle what course would be taken. It was agreed that we would head west-northwest until we were at six fathoms and land could be seen. We would approach the land with the shallops. With these matters settled, the sails were raised, and we got underway with the sounding line in hand so as not to be surprised. At 9 o'clock, we found 10 to 11 fathoms and fine, grayish, and muddy sand; at noon, we took a sight and found 28° 37' of latitude[17] and 282° 47' of longitude. From noon on, we continued our course sounding all the while. Since it was not very windy, we did not make much headway. We came into eight fathoms of water with the *Belle* always running ahead about a half hour by the sun. Then she ran up her flag, indicating to us that she had discovered something. This compelled a few sailors to climb the topmast from where they could see land; it was about six leagues to the northeast. Beaujeu, having seen that the *Belle* had her flag out, sent someone to see what was happening and, when he heard, he decided to set anchor at nine fathoms.

No one among us had knowledge of these waters or had sailed there, but we had all been warned that the gulf was full of currents which run swiftly to the east toward the Bahama Channel.[18] La Salle had been so informed by several knowledgeable persons in Paris, and the chart came closer to our estimation. This greatly diminished our estimated course[19] and caused us to believe that, if we had drifted to the east, the land we were seeing was the Bay of Palache.[20] We were at the same latitude given to it on the charts, and it was the only known place. Meanwhile, with

[16] In Chapter VIII, Joutel explains that the so-called *canot* ("canoe") is what they would call in French *bateau* ("boat"). He uses the term "canoe" more frequently.

[17] The latitude on December 28 of 28°37' indicates that La Salle's party first sighted the Louisiana coast near Atchafalaya Bay about one hundred to 150 miles west of the Mississippi River. See United States Geological Survey (hereafter cited as USGS) *Port Arthur*, NH15-8 and USGS *New Orleans*, NH15-9. However, historians have widely disagreed on where La Salle first sighted land; Fray Juan Agustín de Morfi wrote that on December 28, 1684, La Salle sighted the Florida coast. Morfi, *History of Texas*, ed. Castañeda, I, 121. For a review of studies that have been made about the location of La Salle's sightings and landings on the Gulf Coast, see Weddle, *The French Thorn*, 19–20; and Minet, "Journal of Our Voyage to the Gulf of Mexico," 95, n. 23. The study H. Dickson Hoese prepared agrees generally with the projection Weddle made, which this work supports, for La Salle's location at the first sighting of land. Hoese, "On the Correct Landfall of La Salle in Texas," 5–32.

[18] Although the surface currents in Gulf coastal waters east of the Mississippi run eastward, as Joutel mentioned, the surface currents west of the Mississippi along the Texas-Louisiana coast run westward in winter months. See Swanson, *Geo-Texas*, 149.

[19] The manuscript, which differs here from Margry, was consulted and followed in part in preparing the translation of this passage.

[20] Apalache (Apalaches) Bay, which Joutel called Palache, is on the eastern coast of the Gulf of Mexico (Golfe de Mexique) in Guillaume Delisle's 1701 map "Carte de environs du Mississipi." See Jack Jackson, *Flags along the Coast, Charting the Gulf of Mexico, 1519–1759: A Reappraisal* (Austin: Book Club of Texas, 1995), Plate 14.

this conference it was concluded that we would head west-northwest,[21] coasting along the land, and that Beaujeu would follow, keeping at six fathoms of water. In the morning, he would fire a cannon to weigh anchor and that, whenever there was wind, we would take advantage of it. So we got underway.

As we sailed closer to the land than the *Joly*, sounding all the while, we found ourselves in four fathoms of water, then five, and six fathoms. We continued on course, and at noon a sight was taken again and found to be 28° 44' of latitude and 282° 23' longitude. It was the 29th of the month; as the wind varied, we did not make much headway. At 6 o'clock in the evening, we came upon the *Joly* which was windward of us. As the wind was against us, it was decided to anchor, and it was agreed that if the wind changed, whether night or day, if it were from the north, the *Joly* should fire a cannon which would be the signal to weigh anchor and that she should steer by our lights, keeping further out to sea at six fathoms. About 2 o'clock after midnight, we weighed anchor and we sailed in several directions with the wind constantly shifting.

A sight was taken again, and found 28° 38' latitude and 286° 36' longitude. That same day, the 30th, d'Hère came aboard us with the second pilot of the *Joly* to discuss our estimated location. They concluded that they must have been mistaken and came to the same opinion as La Salle who insisted that the currents had carried us toward the Bahama Channel. In the evening, the wind freshened a bit blowing from the northeast.

We continued to sail along the coast and, when we found shallower water, we veered to the west. We continued until the first day of January when we were becalmed but noticed that the currents were moving toward land, making us drift there. We therefore set anchor in six fathoms. At 10 o'clock in the morning, when the weather cleared, we saw the *Belle* run up her flag. We had a man climb the mast from where he saw land that extended north-northeast and southwest about four leagues from us. As the *Joly* was in the rear, she could not see it nor had she even seen the signal from the *Belle*. La Salle ordered the shallop from the *Belle* to go and advise Beaujeu. The wind had freshened a bit. The commander of the *Joly* approached with the shallop manned, and d'Hère embarked with several men from his ship intending to go ashore. D'Hère came aboard us to meet with La Salle who embarked with them in the same shallop and ordered us to man ours. He also ordered the *Belle*, on leaving, to set sail and to approach land as near as it was possible so that, if the wind arose, they would be able to return on the *Belle* most promptly, not to lose any time. As soon as the shallop was equipped, some 10 to 12 boarded her, of which I was one, to go join La Salle who had landed but had had no time to inspect the country because the wind arose as soon as he was onshore. He saw only a large and vast country, flat, full of pasture land and marsh. When we were nearing shore, we met the shallop of the *Joly* which he was aboard. We returned without landing. All that I saw were great trees which had been cast along the shoreline and which appeared to have been carried along by the river

---

[21] As La Salle and Beaujeu apparently assumed that they were east of the Mississippi River, they continued to sail west and closely followed the coast as they searched for La Salle's river.

currents; the winds from the open sea had thrown them up on the seashore. When we had joined the shallop, we all headed off to board the *Belle* that, following orders, had drawn near shore. After this we weighed anchor and set sail at one o'clock after midnight.

We sailed west–¼-southwest [west by south], and at noon a sight was taken which determined 29° 20' latitude[22] and 279° 59' longitude. This was the second day of January. As the wind varied several times and almost came from straight ahead, we had to anchor. A fog arose that lasted until the next day (January 3rd), whereupon we lost sight of the *Joly*. The next day, the 4th, the weather cleared, and a few cannon shots were fired which she answered. In the evening, we caught sight of her to the windward of us, but because the wind was against us, we could not join her. A few sailors said they had seen her under sail as if she wanted to come to join us,[23] but this turned out not to be so. A signal light was put at the top of the flag staff and another at the top of the yard of the fore-topsail so that they could see us. Between 10 and 11 o'clock in the evening, when a fresh wind began to blow from the north, we fired a cannon shot to advise the *Joly* that we were going to weigh anchor. She answered us, and when we were under sail, we put a lantern on top of the mizzen mast and another at the top of the flag staff so that the *Joly* could see us by the two lights.

[22] The latitude reading 29°20' indicates that the three ships were still along the western Louisiana coast on January 2, 1685, and that landfall (on January 1) occurred over fifty miles east of the Sabine River. See USGS *Port Arthur*, NH15-8.

[23] We have substituted this phrase from the manuscript, since the phrase was misprinted in Margry's version.

# CHAPTER III

# La Salle Lands on the Texas Coast

fter that we set course west and west–¼-northwest [west by north] until 2 o'clock in the morning [January 5] when, in sounding as usual, we found that the water was shoaling. So we made a sudden course change to the southeast for a fresh breeze was blowing again, and we were better off farther out to sea. After sailing in that direction for about a half-hour, we veered about at seven fathoms of water and continued west until about 7 o'clock in the morning when a fog arose as it had the day before. We set the same course, running always with the sounding line in hand. When we found that we were in more than six fathoms of water, we headed west-northwest, risking even northwest. When we found the water shoaling again, we sheered off.

When the weather cleared a bit, we glimpsed land and continued underway until 6 o'clock in the evening when we anchored in sight of land which lay about two leagues to the north of us. We were anxious, meanwhile, about the *Joly* that we had not sighted at all. About one o'clock in the afternoon, we set sail on a course west–¼-southwest [west by south], always coasting along land as much as possible in order to gain some familiarity with it. We sailed until about 6 o'clock in the evening when we noticed that we had gotten into shallow water. We tacked about and headed south about a league until we were at about five or six fathoms. Then we resumed our course. We anchored for several hours after that at four fathoms; we spent the night and the next morning. As a fresh breeze was coming from the east, we wanted to get underway. But, while we were weighing anchor, our pilot noticed a reef behind us where the sea was crashing with great force, and he warned us not to wind the anchor capstan any more, because [both] wind and calm were driving us toward the sandbars. Therefore, instead of raising anchor, we set another anchor and decided to stay there until the wind calmed or at least abated.

We spent January 6, the Feast of the Three Kings, there. The Sieur de La Salle had given orders to the masters of the *Belle* to follow the coastline as closely as possible and to observe what they saw.[1] They said that they had seen a bay that appeared deep to them and they saw there a small island that made them believe this was Holy Spirit Bay. The charts [of this Bay] indicate an island in the middle of the points or very close. When the weather cleared a little more, someone was sent up the topmast to determine what this might be and thereby discovered the bay with this small island. On one of the points there appeared a very leafy tree and, to commemorate the feast-day, we called it by the name of "Gasteau," but [we thought it was the point][2] of Holy Spirit Bay.

La Salle would have liked the pilots' conjecture to be true. He resolved to set sail as soon as the weather permitted. When the wind moderated a bit, we began to distance ourselves from the sandbanks (the area not being worth anything), and at 2 o'clock in the afternoon we set sail to the south-southeast, sailing about a league and a half. We again cast anchor in six fathoms of water, that depth a common advantage along this coast. For that reason, anchorage is very good there. The wind turned to the northeast and blew cold.

At 9 o'clock the next morning [January 7?], rain fell which made the weather more gentle. Between 10 and 11 oclock, La Salle ordered the masters of the *Belle* to weigh anchor and go with our shallop to reconnoiter the sandbanks and bay. But, as the wind had calmed, the frigate could not proceed farther; only the shallop went in shoreward with the pilot from our ship. On his return, the pilot said he had just reached the sandbar when a fog arose, and he had to return for fear of getting lost. He added that the sandbars were the kind of shoal that extended the length of this coast. Not seeing anything, he had sounded and measured just one fathom of water. He had seen a small island. This was all that he reported to us.

Based on this report, La Salle examined the navigation logs of the coast to identify our probable location. He found neither shoals nor reefs; at least the charts did not indicate any. This further confirmed La Salle's idea that we had landed in the Bay of Apalache at the Cape of Barques although, by this reckoning and the logs, we should have landed on the small island. But as he was still determined in this thinking, it was necessary to adjust the latitude and the reckoning according to what he thought appropriate and to believe that we were just at one of the first two islands. La Salle displayed a chart he had that was specifically of the Gulf of Mexico which showed only this one place where there was a shoal and a reef. On this notion, it was concluded that the present course be continued, as formerly, coasting [westward] in order to locate the other three islands that were farther along according to the charts.

On Wednesday, January 10, the weather cleared a bit and we took a latitude of 29° 23'.[3] At 2 o'clock in the afternoon, the wind having picked up, although not

---

[1] La Salle's command seems to confirm that he was uncertain of his location on the coast.

[2] As the manuscript is unclear, this rendition is uncertain. We have inserted in brackets Margry's footnoted guess.

[3] According to the USGS *Houston*, NH15–7, Joutel's citing of 29°23' north latitude places the ship near the entrance to Galveston Bay. Parkman agrees, commenting that the "wide opening—between two low points of land" reported on January 10 was apparently the entrance of Galveston Bay. Parkman, *La Salle and the Discovery of the Great West*, 374.

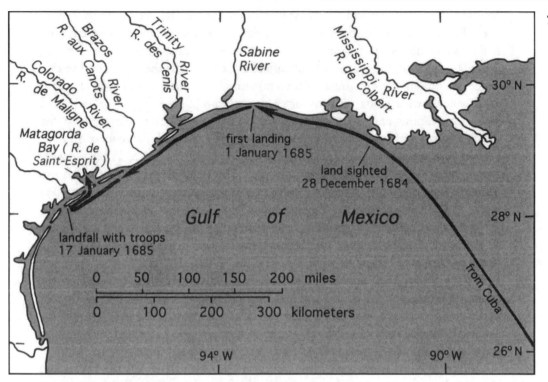

R. aux Canots
R. Brazos River
Trinity River
R. des Cenis
Sabine River
Mississippi River
R. de Colbert
30° N

R. Colorado de Maligne

Matagorda Bay ( R. de Saint-Esprit )

first landing
1 January 1685

land sighted
28 December 1684

Gulf of Mexico

28° N

landfall with troops
17 January 1685

0    50    100    150    200  miles

0    100    200    300  kilometers

from Cuba

94° W

90° W

26° N

The La Salle expedition's route along the Gulf Coast, 1684–1685

constant, we got underway and set sail. Not much headway was made because the wind varied and changed several times; then it fell again all of a sudden. We had to anchor because the currents were drifting us toward land.

The next day, the 11th, the calm continued and La Salle decided to go on land to see if he could discover something to identify this reef. As we were preparing to depart, the pilot murmured that La Salle was taking too many people with him. However, we were only six or seven. It would be more worthwhile, said the pilot, to take casks on board for fresh water. Although La Salle was master of what he judged best, he nevertheless had the deference to indulge this man, churlish by nature as he was. La Salle had decided, a few days previously, that if this was Holy Spirit Bay, he would land 30 men who would march the length of the shore, followed by the shallop to transport the casks and to help them cross the rivers they might encounter. The ill humor of the pilot made La Salle change his mind; he sent the pilot himself there with one of the frigate's masters to see what this bay was. They returned as little informed as the first time; another fog arose and forced them to return. The frigate's master told us only that he believed that the water on the other side of the reef was a river, which was probable. They had found the same depth as on the preceding day.

On Friday, the 12th, the wind began to blow a bit coming from the east. We weighed anchor, and at 6 o'clock in the morning we set sail, steering south-southwest, to stand off from the sandbanks. But the wind again dropped, and we only traveled about a league and a half. At noon we took our latitude at 28° 59'.[4] Since the calm came from the south and the currents were carrying us toward land, we had to set anchor at five fathoms of water where we spent the night. The next day, Saturday, the 13th, the captain of our ship told La Salle that the supply of drinking water was low and that it would be advisable to send the shallop to land to look for fresh water. I went along with five or six others who offered to go. We embarked with our weapons and some casks and, following La Salle's order, we took the *Belle*'s shallop with several volunteers aboard. We pursued our course straight toward land; we saw 20 to 30 men moving with us along the beach. When we were closer, we could see that they were Indians.[5] The wind blew fresh, although not violently, but the waves remained quite high because they came from the open water and the shoreline along the beach was flat. There was no way to turn aside. Therefore, we anchored a grappling iron which the wind carried to rest at the edge of the beach. Seeing that we had stopped, the Indians made us a sign to come to them so they could show us some animal skins. When they saw that we were not making a move, they showed us their bows which they then lowered to the ground.[6] We judged this to indicate that they did not want a battle. I knew that we could not go to them without running the risk of destroying the shallops, but the Indians continued to make signs urging us to approach. So I attached my handkerchief to the end of my musket like a small flag and signaled them to come to us.

After they had spent some time deliberating, nine natives left the others and entered the water up to their armpits. As they saw that the swells were sucking them under, the Indians left the water and searched the beach for a large log, which they found and carried to the water. The nine men stationed themselves alongside the length of the log an equal distance apart supporting themselves with one arm and swimming with the other. With this equipage, the Indians came alongside our shallops. When I saw them approaching, I warned our men to be on guard when the Indians tried to come into our shallops,[7] that they did not take

[4] According to USGS *Bay City*, NH15–10, the reading of 28°59' north latitude places the *Aimable* on January 12 in the coastal waters off Brazoria County. It should be noted that in Michel's condensed version of Joutel's journal, a mistaken reading is given of 25°50' north latitude, a reading that would seriously confuse any reader attempting to track La Salle's marine route. See Cox (ed.), *Journeys of La Salle*, II, 26.

[5] The Indians may have been members of one of the tribes that Cabeza de Vaca encountered in the same area after his Spanish expedition party landed on the Texas coast in late 1528. Alvar Núñez Cabeza de Vaca, *Cabeza de Vaca's Adventures in the Unknown Interior of America*, trans. and annot. Cyclone Covey (New York: Collier Books, 1961; reprint, Albuquerque: University of New Mexico Press, 1983), 54–69. See also Thomas N. Campbell's entry "Han Indians," in Tyler, et al. (eds.), *New Handbook of Texas*, III, 440. When Cabeza de Vaca landed on the Texas coast, the local Indians also used signs in an attempt to communicate with the Spanish visitors. La Salle was familiar with one or more Indian languages that he had learned on his explorations of the Great Lakes region and in Canada, but as Joutel's account later clearly indicates, the Frenchmen were not at this time proficient in the use of Indian signs, the means of communication Texas Indians frequently used when a common tribal language was not available.

[6] Although there was a misprint in Margry, the manuscript clarifies this rendition.

[7] About ninety years after La Salle's expedition to Texas, Spaniards sailed along the Pacific coast north of Monterrey Bay to land and formally take possession of the territory in present-day northern California, Oregon, and Washington. The marine expedition diarist Padre Miguel de la Campa writes that the Indians paddled out several miles off shore in dugout canoes to trade with the Spaniards. Like coastal

hold of the boats all at once, which would make them capsize. When they were near and almost ready to join us, we paid out a little of the hawser in a way that only the one in front could put his hand on my boat. So, in that way, five were taken on board, paying out the line as soon as one had boarded. After that we made a sign to the other four to go to the other shallop which they boarded in the same manner. We headed for our ships. The rest of the tribe [on shore] returned to their territory inland.

As a chilly wind was blowing and these poor men had come out of the water (they were trembling cold), we gave them some clothes to wear. The natives gave us a few signs of gratitude in their way; but as we could not understand them at all, we did not gather much from them. The Sieur de La Salle was pleased when he first saw them, hoping that they could give him some news of the Indian nations that he had met on his earlier exploration [of the Mississippi].

As soon as they arrived on board, the Indians were given some tobacco to smoke. (I have learned since by experience that this is the first civility of the country.) Afterward they were given something to drink. They ate and drank with the same ease that they had when they were aboard our shallop. As they were a little rocked by the agitation of the sea when they arrived in the boats (and even the ship tossed a little bit), they all felt a queasiness. When they felt a little better, La Salle asked them about several matters, particularly about the tribes he had seen on his exploration. But he did not know their language, although he knew several other native languages, which he spoke to them, but none of them did they understand. They made signs indicating that they did not understand anything we were asking them.

After having them smoke and eat, we showed them our arms and the vessel. When they saw at one end of the vessel some sheep, pigs, chickens, and turkeys, and the hide of a cow we had killed, the Indians made signs that they had all these animals where they lived. We began to understand what they were saying to us by signs, that there were many animals on land; they indicated also, answering the signs we made to them, that they had fresh water there too. We believed, moreover, that they were telling us that there was a river near the sandbars.

With evening approaching, La Salle gave to each Indian a knife and some strings of glass beads and told us to take them back to land. We gave them the signal to re-embark, which they did; after that we set our course for land and headed toward the place where they had met us. Arriving there, we gave them signs to strip and return the clothes that we had given them to cover themselves. As they had no way to fasten the items on themselves which La Salle had given them, we

---

Texas Indians, the California coastal tribe had bows and arrows, lived in small huts, communicated by signs, painted their bodies and faces, wore animal skins, smoked tobacco, and were eager to trade. Unlike Texas coastal tribes, they had canoes for use in open ocean waters. Campa, *A Journal of Explorations* ed. Galvin, 27–43.

Mayan seamen used oars to propel large freight vessels across the open gulf waters and had boats under sail. See Weddle, *Spanish Sea*, 78, citing Bernal Días del Castillo, *Historia Verdadera de la Conquista de el Nueva Espana* (2 vols.; Mexico City: Editorial Porrúa, 1955), I, 45–46, and Gonzalo Fernández de Oviedo y Valdés, *Historia general y natural de la Indias* (14 vols.; Asunción del Paraguay: Editorial Guarania, 1944), III, 301.

74

attached the gifts to their arms and neck, and then made signs for them to enter the water. They hesitated a bit, apparently because the air was cold and they had been wearing clothing; however, they jumped in, after making us signs to come ashore and that they would give us meat and skins.

When they were on land, other members of their tribe came to meet them, and when they were re-united, they gave us signs to approach which we could not do because of the high seas. After we had watched them a while, we reset our course to return on board. As soon as we arrived, the wind blowing fresh again, the anchor was raised and we set sail about 7 o'clock in the evening. We steered south to stand off, and then sailed to the southwest, sounding all the while until about 8 o'clock the next morning.

On that day, the 14th, we again had calm weather, and at noon we determined a latitude of 28° 51'.[8] From noon on, the wind blowing fresh again, we sailed west until about 3 o'clock, when, finding that the water was shoaling and that the wind and waves were carrying us toward land, we tacked about and anchored in six fathoms of water. The calm having overtaken us, we embarked in the shallop to return to land to procure fresh water. We were again impeded by the swells, but we anchored the grappling iron. We planned that a party of us would go ashore stripped down. Now we had more desire to go ashore than we had previously, seeing this time herds of deer roaming the countryside.[9] Twenty bison also came as far as the shoreline. These were the first bison I had seen.[10]

Some of our sailors got into the water to sound whether we could go ashore. Somewhat ahead, they found a sort of channel, quite deep, between land and us, causing us to believe that some river ran the length of this shore and formed a sort of shoal on which we were anchored. We wanted to follow the length of the coast to see if the shoal ran far and if we could find some entrance; but we were prevented from doing this by the sudden appearance of a large cloud that threatened a squall. At the same time, a cannon shot from our ship recalled us. Thus, for that day, we did not press farther. We made our way back with great regret.

[8] According to USGS *Bay City*, NH15–10, La Salle was coasting along present-day Matagorda County at 28° 51' north latitude.

[9] The identification of the deer-like animal that Joutel called a *chevreuil* is not clear, but it is likely either (or both) the whitetail deer or pronghorn antelope. According to McDermott, *chevreuil* was a small or "dwarf" deer and *cerf* was an elk. *Mississippi Valley French*, 46, 51. We have translated *chevreuil* as deer.

Spaniards reported pronghorn antelope (*berrendo*) ranging as far south as Parras in southern modern-day Coahuila and north to the San Antonio River. See entry "Pronghorn Antelope (berrendo)" in Foster, *Spanish Expeditions into Texas*, 242–243. In 1828, the European scientist Jean Louis Berlandier met a small band of "Tancahueses" (Tonkawa) Indians about eighty miles north of Lavaca Bay in western Colorado County, and he reported that antelope was the natives' principal game. Berlandier, *Journey to Mexico During the Years 1825 to 1834* (2 vols.; Austin: Texas State Historical Association, 1980), II, 313. William B. Davis and David J. Schmidly illustrate by a distribution map that the former range of the pronghorn antelope in Texas extended into DeWitt, Goliad, and Bee counties in southern Central Texas, but, according to the authors' map, the pronghorn range did not extend to the coastal areas near Matagorda Bay. William B. Davis and David J. Schmidly, *The Mammals of Texas* (Austin: Texas Parks and Wildlife Press, 1994), 284–285.

[10] La Salle and Père Membré, who traveled down the Mississippi as a member of La Salle's 1682 expedition party, saw bison on the trip along the middle Mississippi. Cox (ed.), *Journeys of La Salle*, I, 134.

When I told La Salle what I had seen, the news of bison and deer delighted him, for he reckoned that the country that he had earlier discovered could not be far. I mentioned that, if we could land, we would be able to secure fresh meat, which would please everyone on board. We very much wanted to land although the country seemed inundated. The cloud that concerned us dissipated without any effect, and we spent the night there.

The following day, the 15th, the wind blowing fresh again from the north, we set sail about 6 o'clock in the morning, steering to the west-southwest. With the sounding line in hand all the while, we sailed until 7 o'clock in the evening when we set anchor in six fathoms of water. Coasting along land all during that day, the country seemed quite beautiful; there were small hills of sand, in the form of dunes, on which there was some fog. We could distinguish everything, even some Indians whom we saw on the shore following our route. We also saw some bison which La Salle's Indian [Nika][11] brought to our attention, for these people have much better sight than we have.

We stayed there until Tuesday, the 16th, when the wind freshened a bit, and we got underway, setting sail about 7 o'clock in the morning. With the wind from the north-northeast, we sailed west-southwest, and at 10 o'clock, as we were coasting about one league off shore, the shoreline seemed to us to be higher than usual. We saw in front of us a point of land extending into the gulf, where there were some sandbanks and breakers.[12] That is to say, the seas broke, and there must have been either shoals or sandbanks there. The sandbanks eventually advanced into the sea and, as it was feared the wind was about to strengthen and change, this could throw us upon the shoals, so we tacked about in order to put out to sea. We headed southeast until we were ready to clear the point, after which we took up the same course, and at noon, having taken our latitude, we determined we were at 28° 20' north latitude.[13] This reduction in latitude suggested that the coast was extending southward a little. We continued our course until 6 o'clock in the evening when we set anchor as usual.

[11]  Joutel later refers to the guide as the Shawnee Nika. La Salle's Indian companion had been found when La Salle was in Canada; La Salle took Nika and another Indian guide and hunter with him on his return to France and then brought Nika to Texas. On Nika's role, see Parkman, *La Salle and the Discovery of the Great West*, 412, 421, 425. See also Chesnel's comments that La Salle had purchased Nika as a war prisoner in 1669 and that Nika was with La Salle when he found the Ohio. Chesnel, *History of Cavelier de la Salle*, 29, 35, 95. On the special relationship that developed between the French and Shawnee Indians during the late 1600s, the period during which La Salle found Nika, see Robert S. Grumet, *Historic Contact: Indian People and Colonists in Today's Northeastern United States in the Sixteenth through Eighteenth Centuries* (Norman: University of Oklahoma Press, 1995), 226, 229, 312.

[12]  The similarity in the description of Pass Cavallo Cabeza de Vaca's companion Dorantes related and that Joutel gave is striking. Dorantes reports that his party of nine reached an inlet (Pass Cavallo) that "was broad, more than a league across, and made a point toward the Pánuco side which went out to the sea a fourth of a league, with some large mounds of white sand, for which reason it must have been visible at a great distance in the sea; and for this reason they suspected that it must be the river Espíritu Santo." Harbert Davenport (ed.), "The Expedition of Panfilo de Narvaez," *Southwestern Historical Quarterly*, 27, (Jan., 1924), 237.

[13]  According to USGS *Beeville*, NH14–12, Pass Cavallo is located at approximately 28° 20' north latitude. Joutel's description of the coastline jutting into the Gulf and the high sand dunes in the immediate

On Wednesday, the 17th, the wind being the same, north-northeast, we got underway and sailed to the southwest until 10 o'clock in the morning, when, the wind having fallen, we had to anchor in five fathoms of water. Because we had navigated in sight of land and had seen what was apparently a river[14] toward the north-northeast about a league and a half, La Salle decided it advisable to send a party to determine if we could enter there and procure fresh water. He ordered eight or ten of us to set off in the shallop and told us that when we had landed to give a smoke signal, so that he could embark in the shallop of the *Belle* to come ashore also. As we approached land, we found that the waves were very high and rough and that we were unlikely to draw nearer. Therefore, we anchored with our grappling iron. One sailor then entered the water to see if he could find some entrance. Having searched to the right and left, he shouted to us that there was a channel, but that it was not very wide. We approached by the way that he indicated, even though the waves were very rough, and crossed rapidly taking several waves until we had entered. Once in the channel, we were in calm waters and went a little farther to set foot on land. First, I sent the smoke signal to advise La Salle, after which I ordered a search for fresh water. After that we headed to the right and the left, not however wandering too far, so that if La Salle came we could join him. La Salle set off, but when he came to the entrance that we crossed, he did not want to risk the shallop at that point to explore the countryside. The shallop belonging to the *Belle* was smaller than ours, the one that belonged to the cargo boat the *Aimable*. Therefore, he returned on board.

The country did not seem very favorable to me. It was flat and sandy but did nevertheless produce grass. There were also several salt pools. We saw hardly any wild fowl except some cranes[15] and *outardes* [Canada geese][16] which were not expecting us. There were tracks of deer which had roamed this area. We killed some ducks and even saw some herds of deer, but they moved away a considerable distance. It appeared that the region became inundated at certain times. We went

area of the pass support the contention that the location of the *Aimable* on January 16 was near the entrance to Matagorda Bay.

[14] Cedar Bayou is the outlet (which Joutel called a river) that separates Matagorda Island from St. Joseph Island in the southwest. Weddle also identifies Cedar Bayou as the outlet stream reported by Joutel on January 17 in *The French Thorn*, 21. See also Minet's map, which indicates the location of the outlet (modern Cedar Bayou) in relation to the entrance to Matagorda Bay. Minet, "Journal of Our Voyage to the Gulf of Mexico," 101, Plate 7.

[15] Two species of cranes are found today in the Matagorda Bay area—the brown-gray sandhill crane, with a statewide population sufficient to permit a state and federally sanctioned hunting season in certain areas of Texas, and the slightly larger endangered white, with black-tipped wings, whooping crane. See Rappole and Blacklock, *Birds of Texas*, 780, and Wayne H. McAlister and Martha K. McAlister, *Matagorda Island: A Naturalist's Guide* (Austin: University of Texas Press, 1993), 242, 246. The padre Isidro Espinosa identified the two different colored cranes that visited northern Nuevo León and Coahuila in the early eighteenth century, although Joutel makes no such distinction. Isidro Félix de Espinosa, *Crónica de los colegios de propaganda fide de la Nueva España*, ed. Lino Gómez Canedo (Washington, D.C.: Academy of American Franciscan History, 1964), 767.

[16] *Outardes* or *bustards* were Canada geese. McDermott, *Mississippi Valley French*, 110. Canada geese continue to flock to Matagorda Island in the fall and winter. McAlister and McAlister, *Matagorda Island*, 228–229.

a good half league inland and in the evening we returned to re-embark. The people in the shallop had returned also, not having found any fresh water, although they searched farther than a league inland. As the country is flat, the sea is higher.[17] In re-embarking, I found that we were missing one man, an English sailor whom La Salle had engaged at Petit Goave. If the country were not flat and open, one might have believed that he had lost his way. We thought that perhaps he was asleep, so I had several gunshots fired to awaken him or, in any case, to warn him. We searched for him until sunset when I again had some gunshots fired. Finally, not seeing him, we returned to the ship.

We came out more easily than we had come in. The waves had receded, and we met the *Belle* which La Salle had ordered to come to meet us. We positioned ourselves upwind as she came alongside. I gave La Salle an account of what we had seen, but he was angry to hear that we had left a man behind, fearing that some Indians would attack and kill him. However, at midnight we saw a small fire on land causing us to believe that the lost man made it to signal that he was there. We stood guard watching the place where the fire appeared so we could return there the moment it was daylight, which was done the morning of the 18th. The shallop was sent straight to where the fire had been seen, and it was indeed our man. They then returned on board. What caused the Englishman to be left behind was that he had gone to the left of the river, come back a little while later to the shore, and then he saw the shallop on which La Salle had embarked return without being able to enter. He thought it was our boat. Consequently, he left the river course where we had entered and returned to a point in front of the ships where he camped. Here he made the fire that we had seen to advise us that he was there. He fetched some birds which he had killed which are similar to Canada geese but better.

The north wind having freshened a bit, we set sail steering to the southwest to clear a point that appeared in the distance. We went a league and a half perhaps, but the calm overtook us again and we were obliged to anchor. We found that the land extended still farther toward the south which gave La Salle some concern that he was too far into the Gulf. The ship's captain reported that it was necessary to secure fresh water, so he [La Salle] turned back toward the river from which we had departed that morning and ordered the shallop to stand ready for the next morning. We set sail again to get closer to the river and cast anchor at six fathoms of water about one league from the river. La Salle gave the order to prepare to land one hour before daylight and to carry rations for several days. He gave the same orders to the shallop of the *Belle* and directed that the moment they had landed, the shallop of the *Aimable* should return, so that he could go there too. The other shallop should stay to refill the casks if fresh water could be found. As I was preparing to leave with the others, La Salle told me I should go with him.

On Friday, the 19th, the shallop left with six or seven casks and the men who had been named. There were ten men from our ship and five or six from the *Belle* in addition to the shallop's crew. As there was a thick fog, they took a compass. The fog dissipated a few hours later by a small wind that blew up from the north. When

---

[17] From sea level, or perhaps a few feet below, the sea appeared higher to Joutel.

it was full daylight and the fog had entirely lifted, we saw a ship coming directly toward us from the southwest. We had to work promptly to prepare the cannons and pull all the arms out to go on the defense, although we suspected that the vessel was the *Joly*. But, since it was forging ahead and we were in an area where it was wise to be on guard, nothing should have gone unheeded. We began by firing a cannon shot to advise the shallop to return. Upon seeing us, the ship came up broadside, struck her mainsail, then her mizzen, and approached us under her two topsails. When she was within range of better view, we recognized that it was the *Joly*. She anchored near us, and as all the arms had been brought out to prepare for combat, La Salle ordered that they be cleaned and put away.

A little later, their shallop, with d'Hère aboard, came to our ship. He complained, on behalf of Beaujeu, that La Salle had, by a premeditated act, abandoned the *Joly*. This was a criticism that he [Beaujeu] should not have considered. If Beaujeu had held exactly to the course as we had, one on which we had agreed, he should have sailed in six fathoms of water . . . When we lost sight of them, we shot our cannon and he responded to it . . . Moreover, his ship was a better sailer and it was for that reason that we were going ahead, and it would have been easy for him by this time to join us again, being faster.

Let us say that they had noticed that the coast extended southward which was proof that we were farther [west] than we had believed, and that the currents, of which we had been given such assurance, had not carried us to the east, as had been declared, then we likely had landed on the islands rather than in Apalache Bay. This caused us to review the ship's logs. Having examined them all, we found that we must have landed on the small islands and that, according to the reckoning, we should be twenty or thirty leagues from the Magdelaine River.[18] The pilot of the *Belle* had always been of this opinion and, in spite of the opinion of others, he had continued his navigation and reckoning on that. He was assured that we were at the distance that I just stated from the Magdelaine River.

D'Hère returned to report to Beaujeu. The same day La Salle visited him to make him understand, after a few arguments (as usual), that the question to discuss was the proper course to set and at what position we might be. La Salle thought that the sandbanks seen near where we had anchored the 6th of this month could be one of the branches of the river for which we were searching; on his earlier exploration coming downriver, he had left a branch of the river [the Mississippi] on the right at about sixty leagues from the mouth of the river. Accordingly, he proposed to Beaujeu to return to these sandbanks. For his part, the Sieur de Beaujeu requested more provisions.

As we had come there to obtain the fresh water we needed, La Salle, on the 20th, sent his shallop ashore for this purpose. For his part, Beaujeu sent his shallop

---

[18] The river Joutel referred to as the Magdelaine cannot be identified with certainty. Some authors have suggested that the reference to the Madelaine or the Magdelaine was to the present-day Guadalupe River that enters San Antonio Bay. See Weddle, *The French Thorn*, 193, 376, n. 11. The name is used on European maps of the period to identify some river west of Espíritu Santo Bay and northeast of the Palmas River. See, for example, Nicolas Sanson's 1656 map of North America in Jackson, *Flags along the Coast*, 10.

to get wood. At noon La Salle embarked on the shallop that had returned to carry the men and the casks, and he took me with him. We met Beaujeu who was returning in his canoe with the Sieur Minet, an engineer[19] who had been appointed for our settlement. They had instruments for taking latitude and La Salle found out from them that we had reached 27° 50'. They also told La Salle that there was a kind of lake inland a little farther at about two and a half leagues from the ships; we continued on our way.

Arriving on land, we learned that the shallop of the *Belle* had gone up the river one and a half leagues without finding fresh water; but heading inland to the right and left, several pools of water were found. From these pools some of the casks were refilled and sent on board. We slept on shore. The hunters killed several ducks, Canada geese, teals,[20] and other wild fowl. These hunters were La Salle's Indian [Nika] and a Canadian named Barbier, who was an infantry lieutenant. The next day, the 21st, they returned to hunt and killed two deer and a quantity of other game that La Salle sent to Beaujeu. There were several officers from the *Joly* who hunted, among others, the Sieur Duhamel (ensign of the vessel) and the King's scrivener. We stayed at that place several days refilling casks, and Beaujeu did the same . . .

D'Hère went on land where he conferred with La Salle about the provisions of which I have spoken. They still could not agree, whereupon La Salle decided to land there. However, he could not do so immediately because of the high swells and because the river, which was small, had almost no channel.[21] While we were there, we hunted every day and lived well off the game. La Salle decided one day to reconnoiter a little farther inland to see if he could find another river. It was somewhat foggy, departing in the morning at daybreak, and five or six of us became separated from the others, but we kept going across some open country which was quite vast. We found several salt water pools, some that were too deep to see the bottom. However, there seemed to be an abundance of fish in them. The soil was sandy and dry, but firm. There were, however, some places where the soil was rich, and everywhere there was grass. We saw many deer tracks and many ducks and other water fowl, but little fresh water. It appeared to me that the region flooded at times. We continued on until 2 o'clock in the afternoon when we saw the party at a distance where La Salle was. Then we returned to camp without having learned much from our exploring.

During our time there, when the weather permitted,[22] a few men always came ashore. However, we were concerned when there was a thick fog for two days

[19] Parkman refers to Minet simply as the engineer. *La Salle and the Discovery of the Great West*, 373.

[20] Blue-winged teal is a small duck that annually visits the bay area today. McAlister and McAlister, *Matagorda Island*, 229.

[21] Minet wrote that the channel of present-day Cedar Bayou measured fifteen fathoms wide and was one foot deep at low water. See Minet, "Journal of Our Voyage to the Gulf of Mexico," 99, 100.

[22] Although Joutel does not mention specifically the norther that blew in during this time, Minet describes the cold snap in some detail. In his brief account of the voyage aboard the *Joly* with Beaujeu, the engineer Minet wrote that on January 27 and 28 a norther struck the coast leaving frost on the land up to six inches deep. See Minet's shorter account, "Abstract from the Journal of the Voyage We Made to the Gulf of Mexico," in Margry (ed.), *Découvertes*, II, 591–601. In a more extensive version, Minet wrote that

80 because we could not see the ships. La Salle feared that Beaujeu would put out to sea, especially as he had a fresh breeze, which would leave us there without provisions. The misunderstanding between them caused La Salle such a fear, but it dissipated on the third day as did the fog. We saw the ships in the spot where we had left them. When the *Aimable*'s shallop came ashore, La Salle returned on it to the ship. On board, he gave orders to unload powder and musket balls proportionately, and also bullets for hunting, as well as some casks of wine and brandy. He gave the captains and masters of the *Aimable* as well as the *Belle* their orders, and he left several men to stand guard over everything after which he returned to land.

As our men had been hunting every day, we were not lacking for game, as many as four or five deer in the hut and more than 150 head of other game. That evening when La Salle returned from on board, the wind, having changed to the northwest and become very cold, somehow caused the sea to recede. The shallop thus missed the channel, and it was necessary for the men to get into the water to take the wine and brandy ashore. I had several soldiers do this and had them roll the casks on shore. Then I pierced the wooden casks with a hot iron for want of a proper piercer; a timely treat . . .

---

there was a hard freeze and some pails and tubs of water froze on the ship. Minet, "Journal of Our Voyage to the Gulf of Mexico," 102.

Based on the best available information on temperature averages for nearby Port Lavaca, Texas, the local coastal area currently suffers from short-term freezing conditions, but the average daily minimum temperature has not been below forty degrees during the last quarter century. McAlister and McAlister, *Matagorda Island*, 14, 15. This report of a colder event than the normal recorded in recent years is repeated in numerous winter weather reports found in Spanish expedition diaries prepared during the Little Ice Age, a period of cooler and wetter weather that continued until about the 1850s. See Foster, *Spanish Expeditions into Texas*, 226, 228.

The significance of the Little Ice Age on European exploration in North America is noted by James E. Fitting in the *Handbook of North American Indians* that there was a warming period from about 300 B.C. to A.D. 1000 but that around A.D. 1450 there was a period of cooling, the Little Ice Age that occurred between A.D. 1550 and A.D. 1880. James E. Fitting, "Regional Cultural Development, 300 B.C. to A.D. 1000," in Bruce G. Trigger (ed.), *Northeast*, vol. 15 of Sturtevant (ed.), *Handbook of North American Indians*, 44. The increased moisture associated with the Little Ice Age was indicated in the increase in the size and movement of glaciers in the Rocky Mountains and could be detected clearly in the increase of rain and in the size and flow of rivers and the abundance of plant and animal life in the areas that were being explored in South Texas and Northeastern Mexico.

# CHAPTER IV

# *Beaujeu Returns to France*

❦

hile[1] we were living at ease, La Salle was waiting impatiently for some decision from Beaujeu. Was he going to the place where he expected to find the Mississippi or was he going to take some other direction? Finally, realizing that his project was not advancing, La Salle decided to proceed with his own design which was to land 120 to 130 men and have them march up the coast until they encountered another river.[2] At the same time, the *Belle* would follow the same route by sea, coasting along the land to give assistance to those on land in case of need. La Salle gave the command of this small company to Morenger[3] and me. He supplied us with provisions of all kinds for eight or nine days including arms, tools, and utensils that we might need. Each man prepared his own pack with a memorandum of what we had to do and signals that we would use. We set off on February 4, 1685.[4]

I was in the vanguard; Morenger followed in the rear. Although our men only totaled about one hundred, they occupied more terrain in marching than a

[1] Margry notes that Joutel's manuscript becomes illegible at this passage and that he has relied principally on Michel's version for this paragraph.

[2] Although Minet's more complete journal has been translated into English ("Journal of Our Voyage to the Gulf of Mexico," 83–126), a shorter and slightly different account that has not been translated into English is found in Margry's compilation. This shorter version notes that the troops were dispatched toward the northeast. Minet, "Abstract from the Journal of the Voyage We Made to the Gulf of Mexico," 591–601.

[3] Crevel Morenger, La Salle's nephew who was serving as a lieutenant, is described by Parkman as young, with a "hot and hasty temper." Parkman, *La Salle and the Discovery of the Great West*, 424.

[4] On his march up Matagorda Island, Joutel gives no daily account of the number of leagues and direction traveled, the type of route information that he provided on the 1687 march from Matagorda Bay to the Mississippi. Parkman agrees that Joutel and his troops proceeded until they were stopped by "a river, but which in fact was the entrance of Matagorda Bay." *La Salle and the Discovery of the Great West*, 379. Minet's map of the coastline and entrance to the bay also supports Parkman's conclusion (and mine as well). Minet's map is reproduced in Weddle (ed.), *La Salle, the Mississippi, and the Gulf*, 107.

thousand would have done. We stopped from time to time beside the salt pools. We rested for the evening on the side of a small rise on top of which I placed sentries. Guards were also posted at other points where someone could approach.

At 11 o'clock in the evening on the 5th, I was surprised to hear a few cannon shots fired from our ships. The troubling misunderstanding between La Salle and Beaujeu caused me to fear something, more so because the *Belle* had not followed us since the [previous?] night.

Despite our concern, we continued our march. Our men did not always conduct themselves well. As I said before, each had his little pack of food. When it was time to eat, each would take a measured quantity and cook as much as was needed to pass the night. But all these men had large appetites because the provisions had diminished during the crossing. They would eat meal and other rations during the night. Noticing this, I had all the packs gathered at a central location each night and a guard posted there. As for water, when we could not find any pools, which happened often, we found water holes along the seashore. Almost always, out of every five or six, one or two were passably good, and it was not necessary to dig deeper.[5]

On the evening of the 6th, we camped in a small place outside pistol range of the sea because of the convenience of water. Our men then went to search for wood along the shore, where the sea cast a large quantity from very large trees of several kinds. Some logs were more than 100 feet in length. I noticed that the men were gathering a fruit or grain resembling small reddish-yellow beans that they were eating. I had difficulty making them abstain. Those who ate the fruit became sick, vomiting for one or two hours afterwards until they vomited blood.[6] The next day they were incapacitated.

We continued to march short day's journeys until the 8th when we reached the bank of a big river or the shore of a bay.[7] We were not able to cross, and I now had

[5] The lack of fresh water on the island can be a current problem for visitors to Matagorda Island, but shallow "perched aquifers" are found eight to ten feet below the surface. McAlister and McAlister, *Matagorda Island*, 13.

[6] The fruit or grain resembling small reddish-yellow beans may have been the yaupon (*Ilex vomitoria*), which, according to the authority Robert A. Vines, has "emetic and purgative qualities" and was used by local Indians in preparing a ceremonial tea. *Trees, Shrubs, and Woody Vines of the Southwest* (Austin: University of Texas Press, 1960), 646–647. See also the description of how Indians used yaupon as a drink to induce vomiting as part of a purification ritual. Charles B. Heiser Jr., "Ethnobotany and Economic Botany," *Flora of North America North of Mexico* (3 vols.; New York: Oxford University Press, 1993), I, 205. According to Scooter Cheatham and Lynn Marshall, there are also toxic legumes on the Texas coast, and probably on Matagorda Island, that could be called "beans," including *Sesbania* species.

[7] This was the entrance to Matagorda Bay. According to USGS *Beeville*, NH14–12, the distance traveled by Joutel's troops during the five-day march from Cedar Bayou to the hook of Matagorda Island at Pass Cavallo is approximately thirty-four miles, requiring an average daily march of about seven miles.

After Dorantes, the companion of Cabeza de Vaca, crossed Pass Cavallo in a canoe that they found and repaired, his party moved southwest along the same coast (the length of Matagorda Island) to a smaller inlet (Cedar Bayou), covering a recorded twelve leagues. See Davenport (ed.), "The Expedition of Panfilo de Narvaez," 237. This reported distance plus the distance recorded earlier between the major rivers crossed along the Texas coast are critical in establishing the Spanish league that Oviedo was using in his writings and that possibly other Spanish diarists and chroniclers were employing in their expedition accounts in the 1530s and 1540s. According to USGS *Beeville*, NH14–12, the distance from Pass Cavallo to Cedar Bayou is approximately thirty-two miles. Using the customary Spanish common league of 2.6 miles, Dorantes would have traveled 31.2 miles, a figure very close to the measured distance on

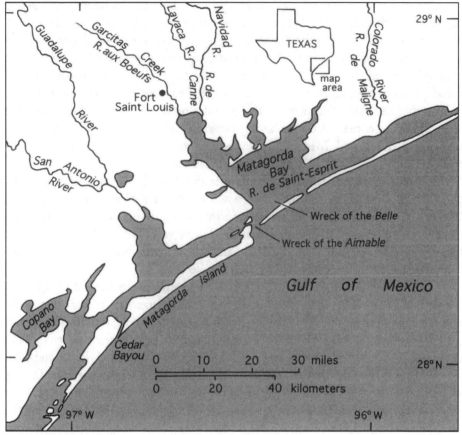

The Matagorda Bay area

supplies for only a few days. As I found a rather suitable area where there were small sand dunes fifteen to twenty feet high, I had two fires made, following the orders of La Salle, so that the vessels could see us. Then I had the men camp as well as was possible, having them make huts or sheds which they covered with grass from a nearby prairie which the Indians had earlier set afire.[8]

---

contemporary maps. The translation of the sixteenth-century Spanish league as measuring 2.6 miles fits very well with other distances reported in leagues by Oviedo along the upper Texas coast and on Cabeza de Vaca's journey across South Texas and northeastern Mexico.

   [8] In Chapter VIII and IX, Joutel again refers to grass fires set by Indians. Cabeza de Vaca gave several accounts of Indians setting grass fires in South Texas to drive away mosquitoes, to drive out lizards from the earth to eat, or to influence the movement of deer and bison during a hunt. See Cabeza de Vaca, "The Narrative of Alvar Nuñez Cabeza de Vaca," 67.

   William M. Denevan has reviewed the recent literature on Indian burning of woodlands and grass-lands; although several contemporary authorities consider regular and widespread Indian burning as an unlikely hypothesis, Denevan disputes this and concludes that Indian burning occurred frequently and for many reasons. Denevan, "The Pristine Myth: The Landscape of the Americas in 1492," in *The Americas before and after 1492: Current Geographical Research*, guest ed. Karl W. Butzer, *Annals of the Association of American Geographers*, 82 (Sept., 1992), 371–372. Joutel's journal account and Cabeza de Vaca's narrative support Denevan's conclusion that Native Americans set grassland and woodland fires frequently and for various reasons.

One of our men had gone astray and was missing. The unfortunate man had lost his sight since he had left France. I had given orders to several men to watch after him, and he had always followed along behind. Now, whether he had become caught in some brush or otherwise, we had to return to look for him. Five or six men volunteered to go search for him, happily for him. He told us that he had spent quite a painful night, that he had not dared to leave the place where he was, fearing that he would fall in the hands of some native. Moreover, he hoped that someone would come to look for him by returning along the same route as the one that they had followed. Meanwhile, he became bored and strolled into the countryside. Luckily for him, he had not made much headway.

But we had a more serious concern: indeed we feared that something had happened to the vessels or that they had passed on ahead without our seeing them. Besides, we were, so to speak, hemmed in by this big river[9] before us, and could find no way to cross it. It appeared to us to be quite wide and, furthermore, part of the countryside seemed to be flooded such that we could not see the other side. Nevertheless, it was necessary to initiate some action.

I gave orders to each man to clean his weapons and to keep them in good shape. I also had racks made to place all the weapons together, as was done in the army to inspect companies.[10] Likewise, we took care to be on guard for fear of surprise from some natives. We killed enough ducks the first day that we arrived, but that came to an end. However, as we had taken supplies for only eight or nine days, we could see no opportunity to get out of this difficulty. As we saw no sign of them, we therefore decided to reduce rations by one meal. We did not have much and it was necessary to consider what might happen. We spent several days there, and the time did not pass without considerable worry. None of us knew how to handle ourselves in this kind of country. Further, each of us conjectured, in his way, what might have happened, why we had not seen our ships. Some said they could have absconded the same day we set out; others thought that perhaps they got rid of La Salle. Thus, each theorized in his own mind, but this did not lead to anything.

The question being how to remove ourselves from there, I offered a proposal to Morenger and several others of the most reasonable and resolute volunteers, who were Messrs. Desloges, Oris, Thibault, La Villeperdrix, Declaire, Arboul, Gayen, and a few others. I had heard La Salle several times, when telling about his journeys, speak of rafts that he made for crossing rivers. I followed the idea that he had given me and worked to construct one. Moreover, we had noticed a very attractive tree about the range of two gunshots from our camp, and we set out to see if there was a way to make a canoe from it. There were some carpenters; we put them to work with two large axes. We apportioned to the carpenters a double ration of the food, although we had treated all men equally up to that time, so no one could complain about the reduction in food. In this way, we were determined to try to get across.

Our large number of people was the entire problem. Only a few were able to

---

[9] This was Cavallo Pass.

[10] This is one of the few comments Joutel makes that reflects his earlier career in the army.

do anything at all. Truthfully, although we had 120 to 130 men with us, 30 good men would have been better and would have done more and perforce eaten less, to which end they were without rival. As I mentioned, these were all men who had been taken by force or deceit. In a way, it was almost like Noah's Ark where there were all sorts of animals. We likewise had men of different nationalities. The soldiers had been recruited by the lower ranking officers of the Navy, who received a half *pistolle*[11] for each man, by whatever means possible. That is why they took in all that they could entrap.

Our immediate problem was to transport everyone across the river [the channel]. We had resolved not to leave any men behind, unless we could leave them with some Indians whom we would compensate for feeding them while we tried to find the Illinois country, of which La Salle had so often spoken and described as very fine.

Thirty of us could first undertake crossing the river. We even brought some goods, in case we encountered some Indians, to exchange for peltry so each party would benefit. With this idea, we worked hard on our raft and our canoe. As I said before, I put the carpenters to work on the canoe. Because there were only two axes and there were four men, they relieved each other, one after the other. They did not have that much to eat even though they had double rations. As for the raft, I too worked on that, having several logs hauled which I fastened together although the problem was finding something to use to tie the logs together as there was no green wood. As a substitute, I used a local rambling vine which was as thick as a finger.[12] First the vine had to be spread out to dry because, if one used it green, it broke off. The dried vine was not much good, but it was necessary to use what one found.

While we were at work, each doing our share, Morenger with several of our men had gone about one league back up the river in search of a narrower crossing. However, he did not find much of a reduction in the width of the river. He told us, upon his return, that the river spread out in a kind of large lake[13] that extended east and west. The land behind seemed to be almost all under water. That did not make us very happy, but we had to remain patient. This discovery was made on the 11th; meanwhile we still had some hope.

Only the large number of men hampered us. We hoped that if we found some Indians, we could leave some of our men with them by giving them a few hatchets and knives. La Salle had even directed us, in case we should encounter some tribes, to contrive to make peace with them, being wary, however, and keeping well on guard. But we did not have to trouble ourselves as we did not see any. It had not been long since they were there, however, as we saw tracks indicating that they had passed that way. Our men had even seen places where the Indians had made fires.

---

[11] There is a discrepancy between the word used by Margry (*demy-solde*) and the word that appears in the manuscript (*pistolle*). A *pistolle* was a ten *livres* (later francs) coin. Although Margry says *demy-solde* (half-pay), the manuscript says *pistolle*, which we have adopted here.

[12] The large goat-foot morning glory (*Ipomoea pes-caprae*) sends vines about the diameter of an index finger across the beach on Matagorda Island. McAlister and McAlister, *Matagorda Island*, 128.

[13] This was Matagorda Bay.

Morenger also saw a sort of small island that was flat in the middle of and far up [the channel].[14]

Thus we had thoroughly considered various ways when we were relieved of our worry. On the 13th of the month, we saw two ships coming toward us from the southwest which was the direction from which we expected them. Thus we were convinced that they must be our ships. They came to anchor near the entrance to the river or bay, or rather across the inlet, which formed the way out. We recognized then that they were the *Joly* and the *Belle*. We signaled to them according to the orders given us; but, as it was evening, they did not see the signals.

On the next day, the 14th, we again sent signals to the ships, so that they would come, for we needed the shallop. Even more, we were impatient to learn the events which had left us in such trouble. At 9 o'clock in the morning the shallop landed with the Sieur Barbier. The *Belle*'s pilot Richaut made a sounding of the entrance of the river where he found 10, 11, and 12 feet of water on the bar. I say 11 or 12 feet of water on the bar as there were five or six fathoms of water and an eighth of a league across. After this, Richaut went the length of the small island that I have mentioned, where he found nearly the same depth, five or six fathoms. As I have described, this was a very wide channel, more than the range of two musket shots. He also saw a number of dolphin[15] coming and going. On the other side of the channel, there were some sandbars. With the least wind, waves crashed on the sandbars with great force. But the sea was calm in this channel although it was heavy out at sea. The waves breaking on the sandbars there encountered a great depth and came to rest. The canoe from the *Joly* also came inshore and sounded near these sandbars. I did not notice what they did in the channel and could not say what their intention was.

When I saw only these two vessels, I feared that something had happened to La Salle, but Barbier reassured me and the others that La Salle was coming behind him. Indeed, we saw the storeship [the *Aimable*] appear a short time later and anchor near the other ships. As soon as they had cast anchor, La Salle gave the order to unload provisions as soon as possible to take to us, knowing that we needed them. However, because a contrary wind rose up, they could not come until the next morning. The *Belle*'s shallop remained near our camp during the night, and the next day, the 15th, Morenger, Desloges,[16] and some others set off aboard the shallop to board the *Aimable* to see La Salle.

The *Aimable*'s shallop came as soon as it was morning and, after discharging the cargo, returned to collect La Salle who came ashore the same day. He visited the post and surveyed the entrance of the river or bay [Matagorda Bay]. He thought it was quite favorable, and, after he had considered everything, he decided

[14] USGS *Beeville*, NH14–12, identifies the island near the entrance to Pass Cavallo as Pelican Island, as does Parkman in *La Salle and the Discovery of the Great West*, 379.

[15] The marine mammal Joutel saw was probably the Atlantic bottlenose dolphin, which as adults may be twelve feet long and weigh twelve hundred pounds. McAlister and McAlister, *Matagorda Island*, 181. These dolphins are described as inshore animals that inhabit primarily shallow lagoons and bays. Davis and Schmidly, *The Mammals of Texas*, 322.

[16] Parkman describes Desloges, who was later killed in an Indian attack, as simply a volunteer. *La Salle and the Discovery of the Great West*, 384.

to have the *Belle* and the *Aimable* enter it. He hoped that this would prove to be a branch of his river [the Mississippi River], the right branch which he had not taken in coming downriver. In addition, the pilot had given his report of the soundings in which he had found that the anchorage was good and the vessels would be very well sheltered. To that end, La Salle then ordered that soundings be made again to see if the ships could enter that day.

Beaujeu also came ashore. He had soundings made and slept on the other side of the river [the channel]. He came by our camp again and let us know that they had seen many rampant vines and some woods. He also told us that he had seen many bison carcasses[17] which suggested that there must be some bison nearby. Beaujeu, however, concluded that the animals must have died of thirst because he had not found any water.[18]

On February 16, the pilots of the *Joly*, the *Aimable*, and the *Belle* made a joint sounding of the entrance where they found nine, ten, and twelve feet in the shallowest water on the bar. As the country was flat and sandy, the entrances were marked by sandbars. The sandbar in question ranged a good two musket shots across and, once cleared, the depth was five or six fathoms until reaching the rear side of the small island. That is to say, the channel of the river was five or six fathoms in depth. It also was about the same range across as the sandbar. Good anchorage was everywhere. When the pilots had completed the soundings, they prepared an official report which they gave to La Salle and Beaujeu.

On the 17th, the pilots by common consent planted buoys with big pieces of wood and floated some casks to facilitate the entrance of the ships. On Sunday, the 18th, the *Belle* got underway to enter, and at 2 o'clock in the afternoon she anchored about a half league to the south of the small island. She was in five and a half fathoms of water, well sheltered from the north and east by the island and the sandbanks, and from the south and southwest by land. When La Salle wanted the *Aimable* to enter, he ordered the captain to have the heaviest things unloaded, including cannon, iron, shot, and similar things that were the most handy. I was rather happy that my trunk was among the cargo taken ashore because it was considered cumbersome. Thus, I did not later lose much. The same day, Chevalier d'Hère went ashore to confer with La Salle.

On the 19th, eight cannon were taken off the storeship, along with several thousand lead shot and some iron, and a number of other things. This continued until the captain said it was not necessary to unload anything else. He was drawing only eight feet of water, or less, and he could thus enter easily. On the 20th, La Salle ordered the captain to approach the bar, adding that when the sea was high, he should signal to him to be towed. La Salle also ordered the pilot of the *Belle* to help the captain of the *Aimable* with what he had to do as that ship had already

[17] Minet described the location where the bison carcasses were found as being on land that was only about six feet above sea level, dotted with low trees with large vines and prickly pears; it was more than ten leagues from the channel entrance. Minet, "Journal of Our Voyage to the Gulf of Mexico," 105.

[18] Despite Beaujeu's conclusion, it seems extremely unlikely that the bison died of thirst as they were very resourceful survivors and water was plentiful. It is more likely that the Indians who killed the bison took with them only select parts, not having the means to transport the bodies.

88     entered. But the captain sent the pilot back, telling him that he was capable of
bringing his ship in without him.

On the same day, La Salle had sent seven or eight men to work on a big tree he
had seen on the bank of the river. He thought the tree could be used to build a
canoe. At 7 or 8 o'clock we were surprised to see two of these men returning all out
of breath and terror-stricken. They warned us that there was a large party of
Indians[19] who were trying to capture them and they believed that the other men
with them had been captured. At this news, La Salle had the men arm themselves
as fast as possible and go to investigate what this was about. We saw the Indians
coming directly at us. When they saw that we were advancing toward them fully
armed, to the drumbeat, they turned around as if to flee, believing we were going
to attack them. But, as the Sieur de La Salle knew the ways of Indians, he made six
or seven of us lay down our arms, except for some pistols which we kept under our
jerkins. La Salle set his weapon down likewise. We approached the natives in that
way, and we signaled to them to come. When they saw that we had laid down our
weapons, a number of them laid their arms down. They came straight to us, our
men with them.

United with us, the Indians made friendly gestures in their own way; that is,
they rubbed their hands on their chests and then rubbed them over our chests and
arms. They demonstrated friendship by putting their hands over their hearts
which meant that they were glad to see us. We returned their greeting in as nearly
like manner as we could. All was by signs, for we could not understand each other
otherwise. They made a certain throat or guttural cry when we said something to
them. They also made a sound with the tongue like a hen when she calls her
chicks, or, better said, as we make to a horse when we want it to move or to do
something else.

After we had been there a while, we returned along the trail back to our camp
and six or seven of the most important Indians came with us. La Salle told a few of
our men to remain as hostages with the Indians who were not coming back with us.
When we arrived at camp, La Salle had the six or seven Indian chiefs sit down.
After he had given them food and drink, he did what he could to make them understand him and to obtain some information about the river [the Mississippi] or the
tribes that he had seen coming down it. However, he could not learn anything from

[19]  Joutel did not identify by tribal name the Indians that La Salle first encountered at the bay, but
Pierre and Jean-Baptiste Talon, young members of La Salle's party, identified the tribe that lived in the
immediate bay area as the Clamcoeh. The first English translation of the 1698 interrogation of the Talon
brothers was prepared by R. T. Huntington and published in 1985 in "The Interrogation of the Talon
Brothers, 1698," 100–131. See also Minet, "Voyage to the Mississippi through the Gulf of Mexico," 242.
Pierre Meunier, who was also with La Salle, referred to the same tribe as the Caucosi. See Appendix A.
Alonso de León called them Caocosi. Bolton (ed.), *Spanish Exploration in the Southwest*, 420, n. 7.

The tribe and those linguistically associated were later referred to as Karankawa. However, no French
or Spanish chronicler of the period referred to the coastal Indians near the bay as Karankawa, the name
often used by later Spanish writers, Anglo colonists, and contemporary authorities. See discussion of the
term Karankawa in Ricklis, *The Karankawa Indians of Texas*, 4–10.

Minet estimated that there were four hundred Indians camped near the entrance to the bay, and he
marked their location on his map. Minet, "Voyage to the Mississippi through the Gulf of Mexico," 107,
plate 8, 109.

them except that there was good hunting inland including bison. This they depicted to us by signs.

After they had been in our camp for a while, the Indians indicated that they
wanted to go back. La Salle gave them a few hatchets and knives and they seemed
satisfied with these presents. For our part, we were very pleased that they were
leaving because we could accomplish nothing while they were there.

Now the *Aimable* that had been held back was to enter, the sea being high.
Although, as the tide barely seemed to rise on this coast more than two or three
feet,[20] [to enter] the wind still had to cooperate. At last, with the water level high,
the *Aimable* was signaled to draw near to enter. It was at this moment that the
Indians chose to return. So they were conducted back to the place where we had
met them, and where we expected to find our men whom we had left as hostages.
But we were surprised as no one was there. The Indians had returned to their own
camp and had taken our men with them. One of the hostages was the Marquis de
La Sablonnière, an infantry lieutenant, and three others were with him. La Salle
was angry about this departure which made it necessary to go search for them. As a
result, we went to the Indians' camp which was rather far from ours, a league and a
half. They were positioned on a point where they had about 50 huts, covered with
reed or cane mats. A few huts were covered with dried bison hides. They were constructed with poles, bent like staves of a cask, and they looked like large ovens.[21]

Before entering the Indian village, we saw our ship approaching the bay under
sail which was a wonder to the Indians. As he watched the maneuver that the ship
was undertaking, La Salle saw that they were not handling the ship well. It was
moving toward the sandbanks. This caused him a great deal of concern and not
without cause. But he had no way to influence the situation because we were so far
away. A little while later, a cannon shot was fired which was a bad omen to us.
Hearing the noise of the cannon, all the natives with us lay down on the ground in
fear. La Salle, when he heard the shot, said the *Aimable* must have run aground or
that something unfortunate must have happened to her. However, as we were so
far along, we had to continue on our way. As we proceeded along, we saw the ship
furl her sails which increased La Salle's concern. His fears were only too well
founded as will be seen.

[20]  The normal tidal range at Pass Cavallo is about 1.4 feet. McAlister and McAlister, *Matagorda
Island*, 20.

[21]  The manner in which Indian huts were constructed may suggest whether the tribe moved frequently to hunt, fish, and gather food or whether the natives lived primarily in one location where crops could
be grown and protected. Joutel describes the Indian huts near Matagorda Bay as being able to accommodate only five or six individuals and generally covered with reed or cane mats. Huts constructed with poles
covered with reed mats (or hides) suggests a temporary structure that was easily movable.

Like Joutel, Spanish expedition diarists reported finding evacuated Indian encampments in South and
Central Texas in which only the pole frames of the huts remained in place, the hide or mat covers having
been removed and carried along with the tribe. Alonso de León described Indian bell-shaped huts constructed of grass and reeds in Nuevo León in the middle 1600s. Foster (ed.), *Texas and Northeastern Mexico*,
13. The tribes in northeastern Mexico and the Texan Gulf Coast are described as being highly mobile in
comparison, for example, to the East Texas Caddo tribes, who were horticulturalists and lived in larger
and more substantially constructed thatched huts. See Chapter XI.

On the way to the Indians' village, some Indians in our party supported the young Cavelier (the nephew of La Salle) underneath his arms and stroked him. When we passed a little cove which extended inland, we took a certain pleasure in watching the Indians fish. Some of the natives had landed a dolphin, a fish that is plentiful in this bay. Before arriving at their village, we found several Indians crouched in the grass, as if they were on sentry duty. However, according to what I have since learned and have noticed, this was not their custom. Whatever the case may be, when we arrived at their village, the Indians wanted to show us all their huts. After this, they led La Salle to one that apparently belonged to the chief. La Salle had warned us that one should be wary of these people because they ordinarily are treacherous. We, therefore, were apprehensive of their motive and behavior to see that they did not assemble. I stayed the whole time with La Salle wherever he went.

We saw several women who were naked except for a skin that girded them and covered them to the knees. They had some markings on their faces and therefore were not very pretty. The men were all naked; several had deer skins that they slung across their backs as gypsies do. The women brought us a few pieces of fresh meat and morsels of dolphin. I admired the way in which they cut their meat with one hand and placed a foot on the other end. This custom did not allow for any fastidious individuals among them. I did not notice any objects made of iron.

They brought us several pieces of dolphin meat to take back to camp. Those of our group who had gone initially with the Indians told us that the natives had made them eat meat upon their arrival. In spite of this fine welcome, La Salle was very worried about his ship. Therefore, we could not stay with them very long, and he soon took leave of the natives.

In leaving we saw that the Indians had a large number of canoes, as many as 40 of different kinds. La Salle also noticed that they had been constructed all-in-one piece, the same type of construction that he had seen on the river he had come down [the Mississippi].[22] Thus he decided that he must not be very far from his river. This observation only doubled his concern about the condition of his ship and caused him much grief although I told him several times that perhaps the harm was not as great as he supposed. I said that perhaps it had anchored for fear of coming upon the sandbanks.

When we returned, however, to the river [channel], we learned how the captain had disgraced himself. The incident made one conclude that the mischief must have been by design or premeditated act. For buoys had been placed and one only had to steer by them. Moreover, a sailor was in the topmast for the purpose of seeing better. Although the sailor continually called out "to luff sail," the ill-intentioned captain called out to the contrary and gave the command to bear down until he saw he was on the sandbanks.

Even if the captain had cast an anchor when the ship touched the first time, he could have pulled off. But, to better assure shipwreck, the captain had the mainsail

[22] La Salle was familiar with the Indian birch-bark canoes used by natives in Canada and the Great Lakes region, and during his 1682 expedition, he had also seen the hollowed-log Indian canoes used on the lower Mississippi. See Cox (ed.), *Journeys of La Salle*, I, 136.

taken in and set his sprit-sail in order to bear down all the more. Moreover, when he went aground the first time and fired the cannon in warning, the shallop of the *Joly* was by its side and they set the ship afloat by placing an anchor forward, but no ax was found to cut the line holding the first anchor. According to the report of everyone who was aboard the vessel when the accident happened, no one believed that the incident was not of premeditated design, the handiwork of someone. This was confirmed by the subsequent statements of the pilot and those of the sailors.

As there was no hope of saving the ship, it was a question of trying to salvage some of the cargo that was aboard. La Salle therefore asked Beaujeu to ready his shallop to aid in transporting whatever they could offload. We started by saving the gunpowder, for which there was the most to fear, and after that the meal. But the most unfortunate factor was that when the least wind blew in from the sea, there was no way of approaching the ship, thereby causing us to lose a large portion of the goods on board. When the wind blew in from the sea, the waves dashed with a force that made it impossible to board. The masts made the whole ship rock, exposing it to the danger of breaking up.

It was decided to cut down the masts, particularly the mainmast. As no one wanted to start, Father Zénobe,[23] who had been aboard the ship, made the first cut with an ax which was followed by many others until all the masts were felled. Then everyone was put ashore for fear that some bad weather might blow in and all would be at risk of perishing. There was quite a way to go and these conditions did not allow us to go as quickly as we would have liked. We took things as they came, but it seemed that all misfortunes followed us.

Indeed, when someone went to unload something from the salvaged goods aboard the shallop that was secured behind the *Aimable*, we found that the shallop had gone adrift, either on its own or because someone had unfastened it purposely (which several surmised). Fortunately, with the wind coming from the sea, the shallop beached on land on the same side as we were. This was luck for a sailor who had fallen asleep in the shallop from wine or fatigue. It was dark and he was at great risk of being lost. When the hapless man awoke and found himself on land, he was surprised. But he looked around him and recognized where he was, and he came to the camp to advise us that the shallop was about a half league to a league from there. This consoled us a little but the consolation did not last long; meanwhile, the shallop was quite necessary.

If we had had several shallops, we could have saved the ship in the beginning. The failure in this was not to have taken aboard ship in France a couple of *brisées*;[24] they would have been a great help to us. When the shallop was sent back, the Reverend Père Zénobe was aboard. He wanted to see that certain things were saved, as only a part of the goods and utensils belonging to them [the priests] had been taken off. There were billowing waves and the priest nearly drowned when he missed a rope that was thrown overboard to him. One must be somewhat alert setting foot on board ship when there are billowing waves. Hands as well as feet

[23] Père Zénobe Membré, a Recollet priest, was with La Salle on his trip down the Mississippi in 1682. His account of the trip is in Cox (ed.), *Journeys of La Salle*, I, 131–158.

[24] *Brisée* refers to a type of relatively small French vessel but there is no known equivalent in English.

should be used. That is what prompted the author, whom I have mentioned before, to say that Père Zénobe's zeal nearly caused him to perish when the shallop was dashed to pieces. The author[25] was mistaken because the shallop was not broken to pieces. It was found more than six months later in a cove of the bay. Joy was not with us for long, only a few days. We presumed that some people had set the boat loose on purpose as the rope with which it was secured was found to have been cut. As the proverb says, when one loses a fish, it is better to keep quiet than to speak. Meanwhile, this second loss of the shallop made us well aware of our need because the *Belle*'s shallop was small and not able to hold much.[26]

While we were involved in these unhappy efforts, about 100 to 120 Indians came to our camp with their bows and arrows. La Salle directed us to arm ourselves and to be on guard. About twenty of them mingled among us to look over what we had saved from the shipwreck. There were four sentries posted to prevent anyone from coming near the gunpowder. The rest of the Indians were there in groups. La Salle, who knew their ways, directed us to observe their actions and not take anything from them. This did not prevent some men from accepting a few pieces of meat from them. A little while later, the Indians, wishing to leave, made a sign to us to go with them on their hunt. But, beside the fact that we had reason to distrust them, we had other things to do. However, we took our opportunity to ask them if they wanted to exchange some of their canoes. They agreed and Barbier went with them and made a deal, giving them hatchets, and brought back two canoes.

A few days later, we saw on the plains nearby a fire that spread and quickly burned the dry grass, drawing toward us. This compelled La Salle to have the grass around us quickly uprooted, particularly the grass around the gunpowder. Wanting to determine where this fire originated, La Salle took twenty of us with him and advanced in that direction and even beyond the fire, but we saw no one. We noticed that the fire spread out to the west-southwest and we decided that it had started near our first encampment and by the Indian village near that place. Having seen an Indian hut near the side of a lake, we approached it and found there an old woman inside. She started to run as soon as she saw us. However, when we stopped her and made her understand that we intended no harm, she returned to the hut where we found some water jugs[27] from which we all drank. Soon thereafter, we saw a canoe approaching with two women and a boy. They landed and when they saw that we had not harmed the woman, they came to embrace us in their special way, blowing against our ears. Then they made a sign that their people were on a hunt.

[25] Douay returned to France with Joutel in 1688. His account of the journey was edited, rewritten, and published in 1691 by Chrétien Le Clercq; it was subsequently translated into English and edited (from the 1691 French edition) by John Gilmary Shea in *First Establishment of the Faith in New France*, II, 229–261. As noted in the notes to Chapter II, Joutel considered the account Le Clercq prepared from Douay to be inaccurate in a number of respects and more a product of Le Clercq than Douay.

[26] Margry notes that the following text, covering the period between February and July, is based on Michel since there is a gap in Joutel's manuscript.

[27] Ricklis discusses the production, design, and use of ceramic pottery by Indians living near Matagorda Bay during the time of La Salle's visit in *The Karankawa Indians of Texas*, 27–34, 177–188.

A few moments later, seven or eight Indians appeared who apparently had been hiding nearby in the grass, watching us approach. They greeted us upon their arrival in the same way the women had done which made us laugh. We stayed with them a while, and some of our people traded knives for deerskins after which we returned to our camp. Then La Salle asked me to go on board the *Belle*, where he had loaded a portion of the gunpowder, with the order not to allow fire near it, having reason to fear everything after what had just happened. While performing this duty, food was brought to me and those with me every day. It was during this time that the *Aimable*, which was aground, split up one night. In the morning we saw the buoyant cargo floating all over the water. La Salle sent people from one direction to the other and they recovered thirty casks of wine and brandy and some barrels of meat, meal, and beans. After we had reassembled as much as could be saved from the shipwrecked vessel (of which there was little to find and recover in the water), we had to distribute the provisions that were left proportionally among us. As there was no more hardtack, meal was issued from which a porridge was made with water, but it was not very good. There were also some large beans and corn, some of which had gotten wet; all of this was distributed prudently. In preparing the food, we were inconvenienced by the lack of pots, but Beaujeu gave one to La Salle, who had also taken one from the *Belle*, and those served us well.

We still needed canoes. La Salle sent an envoy to the Indians' camp to negotiate for some. The men who were sent told us that the natives had profited from our shipwreck and that they had some bolts of Normandy blankets. They saw that several Indian women had cut them in two and made skirts from them. The men also saw pieces of iron from the shipwrecked vessel. Our men returned promptly to our camp to make their report to La Salle, who said we must try to get some canoes in exchange and decided to send an envoy the next day. The Sieur du Hamel, Beaujeu's ensign, offered to go with his shallop, which La Salle agreed to, and he also ordered Morenger, Desloges, Oris, Gayen, and some others to accompany him.

These men, who had more passion than sense, went straight to the Indians' camp, arms in hand as if they intended to use force, which made several of the Indians run away. They entered the huts and found other natives, and du Hamel tried to make them understand with signs that he wanted to recover the blankets which they had found. Unfortunately, they did not understand each other. The Indians decided to withdraw and left a few blankets and animal skins which our men took. In returning, the men found a few canoes which they also took and used for transportation back.

They made little progress because our men did not have any oars, and no one knew how to punt a canoe (they only had a few worthless poles which they could not even use).[28] Furthermore, the wind was against them, so they made little progress. Observing their situation and aware that night was approaching, du Hamel, who was in his shallop, went ahead, abandoned them, and returned to camp.

[28] Texas coastal Indians, as well as the Indians on the middle and lower Mississippi, primarily used poles, rather than paddles, to punt or propel their dugout canoes. See the use of poles by the Cappa Indians on the Mississippi in Chapter XVI.

Meanwhile, with night falling, our new and very tired navigators were forced to go ashore to rest. As it was cold, they lit a fire, around which they lay down and slept. The sentry whom they posted did the same. The Indians, returning to their camp and seeing that someone had taken their canoes, skins, and blankets, believed that war had been declared and resolved to take revenge. They perceived an unusual fire and suspected that our people had camped there. A large band proceeded noiselessly toward the fire and found our careless companions asleep in their blankets. First sounding the usual cry that preceded their strikes, the Indians then shot their arrows all at the same time at the sleeping men.

Morenger, who was awakened by the noise and was wounded, got up and fired a shot from his musket. About that moment, some others fired also which made the Indians run. Morenger came to sound the alarm to us, even though his arm was pierced by an arrow below the shoulder and another arrow had glanced off his chest. La Salle sent armed men to the camp right away, but they found no Indians. When day dawned, they found Oris and Desloges dead on the ground and Gayen was badly wounded. The others were unharmed.[29]

This misfortune, which occurred on the night of March 5, deeply afflicted La Salle. Above all he mourned for the Sieur Desloges, a young man full of spirit who had served him well. But after all, it was their fault and contrary to what had been advised: caution and vigilance. We feared that the arrows that struck Morenger and Gayen might be poisoned.[30] Eventually, it was found that this was not the case. However, Morenger had trouble recovering because some small blood vessel proved to be severed.

This new reversal, along with the disheartenment caused by the loss of our vessel, had its effect on most of the worthy men who had followed La Salle. The losses fortified the plan of those who wanted to return to France and leave him. Their number included the Sieur d'Esmanville (the priest from the seminary of Saint Sulpice), the Sieur Minet (an engineer), and some others. The conferences that La Salle's enemies held to discredit his conduct and the supposed rashness of his enterprise contributed more than a little to the desertions. Buoyed only by his own confidence, La Salle understood and expected whatever event with resignation and continued giving orders without being perturbed in any way.

He had the dead brought in and buried honorably; cannon took the place of bells. Then he proposed to establish a more secure settlement. He had all that had been removed from the shipwreck put in one place and had entrenchments made around it to secure his goods. Noting that where we were the waters of the river or channel rushed precipitously to the sea, La Salle thought that this could well be one of the branches of the Mississippi. He proposed to go up the channel to see if

---

[29] Pierre Meunier gave a similar description of this first significant Indian nighttime attack in which several Frenchmen were killed; see Appendix A.

[30] Although Oviedo reported that some natives in the West Indies used arrows that were poisonous and Joutel was concerned that Texas coastal Indians also used poisoned arrows, Spanish expedition documents of the period do not report the use of poisoned arrows by the natives in northeastern Mexico or Texas. See Oviedo, *Natural History of the West Indies*, 26, 27.

he could find some markers which he had placed when he had headed for the mouth of the river by land.

Meanwhile, Beaujeu was preparing for his departure. D'Here had several conferences with La Salle touching upon those matters that the latter had asked of Beaujeu, particularly the one regarding the cannon and balls on board the *Joly* which were intended for La Salle. But Beaujeu refused, saying that all of the items were in the hold of his ship and could not be disturbed without losing the vessel. This he maintained even though he knew we had eight cannon without any cannon balls.

I did not know how the matter ended between them; but La Salle let the captain of the *Aimable* embark with Beaujeu. The captain deserved a rigorous punishment if justice had been done him. The captain's crew followed him, contrary to what Beaujeu had promised, namely, that he would not accept anyone [for the return voyage]. All that La Salle could do about these injustices was to write about them to France and to complain to Seignelay, the minister of State, to whom he made everything known, as I learned on my return. La Salle gave the dispatch to Beaujeu who set sail for Europe.[31]

As I have lost the memoirs that I wrote then,[32] and what I write is from the depth of my memory, I will not give dates for fear of mistaking them. That is why I cannot in truth give the departure date of the Sieur de Beaujeu, but I think it was March 14, 1685.

[31] According to Minet, Beaujeu and his men and passengers (including Minet) departed the Texas coast aboard the *Joly* on March 12. They sailed first back to Cuba (Cape Saint Antoine) for water, where a hostile Spanish ship captured their crewboat and seventeen men. Several friendly English ships nearby provided Beaujeu with water, wood, and provisions. On May 3, the *Joly* arrived off the coast of Virginia and obtained the additional provisions needed for the return voyage to Rochefort on the west coast of France, where the party arrived safely on July 5, 1685. The return trip is covered in Minet's account, "Journal of Our Voyage to the Gulf of Mexico," 114–126.

Although Joutel is critical of Beaujeu in several respects, the captain is reported to have attempted to secure assistance for La Salle soon after he returned to France. Beaujeu apparently requested that Monsieur de Seignelay send La Salle supplies via a French ship that was bound for Saint Domingue to deliver 130 French girls for the French buccaneers, whom the French supported on the island in every way. However, the French minister refused. See O'Donnell, "La Salle's Occupation of Texas," 33.

[32] As noted, Joutel did not give the daily direction and distance in leagues traveled as he marched up Matagorda Island. Here he explains why; he had lost his notes or memoirs (*mémoires*), without which he would not give unqualified specific dates. As Joutel gives the exact date on which the party initiated the march up Matagorda Island ("February 4, 1685") in the beginning of the chapter; it appears that the "lost memoirs" covered only a short period of time. He thereafter gives specific dates, Indian tribal names (over one hundred named tribes in total), daily directions and distances traveled, and other detailed information. Thus, it appears that Joutel, unlike Douay, returned to France with his memoirs covering events before and soon after Beaujeu's departure. It also seems unlikely that Douay would have returned to France with extensive memoirs as La Salle had been openly and forcefully critical of other priests in his party who kept written accounts and had insisted on their destruction.

# CHAPTER V

# The First Settlement[1]

nce Beaujeu was gone, we began the construction of a kind of fort to defend ourselves and everything that had been saved from the shipwreck from any attack by the Indians. This fort was made with pieces of wood, planks, and other things that had been taken from the wreckage of the ship. I neglected also to say that several of our people deserted, some of whom were brought back.[2] As I have mentioned, we had several different nationalities, including a Spaniard who had been engaged as a soldier and who claimed to know how to prepare pelts and called himself a furrier. When the construction of the fort had progressed a little, we prepared to resist and even to attack the Indians with whom we had a sort of war.

After that La Salle decided to leave with a number of men to search for a place that would be suitable to make a permanent settlement. He sought a place where we could plant wheat and other seeds that had been brought along. Next he intended to obtain some information about his river, particularly whether it emptied into this bay. Since he was not sure, La Salle decided to look in the area left [west] of the bay. Although there was no doubt that the river was toward the northeast rather than the west, La Salle, nevertheless, wanted to explore in the area to the west.[3]

[1] As discussed in the introduction, Margry prepared this part of Joutel's account from Michel's published condensation of Joutel's complete work and from extracts of Joutel's manuscript that the French cartographers Claude and Guillaume Delisle copied for their professional use before the material in question was extracted.

[2] Desertion was a problem for both French and Spanish explorers. For the Spaniards, desertion was particularly prevalent among the mulatto and Indian troopers. See Weber, *The Spanish Frontier in North America*, 90. La Salle's earlier exploration parties through Canada and the Great Lakes region also suffered from desertions. On one of his trips, La Salle pursued and captured several deserters and killed two. Parkman, *La Salle and the Discovery of the Great West*, 178, 199–201.

[3] Joutel's observation that La Salle initially explored to the west of the bay area agrees with Abbé Cavelier's report that in the spring and summer of 1685 (and perhaps again later) La Salle traveled west

He prepared for his journey using the canoes that had been obtained by trade with the Indians. The men set about repairing the canoes, the ones that were deficient that is. Clay was found in the area and put to good use. An oven was con structed of the clay as we did not have any bricks. The bricks that had come from Petit Goave remained in the hold of the ship [the *Aimable*] with the cannon balls and the cannon, most of the lead, millstones, the anvil, a large portion of the iron and steel, and several cases of arms including muskets and pistols. In addition, 14 or 15 barrels of salt and a quantity of other goods which had been brought were lost.

When the canoes were ready, La Salle chose 40 to 50 men to go with him. He took along a keg of about 50 pounds of powder in each canoe, shot in proportion, and hardtack that had been made for the trip. He also took some inexpensive goods in case he encountered some Indians other than those with whom we were at war. When all was arranged, he also ordered the *Belle* to enter farther into the bay which she did. He then gave me command of the post and to the Sieur Le Gros the care and distribution of provisions. La Salle asked us to take good care of Morenger, his nephew, and he left his surgeon to tend to him.

La Salle left with five canoes, taking along with him, among others, Monsieur Cavelier, his brother [the Abbé], the priest Chefdeville, two Recollets, and a party of volunteers. About 100 to 120 of us stayed at the camp, but during this period several died every day of scurvy, the disease of the region,[4] or other diseases. It seemed there was a curse on our workers. They had been a poor selection and that was the principal cause of the troubles which we had in this country. Few among them would undertake any labor.

During the absence of La Salle, I occupied myself in improving our fort and putting it in condition to resist the Indians who very often came to prowl around us imitating wolves and dogs. But three or four musket shots would drive them away. One night after six or seven shots were fired, La Salle, who was not far from us, heard them. That made him uneasy, so he retraced his steps with seven or eight men and found everything in good condition. He slept at the fort that night, delighted to see his nephew in better health. After that, he went back. He had left his canoe about one and a half leagues from there near the place where the Indians had camped. He told us that he had found beautiful country suitable for planting all sorts of grains and abundant in bison and other game. He wanted to build a fort

---

toward northern New Spain and the Spanish mining operations in New Biscay. These are some of the facts that authorities cite in support of a contention that La Salle deliberately landed west of the Mississippi to be closer to the Spanish silver mines in Nueva Vizcaya. The extent and duration of the western exploration is not clear, but the Abbé Cavelier reported a westward journey that took place perhaps in July 1685 or soon thereafter. According to this account, La Salle found Spanish arms and materials along with a marker carrying the date 1588. Jean Cavelier's version is found in Cox (ed.), *The Journeys of La Salle*, I, 272–273. The noted Jesuit scholar Jean Delanglez has argued that the Abbé's account cannot be fully trusted and that part of it may have been fiction. In the Abbé's revised and expanded version that Delanglez translated, the reference to La Salle traveling west and reaching a place where Spanish arms and materials were found is omitted. See Delanglez (ed.), *The Journal of Jean Cavelier*, 25–34.

[4] The illness called *de la maladie du païs* has been identified as a venereal disease by some commentators. See Pat I. Nixon, "Liotot and Jalot: Two French Surgeons of Early Texas," *Southwestern Historical Quarterly*, 43 (July, 1939), 42–52.

farther inland. He left me with orders to square as much wood as we could recover from the abundant amount that had been cast onshore by the sea.

La Salle returned to the place where he had left his men. But, as I later learned, his men had abandoned the camp. A panic overtook them. On his departure from the camp, La Salle had given orders to cut down some trees to use either for building or for some other purpose. While the men were at work, a band of Indians came directly to them because those in command had not sent anyone armed to accompany the workers. The men fled in terror to the main camp, leaving their tools. Furthermore, instead of sending an envoy to reclaim the tools from the Indians, the men in camp were also seized with fear and left the post. The men came down the river and camped in another place, having left a note lower down the river to let La Salle know the trail they had taken.

Upon his return to their camp, La Salle found their note attached to a piece of cane that informed him of this incident. The action distressed him mostly because of the loss of the tools, not so much for their value but for the advantage they would give to the Indians for use against us. He pointed out to these men how wrong were their actions because they invited the scorn of these Indians. So he made the men return to the post where the hunting was good.

I returned to our fort. I squared the wood that the sea had tossed onshore; in this place there was only sand. Actually, there were some places where the soil was clay, and one or another place produced good grass for pasturage. Elsewhere there was coarser grass that was suitable only for burning. Our people, who had suffered much, had appetites that could not be satisfied. Unknown to me, they ate snakes without finding them repugnant. The pasturage was so good that sheep could be fattened here in 15 days or three weeks.

Father Anastase and I caught a large quantity of fish nearby. Having observed one day that the water was agitating and boiling with fish darting from one side to the other, I had a net carried to the water and we made an enormous catch of these fish. There was a large number of sea bream, brill, mullet, and others the size of herring[5] from which we lived well for several days. This type of catch was made often and contributed much to our subsistence.

[One day] we saw a small Spanish vessel pass which was coming from the direction of Pánuco or the Magdelaine River and going toward Holy Spirit Bay. The Spaniards had perhaps been advised of our arrival and wanted to see where we had landed. We shut ourselves up inside the fort which was hidden by sand dunes. This forced us to be on guard. We all resorted to the fort and kept our arms ready. After that, we saw two men appear onboard the ship that went toward the other headland instead of coming toward us. They passed thus without noticing us.[6]

It was during this time, on Easter Day of that year, that the Sieur Le Gros had an unfortunate accident. After divine service, he took a musket to go near the fort

[5] There are over four hundred species of fish in the brackish and marine waters of the Matagorda Bay area, including white and striped mullet and Gulf menhaden, both the size of herring. McAlister and McAlister, *Matagorda Island*, 283–289.

[6] Weddle suggests that the vessel was Captain Juan Corso's trading galley. *The French Thorn*, 43, 357, n. 11.

to shoot snipe.[7] After he had shot one, which fell in a small marsh, he took off his shoes to go find it. On his return, he stepped by chance on a rattlesnake, named for the sort of scale that it has at the end of its tail with which it makes noise.[8] The snake bit him above the ankle. We carefully tended to him but, after much suffering, he eventually died, as I will mention in due course. Another accident happened to us: one of our fishermen, swimming around a net to catch fish, was carried off by the currents and drowned without anyone being able to assist him.

On occasion, our people went around several small salt lakes near our fort and found near shore certain flatfish like turbot[9] sleeping, and they speared them with big pointed sticks. This fish was very good. Providence disclosed to us a bed of salt that the sun produced on the small basins of salt water scattered in different places. Seeing that a sort of white cream formed on the water, I sent someone every two days to skim the froth off this water. This turned out to be a very white and very good quality salt which I gathered in a large quantity and was of great use to us.

Some of our hunters saw some frightened deer running and concluded that Indians were chasing them. The hunters returned to take refuge in the fort and told me of this. Indeed, some time afterward, we saw some Indians gathered together on a point within range of our cannon, and a few among them approached along the dunes. As soon as I saw that, I had our people arm themselves, and, to avoid fire that the Indians sometimes start by shooting arrows, I had wet blankets placed on our huts. Meanwhile, the Indians who had detached themselves from the others (three of them), approached us, making signs for us to come to them, but La Salle had forbidden me to have any dealings with them. Nevertheless, as they had no bows or arrows, we made signs to them to approach which they did without hesitating.

We went out to join them outside the fort. Morenger made them sit, and they told us by signs that their people were hunting nearby. Unable to learn more from them, Morenger was of the opinion that we should kill them to avenge the massacre of our companions. But I did not approve as they had come to us in good faith. So I made a sign[10] to them to leave which they did at once. A few gunshots fired in the air made them run, and a cannon shot that I aimed toward the point where the rest of them were made them all run. These encounters made us redouble our guard, as we were at open war with this cunning tribe that would not fail to surprise us if we were not alert. That is why punishment was ordered for those found sleeping on guard. The wooden horse[11] [*le cheval de bois*] was mounted for

---

[7] Joutel identifies the specific shorebirds as bécassines. Matagorda Island has in residence thirty-five shorebirds, several with long, slender bills such as the snipe, avocet, dowitcher, and sandpiper. McAlister and McAlister, *Matagorda Island*, 248–249.

[8] The western diamondback rattlesnake found on Matagorda Bay is one of the most irritable and dangerous snakes in the United States. Ibid., 276–277.

[9] A Gulf flatfish similar to the turbot is the flounder, which is found in large numbers in Matagorda Bay. Ibid., 285.

[10] This is one of the earliest occasions in which Joutel indicates that he also used signs to communicate with natives.

[11] The term *le cheval de bois* referred to a device used to punish and publicly embarrass those who had committed minor indiscretions. See Parkman's comments on the wooden horse in *La Salle and the Discovery of the Great West*, 288.

the punishment of those found negligent, and there was no pardon. It was with these kinds of precautions that we were able to preserve our lives.

Toward the beginning of June, two canoes arrived with La Villeperdrix and others, carrying orders from La Salle for Morenger along with his surgeon to proceed to join him. Everyone else was to march by land, except 30 men who were to stay with me at this same camp until the *Belle* could come to load what there was at this post. La Villeperdrix told us that the frigate was to unload at a place that was to serve as a staging area about midway between this post and the place where La Salle intended to make the settlement. La Salle had camped 10 to 12 men at this staging area under the command of the Sieur Hurié. From this area, goods were to be transported by canoe to the settlement location where La Salle was. Villeperdrix informed us also that La Salle was having the ground dug to plant the seeds that he had brought from France and some of the men were employed with that. The others were posted about a league or a league and a half from there, in an area where bison were in abundance and where they were to smoke the meat to preserve it.[12]

I kept 30 of the most vigorous men, and 70 others (who were not worth my 30) left on the 10th or 12th of June with Morenger. As there were only a few of us remaining, I had the perimeter of the fort reduced so that not as many sentries were required. Our little group began to find some contentment in the availability and quality of the rations which earlier had not been available in great quantity. We had game and fish in greater abundance and hunting and fishing were our major occupations. We were content enough awaiting our transfer.

It turned out, however, that there were some malcontents who tried to desert. But they found the execution of their plan of desertion thwarted because they were not able to get arms, powder, or shot. Because Le Gros and I kept everything locked up, and we were on the watch precisely so that nothing could be carried off improperly, they cruelly decided to get rid of us.

This bloody massacre was to have begun with me while I was sleeping, followed by Le Gros who was bedded down at the storehouse. He was not in any condition to defend himself because of his injured leg which was swollen and painful. The dagger was to serve for the execution of their scheme. One of the conspirators confided in Davault, a hunter, who came immediately to warn me. I gave no indication of being informed of their plan. But, on the evening of their return from the hunt, I had one of them arrested. He immediately confessed all and his accomplice was also arrested. This required us to spend the effort and care necessary to guard them until we abandoned the camp.

Around mid-July, the *Belle* came to anchor near our camp with orders from La Salle asking me to construct a raft of the wood that I had had squared and then to hide the remaining wood and the planks (of which the fort was constructed) in the sand to conceal from the Spaniards our entry into this country. Our two prisoners were put aboard. Le Gros and the surgeon went too with all of our belongings. The raft was begun, taking infinite pains, but bad weather hit us. The weather was so

---

[12] "Le Boucan," a place that was used for smoking meat, was located on the east side of Garcitas Creek about three to four miles north-northeast of the settlement.

violent and lasted so long that I was forced to discontinue what had been begun and to bury the wood in the sand, as well as we could, to conceal it from the Indians.

When the frigate was loaded, she went to anchor near the small island that I mentioned. The sea was so rough and heavy that it created an island of the place where we were. We set course for the point near the small island where the Indians had previously camped. As a result, we called it the Camp of the Indians, while the one that we were leaving was called the Big Camp. When we arrived at the Camp of the Indians, it was rather late and we still had to cross the cove of water which formed this long bay that we saw. When we found a lone Indian hut and saw that the Indians had set fire to the grass in the area, I decided to camp at that place. The shallop having come to shore, I went aboard the *Belle* where I learned that the men had found two casks of brandy that had been sunk in the sand on the small island when the ship perished.

The next day we crossed the cove of water and went along the right bank to Hurié's camp, the storage area where La Salle had directed that all the cargo be deposited. Its fortifications were nothing but chests and casks, but there was nothing to fear except from the Europeans.

We spent the night at this post. On the following day when two canoes arrived, I embarked with some members of my company to join La Salle at the place where he had decided to establish his new settlement. I gave him an account of what had happened and was surprised to see that things here had gotten such a bad start and so little progress had been made. The plantings of grain and seeds had been almost ruined by drought and wild animals. Several settlement members had died, among their number the Sieur de Villeperdrix. A great many men were sick, among them the Abbé Cavelier. There was hardly any shelter except a small square of stakes where the powder and some casks of brandy were kept. Several other problems made it appear that everything was in a sad condition.

It was necessary to construct a large lodging. La Salle had a drawing of it, but the problem was obtaining wood. There was a small woods from which we could take a few trees, but the location was a league farther inland, and we had neither carts nor horses to transport it. Nevertheless, La Salle sent laborers and other men as helpers and escorts.

Although logs were cut and squared, the ignorance of the carpenters was such that La Salle was forced to act as a master builder and mark the pieces of timber for the building design that he had in mind. Several logs were dragged to the camp through the grass that covered the plain; later we made use of a cannon carriage. All of this was done with such difficulty that even the strongest were overcome. The work was excessive, and the rations for the workers were limited and too often cut back for having failed in their task. La Salle's disappointment at not succeeding as he had imagined led him to mistreat his people at the wrong time. All this brought a cheerlessness upon many workers who declined visibly.

I[13] told La Salle several times that it would be more worthwhile to gather the pieces of wood that we had squared on the seashore, as there were quite a number

---

[13] Here Margry resumes Joutel's original text.

of them. In addition, they would be more portable. As the wood could be carried by water, it could be moved without tiring workers so much. But La Salle was interested only in his own opinion, having said as much to me several times, as well as to others, and had had no intention of bringing advisers along with him. So I did not insist further in speaking to him about it. The difficult work continued for some time and caused the death of several men.

One evening when I was, as usual, escorting the workers on their return to camp, I strayed off a short distance to pass by some small thickets that were between the woods and the settlement. I planned to kill some birds to bring to the Abbé who had been ill for some time. I had told the carpenters to go ahead, and I expected to find them all at the camp when I arrived. [When I returned], I asked where the master carpenter was and was told that he had not arrived. I was obliged to retrace my steps to see if he had fallen asleep along the way. However, I found no trace of him although I shouted here and there and fired several gunshots for him to hear. I found nothing, which worried me. The night passed without learning anything of him, and the next day we went in different directions to see if we could find him. However, we could not find out where he had gone or what had become of him. He remained lost. I was disturbed by this loss because I was with him; but there was nothing to do. La Salle told me that I should not have left him, but there was no reason to expect that this would happen.

Eventually, when we had secured nearly as much wood as was needed for this house, La Salle laid out the pieces so they would fit, marking the mortises and tenons. During this time, the men were always traveling to the staging area and the *Belle*. I made several trips to the place. We transported eight iron cannon[14] of about six pound shot that had been taken off the cargo boat. We also brought 100 kegs of powder, but we did not have a proportionate amount of shot for we had been unable to retrieve it from the bottom of the hold. The cannon balls, too, were lost as were the anvil and all the other things mentioned earlier. There were at this point only about 3,000 pounds of lead shot and 30 kegs of flour.

I will return to the construction of the house which La Salle had made ready to be erected. He recalled the pieces of wood on the seashore that I had squared and left buried in the sand and thought that the wood could be of use, particularly for roofing. La Salle ordered me to return there with 20 men, three canoes, and some rations, and he told me to take the *Belle's* shallop with some rope, anchors, and other things I would need which would be useful to make the raft. At length we left with these orders. I went to the *Belle* and took a small anchor with a grappling iron, a sail, and some tools, and set out for the place called the Big Camp.

As soon as we arrived, I went to see if the cache was still there and found that someone had discovered it. The Indians, it must have been, had taken some planks to remove the nails from them. I proceeded next to inspect another cache where I

---

[14] In early 1997, the Texas Historical Commission announced that the eight cannon Joutel discusses had been located, buried together on the west side of Garcitas Creek in Victoria County apparently near the Fort Saint Louis site Bolton identified and Kathleen Gilmore studied. "Texas Historical Commission Announces Discovery of Eight Cannons—Find Confirms Site of La Salle's French Fort," press release, Feb. 10, 1997 (Texas Historical Commission, Austin).

had left a good amount of rope that was necessary to secure our pieces of wood. No one had touched that. As the rope had been put in barrels, it was preserved. After we had taken everything out, we worked to construct our raft. I had the longest pieces of wood placed on the bottom and secured at the ends, and others were secured in the middle by pieces which spanned them crosswise. After this had been done, I had the anchor (which we had taken) carried a short distance into the water to maintain our raft afloat. The raft was both tied on land and attached to the anchor so that it would always be steady. If we had not had the anchor, the least wind would have beached it and we would have been required to do everything over again. After we had placed the largest pieces of wood on it, we put the rest of the wood on top of the planks and everything else that was at that place. It took four days to construct our conveyance, and when all was ready we took advantage of the tide to leave. Otherwise, we would not have been able to master the currents which were rough in going out of the bay even though we had the three canoes to help us. The tide was more favorable to us. I had a large piece of wood put aft to which I had a plank nailed to serve as a rudder. Also I had a mast erected for the sail, which I had had put on the *Belle*, and the raft carried us right away. We moved forward quite well.

I forgot to say that in the evening we saw some Indians in canoes crossing toward the bay. They were coming to their usual camp. After they had crossed, several of them came to investigate us and seven or eight of us took arms to confront them. The plan was to aim at them if they tried to advance. But when they saw us, they ran away. I also forgot to mention that the pilot of the frigate had come with us.

The next day, we made a sounding of the entrance to the bay and confirmed the one made the first time. There were nine, ten, and eleven feet of water on the bar, and once the bar was crossed, there were five or six fathoms of water and a good bottom everywhere. The entrance was a good two musket shots in breadth, on the bar as well as nearly across. The ill will of the captain of the storeship who had so wickedly gone aground was thus made clear, considering that there was nothing easier than entering this bay. We again made an official report of the sounding which I gave to La Salle on my return. This occurred on the 10th of August.

Now, when we were under way on our raft, going under sail, we passed just in front or rather to the right of the Indians' camp. They were there and were in wonder of us. Our canoes followed behind and when we rounded the point to the right of where the Indians were, I had the anchor cast, intending to land. But when the Indians saw that we were preparing to visit them, they decided to run. This caused me to change my plan, for there was nothing to be gained in running after them. Moreover, since the wind was rather favorable, I was glad to take advantage of it, so we reboarded and lifted anchor. We continued on our way, but, since we did not know the navigation of this bay perfectly, we coasted a little too close to the point. This caused us to run aground on a kind of sandbank where we had to stay some time in great fear of being forced to abandon our raft. This would have been a serious setback. We all got in the water to free ourselves. It was with great joy that we pulled ourselves off that bank after about five hours when the water had risen a bit. We knew that if we had had to abandon our raft, we would have been quite far from land.

As night fell shortly thereafter, we anchored in a small cove that had been named the Cask because a cask of wine from the wreck of the ship had been found in the sand. We all lay down to sleep on our raft, having attached the canoes to it. Some of our men had apparently poorly tied one canoe although I had given the order to take great care. I had even posted a guard all night. But these precautions did not prevent our finding ourselves in the morning with one canoe lost. It was the largest canoe, the one in which there were two adzes which are a ship's carpentry tools. This loss bothered me a great deal because we needed canoes. As I saw that the tide was higher and that there was not much wind, I sent some people to shore to see if they could find it. The loss of the canoe was the fault of the one who was steering, a pilot from La Rochelle named Sellié. When I realized that we could not get any further sign of the canoe and I did not know for certain which shore it could have reached, I decided to proceed because the wind blew favorably from the sea allowing us to enter into the river.[15] This done, we arrived at the settlement the next day. I had sent the canoes ahead when we entered the river to tell La Salle that we were coming.

La Salle saw us at a distance and came to the water's edge. He was very glad to see us with the wood that we were transporting. It was only the loss of the canoe that dampened his joy somewhat. The wood that we brought was of much more use than all the wood that we had collected before that had cost the lives of many people. I can indeed affirm that that work caused the deaths of 30 people, as well as creating trouble and vexation.

The question was what would be done with the new wood. First, it was unloaded as soon as possible and each man was put to a particular task. As there were a number of pieces of wood of considerable size, large enough to construct a house, La Salle had all the pieces cut to the length he decided was correct. He had a building made from them, joining the other building that had been begun. This last one proved to be the larger and nicer although there was only new wood for the most part, and the pieces were heavy. The first building was constructed in the Canadian manner and the other almost the same way. As the pieces of this latter one were quite straight and thick, they were much better fitting. The pieces were closed with dovetailed corners with a good peg so that they would be most unlikely to slip. This house was ready first. It was roofed with old planks which we had brought, and on the roof we nailed buffalo hides for cover from the rain as a good number of the planks were damaged or had holes. Our bison hides were not as satisfactory as we had expected; they shriveled in the sun and split apart from the nails.

When the house was completed, it was divided in four rooms. One quarter was the Sieur La Salle's lodging; another that of the Recollet fathers; another was for several of the gentlemen; and the fourth served as storeroom. We were not worried about lodging at that time because it was not cold. In addition, some of the gentlemen had made sheds for themselves. The crew were almost all in the open air.

---

[15] This is Garcitas Creek.

While the work was under way, I again made several trips to the *Belle* as well as the staging area to bring several things to the camp. I also went to collect Le Gros who was not recovering from his snakebite. La Salle decided to bring him ashore where meat was available to cook bouillon and it was easier for the surgeon to dress his wound.

On one of my trips, having arrived at the staging area with a canoe and five men, we saw some Indians at a distance of about the range of two musket shots from the post. The Sieur Hurié told me that they had come the previous day to a certain spot, where they went for water, and they had staked some arrows on the banks. As there were not many men at the post, they had not confronted the Indians. I took the five men who had come with me and proceeded in the direction of the Indians. When they saw us coming, they slowly withdrew. It seemed that they wanted to talk; but, as La Salle's order was to fire above them, there was no reason to talk to them. Some of our men, nonetheless, made a sign to them to approach. Seeing some of them in range, I took aim at them; but as I had not recently primed the musket, it did not fire. I then corrected it. Then whether I was not accurate enough to hit one of them with the shot, or whether they were wounded, they did not stay. Two or three of those who were with me fired also although I had warned them not to shoot all at once. As we were in a thicket, I reloaded my musket calmly, thinking nothing. I was taken by surprise when the Indians attacked us and particularly me. They shot at least 10 or 12 arrows at me which came at me in force. One even grazed my arm; I needed to keep a sharp eye to avoid them. Seeing the Indians coming, I cried out to our men to advance, and we bore down directly on them even though I had no more shot in my musket, not believing that they would come back to charge. Here I lacked prudence, it is true. I remembered that La Salle had told us several times that one must not shrink from the Indians because, if we had fled, not one of us would have escaped. They run much faster than we do.

When they saw us coming at them, they took off on foot, and I told our people to move out of the thicket for fear that some of them would come from the shelter of the brush and could surprise us. We moved to the plain, where we were exposed, and waited for them, but they did not want to approach. They gathered the arrows that they had shot at us, but it appeared that they had only shot at me. This may have been because I had fired on them first, or perhaps for some other reason. A man who was not of their tribe was with them; he seemed lighter than they. After we had lingered some time in that place and saw that they had retreated, I returned to the Sieur Hurié's post where we spent the night.

The following day we proceeded to the *Belle* where we learned that the Indians had left during the evening. Perhaps they feared that we would attack them during the night, for they had been camped to the right of the frigate. They had with them 18 or 20 canoes. We loaded what we had come to get and retraced the route back to the settlement.

Some time passed without anything out of the ordinary happening except in regard to the Sieur Le Gros whose leg was still very swollen. The surgeon told him that gangrene threatened to set in and that he could find no remedy other than cutting off the leg. Initially, Le Gros did not want to hear of it; but eventually he accepted this course of action. Several people persuaded him and assured him that he would not be left alone to walk with a wooden leg. In the end he accepted it all although the surgeon had not previously performed such an operation. When everything was prepared for the operation, his leg was cut off. This happened on the 27th of August.

The amputation was made very close to the knee, and a fever overtook the patient. He lasted only two more days and died the 30th, the Day of the Beheading of Saint John. The loss was to everyone's regret, particularly La Salle's. Indeed, his death was a great loss to La Salle for no one else had such knowledge of La Salle's affairs. For my part, I can say that I lost the best friend that I had in the country. Although we had only met on the voyage, we had established a firm friendship. He left several items, in goods as well as clothing. He also left 900 or 1,000 *livres* [16] in gold *louis*.[17] La Salle took charge of these. He then had some of his clothing sold at a valuation to different individuals. He had done the same with the belongings of others who died here including Desloges and Lecarpentier.

Meanwhile, La Salle wanted to make a trip and attempt to gather some information about his river. He only had to await the recovery of his brother, the Abbé, who was to go with him and whom he would not leave. But his brother did not recover as soon as La Salle wished. During the interval, La Salle made some short trips of about two or three leagues from the settlement from which he did not draw much information. However, he did discover some very beautiful country, ending in one direction with a high hill that appeared to be about 15 to 20 leagues away.[18]

This country was crossed by many rivers that flowed through it. The one on which we were, and where the settlement was situated, is one of the smallest.[19] It was called *Rivière aux Boeufs* [Bison River] for the number of bison there and the bison we had killed nearby.

About the middle of September, La Salle ordered me to go to the *Belle* to take some utensils and clothes to the ship. He wanted all of his belongings to be put

[16] The term *livre* is translated as about a pound in weight.

[17] Apparently some of Le Gros's gold *louis* fell into the hands of young Pierre Talon, who had a pocketful of French gold coins when he was captured by the Spaniards. Bolton (ed.), *Spanish Exploration in the Southwest*, 375. The relative value of the *louis d'or* to other French monetary units during this period is found in McDermott, *Mississippi Valley French*, 94–95.

[18] The noticeable high hill was likely the high and prominent ridge on the west side of the Colorado River across the river from the present-day city of La Grange. The hill, which is approximately thirty-two leagues north of the bay, rises abruptly to an elevation of over five hundred feet from the riverbed of the Colorado, which is at an elevation of under two hundred feet. On his journeys to East Texas in 1686 and in early 1687, La Salle used the same Colorado crossing near the high hill that was named Jesús, María y Joseph Buena Vista by Alonso de León in 1690 [Bolton (ed.), *Spanish Exploration in the Southwest*, 412, n. 2, 419] and was later shortened to just "María" by Anglo settlers. See Bonnell, *Topographical Descriptions of Texas*, 59. Today the hill is called Monument Hill.

[19] The small stream was Garcitas Creek. Although Joutel usually refers to the stream on which the fort was established as a river, Pierre Meunier calls it a creek. See Appendix A. Kathleen Gilmore has conducted a study of the artifacts from the excavation of the site; see Gilmore, *The Keeran Site: The Probable Site of La Salle's Fort St. Louis in Texas*, Texas Historical Commission, Office of the State Archeologist Reports no. 24 (Austin, 1973), and Gilmore, "La Salle's Fort St. Louis in Texas," *Bulletin of the Texas Archeological Society*, 55 (1986 for 1984), 61–72.

aboard ship. He hoped that the Colbert [Mississippi River], that is to say, one of its branches, emptied into this bay, and he wanted to take the frigate a littler farther up into the bay. So I left with five men in a canoe. Once we were underway, knowing the route, we did not have difficulty traveling by night. We headed for a very large cove that was about one and a half leagues across and we made good headway, going by water from one headland to the other. If one went around the cove by land, the route was more than doubled. But when we were in the middle of this cove,[20] we were taken by a gust of wind from the northeast. It was blowing quite strongly from over open seas, and it was not long before the waves began to increase. As the wind caught us on the beam, we were forced to make our way to the farthest end of the bay. But, with such high seas, we could not find a suitable place to land, and we were in quite a predicament.

After having searched, with the waves getting higher all the while, we finally landed in a small inlet. As we were able to take few precautions, we could not prevent the canoe from filling almost halfway, drenching the clothes. But this was not all. After the trunks were unloaded, we pulled our canoe along the shore as best as we could. There was no place to beach the canoe and it was in great danger of being smashed, without our being able to remedy the situation. The waves pulled it to one side, although we persisted for a time in holding the tip of the canoe into the waves. Several times the waves knocked us down, so we finally abandoned it to Providence. Fortunately for our canoe, the wind changed from one side to the other, otherwise the canoe would have been smashed. The wind came from the north-northeast and blew furiously; but because the land sheltered the inlet there were no waves. We spent the night rather ill at ease. First of all, we were not very warm, there not being large wood in this area. Furthermore, we were worried, especially me, who feared for the frigate because the wind was extremely strong.

In the morning at daybreak, we were very surprised to see that the sea had retreated quite a distance. This is to say, the water was more than the range of a musket shot from where our canoe was. Thus we were quite uncertain about our situation. There was no way to drag the canoe because the bed of the bay was too rough, covered by oysters and other kinds of shells.[21] There was less likelihood of carrying it because it was all one piece, made from a hollowed-out tree trunk, and we were only six people. Therefore we were perplexed about what we should do. We had two trunks which we could not carry, and inside were clothes which we could not leave behind.

---

[20] This is probably Lavaca Bay.

[21] The following is taken from a footnote Margry attributed to Joutel: "There were a good many oysters along with stones which we found more often than we would have wished because they cut like knives and this was disagreeable because we had shoes which were inconvenient for this type of expedition where we often had to get in the water, besides which when we came to muddy spots, they could stick to the bottom. Therefore, we had to suffer this discomfort. The hardship was doubled because after being cut by the oysters, the salt water went in the cuts and they smarted intensely. These oysters were otherwise very good and more tender than those in France, but not as big as those from Rouen and Dieppe; they are longer. They are abundant in this bay. There are also mussels but they are not as good as the oysters." Margry (ed.), *Découvertes*, II, 185.

The difficulty we were in was not insignificant, and we had experienced all sorts of weather during the day. The wind went around the compass, and it rained almost all night. The wind veered to come from the sea by the next day which consoled us although we were quite wet. This indeed made us very happy because the wind had caused the water to return in full tide as it was before. What had caused this great outflow of water had been the north winds which were very severe. They had almost emptied the bay.[22]

With the rain over, we set off again on our trip to the *Belle*. But when we approached the location where she was customarily anchored, we saw nothing. This shocked us, particularly me who was apprehensive that she might have perished. We continued farther on a couple of leagues, but we saw nothing. So I made the decision to return to camp to advise La Salle of the situation. The next day, having seen us from the distance, La Salle came to meet us and asked for the news. He had been worried about us as the weather had been as severe in camp as it had been where we were. When he learned that we had seen no sign of the frigate, he decided to head along one side of the bay and ordered me to go by the other side, so that if the ship was aground, we would find her. He also ordered that in case I came upon the ship, I should have three cannon shots fired to give notice, and he would do likewise in case he discovered her first. So we separated, La Salle taking the left side and I took the right which was the customary route.[23]

We navigated until evening when we camped on a point where we had camped several times before. The next day we continued our course, and when we arrived at the site of the staging area, we saw the ship. She was anchored in a place a little farther off from where she customarily anchored. We proceeded toward a place opposite where she was, but as a fresh breeze was blowing and the swells were heavy, we could not go on board. We camped at that place. The next day, when it was full daylight, the men on the ship saw us and raised their flag at half mast to signal us. When they saw that we were not going to them (because the swells were too heavy), they fired a cannon, believing that we did not see them. But the sea was too rough for these canoes which capsized more easily than the ships' shallop. Nevertheless, as I anticipated that they must need something, it worried me as much as them.

Several of our men who knew how to swim volunteered to swim to the ship. They went as a threesome and arrived together and they found Morenger aboard the frigate. He came ashore with another individual and told me what had happened during the bad weather. They had run a great risk of being wrecked. They were driven upon their anchor, having failed to follow La Salle's order who, because there was only one anchor on the ship, had directed the pilot to anchor a

---

[22] As indicated, the normal tides along the coast near the bay are only about one to two feet. From the narrative it is difficult to determine the date on which the storm occurred, but it was clearly within the late summer and early fall hurricane season.

[23] The right side of the bay (as the bay waters move southward into the Gulf) would be along the southwest bayshore, which was the customary and most direct route used between the settlement and Pass Cavallo.

cannon with the anchor in order to relieve it. However, the pilot had not done that; so when the bad weather surprised them and the pilot remembered, it was too late. However, there was enough time to avoid a shipwreck which was a risk without this precaution. They lost their shallop and did not know in what direction it might be. If the wind had continued, they would not have been able to avoid being cast away or, at the very least, run aground. That is why they finally took recourse with the cannon which served to hold them. They kept running for some time after anchoring the cannon because they were underway and the wind was blowing strong. When they realized they were deprived of their shallop, they felt most troubled. Morenger also told me that they were making a raft in order to go inform La Salle when they first saw us. They were making the raft with a few yards for sail and some planks.

During this time, La Salle also sighted the ship from a distance and sent his canoe. He himself landed with a part of his company so that his canoe could be of use in case they needed something on the ship. Morenger told me that he was going to render an account to La Salle of what had happened. He added that it would be best to send someone as soon as possible to the right and the left side of the bay to see if the ship's shallop could be found. Accordingly, it was determined that I stay in that place until someone had investigated the other side and a few casks of water or some wood were obtained in case they needed them. I then sent the canoe with Morenger so he could cross the river that was at the head of a cove that had to be traversed. I remained in the same place until the next day. But when I realized that it was not necessary to stay there too long, I left one canoe with my men and returned to the settlement. I ordered them to send the canoe back when they had finished what was most useful but preferably sooner if they retrieved their ship's shallop. After this I returned to the settlement where we passed some time without anything extraordinary happening, except several more trips which I made to the *Belle*.

CHAPTER VI

# Life at the French Settlement

a Salle intended to search for his river [the Mississippi] and he was only waiting for his brother, Monsieur Cavelier [the Abbé], who was recovering well. La Salle therefore prepared to depart and designated me to stay at the post, giving me its command. La Salle told me several times that he intended that I should receive a salary, which I resisted, insisting that it was not my intention to be so engaged. I also said that I would do my best in all that involved the King's or his service. However, La Salle convinced me that he was proceeding in my interest because if he died, he wanted it settled that I would receive 600 *livres* per year and a quarter of all the hides which would be collected at this post.

After this, he gave me orders as to what I should do during his absence, including the work that had to be done as well as the distribution or reduction of rations. In case some of his people returned after his departure, La Salle directed me not to receive them unless they had letters from him written in a specified manner.

He gave me, in short, many similar instructions in writing as well as an inventory of all that he was leaving in my charge, namely: eight cannon; about 200 muskets and as many sabers or swords; 100 kegs of powder, totaling about 9,800 or 9,900 pounds; about 3,000 pounds of bullets and some 200 to 300 pounds of other shot; 40 or 50 bars of iron (squared as well as flat), 20 bundles of iron rods to make nails; and a quantity of other scrap iron which had been saved from the shipwreck; several kegs of steel; some tool chests; and about 100 hatchets.

We had an edge tool maker who worked a little bit, but he did not accomplish much because the anvil was left in the hold of the ship. We, therefore, used a cannon to pound upon. Moreover, the tool maker died soon thereafter, and several others died as well. At that post, I was also left with 20 barrels of flour, a cask and a half of wine, and about three quarters of a cask of brandy. I myself bought two small casks in Rochelle and had saved some in a case that La Salle had given me. He left me orders regarding what rations I should hold in reserve for the Recollets who remained at the post as well as for different individuals who were favored at La Salle's table.

As for the livestock, we had all kinds. This subject was discussed by the author of a book entitled *The First Establishment of the Faith in New France*.[1] The livestock consisted first of two boar. One died and we found it in the river. There also were a few sows. La Salle had brought eight young ones on board the *Belle*, hoping to unload them at his river if he found it. Since they were over five or six weeks old, it was easy to raise them. There also were a hen and a cock which had reproduced. Beaujeu, in the end, had given us a billy goat and a nanny goat, but the female was sterile so we killed them both during the Abbé's illness. Those were all our animals; there were no others.

The diverse livestock that the author of the *Establishment of the Faith* mentioned is as imaginary as the fort that he said had been built in so little time and put in condition for defense. Indeed, there was only the house that I have mentioned before, having eight cannon in the four corners unfortunately without cannon balls. When we left there was no other stronghold. As for the families, the author said that there were nine or ten, but we were far short of that count. There was only, at that time, the wife of the soldier named Talon[2] who had died.

To return to our discourse, La Salle gave me written instructions on what I should do in his absence. He also directed me, in regard to what might happen, to do my best without seeking advice from anyone. After that, he thought of nothing but his departure. For the journey, he had some breastplates made of barrel staves which our men attached together to protect themselves from arrows in case they undertook an engagement with the Indians as La Salle indicated he was planning. When all was ready, La Salle left with all the canoes. He promised to send me back one canoe with four men, including the hunter named Daneau [or Davault] whom I had with me earlier on the coast.

After we said farewell and they were enroute, I had five of the cannon fired, fired rather with powder only, to salute La Salle on his departure. He took his route downstream, planning to have his ship [the *Belle*] proceed as far as the end of the bay which we called Saint Louis in honor of the King and the country named Louisiana. La Salle intended to follow the length of the bay in the hope that there could be a branch of the river called the Colbert River emptying into this bay.[3] His

[1] The following is a note Joutel added: "The author of this book, who treats M. de la Salle's voyage, indicates having drawn what he alleges from the memoirs that were provided him by Reverend Father Anastase with whom I returned to this country. I did not notice that the Father was at work on this subject. I will say more: I did not notice that he wrote a single word during our return; he even expected me to give him a copy of what I had written. I do not know that he wanted to assert so many falsehoods. But that there is falsity in it is evident and can be perceived without necessarily having been in that country."

[2] The husband, Lucien Talon, was lost; he failed to return from one of La Salle's earlier explorations from the settlement. Lucien's wife, Isabelle, along with their children survived him. See an account of the Talon family members in Robert S. Weddle, "La Salle's Survivors," *Southwestern Historical Quarterly*, 75 (Apr., 1971), 413–433.

[3] Although Joutel reports that La Salle departed eastward in October 1685, a number of Texas historians, including Henry Folmer, John F. Bannon, and Robert S. Weddle, have argued that during the period from the fall of 1685 to the spring of 1686 La Salle personally explored the Rio Grande. In 1953, Folmer postulated that La Salle did not explore eastward in the winter of 1685–1686, as Joutel recorded, but rather

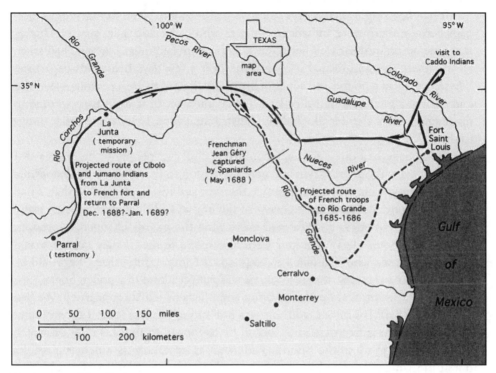

Northeastern New Spain

departure occurred at the end of October, a few days before the feast of All Saints. There were thirty-four persons who remained at the settlement; in this number there were three Recollet fathers, the Sieur Hurié (to whom La Salle had given command during my absence), one of the Sieurs Duhaut, and the Sieur Thibault, a surgeon.[4] The others who remained were soldiers along with young boys and enlisted men. The girls and women, whom I mentioned before, came from Paris. One even called herself a kinswoman of M. le Curé de Saint Eustache. There were also two girls named Talon, and another from Saint Jean d'Angely who was taken on at Rochelle.[5]

---

explored to the west, and visited an Indian village that Folmer estimated was located "less than seventy Spanish leagues from the mission of La Junta de los Rios" at the junction of the Rio Grande and the Conchos River in the Big Bend region. Folmer, *Franco-Spanish Rivalry*, 162–163. In 1970, Bannon stated that La Salle and his small party went west as far as the lower Pecos on the Rio Grande in *The Spanish Borderlands Frontier*, 96. Weddle agrees with Folmer and Bannon that during the winter of 1685–1686 "La Salle reached the Rio Grande." See Weddle, *The French Thorn*, 30, and Weddle, *Wilderness Manhunt*, 34. These projections of La Salle's travels west in late 1685 and early 1686 are based in part on Spanish sources of Indian reports that an unidentified group of approximately eight to ten foreigners dressed in armor who sought information on the location of Spanish mines were met on several occasions near the Rio Grande in West Texas. Joutel's account neither confirms nor denies the interpretation that La Salle personally was among the group of foreigners, as discussed in more length in the introduction.

[4] Two surgeons were with La Salle at the settlement. One named Liotot played a prominent role; the second was Thibault. See Nixon, "Liotot and Jalot," 42–52.

[5] Marie-Madeleine was one of the Talon daughters who survived the Indian massacre at the settlement and in 1690 was recovered from the coastal Indians by the Spaniards; the second daughter, Marie-

It had been eight or ten days since we had seen any bison in our region, perhaps because there were Indians in the area who had made them scatter. During this time we did not eat well because we had no smoked meat. La Salle had taken all that there was and loaded it aboard the *Belle* a few days before his departure. Therefore, I had a pound and a half of bread distributed to each person. As we also had the remainder of a barrel of lard, I gave out a bit of it from time to time to make soup. As for the Recollet fathers, I distributed wine, brandy, and other things to them.

As La Salle had directed me, I commanded all our people to be on guard. I enforced this without exception and gave no pardon to those who fell asleep while on sentry duty. This made them realize that our survival depended on that. I had four guards posted, one at each corner of the house, and they were relieved every two hours. I wanted to be informed every time the guards changed. Moreover, when I cried out: "Alert!" the four were to respond to me. If they failed I would directly go to see who had failed to respond. If I found him asleep, he would be punished without mercy, that is to say he was put on a kind of wooden horse.

During this interval we saw no bison and I became a little concerned. We had only twenty barrels of flour, and this was not enough to last long. I foresaw that we would not hear from La Salle soon if he happened to find his river, in which case he would go up to the Illinois. Patience was necessary, as much as possible, but at the same time, one had to consider what action to take. I was not lacking for opportunities.

One day when I was going with some of our people to a spring for water (which was about the range of two musket shots[6] from the house), I saw something in the distance moving on the plain, a good league and a quarter away. I decided that it could be bison. So, when I returned, I climbed to the roof of our house to investigate further. Having made the same observation, I ordered seven or eight of the most alert men to take their weapons and follow me to see if we could catch the bison. The trouble was that we were not very expert in this sort of hunt. As for me, I had only once been with the hunters on a bison hunt, so I did not know how to go about it. However, I set out, and we proceeded toward the place where I had seen the animals moving.

When we arrived there, looking to the right and the left, I saw two bison lying down in a hollow. I told my companions to stay while I approached them. A Recollet father named Father Maxime was the only one who came along with me, and he approached closer as well. When we were within range, one of the bison stood up. Whether it had noticed something or otherwise, I took aim and fired at

---

Elizabeth, died at the settlement. The name of the girl from Saint Jean D'Angely is unknown. See Robert S. Weddle, "Talon Children," in Tyler, et al. (eds.), *New Handbook of Texas*, VI, 197–198.

[6] The generally accepted distance for a late-seventeenth-century Spanish or French musket shot is approximately seventy-five to one hundred yards. However, the meaning of the expression, "range of a musket shot," used in both French and Spanish literature, varied according to the author and location. Professor Stephen Hardin of the Victoria College and Dr. Pat Wagner of Shiner graciously directed our attention to several documents and studies relating to seventeenth-century French and Spanish armament and the effective range of weapons of the period.

it. We could not keep it still because of the two dogs we had with us. One dog had been brought from La Rochelle by the deceased Le Gros; the other was a small dog that had been found in the forest nearby. The dogs ran after the bison, causing them to run. As a result, we accomplished nothing, so we returned to the house.

The next day, when it was full daylight, I noticed several bison near the area where we had been the previous day. That gave me occasion to return there. I took the same men with me as I had taken the day before, and when we had proceeded about a league and a half from the house, we saw a number of bison. I was able to get near a few herds and I fired several shots at them. Whether I missed or whether I did not wound them in a vital part, I was unable to bring down a single one. Meanwhile, I noticed that I had shattered the shoulder of several that escaped on three legs. I was still not discouraged. I approached several other herds, not without difficulty because it was necessary to crawl to avoid notice by these animals.

That day I found myself in the middle of 5,000 to 6,000 bison.[7] But, to my great disappointment, I still did not kill any. These animals, having a very good sense of smell, could detect us and would scatter to the right and left. Meanwhile, evening was approaching and I had not killed anything. Although very fatigued, I again approached a herd and again fired several shots. Not one bison fell. Should I have troubled myself uselessly? My knees were all raw from crawling about on them. Finally, when I was returning to join our people, having looked to the right and left around me, I saw a fallen bison lying on the ground. I approached it and found that it was dead but still warm. I examined it and found it was pierced by a bullet through the shoulder where I had shot it as I had several others. I signaled then to our people to hurry. They were rather displeased that I had not killed anything sooner, and I was even more so considering that birds were a rather easy target.

At length we worked to dress our bison, a task at which we were rather new, every one of us. Finally, the dressing of our animal complete, we each took our share of the burden. For fear that some animals might find the carcass, I had the rest wrapped in the skin so someone could collect it the next day. We retraced our route to the settlement which we could not reach while still daylight. Fortunately, Hurié, who had stayed at the post, had made a fire to guide us which served us

[7]   The report of five to six thousand bison is not surprising, as Spanish expedition diarists in the late seventeenth and early eighteenth century reported bison herds of a similar size roaming between the lower Colorado and Guadalupe rivers. In 1691 Terán reported over four thousand head of bison in nearby Fayette County and up to three thousand head in congregations on the lower Lavaca River. Mattie Austin Hatcher (trans.), "The Expedition of Don Domingo Terán de los Ríos Into Texas," *Preliminary Studies of the Texas Catholic Historical Society*, 2 (Jan., 1932), 22, 23, 25, 46. In contrast, Cabeza da Vaca, who lived for several years (1528–1534) near the central Texas coast where Joutel lived for two years (1685–1687) reported seeing bison only on three occasions. See Cabeza de Vaca, "The Narrative of Alvar Núñez Cabeza de Vaca," 68. It should also be noted that Cabeza de Vaca reported relatively dry weather in Central Texas whereas other Spanish chroniclers reported wet and cool weather in the same region about one hundred and fifty years later.

A similar contrast can be made in reported bison sightings in the 1540s (as recorded by chroniclers of the De Soto expedition) and in the 1680s by Joutel in southeastern Arkansas. Chroniclers on the De Soto-Moscoso expedition differed on whether bison were seen in southeastern Arkansas. However, one hundred and forty years later, Joutel saw and killed bison on several occasions between the Ouachita River in central Arkansas and the Mississippi River.

well. As there were no trails in this area (other than the ones made by the bison), it was easy to get lost in the open plain that extended beyond our view and was covered with tall grass.

The late hour at which we arrived home caused me to wait until the next day to distribute the meat to all our people. Everyone was rather hungry inasmuch as it had been three weeks since we had had any fresh meat except a few turkeys, some ducks, and other fowl. But that had only been for the Recollet fathers and the officers. I had the meat distributed to everyone. La Salle's instructions were that a pound and a half be given them each meal (not counting the bread) and to have three meals a day, with the exception of the fathers, a few gentlemen volunteers, and us. We were to have a pound and a quarter per day with a pint of wine as long as it lasted. When the wine was finished, I was to give out a little brandy. Regarding those to whom La Salle ordered me to give bread, they each should have a half pound of it a day, and those who were sick were to be given as much as was reasonable.

The people whom I had sent to collect the rest of the meat returned at noon. I was afraid that the wolves would have eaten it because there were a large number of these animals in this area as well as wild dogs. But the wolves were not large like those in France. My fear, fortunately, was not realized. Our people brought back the rest of the meat and the skin which I had the men stretch [to dry]. From that day on, we no longer lacked meat; the bison that were in the vicinity furnished our needs. In all likelihood, we had been without bison so long because the Indians had scattered them. After that, bison remained in the vicinity of the settlement, that is to say, at a distance of a league or a league and a half away. Besides, I learned how to approach and kill them.

A few days later, a canoe arrived with three men aboard: the Sieur Le Clercq[8] and two soldiers. None of the three had much strength left although Le Clercq, who was young, was strongly built. However, he was not accustomed to hard toil, never having experienced anything tiring except what they had done during the voyage. When I asked them where the hunter was whom La Salle was to send me, they told me he was dead. He had been a very good man who well understood how to hunt. But it seemed to me that La Salle appeared displeased when, upon his return from a hunt at which he had exerted himself, I would sometimes give the hunter something. Also, I found him quite friendly which moved me from time to time to give him something to drink.

I was therefore very sad to learn of his death and of the manner in which it happened. In returning from a hunt in which he had killed two or three geese, he was fatigued and in a sweat, and he stopped to rest. At that time, the wind was from the north and consequently it was quite sharp. In all likelihood, he gave into his need to rest and the cold seized him. He could not move out again and stayed in a depression in the ground where some of the others found him. They informed La

---

[8] Père Maxime Le Clercq was a Recollet priest, who Parkman noted was a relative of Chrétien Le Clercq, the author of *First Establishment of the Faith.* See Parkman, *La Salle and the Discovery of the Great West,* 353, 418, n. 2.

Salle who sent some men to find him and help him, but they could not rescue him in time.

I also heard from these men about the attack that La Salle made against the Indians. It was not as great as the author, whom I mentioned before, has told it, as the whole thing consisted of only the capture of one woman, a little girl, and one other woman who was wounded and found in the field. I do not doubt that there were others wounded, but they escaped.[9] This victory was not very advantageous to us, and I can even say that it cost us dearly, as will be seen in due course. We learned also that the Indian woman who was wounded did not live long afterwards. La Salle had her wounds dressed. But, whether from caprice or for glory, she tore away the dressings and the bandages that had been put on her wound; nor would she eat.

What was most advantageous to relieve us at the settlement was the canoe brought by Le Clercq. It was a great help in the transportation of meat which we had to carry for a league and a half sometimes. This had been most tiring. Afterwards, we went up the river, on one side or the other, and when we killed a few animals, we only had to transport them in our canoe and then to the settlement. That meant we had an abundant supply of meat.

I had to make a pit near the settlement to smoke the meat so we had a supply to save in case of need or if the bison happened to wander off as they had done before. I did not miss the opportunity to have the meat smoked and to have the fat and tallow collected. This served to season the smoked meat when it had aged. I noticed that the fat did not smell as much as the tallow that was produced in France. The meat even had a much better taste. I took care to set aside the marrow and the grease from the top of the pot which I found to be as good as butter. Circumstances made us think so at least.

Thus the time was almost entirely engaged with these sorts of activities. Indeed, it was necessary first to go search for wood elsewhere and then to cut the meat into very thin pieces. Moreover, our people were not too ready to go, and it was necessary to urge them to get started.

Before his departure, La Salle had laid out work for us to do in case he was away for some time. He wanted a large trench dug. I had it begun, but it only served to become a pond where the pigs wallowed every day.

Our people were not too active, but it was important that each one contribute his part. For this reason, when I went out, often one of the Recollet fathers accompanied me with a musket. We did not go out without this weapon. One day when Father Anastase accompanied me, I was approached by a herd of bison. One strayed a little, and I shot him and broke his shoulder. That did not prevent him, however, from taking off which forced Father Anastase to run in front of him to make him turn around while I reloaded my musket. The good priest did not know the fury of these animals any better than I, but he quickly learned. When the priest

[9] Pierre Meunier, who was with La Salle on the raid, testified that the French party in late 1685 attacked four Caucosi villages near the lower Guadalupe River and killed four Indians. See Appendix A. We have no further record regarding the disposition of the other Indian captive woman.

approached a little too close, the bison proceeded to charge him in a fury, and the priest's robe, as well as the tall grass, hindered his running. The bison overtook him, threw him to the ground, and trampled him. By luck the father was not gored by the horns. What bothered me was that I dared not shoot for fear of wounding the priest along with the bison. I cried out for him to retreat, which he did, after which I fired a second shot that stilled the animal. The good father was indisposed for more than a month or six weeks by this episode, although it did not prevent him from coming and going around the settlement.

There was another priest named Father Maxime [Le Clercq] who was well suited to such a venture, that is to say, for a hunting trip. He was fit for anything whether it was dressing a bison or some other thing. As I have said, it was necessary for everyone to have a hand in work. As there were not enough of us to suffice, I made the women, girls, and children work. Everyone wanted to eat, so it was quite right that they be productive; the more so because the work was for survival.

We spent a while without anything remarkable happening. Two or three people died, among others, the Sieur Thibaut. His death greatly saddened me. We were good friends. He was from Rouen, and we had begun the voyage there together from the start. I had him buried as honorably as the conditions of the place would permit. Before dying, he made a sort of will in which he disposed of a few of his belongings, some to the Recollet fathers and some to other individuals. However, the return of La Salle changed matters. Thibaut also entrusted me with a letter that, in all likelihood, was some bequest favoring one of his sisters. On my departure from the settlement, I left the letter with the Sieur Chefdeville, not expecting not to return. Thibaut also ordered a number of masses which were said by the Recollet fathers. The soldier who was married died also, so the number of families consisted only of two wives widowed some time later.[10]

Another day, when I was hunting in the area, I killed several bison. When we were to return, each with our load, the question arose of who would go back to find the meat that I had left and had covered with hides. Father Maxime told me then that he was going to take his musket and serve as escort as it was necessary to guard in case the natives surprised them. He accordingly left with several men. But that evening when the others had returned, Father Maxime was missing which worried me a great deal. I had a large fire made outside so that he could see it; but he did not return that night. The next day, which was the feastday of Saint Thomas, the wind was from the northwest and it was very cold. We were closed up inside the house where a fire was made in the middle of the fathers' room. We were most troubled about the father, about what could have become of him and how he could have gone astray. At 10 o'clock the following morning we saw him returning

[10] Authorities have characterized La Salle's expedition as one intended to colonize the lower Mississippi and have often referred to the members of the expedition as colonists. According to Joutel's count there were only two families with La Salle, both of which had children. In addition, there were perhaps five or six unattached young women. The composition of the expedition party suggests that the primary mission was a military exercise, and that the establishment of a colony for settlement was secondary. Joutel reports no significant effort by the French priests to evangelize the natives. In contrast, on Spanish expeditions into Texas in the late seventeenth century, Spanish clerics busily and aggressively attempted to convert the local Indians. See Foster, *Spanish Expeditions into Texas*, 17–95.

along the river. When he arrived, he told us that he had taken a bison trail to the left and had gone astray chiefly by walking toward a star that he had seen on the horizon, thinking it was a fire lit in the settlement. He walked until he encountered the river which he recognized. As he was tired and he was not quite certain where he was, he waited for daylight. But he was not very warm. Everyone was joyful at his return, and I was in particular.

Yet another time, one of our girls, having fallen behind, likewise strayed. We thought she was lost, for she was outside for two nights even though I sent people right and left to find her. After we fired several gunshots, I had a cannon fired, but still there was no trace of her. But she returned the second day. It was also the river that put her straight. After Father Maxime had recounted his adventure to us and had rested a bit, a mass was said. This was a benefit we had everyday, as well as vespers on feastdays and Sundays and common prayers everyday, evening and morning. In this manner, we spent a space of time without anything out of the ordinary happening.

I should mention that there are some reflection phenomena in this country when the sun begins to rise above the horizon. Trees are made to appear, as are very high mountains and brushwood, and woods of full-grown forest trees at one time or another according to the weather conditions. One morning, the sentry informed me that he saw men in the field. I climbed on top of the house to see better and, after looking carefully, I noticed what appeared to be bands of men here and there. They seemed disposed to attack us and in the line of battle itself. I was compelled to have our arms and munitions prepared and our cannon as well. In each cannon I had a small sack of shot placed because we had no cannon balls. Each one considered how best to defend himself, and there was not one person who did not believe that these were men. They appeared to be walking. We firmly held this belief until the sun was a little above the horizon and the illusion dissipated. Even then, as they were withdrawing from us, they seemed to be returning. Even if I had not seen the like since, I would still believe that these were men. Why, I noticed after that that trees of a prodigious height appeared which eventually were only brush or thickets. Some times rocks appeared to us, scarped like those that are at the edge of seas or rivers. I observed that even a little bird on a branch or a small plant seemed as large as a man.

Toward the middle of January [1686], when we were all at the settlement, the sentry told me that he heard some voices on the river where we proceeded to go as fast as possible. We saw a man in fact in a single canoe who cried out: "Dominique?," which was the name of the Sieur Duhaut who had stayed at the settlement with me. When we went down to the riverbank and he came closer, we recognized him as [Pierre] Duhaut, the older brother of the one who had stayed at the place. He had parted with La Salle. Seeing him alone, I was seized by fear that some misfortune had befallen La Salle. I first asked him if he had letters from La Salle, and he told me that he did not. This gave me reason to suspect even more. Consequently, I was quite confounded about what conduct to take at this conjuncture. La Salle had given me orders, and I had pledged not to receive any of his men unless they had his letters. La Salle had even left me an inscription to find. This was:

"in the name of the three persons of the Holy Trinity." Moreover, he had given me orders to have those arrested who might come in order to call them to account on his return. However, after having weighed and understood why he had left La Salle, or rather the way in which he had been left behind, I found no reason to hesitate in accepting him. We were surprised that he had escaped the hands of the natives. He gave us the following detailed account of the way in which he had gone astray.

La Salle had spent some time at the place where he was camped before he sent back the three men to me with the canoe. He had some meat smoked there for provisioning the *Belle*, and he had the ship advance farther toward that end of the bay, hoping to find there the right branch of the Mississippi River, that is to say, the branch that he had left on the righthand side when he came down the river on his discovery. But prior to having the ship advance, he sent the pilot of the ship in a canoe with five of his best men to sound and determine how far upriver the *Belle* could go. Now, after the men had sounded and viewed the situation from several sides, they felt fatigued and landed to rest. As night was approaching, the men decided to sleep on shore and made a fire to warm themselves and cook something, as usual. Unfortunately they lacked prudence. Apparently, the men were not on guard and let themselves be surprised by the natives who gave them no mercy, killing all six and even destroying their canoe.

Judging from the position in which La Salle found his men when he went ashore, they must not have defended themselves, nor even taken out their arms. The corpses, scattered here and there, were by that time stripped of flesh, eaten some by wolves and some by wild dogs. This was a considerable loss as these were, so to speak, the six best men of the company. One was the pilot, a very able man. In addition, this incident showed the natives our weakness. Thus, I do not doubt that this loss very much saddened La Salle, and I believe that the natives felt well revenged for the way they had been dealt with in the previous incident.

La Salle, not to be discouraged, had the smoked meat put aboard the ship along with a number of men to guard it, among whom were Messrs. Chefdeville, a priest, and Planterose. Chefdeville [was too tired?] to endure the journey. La Salle also put aboard the young native girl who had been captured in the action that I mentioned. The wounded native woman had died. After furnishing them with the necessities, La Salle gave orders as to what they should do, in accordance with what the conditions of the place would allow. He entrusted the command of operations to a man named Tessier[11] who had been along on the journey from the beginning in Rochefort. La Salle directed him to stay in that place until he had received word from him. He put them under firm obligation, when they went to bring water on board, to stay on guard for fear of surprise and to take people ashore as escorts. After this La Salle left with twenty men to see what he could learn about the river.

With two canoes remaining, La Salle took them along as far as the point where they would continue by land. They had, a few days before, lost one canoe that had

[11] According to Parkman, Tessier was a pilot (*La Salle and the Discovery of the Great West*, 421), but Margry used the term "master."

drifted away without anyone noticing. So when La Salle decided to explore overland, he thought it wise to have the canoes sunk so they could later find them. This
was done, and they set off on their way with each man carrying a heavy load.
Hoping to find some tribes, La Salle had goods taken along to offer them presents
and to trade with them for food. The lot consisted of hatchets, knives, awls, glass
beads, vermilion, and several other things such as some powder and shot, as well as
food provisions that they had to take as a precaution for fear of being caught in
woods where no game could be found. After having walked for some time, the
party found a rather pretty river which afterward was called the Maligne.[12]

La Salle, who walked in the lead, ordered Morenger to stay as the rear guard
with the instruction not to leave anyone behind. But [Pierre] Duhaut had to stop
to repair his pack and his shoes with which he was not too well provided. They
were not in great supply and most men had to manage with pieces of bison hide to
protect themselves from thorns, stumps of trees, and stones.

Seeing Duhaut stop, Morenger told him to walk on, but Duhaut asked him to
wait a little. Morenger could not be persuaded. It was difficult to catch up with
those still walking as seldom as the party rested. As it turned out, when Duhaut
continued on his way, he was unable to rejoin them. He took another route, as
would be expected, there being only bison trails which here go in one direction,
there another. Eventually, evening came and Duhaut found himself alone, and, for
good reason, worried about his safety. At nightfall, he fired several gunshots so that
if he were heard, someone would respond. But the night passed without his hearing anything. The next morning he arose confounded by which route he should
take. Not knowing in which direction to go, he thought that it was best to retrace
his steps so that, if someone came after him, he could be found. With that in mind,
he decided to spend the day in this same place again. But, as he neither heard nor
saw any sign of them, he made his return to the settlement from there.

On his way back, he became very hungry. He had eaten his supply of smoked
meat, but he had a few shots left, so he killed a large turkey when he saw it within
range. He dressed and cooked it with two cakes of hardtack which, he confessed to
me, he ate all in one meal. After that he headed toward the place where the canoes
had been left. As the canoes were sunk, it was difficult to recover one. However, he
managed to pull one up and empty it with his pot which was very useful to him for
this as well as for cooking his meat. In this way, he decided to try to find the ship

---

[12] According to my projection, the Maligne is the present Colorado River as indicated in Joutel's
account of La Salle's last journey to East Texas in early 1687, which is detailed in Chapter VIII. Again,
confusion occurred when earlier historians, such as Carlos E. Castañeda, called the Maligne the Navidad;
see Morfi, *History of Texas*, I, 483, n. 3.

The account of La Salle's trip related by Pierre Duhaut (being told here) is consistent with the account
La Salle gave to Joutel on the expedition leader's return, in which La Salle described going east toward the
Mississippi from the bay in late 1685. Thus neither the Duhaut nor the La Salle account refers to a westward trip by La Salle personally, and in that respect, these accounts do not support recent assessments by
historians who assert that La Salle personally traveled to West Texas in late 1685 and early 1686. This is
noted not as proof that La Salle (nor any of his men) traveled both to the west and the east during this
period because Duhaut reported only on his brief trip and La Salle, as Joutel says, did not explain all of his
actions to Joutel, or perhaps to anyone else.

(the *Belle*) or to return to the settlement where I was. But the trouble was subsistence. He did not even have a knife so that, when he killed a bison, he could only partly dress it. He could only pull a few pieces of entrails from it by tearing it, having made a little hole with the flint of his musket. What was even more of a handicap for him was that he did not dare travel by day for fear of being surprised by the natives. Therefore, he only traveled at night, and during the day he hid in the canes and the water willows. A few days later, he came close to some deer and killed one which he dressed with the gunflint, the hide not being as tough as that of the bison. The deer served him well for continuing his trip. He spent about one month on his journey. When the wind blew a little, he used his shirt as a sail. It came about in this way that he joined us, having escaped death. (But it would have been better had he perished than commit the assassination of which I will speak later.) After examining all the facts which he explained to me, considering that it was by accident that he had strayed, I found it acceptable that he stay, not being able to do otherwise, so to speak. However, I observed his conduct a little more closely than that of the others.

We again passed a long period of time without significant event. We proceeded as usual with hunting. We only noticed the natives once coming close to the settlement and also coming to the spring where we went to draw water. As the Indians had staked arrows on the banks of that spring, I was obliged to take care and to be watchful that our people stood guard and kept a good look out. Sometimes, when we were hunting a distance from the settlement with our canoe, we had to sleep outside. I took care to construct a small barricade of brush around us so no one could approach without making noise.

As our people were not very well sheltered, I decided accordingly to construct a kind of room made of stakes planted upright and close together which we did. But we only had wood fit for firewood in our vicinity. I took the opportunity of having wood cut when we went hunting and putting it in the bottom of the canoe, so that little by little we managed to have it carried back. After this was done I had a separate structure built, with one side set aside for the women and girls and the other side for the men. I had this building covered with reeds which were in abundance in the area. After that I had the roof covered with clay which I had mixed with other soil because, when the pure clay dried up, it cracked too much. It was like potter's clay. I did something else: several large trees near the house, particularly on one side, screened our view of an area and could facilitate the approach of natives who could surprise us one day and kill someone. I found it best therefore to have them cut down.

I will add a few details of little importance to the reader but which were not without interest for us. Our pigs were multiplying, the sows each having had a litter. Since the hunting was plentiful, the pigs benefited from it for they also ate meat. All the animals adapted well to eating meat, even the hen and the cock. Another detail: I mentioned that we had a man with us who had lost his sight. But there was a second person who was one-eyed, and unfortunately, a film came over his other eye which rendered him blind. He was a soldier.

As I have not yet spoken of the settlement's surroundings, I will say something about them. The settlement was located about two leagues inland on the banks of a river[13] which had been named *Aux Boeufs* [the Bison].[14] We were on a small rise from which one could see a long distance. Toward the west and the southwest there was prairie, very level, that continued beyond our view. Beautiful, good grasses grow here serving as pasturage to an infinite number of bison. I should not say only to the west and southwest for the country is quite beautiful all around. Toward the north and northeast, there are woods usually found along the river-banks. There are also some ravines. Toward the east and southeast, bearing toward the bay and the sea, the country is also quite beautiful. There are fields of wild flowers here and there which graced our view. It resembled populated country such as one sees, for example, in the Caux[15] region with its small country estates and mottes of trees, particularly oak of several species. Some oaks are always green and never lose their leaves.[16] Other oaks are like ours in France; others have a little different leaf. Some bear small and numerous gall-nuts, and they also have acorns which I ate with great ease.[17] The oaks that bear gall-nuts lose their leaves during winter like those in Europe. The oaks that stay green have a smaller leaf than the others and they bear mild acorns.

There is another species of oak that has leaves similar to the oak leaves in Europe, but these trees have a thick, rough bark. Its wood is extremely soft; but when it is dry, only a good axe can avoid damage. There is also another species of tree that bears a certain small red berry when it is ripe, and it is rather mild.[18] These trees bear fruit up to twice a year, as I noticed; but the last fruit is liable to not ripen because the first cold blights it. It only needs one rather sharp wind from the north; at any rate, that happened the year we spent in the place. They all with-ered as do the walnut trees and the vines in France when frosts come in the month of May. There is another species of tree that bears a fruit somewhat resembling a

---

[13] The French settlement was about five miles upstream on the west bank of Garcitas Creek, as deter-mined by Bolton in "The Location of La Salle's Colony on the Gulf of Mexico," 171–189, and confirmed in recent archeological studies and Spanish expedition accounts.

In one of his more egregious deviations from Joutel's journal, Michel added from an undisclosed source that the settlement was located at about 27° north latitude. Cox (ed.), *Journeys of La Salle*, II, 78. Michel's version gives a false reading, whereas Joutel's unabridged account accurately records the reading of 28° 20' for the entrance to Matagorda Bay. See Chapter III.

[14] The French as well as the Spaniards initially referred to bison as cattle.

[15] Caux is a region in northern France that would have been familiar to Joutel.

[16] These trees are live oaks.

[17] In laying their eggs, wasps stimulate the small oak tree branches to produce galls, which carpenter ants call home. Although acorns are usually processed to remove tannin before human consumption, they are suitable for direct animal consumption. Wayne H. McAlister and Martha K. McAlister, *Aransas: A Naturalist's Guide* (Austin: University of Texas Press, 1995), 40. Joutel later reported in East Texas that he was served a meal that included prepared acorns. See Chapter XIV. The oak with a thick, rough bark may be the blackjack oak (*Quercus marilandica*).

[18] The hawthorn found near Matagorda Bay has a small red berry that is edible. Vines, *Trees of the Southwest*, 334–387. Cheatham and Marshall note that there are several species of hawthorn including *Crataegus texana*, but there are other candidates for this description including the sugarberry (*Celtis laevigata*).

medlar,[19] but it has another taste, very close to that of the cassia. I even noticed that they had somewhat the same property in that they act as a purgative.

One finds here many creeping vines and other vines that climb trees and bear many grapes.[20] But the grapes are pulpy and sour, unlike the ones in France. We consumed much of their sour juice in preparing soups as well as stews. As they are pulpy, I do not believe they would be good for making wine. However, the grapes did not last long, because the animals knew how to find them. Mulberry trees[21] are found along the river. Their berries are like ours, except they are a little smaller, and they are very good, sweeter than those in France. They have very beautiful leaves, good for nurturing silkworms which should thrive well in this country because it is almost never cold here and there is almost no winter.

Also I noticed certain plants similar to those I have seen in France and in the Islands, that we called *raquettes*[22] because they have a leaf of that same shape. They bear flowers around the leaves which sprout fruit that look almost like figs. But the leaves are full of quills, and even the fruit have them all around. One must strip the fruit before eating it because, although the quills are quite small and almost imperceptible, without fail they make one sick once they lodge in the throat and on the roof of the mouth. One of our soldiers even died from having eaten the fig greedily without wiping it. All these small quills caused a tremendous inflammation of the throat and eventually suffocated him. These fruits do not have much taste; they are in several shapes, sizes, and colors.

There is another species of tree which has long branches of about three or four feet and its leaves are like those of palm trees,[23] but are taller and wider. They bear a small fruit, but I do not know how to describe the taste, not having eaten any. One of our men told me that it seemed good to him.

Another kind of tree has a trunk very nearly like the other one, but its leaves are quite different. The leaves are pointed and stiff, formed like spouts, and they must not be approached abruptly because they pierce material and skin.[24] This tree has a tall stalk which flowers and forms a rather beautiful cluster of a white flower

---

[19] On a number of occasions French and Spanish explorers reported finding trees similar to the medlar they knew in Europe. See the entry on persimmon in Foster, *Spanish Expeditions into Texas*, 256.

[20] Large mustang grapevines carrying heavy clusters of purple grapes with pulpy centers are found climbing to the tops of live oak and some other trees in South Texas. Vines, *Trees of the Southwest*, 715, 716. Marshall adds that the grapes make excellent juice, jam, and wine.

[21] The Texas mulberry seldom exceeds twenty feet in height; it has small edible berries that turn red in May and then black within a few weeks. Vines, *Trees of the Southwest*, 219. Cheatham and Marshall add that Joutel is probably describing the red mulberry (*Morus rubra*), whose berries turn blackish as they ripen.

[22] Del Weniger gives very helpful background information on the racket-shaped Opuntias called prickly pear and their spiny, edible but seedy fruit called "tunas" in *Cacti of Texas and Neighboring States: A Field Guide* (Austin: University of Texas Press, 1984), 230–231.

[23] Cheatham and Marshall report that this description reads more like *Sabal texana* (aka *S. mexicana* in some works) and that Garcitas Creek is one of the known sites for *S. texana*.

[24] The Spanish dagger or Spanish bayonet (*Yucca treculeana*), which grows side-by-side with the prickly pear, is a yucca (a member of the lily family), not a cactus. The yucca found near Matagorda Bay grows to a height of twenty-five feet, has very attractive, large, white flowers in the spring, and has a two-to-four-inch-long and one-inch-thick sweet fruit that may be eaten. Vines, *Trees, Shrubs and Vines of the Southwest*, 53, 54.

with a tinge of yellow. Some of these have as many as 60 or 80 flowers to a stalk. The flowers droop rather like Indian corn except less so. After the flower has bloomed, fruits are produced which are the size of a thumb; the longest is the size of a finger. They are full of small seeds and berries spread unevenly along the length of the fruit. Only the surface of it is good to eat, but it is barely the thickness of a coin. They are quite soft and quite sweet but hardly satisfying. I have spoken of the mulberry trees, so I will also mention that there are a great many blackberry bushes[25] which in Normandy are called the mulberry of the fox. But they are much better in this country and much sweeter.

With regard to plants and herbs, there is a certain small sorrel[26] in the fields which has a leaf shaped like a clover; it is tart and as good as that found in France. There is an abundance of them as well as a great many small onions[27] which are not much larger than a thumb but as good as ours in France. When the fields are burned, these are the first flowers that appear at the same time as the greenfinch. Afterwards, the countryside is crowded with other plants of different kinds and colors which create a most pleasing brilliance when they are in flower.

I noticed among [the wild flowers] that one had the flower and scent of the tuberose. However, its leaves are quite different, being like those of the borage, hairy, and full of small prickles.[28] There are a great many white narcissi of the same scent as those in France as well as French marigold, the scent of which is not agreeable. There are as well a great many anemones of diverse solid colors; but their leaves are different.[29] Most of the autumn flowers being yellow, the fields seemed to be this color.

To finish describing the area near the house and the view to the south as far as the bay, I will say that the countryside which bordered to the west and southwest is spacious and lost to view except for a few clumps of trees. On the other side of the river is a prairie, an eighth of a league across, in which there are several fresh water lakes. The grasses there are not very good; they are mostly rushes. At the far end of the prairie a small slope rises, 40 or 50 feet in height, which overlooks another wide

[25] The wild, sweet berry bushes were likely the southern dewberry (*Rubus trivialis*) found in the counties north of Matagorda Bay, although the less frequently found Texas blackberry is occasionally seen in the same area. Ibid., 452–453.

[26] Cheatham and Marshall suggest that the small sorrel is *Oxalis*.

[27] Small wild onion plants (*Allium drummondii*) are found throughout South Texas in the spring. Indians used both raw and cooked wild onions for food. See "*Allium*" in Scooter Cheatham and Marshall C. Johnston with Lynn Marshall, *The Useful Wild Plants of Texas, the Southeastern and Southwestern United States, the Southern Plains, and Northern Mexico* (Austin: Useful Wild Plants, 1995), 206–229. See also Melvin R. Gilmore, *Uses of Plants by the Indians of the Missouri River Region*, enlarged ed. (Lincoln: University of Nebraska Press, 1977), 19.

[28] Cheatham and Marshall suggest that the flower with the scent of the tuberose is possibly the bullnettle (*Cridoscolus texana*). The flowers are white, tubular, sweet-smelling, and the leaves are prickly and sting.

[29] Joutel tried to identify the local wildflowers that were similar in appearance to those found in northern France, such as the marigold, narcissus, and anemones. See Alastair Fitter, *New Generation Guide to the Wild Flowers of Britain and Northern Europe*, ed. David Attenborough (Austin: University of Texas Press, 1987), 43, 114, 128, 242. Cheatham and Marshall advise that neither marigold (*Tagetes*) nor narcissus grow wild in Texas. However, many other yellow and orange wildflowers similar in color to marigold are native to Texas, and the plants Joutel mentions may be *Cooperia* or *Zephyranthes*. Wild anemones grow in Texas. See "*Anemone*" in Cheatham, et al., *Useful Wild Plants of Texas*, 353–355.

plain about a league and a half across ending in a ravine where there is almost always water. The prairie, which likewise is bordered by water to the right and the left, extends a long distance toward the northeast and the northwest. There are not only beautiful fields but more woods as well, particularly on the banks of the river. However, the trees are not beautiful. A border of trees appears about three leagues from there and continues along the river which was named Cane or Reeds[30] because of the reeds on its banks. These woods seemed prettier to us than those around the settlement. Near the upper part of the river, there are several lakes trimmed with rushes in the middle of which are found a great many ducks, teals, coots,[31] and the like. It would be very easy to make fine duck ponds there. Many ducks could be caught there, considering how many there are, as well as other wild fowl.

[A listing of the local game] must begin with the bison which are very numerous, and it could be said that they were our daily bread.[32] After bison, there are the deer, the turkey, Canada geese, other geese, swans, cranes, ducks, teals, coots, plovers, jack-snipes [bécassines], sandpipers, white and brown curlews,[33] and grouse of two kinds, one large and one small (which is the better). The large grouse[34] are like pheasants, and they spread their tails like turkeys and have two cups hanging at the collar of their neck. There also are many large birds that we called large gullets because of their big throats which they sometimes fill with the fish they have caught and after which they go on land to eat. I have been told that there are some similar birds at Versailles, and they are called pelicans.

---

[30] Giant cane up to thirty feet high is found along riverbanks in Texas. Vines, *Trees of the Southwest*, 44. Near Garcitas Creek the predominant "cane" now is phragmites. See *"Arundinaria,"* in Cheatham, et al., *Useful Wild Plants of Texas*, 500–509.

[31] The *poule d'eau* is the American coot, a water bird found in the Texas Gulf Coast area. McDermott, *Mississippi Valley French*, 127; Rappole and Blacklock, *Birds of Texas*, 76, 77.

[32] Some anthropologists have assumed that during the seventeenth and eighteenth centuries bison were found only seasonally in Central Texas. For example, Newcomb incorrectly describes Central Texas as a "region on the southern margins of their [bison] range; bison were usually present in the winter months, particularly on the Blackland Prairies, but in the summer months they moved northward leaving few or no animals in the area." See Newcomb, "Historic Indians of Central Texas," 49.

Joutel's journal account disputes Newcomb's statement, as do reports of bison in South and Central Texas between April and September made by seventeenth- and early eighteenth-century Spanish expedition diarists: Bosque (May 1675), De León (April 1689 and May 1690), and Terán (June 1691) reported bison herds near the Rio Grande. Reports of large bison herds in South and Central Texas during the summer months in the late 1600s continued into the 1700s: Céliz (September 1718) saw them near Matagorda Bay; Rivera (August 1727) reported them in Travis County; Rubí (August 1767) in Gillespie County; and Solís (April 1768) in Goliad and Fayette counties. In addition, Espinosa and other Spanish expedition diarists described large bison herds south of the Rio Grande, over 250 miles southwest of the Central Texas area as Newcomb defined it. See the entry "Bison or American Buffalo (cíbolo)" in Foster, *Spanish Expeditions into Texas*, 236–237.

[33] The manuscript includes mentions of sandpipers and white and brown curlews, which Margry dropped.

[34] In the late seventeenth century, prairie chickens (*Tympanuchus cupido*) were found in large numbers near Matagorda Bay, but today they are an endangered species. See Robin W. Doughty and Barbara M. Parmenter, *Endangered Species* (Austin: Texas Monthly Press, 1989), 61–64; Edward A. Kutac and S. Christopher Caran, *Birds and Other Wildlife of South Central Texas: A Handbook* (Austin: University of Texas Press, 1994), 65.

There is another species which we called *spatulas*,[35] because their beak resembles the same. They are large and fleshy and have a very beautiful plumage of a pale red which is quite lovely. There is a species of small bird of a different kind and color that, among others, is very beautiful with plumage that is part red and part black. There also were some birds which we called *mouches*[36] whose plumage is gray-green but the color varies. They are very pretty, and ordinarily they are circling around flowers.

There are two or three species of eagles [vultures]. The most numerous are what we call *aigles corbins*.[37] They are black and are very much like crows, in appearance as well as for their penchant to kill. They have heads like turkeys.[38] I noticed several times when we were hunting and spotted some animals, the vultures would usually go and roost even though we were far distant. We were surprised that in so little time there would be flocks around us. They would wait until we were gone and then eat what was left. It often happened to me, when I would kill some bison around the settlement, that I would leave the kill to come and instruct the men to go dress it. But, when we went back, we found the vultures had eaten the tongue, or had begun to eat it at the base, and the eyes had been plucked out. There are some vultures which are gray and others which we called *aigles nonnes*[39] because they have a white collar and white on a part of the head. There are also several kinds of birds whose names I did not know and others that are common like the starlings, small crows, oyster catchers, cormorants, herons, and the like.

Just as this country is bountiful in all kinds of animals, so the lakes and rivers are full of fish. I have already spoken of those in the bay which are in abundance and of several species. The most common are the brill, but they are not like those in France. They are something like the "French" catfish;[40] they do not have scales but have two quills on the sides of their gills, beards beneath their snouts like the

[35] The roseate spoonbill (*Ajaja ajaja*) found on Matagorda Bay has a soft spatulate bill that is very helpful in grasping prey. Although the bird was almost wiped out at the close of the nineteenth century, there are now over two thousand breeding pairs along the Central Texas coast. McAlister and McAlister, *Matagorda Island*, 227–28; Kutac and Caran, *Wildlife of South Central Texas*, 57.

[36] *Mouches* (a bee or fly) refers here to one of several species of hummingbirds that migrate through south Central Texas. Authorities presently list twelve species that are found in the area. Kutac and Caran, *Wildlife of South Central Texas*, 77.

[37] Black vultures or buzzards (*Coragyps atratus*) are frequently seen today in the Matagorda Bay area. McAlister and McAlister, *Matagorda Island*, 233. Kutac and Caran, *Wildlife of South Central Texas*, 61. Joutel occasionally refers to vultures as eagles.

[38] Turkey vultures (*Cathartes aura*) and black vultures intermingle near the bay in their common search for dead animal matter. McAlister and McAlister, *Matagorda Island*, 233. Rappole and Blacklock report that black and turkey vultures range from southern Canada to Cuba and South America, *Birds of Texas*, 53; in 1526 Oviedo described the black vulture found in the West Indies in the early 1500s as having no feathers on its neck and having a terrible taste, which he attributed to the fact that the bird only eats "filth, dead Indians, and animals." Oviedo, *Natural History of the West Indies*, 66.

[39] This may be the bald eagle or the caracara, which is a black-and-white scavenger with a distinct white collar neck. John L. Tveten, *The Birds of Texas* (Fredericksburg, Tex.: Shearer Pub., 1993), 147, 148.

[40] Joutel's description fits that of catfish found in Matagorda Bay and in local rivers and larger creeks. McAlister and McAlister, *Matagorda Island*, 286.

brill, and their flesh is flabby. There are also a great many trout[41] or salmon, but they are not as good as those in France. There is a species of fish called *arme* [42] which has a long snout, like an eel, but is much bigger. Its skin is rough and the meat is not very good.

We also had a large number of tortoise,[43] but they are smaller than those we had seen in the Islands. We often caught them on a fishing line. The meat is quite good. Inside their bodies are eggs which are not bad and serve to thicken sauces. There is another species [of turtle][44] that is found inland, but they are smaller and rounder. Their scale is beautiful when it is prepared to make powder flasks. One of our surgeons, while looking for these tortoises in some holes where they had retreated, was bitten on the arm by some animal. The arm became quite swollen, and later he lost one finger and a half of second one. We did not know if it was a snake or some other animal that bit him because I had seen some animals which were shaped like toads[45] with a similar mouth and four legs. But they have skin above the back, raised in bumps and tough, with a small tail. They do not jump; they walk. Whether it was one of these animals or a snake that bit him, I do not know. As we did not have any experience with these kinds of venom, this was very troubling.

Afterwards we had several of our animals bitten by snakes including a dog that survived. She belonged to the deceased Sieur Le Gros. The dog was near me one day when I was on the seashore fishing and she was bitten on the jaw which swelled a great deal. I gave her a little theriac[46] which cured her. It had also cured one of our sows that returned one day with a head so enlarged that she could barely lift it. As I had no doubt that it had been a snake that bit her, I gave her a little theriac with some flour and water. I killed several rattlesnakes while I lived at the settlement using the same dog. Whenever she would discover one, she would sometimes bark for a half an hour around it. This forced me to get my musket. I often found the snake in the brush, making a noise with its tail. When I killed them, our pigs would eat them. I would often take pleasure in seeing them torn to pieces, and when we were at the seaside, where food was not plentiful, if some of our men found one, they would not let it be wasted. Their flesh was very white.

---

[41] Speckled trout, along with the redfish, are today the most popular sport fish in the bay area. Ibid., 284.

[42] The fish was probably a gar.

[43] Joutel's tortoise was likely the green turtle that was caught commercially in Matagorda Bay during the latter part of the nineteenth century. See Robin W. Doughty, "Sea Turtles in Texas: A Forgotten Commerce," *Southwestern Historical Quarterly*, 88 (July, 1984), 43–69. The description also fits the less familiar Guadalupe spiny softshell turtle and the Texas tortoise. See Thomas G. Vermersch, *Lizards and Turtles of South-Central Texas* (Austin: Eakin Press, 1992), 124, 129.

[44] The western box turtle is found near Matagorda Bay. McAlister and McAlister, *Matagorda Island*, 263.

[45] The four-legged Texas horned lizard or "horned toad," with its raised rough scales, is not dangerous but appears so. It is now considered a threatened species in Texas. Kutac and Cavan, *Wildlife of South Central Texas*, 122.

[46] The French term refers to any type of antidote or cure-all against poison.

There also were many crocodiles or cayman[47] in the rivers in this area. When they came out they made me fear for our pigs who were often in the river wallowing to refresh themselves. I killed several of them. I did not spare them when they were found near the house. One day I killed one that was extremely large, almost four and a half feet around and about 20 feet long. I never saw any other as large although I killed several of them. Our pigs lived well off of it for several meals. As these animals have short legs, they crawl with their stomachs touching the ground. So, when they cross a place where the ground is soft or sandy, one discovers their track. They are not as vicious as those of the Nile according to the accounts of different authors.

I had some seeds which I planted in February. I had reserved about a quarter of the big beans, intending to plant them, but before doing that I soaked them so they would not take as long to grow. Whether they were too soaked by seawater or otherwise, not a single one sprouted. Neither did the wheat that we had brought from France which, in all likelihood, must have been past germination. But I planted some other seeds which came up very well including chicory, beetroot, celery, asparagus, French melons, watermelons, and some pumpkins. I also planted cotton seeds which I had brought from Petit Goave; I planted them in various places so that if they failed in one area, they might grow in another. In short, I tried and did my best to make something thrive. My satisfaction was thwarted by the animals who deprived me of it later.

Toward the end of March, when I had climbed up on the roof of the house, as I often did to see what was happening in the country around us, I discerned seven or eight men in the distance coming from the northeast[48] near the spot that we called Le Boucan [the place to smoke the meat]. When I saw that they were coming toward us from our flank, I called to seven or eight of our people to take up arms and join me to investigate them. I ordered the others to stand guard in the meantime. As the men whom I had seen in the distance came nearer, I saw that they were dressed and thus concluded that they were Europeans. I left to go meet them and, when we were within range, I recognized that it was La Salle with his brother and Morenger, his nephew, and some of his other people, all in a rather wretched state with their clothes all slashed. The Abbé's short cassock was in strips, and one would have had difficulty finding a piece to wrap two small pieces of salt. Further, he had an old cap on his head, having lost his hat along the way. The rest of the crew looked the same; their shirts were in the same condition. Some in the group were weighed down with meat as La Salle had anticipated that we might not have killed any bison. When he left there was none around the settlement. This must have troubled him, as he might not have found many people. Indeed, if rations had failed us, we would have been forced to move and go elsewhere. In short, the arrival was met with many embraces and much joy in seeing one another again.

[47] The French generally referred to the smaller alligators as *cocodrie* and the larger ones as *caiman*. McDermott, *Mississippi Valley French*, 40.

[48] This report also suggests that La Salle traveled northeast toward the Mississippi in early 1686.

After regards were exchanged, La Salle saw Pierre Duhaut and asked me in an angry tone why I had received this man who had left him. I told him of the manner in which Duhaut had come and told him how he had recounted to me that he had gone astray. Duhaut defended himself as well, and La Salle's anger did not last long. We then returned to the house. There we first refreshed ourselves with a little bread and brandy because the wine was in short supply. There were, however, still 20 to 30 jugs[49] that I had reserved for making vinegar having told the fathers, who had their portion as I did mine, that it was worth more used that way than as a drink.

After La Salle had rested a bit, I told him all that had happened during his absence and how I had proceeded, and he was well satisfied. He told me that the rest of his company had gone to the bay to see where the *Belle* was. The next day, Captain Bihorel, the Sieur Cavelier, La Salle's young nephew, Lieutenant Barbier, the surgeon Liotot, and several others arrived. La Salle spoke to us of the beautiful country he had discovered with many rivers whose banks were lined with beautiful woods and lovely countryside beyond. The country was well populated with bison and other game. He told us that he had seen a few tribes of natives with whom he had formed a liaison; that is to say, he dealt with them in peace. But he did not find his river.

What turned out to be more unfortunate, and caused even more sadness, was the information given on the following day by Barbier and the rest of the company that they had not seen the ship. Apparently she must have long since departed from the place where they had left her because there was not one sign that they had gone ashore since the parting. This gave La Salle much to worry about. All his belongings were aboard, and he realized the error that he had made in not leaving some of them in this place. As he was not disposed to take advice from anyone and only followed his own impulses, he was at all times deluded that there must be a branch of his river that emptied into this bay. But in this he was mistaken. What caused him the most worry about the disappearance of his ship was that he did not know if she had perished or if she had been taken over by some malcontents. In the latter case, he told me that if she had gone to the Islands, the Sieur Cussy or others would send her back to him. But the situation was uncertain, and because no one knew if she had gone aground, perished, or departed, it remained troubling.

I proposed to La Salle that if he consented to give me ten men and a canoe, I would go to the other side of the bay to try to obtain definite information about this. He responded that due to the war with the natives, who had killed several people, we would risk the same happening to us. I told him that we would take care to keep a good lookout; but he did not consider it wise. He dwelled upon the notion that the ship had been seized and forced to depart even though it was pointed out to him that Chefdeville and Planterose were aboard, and he could be assured they were incapable of such an action. But he told me that [the mutineers] could have gotten rid of these gentlemen. Realizing that he was to persist with this

---

[49] The French word, *pots*, which Margry used, means a small liquid container such as a jug or carafe that holds about two quarts. McDermott, *Mississippi Valley French*, 126.

notion and that he did not consider it worthwhile that I undertake the suggested trip, even though I proposed it several times, I ceased to speak of it. He was much more acutely affected by this third loss than by all the others, since all [his] belongings and apparel were on the ship, as well as all of his papers. If, by misfortune, I had been taken by force at this post by some foreign nation, whether European or natives, they would have been at grave risk. This is why he was so worried during his journey.

I learned this from several people who told me that La Salle had decided, as soon as he should arrive, to have the ship repaired and all the belongings unloaded on one of the rivers he had found. There were more beautiful and more habitable locations than those where we were. Afterward, he would send the ship to the Islands with Morenger and me aboard to try to obtain fresh provisions. We should have, by that point, managed to find the entrance and mouth of the river entering the Holy Spirit Bay. But all these plans were frustrated by our not finding the ship. This forced him to make another decision: to set out again as soon as possible by land and to try to find the river. Thus, after a short rest La Salle prepared himself for this journey.

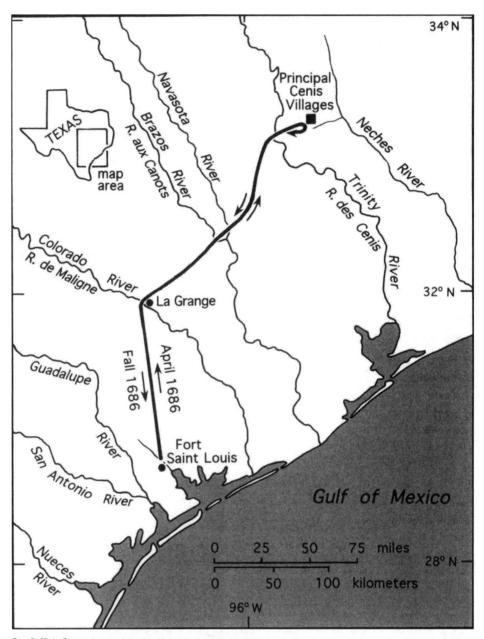

La Salle's first trip to visit the Cenis Indians, 1686

# CHAPTER VII

# La Salle's First Journey to the Cenis

s I have related earlier, when the cargo boat was preparing to enter the bay, some of the heavier items had been unloaded to lighten her load. Under the circumstances, I was quite pleased that my chest had been among the first put ashore for, as it happened, I lost almost nothing. I was therefore able to offer La Salle a cloth coat, almost new, which fit him because we were almost the same size. This he accepted. I offered Abbé Cavelier some linen and a pair of shoes, the only ones I had. I also gave some linen to the Sieur du Morenger. In short, I offered what I had as was appropriate under the circumstances. I also had 10 or 12 pounds of ribbon, a few knives and awls, and similar things which I gave away. The Sieurs Duhaut likewise had belongings which had been left for them here. La Salle took hatchets and other things including some linen cloth that he gave in turn to several individuals to make shirts, because that is what one wore out most in this country where it was not cold. We were most often only in shirts unless one had some lighter short coat.

While everyone was preparing to refit themselves in linen and accommodate themselves with this apparel, La Salle also distributed the belongings of several deceased individuals including the Sieur Le Gros, Monsieur Thibaut, and Monsieur Lecarpentier. This clothing was charged to individuals according to estimated value. I had a shoulder belt of moose skin that was well dressed; La Salle used it to make shoes. Each man was provided with a pair. I only had one pair which I gave to the Abbé along with a sheet to make a mosquito net[1] to protect himself from the mosquitos. Thus everything was put to use to try to get out of this difficulty and effect the success of the venture.

When all was ready, it was proposed that some men should be reassigned because many who had made the first trip were not strong enough to endure the

---

[1] Margry misuses the word *berceau*, meaning cradle, here and elsewhere. In the manuscript the word is *berre*, meaning mosquito net or bar. McDermott, *Mississippi Valley French*, 22.

fatigue of this one. The Sieur de La Salle chose others from among those who had stayed with me. The Sieur Barbier was among those who stayed behind, having been crippled by a splinter that had entered his foot during La Salle's earlier exploration. He continued to limp from the injury and this prevented him from undertaking another long journey. The young Sieur Cavelier also stayed behind with a few others. La Salle chose the replacements, taking a total of 20 men with him.

Two pounds of powder were packed for each person. The powder was wrapped in three different sacks; the first of canvas, the second of cloth, and the third of tarpaulin. One could not take too many precautions in protecting gunpowder. Each one also took three pounds of bullets, a pound of lead shot, and another small sack in which there were five pounds of meal. Besides that, each one took hatchets, two dozen knives, some awls, and similar things. After all had been thus prepared, they thought only of departing.

Before he left, La Salle gave me orders that in case some ship or shallop arrived belonging to Sieur de Cussy or an official of the Islands, I could give them what I had and hand over to them the bison hides that I had dressed. He was of the notion that the frigate [the *Belle*] had left and was going to the Islands from where he would have news of her. He also left a letter with me for Sieur de Cussy in case someone came. Otherwise, he gave orders to Barbier to find some place on the Cane River to hide a few kegs of powder in case of misfortune, whether from fire or other accident. Likewise he gave us orders to go hunting up the same river with canoes in case the bison were scarce in the vicinity. With the canoes we were also to collect some tree bark for repairing the house. I had [the roof] covered with bison hides which I had nailed firmly on the planks. However, once the hides became wet and then the sun beat down on them, they shriveled and cracked only slowing the water rather than keeping it out.

After all had been settled and La Salle had asked me to keep close watch and take care of everything, he departed with 20 men including the Abbé Cavelier, Father Anastase, the Sieur Bihorel, the Sieur du Morenger, the Sieur Ducler, the Sieur Hurié, the younger [Dominique] Duhaut, his surgeon, a gunner named Hiems[2] whom La Salle had engaged in Petit Goave and who was formerly a buccaneer, and his own two servants. At the departure on April 28, I wanted to have the cannon fired, but La Salle did not think that fitting.

During La Salle's stay at the settlement, not much hunting had been done and our provisions of smoked meat had diminished. Thus I decided that it was necessary to replace it with some more. But as there were not enough bison near the settlement, it was a matter of traveling farther. Accordingly, Barbier prepared to leave with two canoes to see if he could find some bison elsewhere. He took along some members of the remaining company to smoke the meat and to carry it back as soon as it was possible. He left the next day, and I remained at the post with the rest of the company. As the number of people was small, each was obliged to stand sentry

---

[2] According to Parkman, Hiems (or Hiens) was a well-educated and well-traveled German buccaneer from Würtemberg who may have served in the British military service. Parkman, *La Salle and the Discovery of the Great West*, 25, 72, 411.

and guard in turn. I even put the women and girls under an obligation to stand guard like the others, it being to every one's interest.[3]

At about two o'clock in the afternoon on May 1, as I was walking around the house, I heard from the lower stretch of the river a voice that cried out several times: "Who goes there?" As I knew that we had two canoes out, I believed this could well be one bringing back some meat although they had not been gone long. I had not given it too much attention when again I heard the same voice. I responded: "Versailles." But, some time later a voice other than the one I had heard before cried out again: "Who goes there?" I responded again: "Versailles," for that was the password which I had given Barbier in case he returned at night. But when I came near the riverbank, I heard voices which I was not accustomed to hearing. I recognized, among others, that of Monsieur Chefdeville. This made me, fear that some misfortune had happened to them. Chefdeville recognized me and called to me so I immediately went down to the water's edge. The first question was where the ship, the *Belle*, was. They answered that she had perished, or rather gone aground, on the other side of the bay, and that only six [seven?] had escaped. They all were in this same canoe, namely: the Sieur Chefdeville, the Marquis de La Sablonnière, lieutenant of a company of infantry, Tessier,[4] who was one of the masters of the frigate (the other having died on La Salle's first expedition), the pilot, a soldier, a girl, and a small boy as well.[5] The girl had been taken at La Rochelle where she was a servant. She was from Saint Jean d'Angely.

After the usual greetings upon such an occasion, I took them up to the house and had unloaded from their canoe a number of things, among others, La Salle's clothes and some of his papers, some linen and glass beads,[6] and 30 to 40 pounds of meal which were remaining. I gave them something to eat and let them rest a bit from their fatigue. Chefdeville, who had believed himself lost, was particularly joyful to be rejoined with us, and for our part we were quite happy to see them as well. But we were distressed by the loss of the ship. The next day, Chefdeville gave me a detailed account of all that had happened since the departure of La Salle when he left them anchored at the place that I mentioned earlier according to the report that Pierre Duhaut had given me.

After [their party] had remained in that same place for some time and the water supply had begun to run low, they decided to send the shallop ashore with

---

[3] It should be noted that the young French women were serving their turn at military service in sentry duty like the soldiers.

[4] Although Tessier was apparently drunk while master of the *Belle*, La Salle selected him for his small party on the final expedition and assigned him to the hunting party that included those who killed La Salle. Parkman considers Tessier an accomplice in the murders of Morenger and La Salle; see *La Salle and the Discovery of the Great West*, 451.

[5] The entry Robert S. Weddle, "Meunier, Pierre," in Tyler, et al. (eds.), *New Handbook of Texas*, IV, 649, states that Meunier returned to Fort Saint Louis with the other survivors of the *Belle*. This is not supported by Joutel's list of survivors, which does not mention Meunier's name but does include an unnamed soldier and a boy, descriptions Joutel never applied to Meunier.

[6] Joutel frequently mentions giving Indians French-made glass beads, rings, pins, and needles in exchange for hides. Archeologists engaged in the recent excavation of the wreck of the *Belle* have uncovered a plentiful supply of small to tiny glass trade beads of blue, red, and other colors and shades, rings, pins, and needles that were apparently left on the ship for future use as trade goods.

four or five casks to fill them with water. For this purpose, the best men were chosen to set off in the shallop. Planterose was among this number. It was he who was the godfather of the small native slave girl taken in the action that I earlier mentioned. The young girl had been baptized by Chefdeville. She alone had had the advantage of knowing Christianity by means of the sacrament of baptism, and she died a short time later.

The shallop left with these orders and headed for shore. That evening, the wind, having freshened a bit, caused the bay to rise. Shortly after sunset, one could see that the shallop seemed to be heading out to sea. They had a head wind and could not make much forward progress. Chefdeville, realizing that night was advancing, told the master of the frigate that it would be wise to put a torch atop one of the masts so that those aboard the shallop could see the ship from a distance more easily. But the master disregarded the advice that had been given him and was content to only light a candle in the ship's common lantern. This did not stay illuminated long because the wind freshened and made the swells heavy, and no trace was had of the shallop the next day. So that day was spent in impatience. It was thought that they must have perished although it could not be known whether the shallop had sunk or gone aground on the shore.

The lack of water added to the loss of the five best men on board (the rest were not their equals) forebode a deadly end for the survivors. Meanwhile, they stayed a few more days in the same place waiting to learn something. During this time, several people among them died from lack of water. They had eight pigs from the settlement that had been put aboard and they ate them, not having water to give them. They began to fade one after another as they saw that their hopes for news were in vain. Also they realized that the longer they waited, the weaker their condition became to save themselves.

They had cooked some flour with seawater; but that did not agree with them at all. They could not even eat it. They still had some wine and some brandy and even a case of Spanish wine that the Abbé Cavelier had put aboard. He had abstained from this in order to say the mass on his return because none was left at the settlement. The ship's master took possession of the wine and filled his gullet well indeed. According to Chefdeville's report, he hardly spent a day that he was not drunk.

Seeing that they were at risk of perishing where they where, they decided to weigh anchor and move near the settlement where I was. But they had only a few men, and the wind rushing from the north drove them off course to the other side of the bay. Seeing themselves approaching land, they cast the only anchor they had. But as the wind was too strong, they were driven upon the anchor. The master could have avoided this if he had had the foresight to anchor a cannon with the anchor. Carried away thus, they soon ran aground,[7] dragging all the while on the

---

[7] The *Belle* ran aground on the north or bay shore of Matagorda Peninsula, approximately five miles from the southwest tip of the peninsula. According to Joutel, the *Belle* was probably beached in February 1686. In 1995 archeologists under the direction of the Texas Historical Commission found at this location the hull of the *Belle* and much of its cargo, including several cannon, muskets, glass trade beads, rings, needles, and many other artifacts. See Texas Historical Commission, *Fact Sheet: La Salle's Cannon* (Austin, 1995), a release informing the public about the discovery of the *Belle*.

anchor. During the night, the wind moderated, and they remained calm enough. If they had only had their shoreboats to carry an anchor forward the next day, they would have been able to put the frigate afloat. Their circumstances thus [lacking shallop and failing water], they considered how to send a few people ashore to see if they could find water. The master contrived a sort of raft with two casks and a few planks upon which two men set off to go ashore. But the planks were not well fastened, the waves disengaged them, and the casks got loose. The two men went in, one to one side and the second to the other side. One did not know how to swim and drowned. Indeed, the one who made land did not have any greater fortune. After having searched to the right and left to find water, he realized that no one was making ready to rescue him. In spite of the wind from the north that was blowing cold as it was February,[8] he plunged into the water again to return to ship. But his strength failed him and he drowned.

Thus, it seemed that all sorts of misfortune occurred to thwart the enterprise. However, all of this happened only because of great rashness and lack of direction, for all this disorder would not have occurred without the drunkenness of the master. But, in brief, the next day it became a matter of making another raft. This one, fortunately, was better constructed with sail yard and planks that were well fastened together, and this provided the means to go ashore. After they had found fresh water there, the task was to unload things from the ship by the raft. As it was not large, not many things could be unloaded at once. Besides, they had to indulge the caprice of the master who was usually drunk. He had put the case of brandy that he had seized on the poop deck, and he alone handled it. This meant that as long as it lasted, he was in no hurry to leave the ship. He used the pretext that he was staying until all the cargo was unloaded. In the end, a number of things were saved among them La Salle's clothes, specifically one scarlet dresscoat and another blue coat with large gold braid, as well as some of his papers, dampened though they were. Chefdeville took care to dry them. They were careful to bring some barrels of meal ashore and a few casks of wine which were the most necessary. After this they tried to save some linen clothing belonging to La Salle, his brother [the Abbé], and Chefdeville. They also saved a few beads and other similar things.

They went on board almost every day for this purpose, bringing what they could each time until a wind blew in from the sea that stirred up the waves and made the hull of the ship settle deep into the sand. The water covered her except for the poop deck. As they had provisions on shore, they did not seek a means to get away. One could say that they were very happy to have escaped and that no natives had come near this place which was, it happened, along their customary route. At least I saw natives come by there several times while I was on the shore [of that peninsula]. Our men would have had difficulty escaping their clutches had they attacked because they were few in number with little defense.

Had our men set out for the settlement immediately after the shipwreck, the frigate could have been saved, or we could have gone with several canoes to unload it with dispatch. But I believe that if their provisions had not failed, they would not

[8]   Here Joutel states specifically that the *Belle* wrecked in February 1686.

have considered coming back to the settlement.[9] They still had some wine left; that is the reason the master was in no hurry. They often shot ducks and caught fish; they found oysters which were in abundance. It was when they realized their meal supplies had diminished that they behaved like the wolf that hunger forces from the forest. Then they had a piece of good luck in [finding] the canoe that had gone adrift when La Salle was camped on the bay shore before his departure. The wind had driven his canoe to the other side of the bay where it had gone aground. They found it, and fortunately it was not smashed. Thus they put what was most valuable inside the canoe and set off to cross the bay to come and join us. If they had not found the canoe, they would have been forced to walk around the bay and they might have encountered obstacles blocking them.

They had remained in that same place nearly three months. Chefdeville told me that they had been near the tip of that long strip of land [peninsula] opposite the place where the natives had camped when we saw them for the first time. I learned that near this same place there was a large pond of fresh water, quite deep, around which there were tall reeds which would be most advantageous if one wanted to build a fort there.[10] This post would guard the entrance of the bay and shelter the ships which would be anchored behind the strip of land where there was room to moor about 50 ships in five or six fathoms of water in good bottom.

A few days after his return and that of his companions, Chefdeville asked the Recollet fathers to say a high mass with him ending with the *Te Deum* in thanksgiving. He was recently ordained a priest and had not said the mass for some time, so he had almost forgotten the liturgical service. Therefore, he waited several days to refresh his memory. And, as I have mentioned, the wine was short and it was necessary to limit the saying of mass to feast days and Sundays, all for the lack of precaution. For had a number of flagons of Spanish wine been kept [at the settlement] and not been put aboard the ship, the mass might have been said as usual. Chefdeville had brought back a piece of ironware to bake altar bread, and as there was some flour, some was made.

To return to our housekeeping, I mentioned that Barbier had left to secure meat. La Salle had also directed him to collect bark for roofing the house because rain was dripping through where the hides covering it had been shrunk by the sun after becoming wet. The water lying in the depressions caused rot, whereas the bark would make a much better covering. I had not seen this method used, but I found it was very effective. Upon his return, Barbier was surprised in his turn to see these men. He was joyful and saddened at the same time, joyful because he had

[9] Joutel writes in summary that the congenial group, which included Tessier (the master of the *Belle*), Chefdeville, Lieutenant Sablonnière, the pilot, an unidentified soldier, the young servant girl from La Rochelle, and a small boy were living well during the three-month period, drinking wine and eating ducks, fish, and oysters. They apparently were not in a desperate situation and were quite content to remain about twelve leagues across the bay from the French post until their meal ran low.

[10] The location was later known as Decrow's Point or Decros Point. Thomas Decrow settled the area in the 1840s. McAlister and McAlister, *Matagorda Island*, 43, n. 2. In late 1861, Fort Esperanza was established by Confederate forces on the opposite side of the pass. Brownson Malsch, *Indianola: The Mother of Western Texas* (Austin: Shoal Creek Publishers, 1977), 161–163. See also Rachel Jenkins, "Decros Point," in Tyler, et al. (eds.), *New Handbook of Texas*, II, 558.

believed them dead, but saddened because of the too real loss of the ship and the goods. However, he had to console himself. He told me that the waters of the Cane River were so high that they were kept from hunting because the bison had moved off. With regard to the bark, he added that he had not found elm trees which were rising. One says "rise" because when trees are not in sap, the bark can not be removed. Only the aspen rises in all seasons, but its bark is coarse and brittle.

As we had almost no smoked meat left, Barbier had to go out again, for the arrival of the others had reduced the provisions by a few days, and it was wise not to wait until none was left. But the day after his departure, a few herds of bison appeared quite close to the house. This was an opportunity not to be missed. I killed five or six of them which yielded us plenty. I took care to smoke as much as I could, and a few more herds appeared which much relieved us. It turned out that when the Sieur Barbier returned, he found us better provided for than he was. Indeed, we had much better meat than he brought.

As the grass was dry, I had a fire set to burn it off in order to regenerate it. This caused the bison to wander off a little. But this was not for long, for when the grass began to grow, they were there almost every day. Thus we worked to provision ourselves the best we could.

When we were all gathered together, we did our best to divert ourselves and chase away our sorrows. I invited our people to make the best of it, as they could, and to dance in the evenings to songs because when La Salle was there, mirth was often forbidden. Now it is better not to mope in such circumstances. It is true that La Salle did not have much reason to rejoice after so many losses and the realization that everything was not going according to his plan. And, consequently, not only he suffered. Although he had directed me to give only a certain amount of meat to each person per meal, this rule was practiced only in times when meat was short, and smoked meat was given out then. As for fresh meat, I gave them as much as they wanted. The air was extremely sharp, and appetites were big. It was necessary then to eat and move if one wanted to be in good health; otherwise one was always uncomfortable. I speak from experience because at times I had a four-day fever, and on the days of my attacks, when I found myself at the house with nothing to do, I became worn out and sluggish. On the other hand, if I was busy hunting or at some other occupation in which I tired, I was downcast less than half as much. That is why I tried to exercise the people as much as possible.

When the weather grew warmer, we had greater difficulty preserving the fresh meat and had to cook it, at the latest, on the third day. During the summer, we had to cook the third day's meat in advance on the second day. Accordingly, I decided to dig a sort of cellar which was easy because the soil was heavy with clay like potter's soil. I had begun making a small cellar that would serve us well for keeping meat which, when fresh and cool, could be kept a few days. But when La Salle came, he decided it was too small. As he only had large schemes, he took measures to make a big one for which he laid out the entrance. But, for the shortage of people to undertake the labor (work necessary for survival occupied us most of the time), this project languished to make room for another.

We had only the house for our stronghold which was not much protection. I consulted with Barbier and it was decided that we should enclose ourselves in a stockade. As there were no suitable woods near us, we decided that whenever we traveled by canoe, several pieces of wood should be brought back in the bottom of the canoe so that little by little we would manage to build it. I ordered that the logs be cut eight feet in length so that two feet could be planted in the ground with six feet above. As we did not often go upriver where the woods were, this work did not progress well.

We moved more expeditiously toward another goal. As mass was said in a passageway of the house, Chefdeville and the fathers suggested that it would be proper to build a special hut to serve as a chapel. They even offered to work on it themselves and it was completed. As it was built longer than necessary, Chefdeville divided it and lodged there to be alone. He had, up to that point, lodged with me. Although this chapel was only made of stakes driven into the ground and roofed with grass or reeds, the gentleman did not fail to adorn the altar with holy images and whatever he happened to have to the extent the conditions of the place permitted.

I neglected to mention that Chefdeville and the others told me that they had buried several things such as sails, rope, some new sail-cloth, and the like in the sand at the place where they had stayed for so long. I told Barbier to return there to bring back what was left if the natives had not found it. He left on this mission in a canoe with 14 or 15 men and the ship's master and a soldier. I gave them provisions for eight days and advised them to stay on their guard. On their return, I learned that the natives had been at that place since Chefdeville and the others had left and that they had taken away pieces of sail-cloth, some scrap iron, and even a swivel-gun. These were lost. Nonetheless, our company loaded what they found, even a cask of wine. I took pains to have all the sails and sailcloth placed in the sun for fear that they would rot. I had acted likewise with the apparel and the papers they had brought on the first trip.

In the end, only our husbandry mattered. Our animals increased daily. It was necessary to take some care for, once the sows had farrowed, the herd was greatly multiplied. Our hen and cock did not produce much, although the hen sat on her eggs several times. One had to believe that the eggs turned out to be infertile. Now, as it was desirable to have some poultry, I wanted to discover the source of this problem. Therefore, when she laid eggs, I put her in a particular place, and after that a chick was hatched which was a relief. All the animals ate meat, the chickens as well as the pigs, when we had plenty. We were worried for five or six days about one of our sows that had gone astray with eight or ten piglets. We thought she was lost and that the natives had found her and killed her.[11] But, on the seventh day she returned with her troop.

I have mentioned before that I had planted a number of things, some of which failed and others grew successfully. The endive was as beautiful as the finest I have seen in France. You could watch the melons and pumpkins grow. Unfortunately,

---

[11] Pierre Talon testified that the Indians near Matagorda Bay thought that the pigs at the French settlement were the Frenchmen's dogs, which the Indians did not kill since they considered dogs inedible. Pierre and Jean-Baptiste Talon, "Voyage to the Mississippi through the Gulf of Mexico," 233.

the rabbits, in great numbers, ate the tender shoots and the fruit. In addition to the rabbits, there were plenty of rats that did the same. However, these animals were not aware of the garden at first, and the plants had an opportunity to grow. The pumpkins particularly grew huge and four or five were too large and too hard for the animals to eat. This gave me hope that I would have seeds from them to sow for the next year. But another animal intruded into the area and situated itself by the riverside near the spring. It had harder teeth and a longer snout. This was the cayman or alligator. Only the cotton remained and thrived the best. I had also planted carrots which came up quite well. But they perished; the cause I did not notice, unless it was too much heat. The celery and the asparagus both came up well; but I do not know what became of them later.

Father Zénobe had also planted a garden in a separate place where he planted several things which grew quite well. He had, among others, beetroot (which were as fat as your arm), beets as well, and other similar plants. He only half succeeded, just as I had, because of other animals. Certain flies, shaped like a cantharis (however not of the same color), attached themselves to the leaves of these plants and ate them. Eventually, rats found the roots and ate them as they had eaten the melons and pumpkins. It was necessary to find an expedient way to destroy all the insects, if we wanted to benefit from what we had planted. For the rats, it would be easy to get rid of them with poison or with cats which could catch plenty if the ground was uncovered and cultivated. This is what I noticed about some cats which slept in our powder storehouse. I would some times find more than a dozen rats whose heads had been bitten off by these animals and left behind because they had small ones in the storehouse. But as for this species of fly, I did not know what remedy could be applied. It seemed that I had heard that once the soil is turned over, very often insects are disturbed for some years. This likewise happened in Canada at the beginning of its settlement. But after the land had been cleared for a time, this was no longer the case. This could also occur in this region. The essential point is that everything grew well there, from what we experienced with what we planted. I will add that the rats often worried me because they carried off everything they found and stored it, even our knives and firebrands. I took care to extinguish the fire before we went to bed for fear that rats would carry some burning firebrand into the powder storehouse and we would be left with all lost and no resources.

As I already mentioned, before the Sieur Barbier went to smoke the meat by the Cane River, the young Sieur Cavelier told me that he would be glad to go along which he did. A number of our people went along who were not engaged in much labor but who ate as much as the others. When someone went outside the compound, I sent them along to help. I also sent a few women and girls, until I learned that some intercourse had come to pass, and I remedied that situation.

By and by, Barbier, having gone up the river about two or three leagues, saw a band of natives on the other side who made signs to him to approach them. He watched them closely and saw that they had two muskets in their possession which must have come from our deserters or our people whom they had killed, or in some such manner. They fired two small shots either because they had little powder or because they did not dare to load it. Barbier, seeing them from the other side of the river, fired several shots at them. I do not know if he wounded some of them for they did not stay there long before slipping away. In any case, considering that he had fired on them, he decided that it was not wise to go upriver any farther as there were forests where the Indians could lie in wait. He decided to return and when the natives saw this, a group of them detached themselves and crossed the river to confront our people. Seven or eight went to hide in a thicket and undergrowth. When Barbier passed by in the canoe, they shot several arrows at those in the boat. Two of our men were wounded. Le Meusnier,[12] who was from Paris, had his arm pierced and several strikes to the head which fortunately did not amount to much. Sieur Barbier took a few hits [which tore] his clothing as did the young Cavelier. Barbier fired a gunshot that ran the Indians off, but when he saw them in another place in the open, he set off on foot to show them that he did not fear them. Then he made them a sign to approach. During this time, our men's wounds were dressed. After this, they set off on their way again without letting it be seen that anyone was wounded. Barbier came back then to the house, and as there were bison in the area, he was comforted.

About 15 days later, we saw bison running in flight as if they were being pursued by natives. This turned out to be the case and some Indians even came near the house, that is to say, within cannon range. Since I did not know their numbers, I had our men take arms. Barbier advanced on them planning to draw them out. But only one of them remained, as if in waiting. The native was withdrawing carefully, apparently wary of Barbier. When I saw them run, I had a cannon shot fired not so much intending to hit them as to frighten them. A small cannon shot fell beyond them, and they could hear it hiss, for I had pointed the cannon as accurately as I could. They took flight having had enough.

A few days later, Barbier left again with a number of his men to go smoke the meat. He wanted also to go inspect the Cane River again. Chefdeville said that it would be good if he too went along and Sablonnière and the young Cavelier as well. This left only a few people at the house, and it was still necessary to beware of surprises. They were away for 10 to 15 days before returning. It seemed that when they were home they dispersed the bison, for they had no sooner left than the bison came near again. We managed to dry quite a bit more meat than they, even though we were fewer people. But they lost much time going and coming.

When he had returned from this trip, Barbier came to me in private, for he knew that I had been told about matters between him and one of the girls.[13] He told me that he had had an affair with her, that he had promised to marry her, and that he was ready to do so provided I would consent. He was apprehensive that La Salle, upon his return, would be displeased with him. He thought (correctly) that La Salle would not be happy to see that he had seduced one of these girls whom the gentleman had charged me with chaperoning. I told him that his inclination

---

[12] Le Meusnier was perhaps a reference to Pierre Meunier, who was from Paris. Although Joutel is clear that the injury to "Le Meusnier" was minor, a subsequent report (see Chapter VIII) suggests that a man named Meunier was wounded (or, as Margry incorrectly says, killed) on this outing.

[13] The girl was later called Princess. See Chapter VIII.

was good and Christian, but as for marriage, I did not advise it. Although he was not from a distinguished family, he was an officer. His status as an officer placed him above the girl who was unknown when she embarked. In closing, I made the observation to him that it was for this reason that I withheld my consent to his request. I asked him to await the return of La Salle.

This did not satisfy him. Chefdeville and the fathers appealed to me saying that the two so much wanted each other, matters had already gone far, and it would be much better to marry them. Likewise, this would prevent the disorder that could occur otherwise. Thus, after reflecting, I gave into their appeals and told Barbier that he was his own master and could act according to his own wishes. Thus, they were married; Chefdeville performed the ceremony. In this he reaped the first fruits of the new country, for earlier he had baptized the young captured Indian girl. A small apartment was made for Barbier and his wife to separate them from the others.

A short time afterwards, this marriage was followed by a similar request. The Marquis de La Sablonnière asked to wed the young girl from Paris who had been given the same name.[14] Whether she wanted to conceal her own name or otherwise was unknown. Paris was quite young and not uncomely, but I told our suitor that he should not consider the matter seriously because his status would not allow the marriage. I even forbade them to talk to one another, adding that La Salle would decide the matter upon his return.

We spent then a period of time without anything extraordinary happening. Some time later, Barbier headed upstream as usual to smoke meat. This time I asked him to take along four of the pigs belonging to one of our sows which were already grown and who would not leave their mother alone. I decided it was time to wean them so that the sow would produce others for us sooner. But our people returned with only three of the pigs and told me that one of them had escaped into the grass when they were unloaded and that they had not seen it since.

During their absence, a somewhat unfortunate accident happened to Father Zénobe, Superior of the Mission. One morning, seeing a bison about a quarter of a league from the house, I took my musket to try to kill it. I asked a few men to come with me to keep watch on both sides for fear of some surprise because the approach to these animals was not easy. Indeed, one must be careful to always position oneself downwind of them. Also, once they are seen approaching, one must crawl on one's stomach like a snake, sometimes for more than a quarter league according to where the animal moves and the layout of the terrain. That is why it was best to have a few people on the lookout for fear that some natives would slip furtively through the grass and suddenly spring upon me after I had fired my shot or upon someone else in the same circumstance who would not be able to fend them off.

When I drew nearer the bison, I shot it and broke its shoulder. As I have said, although these animals may be fatally wounded, they may keep walking and continue for some time longer. Sometimes they go off to die two or three leagues away

14 Paris is the only name we have to identify this young girl.

depending on their strength and the loss of blood. My bison with the broken shoulder still did not stop walking, laying down only from time to time. I tried to catch up to it to give it the final shot but, whether because it spotted me or otherwise, it took off as soon as I approached. I could see the animal was lying down often and could not go far from the house (from where it could be seen). Also it was extremely warm and the sun was shining directly down on the dry grass which made the hunt uncomfortable, so I left the bison.

When I returned home, I ordered the sentry to keep watch where the animal was circling. As soon as it went down, it was to be field dressed. In the evening, I left again to finish the kill, for the animal had remained in almost the same place. Father Zénobe accompanied me. But when we were near the animal, it saw us and limped away, so I told our people that we should drive it toward the house which we did with some difficulty. When it was within gunshot range, I realized that it would soon be night and that we could not see to dress it. I decided then that it was better not to dress it until the next day. So that it would not go any farther, I shot it in the haunch to stop it. As soon as it was hit, it fell. Then Father Zénobe went up to the animal and poked it a few times with his musket. As I said, we did not go out unarmed. Now in the animal's perception, the priest was goading him. Although I told him not to trust the animal, he nevertheless insisted on poking it. The wounded animal rose up in fury before the priest had time to retreat, and it trampled him, scraped the skin from his face in several places, and broke his musket. The poor priest had great difficulty getting himself safely away. Afterwards he was indisposed for more than three months, unable to do much of anything. Even though this accident was unfortunate and the priest suffered from it, he made jest of himself because of his rashness in wanting to goad an animal enraged because it could not escape our hands. Meanwhile, the priest escaped, but not without harm.

Some time later, there was another incident involving Father Maxime who had written about what took place. Chefdeville informed me that he had seen a report by the priest in which things were said against La Salle. I told the Sieur that I must seize this report which was done. The priests were much embarrassed, particularly the author of the report who consequently had to fear the return of La Salle. For this reason, Father Zénobe begged me not to carry this too far. I told him that I could not conceal this and that I was obliged to protect La Salle's interests, besides which it was not within their authority to write things of this nature. Furthermore, I was not the only one who had knowledge of this. Meanwhile the priests made sure to burn the report so that it would not come to light. Father Zénobe had fallen into a similar error with regard to Beaujeu. As these gentlemen are extremely fond of writing, they have difficulty restraining themselves. However, it is not appropriate to say certain things, and there are some who exaggerate. That happened in this case.[15]

---

[15] This passage is another example of Joutel's ability to criticize authority that he respected. Although he held both the church and La Salle in high esteem, Joutel expressed his independent judgment regarding their actions as neither La Salle nor the clergy were infallible in his eyes. This willingness by authors to challenge church and state representatives was seen in more pronounced forms in works written during the Enlightenment as it developed in the early eighteenth century.

Because we were few, it was important that each person be able to protect himself in case of attack. Therefore, I took the trouble to have our people practice shooting. To this end, I had a hillock made so that our bullets would not be lost, for we had few shot in proportion to the powder we had. Also in trying to conserve shot as well as I could, when we dressed and cut up the bison, we searched for the bullet and often happened to find it. There were some hunters who had killed as many as three bison with the same bullet.

I even made the women and girls shoot. To tempt them more to practice, I made sure to give some small trifle to him or her who won the closest shot to the mark. To the men, I gave a few draughts of brandy, and to the women and girls, some other trifle which would occasion each to do his or her best. One day, when I was at this practice, an accident occurred to Father Maxime. I do not know what grudge a certain large boar had against the father, whether he had mistreated or beaten him, but I saw the priest take flight, crying out as the boar chased him. I went to the rescue; but I was somewhat far away and not able to arrive in time to prevent the boar from striking the priest's arm a blow in defense. The animal was moving faster than he was. The priest had leaned over to free his legs from his robe and had thus exposed his arm. The blow tore some tendons which left a few fingers and a part of his arm disabled even though the surgeon gave him every attention. Thus, our three good fathers fell victim to animals.[16]

I neglected to say that when I reached the boar, I began to hit him on the head and body with a big stick. Feeling himself mistreated, he wanted revenge against me. Whereupon, when I saw him in such a fury, I myself fled to the house and shut the door behind me. Chefdeville, who was in the house, saw that I was overheated and had heard that Father Maxime was wounded. He thought I had wounded the father for he had heard a gunshot fired just a little beforehand. After this, I considered whether I should have that old boar killed. As I was not eager to give La Salle a reason to be displeased, and the animal had not harmed anyone before, and what he had done to me was only a reaction to the number of blows I had given him, his life was spared. His salvation was a great vexation to Father Maxime, his enemy. But the father was the only one opposed to him.

To return to our discourse, nothing extraordinary happened. We went hunting sometimes in one direction, sometimes another, always bringing back some stakes for our stockade when we went near the woods. What was troubling about our situation was that several of our people were becoming restless at hearing no news, and were despairing to leave the country, in view of the accidents that had happened. One day, when they were conversing among each other about this, saying that they did not believe La Salle would return, I learned from a few people that [Pierre] Duhaut had told them that they only had to take the trouble and he had the power to help them. He said that he would find a means to lead them out, one way or another. I warned Duhaut not to hold such discussions which could lead to

---

[16] In summary, Fathers Douay and Membré, on separate occasions, had been trampled after goading injured bison; Le Clercq was gored by the boar. The fact that the boar had dangerous tusks suggests that this import was not fully domesticated.

some rivalry. I then reassured our people that they should not be impatient because, if La Salle had found his river and went up it to the Illinois country, he would take a good deal of time. I added that we could wait a year and more without losing patience; and with respect to the food supplies, they had nothing to fear unless something happened to our powder of which we had more than we could use in our lifetime. I was quite fearful that a fire might be set by accident or by lightning which struck frequently in this area, and I had noticed several times that the fields were on fire. That is why I put the powder in different places to prevent unforeseen mishap and to have it to draw from and subsist upon for a while.

When everyone was at the settlement and we were not fully occupied, I employed a party to cut down water willows[17] which provided an easy approach for natives and could allow them, hidden behind trees, to kill some of our people. That, in part, was what compelled me earlier to cut down some trees that concealed our view. In addition, the water willows provided a refuge to mosquitos, or what we called *cousins* [midges] in France. They are quite annoying in this country when the weather changes for the worse and threatens to rain. I am sure that I found no difficulty more troublesome to surmount than that of these insects that prevented rest. It is not that it would be hard to protect oneself in a house that was securely closed or if one had a canvas or light bunting to make oneself a net that these small creatures could not enter. As they liked neither cold nor great heat, we often hoped for the wind to turn toward the north to give us a chance to rest.

I had a large square cleared and, when a breeze blew, it was much more pleasant for us. I had the grass cut back a certain distance around the house and in the evenings I encouraged our people to divert themselves as they saw fit and, for our part, we tried not to become discouraged. We were in our group the two Recollet fathers, Chefdeville, the young Cavelier, and me. Barbier, being married, kept company with his wife. Each amused himself in his own way. In this country, [the temperature during?] the nights was almost like the days which was why one had the leisure to sleep.

One evening we were amusing ourselves when some voices were heard from the other side of the river. I then cried out: "Who goes there?" Someone responded: "France!" which at first made me fear that some other accident had occurred. But, a short while later, I recognized the voice of La Salle who shouted to us that he had some horses. I headed with all speed to the riverbank to take a canoe across. There were the initial embraces back and forth. It had been some time since we had seen each other.

The Sieur de La Salle told us that he had left his horses about musket shot range away, in a place where the grass was good, because it was too late to make them cross the river. Furthermore, he said that he did not know in what state matters might be if we were even still there, for several times he had not found people in places where he had posted them. At length the evening passed in recounting the numerous adventures which had happened during their journey. Although I

---

[17] Margry uses *hallier* (thicket), but the manuscript says *ozier* (willow), a plant common to the area today. Cheatham and Marshall suggest probably black willow (*Salix nigra*).

had reason to rejoice that La Salle had returned in good health, I perceived that his journey had still not advanced matters for all the length of time that we had been in this country. Before he had told us a thing, I realized that he was not able to reach the Illinois country. Consequently, he had not accomplished anything.

Sieur de La Salle asked me first if the younger [Dominique] Duhaut, Hurié, and two others, to whom he had given permission to return two or three months ago, had arrived. When I told him that I had no news of them, he said they must have been killed by natives. After some discussion and when the Sieur had refreshed himself a bit, I left him to rest. The next day, I oversaw the arrival of the five horses carrying maize, beans, and pumpkin and watermelon seeds which were put inside the house. But I only saw eight of the twenty men who had left with the gentleman; I wondered what had become of the others. I learned that Bihorel, an infantry captain, had become lost shortly after their departure, as had Duhaut, and no news had been heard of either one. It was not known whether they had been killed by the natives or whether they had died of hunger. I also learned that another man had perished, having been dragged under water by a crocodile while crossing a river. He was one of the servants of the gentleman [La Salle], a man called Dumesnil, who had deserted him in the village where the horses and maize had been found.[18] All of this news did not fill me or the others with joy as we were such a small number remaining. However, there was no remedy for it; one had to be resigned.

La Salle was very pleased to see Chefdeville and at the same time to recover his papers and some of his clothes. Thus he also had a way to replace the clothes of his nephew Morenger whose clothes were good for nothing. First it was a matter of recovering themselves a bit; then, as the journey had produced nothing, it was proposed to undertake another one to the Illinois country to successfully find the river. However, the heat was uncomfortable and La Salle found it best to wait for it to pass. After that they would leave and return directly to the village where they had procured the horses and seeds. The gentleman described this village to me as quite large.

After several days had passed, La Salle, who had brought seeds intending to plant them there, was persuaded that this could not be done without an enclosure to protect them from the pigs which we had in large number. Accordingly, he directed that stakes be cut in the neighboring small woods closest to the river so that they could be transported by canoe. Among the stakes that I had had gathered to fence us in, there were some that were ten feet long which I would have to plant three feet in the ground. La Salle set these aside to make another storehouse because the one where the powder was stored was not very strong. That was eventually done. Thereafter when anyone went hunting nearby, a detachment of people was sent to cut stakes.

One day when Barbier and Nika were hunting with seven or eight others, they encountered a band of Indians who, seeing that our men were few, tried to attack them. But when our men saw the Indians advancing, they took positions to fire upon them. One Indian was wounded and the others carried him off dead or oth-

---

[18] This passage is confusing unless Dumesnil's desertion attempt was unsuccessful.

erwise. Our men could not tell for sure. The natives, seeing that our bullets traveled farther than their arrows and realizing that they had wounded among them, did not press their attack. When the Indians had withdrawn, our people resumed their route. But, as I have mentioned, these people are vindictive, and we could not long be boastful of this apparent victory. Indeed, a few days later, the natives killed one of our men very close to the settlement.

Nearly every day, [to build a fire?] for cooking, a few people went to look for wood in a small grove that was the range of a musket shot away. One or two men served as an armed escort while the others gathered their bundles of sticks. Upon their return, one of our group stopped to pick some herb, like purslane, which was plentiful in the country. The Indians, who in all probability had been lying in wait among some willows, found this man alone and, to get even, shot him with two or three arrows. After this they fled, but someone who saw them running came as soon as possible to give warning, but it was too late. To run after them, so to speak, was time lost. Nevertheless, a dozen of our men took arms, but the natives were much better runners than we were. There were ten of them. We took such action for a man who died for a number of stakes. This stockade or rather the enclosure for the Indian corn and other seeds was commenced.

The care I had taken to set fire to the grass served the horses well for when the grass returned it was tender and good. This demonstrates that a large number of animals could be kept in this country where one need only make hay for their nourishment. Indeed they could pasture all year long and always have grass for there is almost no winter. Caution, however, would be necessary. For example, I have mentioned before that we had several animals bitten by rattlesnakes. One of our horses was bitten on the jaw, beside the jawbone that is to say. We did not know whether the horse had stepped on the snake or otherwise. Whatever the case, we noticed that he often would lay down without resting long. After that, we discovered that one side of his of head was swollen. He was given a dose of theriac; then we lanced the place where he had been bitten and cleaned it with pickled bacon, vinegar, and some soap. He was cured but not without suffering for seven or eight hours when he had to stay in place. I noticed that drops of water were pouring from all over his body. The drops were thick as a finger; this shows how strong and malignant the venom of these snakes is. However, there is a cure for it. There are also scorpions[19] in the region, but they are not very dangerous. They are similar to those in Europe where I have seen several people stung by them when handling some piece of old wood where they are found. But they escaped with a little pain and slight swelling that smarted for an hour or two.

While we were laboring with everything I have mentioned, we did not cease to consider the journey that must be undertaken to gain knowledge of the Mississippi. La Salle asked me one day if I would be inclined to take this journey, to go to Canada afterwards, and from there to France to bring back a ship, for I had some knowledge [of navigation?].[20] He told me that if I had some distaste for this country, I could tell him, so that he would not count on me. I told him that he

---

[19] Margry refers here to a snake, but the manuscript clarifies that the reference is to a scorpion.

[20] This is Margry's question "of navigation?"

could rely on me for everything it was in my power to do. Hence, it was proposed that preparations be made.

Because Duhaut, as I have several times said, had hatchets, knives, and other things including some cloth to trade or barter, La Salle took possession of these to distribute to different individuals to make shirts. Most of the soldiers had well worn clothes, so others were made from the sails that were saved from the *Belle*. For my part, I had two pairs of sheets of coarse cloth, which the gentleman told me to give to him. Thinking that in such circumstances nothing belonged to oneself exclusively, that each one must help the others with what one had, I likewise gave Morenger several shirts along with some pairs of breeches. Furthermore, Hurié, on his departure, left to me a portion of his belongings in case he did not return. I showed this document to La Salle, but as he needed these things, he took possession of them, all except a pair of sheets from which I had shirts made.

While preparations of this kind were being made, La Salle became indisposed with a hernia which he had had during his youth and which, he said, had not troubled him for twenty-five years. Naturally, this unfortunate occurrence delayed the journey. He even told me that it was not likely that he could undertake the journey unless he recovered. I proposed to him that, if he wanted to give me Nika and 15 men, I would do my best to proceed. I asked for Nika because he was necessary for hunting which was what was most useful for such an enterprise; it was impossible to travel without food. But he replied that his presence was necessary in the Illinois country and that I could not do what he intended to do. In addition, he said it was best that the Abbé proceed to France, and that he could not abandon him until he was placed in a secure and familiar place. Finally, I told him that I would do my best and all it was in my power to do in case he considered my going feasible. But he did not find it so. Accordingly, it was necessary again to wait. It would be wished that he had issued these orders to us, and then the disaster that occurred later would not have happened.

We remained at the settlement for again some time. La Salle, wishing to avoid unrest, had the boar killed that had wounded Father Maxime although he was master of 15 or more sows. He would not let any of the young boars come close to them. The boar's meat proved to be very good; indeed, he had always been kept fat because our animals often had meat and in the fields they found grasses and roots which provided them sustenance. A short time later, we found the pig that I have noted was missing. It had been lost for three months. This suggests that the wolves and wild dogs, which are numerous in this region, must not be as vicious as those in Europe or perhaps that they did not recognize the animal, not having seen one before. It could not have defended itself because it was not more than a month or six weeks old when it was lost. As we found it during a hunting expedition, and it had become as good as wild, it was killed with one gunshot and eaten. A few small suckling pigs were also eaten. Although they had done as their mother and eaten meat, they were nonetheless very good. This will be a great advantage in this country; all kinds of animals will be able to find food easily without much effort.

I mentioned that I had planted several things, among others, cotton plants. They had come up very well and were quite beautiful. We even had the pleasure of seeing them bloom with many flowers. But when the north winds rushed down during the three or four months of winter in this country, they were extremely cold and sharp.[21] We, therefore, did not get the promised success from our cotton. In planting the bushes, I did not take the precaution of protecting them from the north wind and, what's more, I was not aware that this kind of bush was so sensitive to cold. One time, after the wind had remained very cold for three or four days, I had the unhappy experience of seeing my poor cotton bushes all blighted. All the flowers, of which there had been so many, were blackened and the leaves also, just like the leaves in vineyards and walnut groves in France when a frost occurs. I do not know what became of these bushes afterwards for we left a short time later.[22] La Salle was displeased about this, for it was such a pleasure to see them so big in so little time. This was another commodity to make use of in this country even if it were only for making [wicks for?] candles, but it would have served well for some other purpose as well. There would surely be good reason to plant it in spots which are not exposed to the north wind.

I must not forget to say that La Salle learned from someone that Father Maxime had written something about his leadership and he made a bit of a stir, and for a while the gentleman did not eat with the priests. He reprimanded me a little, saying that I should have informed him of this as well as some other matters upon his arrival, namely the disputes I had had with [Pierre] Duhaut. But I told him that I knew quite well he would learn of these from others. Besides, these matters were past, and it was not necessary to revive them in view of the many other matters we had to consider.

I will mention another dispute that occurred at that time regarding the privilege that the King bestows upon the first born in a newly settled country which is to raise them to the rank of nobility. As I mentioned, there was a man named Talon who had formerly been in Canada and who had a family. His wife was pregnant when they embarked and she delivered the child on board the ship.[23] La Salle was asked to give her child a name. The child was nurtured during our voyage and was still living when we left the settlement. However, his father died during the beginnings in this country. The widow still remained with her children. Now the wife of Barbier, who had married during La Salle's absence, was pregnant. Barbier claimed that if his wife delivered a boy, the child should enjoy the privileges that the King granted first born. But the widow maintained that her son, born en route, must be considered the oldest and as if he had been born in this country. Thus there was a dispute between the two parties. Barbier also argued that, as an officer, the privilege should rightly belong to him. La Salle, who was not pleased with Barbier's marriage and viewed with distaste the beginning of the colony with a child born

---

[21]  This is one instance in which Joutel describes the bitter cold winter weather.

[22]  When De León and his party reached the French settlement in 1689, they made no reference to seeing any cotton. The fact that Joutel planted cotton in the fall indicates that this was a native American plant unfamiliar to the French. Massanet reported that endive, asparagus, and corn were found. Bolton (ed.), *Spanish Exploration in the Southwest*, 362.

[23]  Robert Talon was born during the voyage from France. Robert S. Weddle, "The Talon Interrogations: A Rare Perspective," in Weddle (ed.), *La Salle, the Mississippi, and the Gulf*, 211.

before the proper time, did not judge it appropriate that he enjoy this privilege. These kinds of matters served us as opera for a time. But the dispute was ended with Madame Barbier's miscarriage.[24]

The Sieur de la Sablonnière, whom I had told to await La Salle's decision regarding his intention to wed the young girl from Paris, asked his permission but La Salle told him that being from the distinguished family that he was, this could not be. His parents would not consent to it and neither could he. That, far from consenting to it, he forbade it. Thus the matter faded away.

Some time later, La Salle, feeling relief from his discomfort, proposed to take up his journey again. Meanwhile, we spent the feast of Christmas again at the settlement. Midnight mass was solemnized with as much decorum as possible as was the rest of the divine worship. Each made his devotions to offer our vows to God and beg Him to guide us. We also passed Twelfth Night which was celebrated with presence of mind, drink not leading us astray. We kept toasting the King with water. Although I still had a bottle or two of brandy, it was better to save it in case anyone was wounded or for some other necessary purpose. After that, it was only a matter of departing and outfitting ourselves accordingly.

As I was nominated for this last journey, La Salle gave command of the post to the Sieur Barbier. At the settlement there remained, along with the Sieur Barbier, the Sieur Chefdeville, and two fathers, namely: Father Zénobe Membré and Father Maxime Le Clerq, the Marquis de la Sablonnière, a surgeon, and others numbering 20 or 21 in all including the girls and women of whom there were seven. At that time only the Sieur Barbier was married.[25]

Those who stayed at the settlement should not have to fear death by hunger because there were plenty of pigs, not less than 75. Besides that, the Indian corn that was left them was growing well, and there were still 18 or 20 hens. Thus they only had to beware and keep a good lookout.

The Sieur de La Salle having given his orders to those who remained, on January 12, 1687, we left the settlement situated on the Bison River near the Bay of Saint Louis. About 100 pounds of powder were brought along with a proportional supply of bullets, seven or eight dozen hatchets, a few gross of knives, and other similar things that had come from the ship. The hatchets and knives belonged to Duhaut, as all of La Salle's effects had remained in the frigate. We provisioned ourselves with some meal; a few barrels were left at the settlement for the sick and in case of need. La Salle took his clothes and his papers which had been saved from the shipwreck. Each one brought, for his part, a portion of what he had that was best. I myself brought a few shirts, some cravats, handkerchiefs, and also the remainder of the glass beads and knives that I had to trade in case of need and an encounter with some tribes. As I still had some linen and worn attire and some goods such as knives and similar things, I delivered them to Chefdeville. Morenger

---

[24] The dispute ended with her miscarriage, but the topic may have arisen later when Madame Barbier delivered a healthy child after La Salle departed.

[25] As the Marquis de la Sablonnière and his young lady called Paris along with at least four other girls remained together at the settlement after La Salle's departure, there was an opportunity for other marriages to take place, as Joutel may be suggesting.

needed linen so I gave that to him. La Salle had already given him the jerkin that I had offered to him. When everything was ready, La Salle gave orders to go camp at about a league and a half distance, at the meat smoking place to supply ourselves there. Thus we took our leave which was not accomplished without sadness on everyone's part. Father Zénobe said he had never had such regret upon leavetaking as this one.

Finally, we set out to camp at the appointed place. Our horses' burdens were made ready as securely as possible; then we made them swim across to the other side of the river. The clothes and what was left were transported across by canoe that Barbier and a few others brought from the settlement and returned after we had crossed. La Salle enjoined him once more to take care of everything, to stay wary, and to plant the corn and beans we had left.

# CHAPTER VIII

# La Salle's Final Journey

e set out, numbering seventeen, namely the Sieur de La Salle, the young Cavelier, Father Anastase, the Sieur [Pierre] Duhaut, his surgeon, and others, among whom was a young son [named Pierre] of this Talon who had been in Canada. La Salle planned to leave him as well as Father Anastase and a few others with the Cenis to learn their language. We had not made much headway before we were forced to stop and readjust the load on one of our horses. We rested near the place where we had previously camped because there were numerous bison in the area and this was where we had smoked the meat.[2] Our camp was located in a motte of trees and we kept a close lookout for we noticed a number of fresh human tracks in the sand and there were several smoke trails in the vicinity.

On Monday the 13th, we crossed open country, about one and a half to two leagues across, in which we saw several herds of bison and many deer, turkeys, Canada geese, and other kinds of game. This land seemed very good to me although we encountered marshy stretches of stagnant rain water in places where there was no drainage because the land was somewhat sunken. The tall grass prevented the sun from penetrating and was tiring for us as well as our horses because

---

[1] La Salle's line of march is traced as precisely as possible from Matagorda Bay to the middle Mississippi River on contemporary government maps (USGS *Beeville*, NH14–12; USGS *Seguin*, NH14–9; USGS *Austin*, NH14–6; USGS *Beaumont*, NH15–4; USGS *Palestine*, NH15–1; USGS *Tyler*, NI15–10; USGS *Texarkana*, NI15–7; USGS *El Dorado*, NJ15–8; USGS *Greenwood*, NI15–9; and USGS *Helena*, NI15–6), based principally on Joutel's account of the directions and distances (in leagues) traveled each day, and as supplemented by other relevant information regarding terrain, vegetation, wildlife, the relative size of the larger rivers, and other route information given by Joutel and Douay. Calculations of distance traveled are based on the French league, which is the equivalent of 2.4 miles. See McDermott, *Mississippi Valley French*, 93.

[2] The smokehouse (*le Boucan*) was about one and one-half leagues northeast of the settlement in Jackson County, according to Joutel's account. See Chapter VII. Douay reported that on the first day the party met the local, apparently friendly, Bahamo (Bracamo) tribe. Cox (ed.), *Journeys of La Salle*, I, 238.

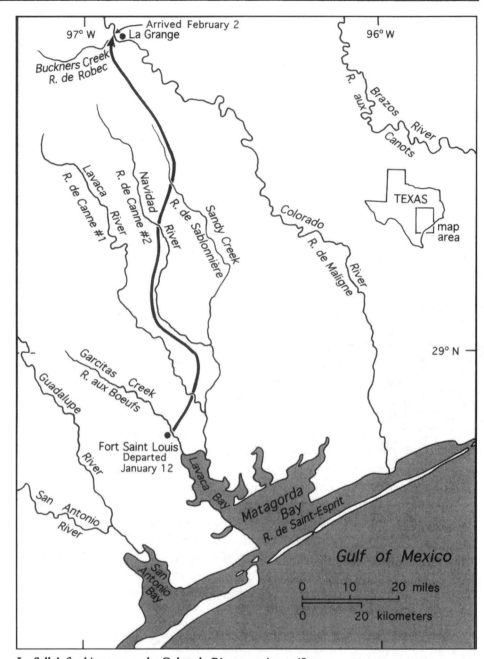

La Salle's final journey to the Colorado River crossing, 1687

it caught our legs. In the grass were also sword-like plants[3] which caused us quite
a bit of trouble as did the water that sometimes came to our knees because of
recent rainfall.

This country is bounded by great woods where there are all kinds of beautiful
trees including large oaks which would be excellent to use for construction.
Through the middle of the woods flows the Cane River.[4] These cane, properly
speaking, are only large reeds. They are hollow and can be quite annoying in
places where there is a heavy growth of them. Where they grow thick and tall, one
cannot pass through them unless an opening is cut. The name of this river was
changed by La Salle to the "Princess" because on its banks the Sieur Barbier had
expressed his passion and had courted his belle as Princess and Darling. The
proverb is quite true that there is no unbecoming love even if the object is not
charming. As customarily one names rivers and other places for the adventures
that happen to individuals, whether one has fallen into it or been misled there, or
some similar case, thus was this river named the Princess.

About five leagues below the place where we were, the river empties into the
Bay of Saint Louis after joining the other branch which forks and separates above.[5]
If we had come here to build the settlement, there would not have been as many
dead because wood was available and there was an abundance of several species of
trees quite suited to what we wanted to do. This river is navigable by medium-
sized boats to this point. Five bison were killed on the edge of the woods. We forded the river with our horses' loads and camped a half league farther on.[6]

The land seemed quite good in this region, producing very fine, high grass
which caused me to believe that wheat and other things would grow well here if
they were cultivated. We noticed that there had been a large number of natives
encamped there, judging from the disposition of their camp and the number of
huts they had made. Bison and turkeys were numerous.

After we had made camp, La Salle sent a party with horses to retrieve the bison
meat from what we had killed on the other side of the river, as well as the hides to

---

[3] Perhaps small soapweed yucca. Vines, *Trees of the Southwest*, 67–68.

[4] Joutel described the Lavaca River, which he and Pierre Meunier called the Cane River and Douay
called the First Cane River, as being about three to four leagues northeast of the settlement, which was
about two leagues upstream from the mouth of Garcitas Creek. Spanish diarists also described the distance and direction between Garcitas Creek and the Cane River. Governor De León traveled about three
leagues from the stream where the French fort was found to a large river (the Lavaca or Cane River),
which the governor named the San Marcos. Bolton (ed.), *Spanish Exploration in the Southwest*, 401. In 1691
Captain Martínez, who was with Governor Terán, identified the Cane River with the help of his guide,
Pierre Meunier, and recorded traveling about six leagues from the point at which the Martínez party
crossed the Cane river to the fort on the "Creek of the Frenchmen" (Garcitas Creek). Foster, *Spanish
Expeditions into Texas*, 61.

[5] Joutel very precisely and accurately described his location as five leagues upstream from the mouth
of the river (where the Lavaca River enters Lavaca Bay) and above or upstream of the junction with "the
other branch" (the Navidad, also called the Second Cane), which he says, correctly, forks farther upstream
(to form Sandy Creek). See USGS *Beeville*, NH14–12.

[6] The party forded the Lavaca (First Cane River) in southwestern Jackson County. The manuscript
includes, but Margry omits, that the party camped a half league farther on.

make use of them as cover for the clothing and shelter in case of rain.[7] As rain did not fail to fall, the hides became quite useful.

On Tuesday, the 14th, the rain having ceased, we got under way and crossed an open prairie, about three leagues in width and six or seven leagues in length, going toward the north. We saw more bison and other game, and many courses or beaten paths, going in one direction or another, made by the bison. We noticed that the bison kept moving without stopping to eat, and a few herds were even running. We suspected that they were being followed by a band of natives, heading all in the same direction and taking the same route to the east. We were not mistaken in our supposition. One of our horses broke down, and we were forced to stop while he was reloaded. During that interval, we each looked around to all sides. Then we saw a herd of bison running very fast. Shortly after that we noticed a native closely following them. La Salle, having spotted him, dispatched a man on a horse to chase the Indian.[8] This was done and because the native was busy with his chase, he did not notice our horseman pursuing him until it was too late although he did change his direction. When the native saw our man within range, he stopped, and because the horseman had overtaken him and given him a sign to move ahead, the native obeyed. The horseman led him directly to us.

Upon his arrival, the Indian was extremely ill at ease. Now I can assure you that he was not alone for fear kept him good company. His fear was not without reason, for, among the natives, when they fall into the hands of their enemies, no mercy is given. Some of our party favored his death because the Indians had killed many of us. But La Salle took into consideration that not many of our people remained at the settlement and that we had never done anything to the natives for which they did not seek revenge. Indeed, there had been more loss on our side. Accordingly, he decided to treat the native with kindness and do him no harm. With signs he told him that we did not want war with anyone and that we came in peace everywhere. After this a fire was built, and he was given something to smoke. But despite his best efforts, he could not keep from trembling. After he had smoked, La Salle gave him a few bits of tobacco, and we indicated to him that it was fitting for him to leave. If we had treated him as an enemy, the people at the settlement would be at great risk as they were obliged to go out hunting. In addition, the native could have been from a tribe other than the one with which we had been at war although he made us understand that someone had fired gunshots at them near the mouth of the Cane River. This must have been the Sieur Barbier when he headed out with three canoes to the mouth of the river where the man

---

[7] The Abbé Cavelier reported that the crossing was made on a raft, which perhaps was required to carry the bison meat and hides across the river. Cox (ed.), *Journeys of La Salle*, I, 289. The abundance of bison all along the route from the bay to the Brazos will be noted, since the animal was a significant source of food for both the Indians and the Frenchmen.

[8] Douay says the Indian was a Quinet. Ibid., 239. Douay wrote that the party met members of the Quaras and Anachoremas tribes at some point between the First Cane River (the Lavaca) and the Second Cane River (the Navidad). The party was near Edna. On the fourth day out, the Abbé Cavelier says the party arrived at a village of Kouraras. Ibid., 289. The tribe may have been the same as the Quaras, which Douay reported had about eight hundred warriors.

named Meunier was wounded[9] as I have mentioned elsewhere. As Barbier had fired on them first, the natives were not at all in the wrong to seek revenge, having this practice among themselves. After La Salle asked him several questions and gave him a few trinkets, he gave him the signal to leave which he did. We admired his manner: he took his leave very slowly until he was a distance away and out of range. Then he doubled his pace with great speed.

The Sieur de La Salle told us that it was best to make peace with these people so they would have no cause to harass those at the settlement. If these precautions had been taken from the moment we arrived in the country, the natives would not then have killed so many of us. In a short time, we also could have gathered much information from these people that would have served us well, whether it was about the country for settlement purposes or for news of the big river about which the gentleman still had no information at all.[10] Besides that, if we had known the country, we would have settled in a more advantageous place than where the settlement was located. The woods was too far away, and the water was not very good, often proving to be brackish particularly when the winds came in from the sea. This contributed in no small way to the deaths of some of the people; hence we were no further advanced than on the first day. On the contrary, we fared worse for we were weaker in every way. The food supplies had been eaten, property lost, and most of the men were dead without anything having been accomplished.

To return to the account of our journey, after the native left, we loaded our horses again and proceeded on our way, but we had gone only a half league when we saw another native pursuing a herd of bison in a similar manner. Again, La Salle had two men mount horseback and sent after him. They overtook the native, as the first one had been overtaken, and brought him before us. He was given the same treatment as the first one after which he was sent on his way, and we proceeded on ours.

We had not made much progress when we saw a group of men coming toward us from our left. We did not stop walking until they were within range at which point La Salle told us to halt and wait for them. When they saw us stop, they stopped as well, not daring to advance. As La Salle knew how to conduct matters with these people, he dropped his musket and moved toward them, making a sign to them to come forward. Immediately, the leader of the group came forward. He had a fine physique and seemed to be quite human. La Salle had given us orders to stay on guard, and after the leader came toward us the others also approached and gave us a few caressing strokes. It was then in order to have them smoke, for that was the first way to regale the natives. After this, La Salle made them understand with signs that we were going to the Cenis and after that we would return to our country. He demonstrated to them that upon our return we would bring them

---

[9] In Chapter VII, Joutel reported that a man named Meusnier (Meunier?) was slightly wounded by Indian arrows on an earlier excursion to the Cane River with Barbier. Here Margry miscopied Joutel's manuscript, which clearly records that Meunier was only wounded and not killed.

[10] This statement conflicts with La Salle's report in his *procés verbal* that he had earlier reached the Mississippi River from the bay.

things that they needed such as knives, hatchets, beads, and the like. They indicated that they understood for the most part. The gentleman then gave them a few bits of tobacco, dismissed them, and made them understand that we wished to have peace with everyone. With this they seemed quite satisfied and contented, and they each headed off in their directions toward several mottes of trees that were about a league away from us.

We moved on again about half a league to reach a motte of trees where La Salle had camped the previous autumn.[11] The woods were protected on one side by a large marsh and otherwise were bordered by open fields. We fortified the camp with a barricade of wood which we set up all around us because there were many natives in the vicinity, and we had seen those who came to meet us take several directions when they departed. So we believed they must have gone to warn some other bands of their people.

We were not mistaken in our conjecture, for hardly had we completed the larger part of our barricade than we saw one man, then two, then three who came one after another. In a short time, we saw fourteen near us. La Salle ordered some of us to take arms while the others continued with the work. The gentleman then advanced toward the natives to speak to them and warned us to stay on guard because he had noticed that when they planned to make a spiteful strike, they acted in about the same way. That is to say, they would approach one after another as these had. Accordingly, he positioned people in different spots within range of one another, for natives are not daring enough to attack when there is risk but only when they see their advantage. At that point, they make their strike by means of some signal among them either by shooting an arrow in the air or by uttering some loud shout or cry.

When the gentleman came even with them, the natives indicated that they had come to visit us, having learned from others of their people that we were making no trouble for anyone and that was good. La Salle gave them some tobacco to smoke and let them understand that we were going to the Cenis and, after that, to our country to procure many things and, among others, men to join with them in going to war. After we had stayed a while, we made them understand that night was approaching and we must rest. The gentleman gave them something, for it was always necessary to make some small present to them as they only have a few wretched, dressed skins with which they cover themselves when it is cold. In this

[11] This is the first of numerous comments by Joutel that La Salle's party passed or camped at a place used earlier by La Salle. Obviously, as an experienced woodsman, trapper, and explorer, and with the help of local guides and his Indian hunter-guide Nika, La Salle could retrace the route he had followed the year before, and possibly at some earlier time in his explorations. As a seasoned explorer in the Great Lakes region, La Salle (with Nika's help) probably sought local Indian guidance when they first searched for a route to the Cenis, and local Indians likely led the Frenchmen to the same crossing of the Colorado and Indian trade route that they showed De León in 1689 and 1690.

The Spanish expedition route study prepared for Foster, *Spanish Expeditions into Texas*, identified an ancient trade route that ran from northeastern New Spain through parts of South and Central Texas to East Texas. That route did not go to Matagorda Bay but ran north of the bay and crossed the Guadalupe near Cuero in DeWitt County and the Colorado near La Grange in Fayette County. La Salle was marching toward the same Colorado crossing, but there was no established Indian trail to follow between La Salle's post on the bay and the Colorado crossing.

region, it is seldom cold but when it is cold, the nights are almost as long as the days, and the nights can be quite cool. After we made signs for them to leave, each headed off in his own direction. They saw clearly that we were fortifying our encampment. I noticed, in fact, that they often turned their gaze in that direction. La Salle told us to keep a good lookout but principally to watch our horses for fear they would come and steal some of them. We noticed that, among this last group of natives, there was not one of them whom we had seen with the first group. Meanwhile the night passed quite calmly without seeing or hearing anything.

On Wednesday, the 15th, we proceeded on our way and looked for the ford where they [La Salle's party] had crossed the river last spring. However, because at that time they had traveled by night through the woods where the river made its course, we missed the ford. Also, the river had risen because of the rains so we did not want to endanger the horses at the crossing they had used the previous autumn. For that reason we continued going upriver headed toward the west and west-northwest.[12] We found country of all kinds, sometimes fine open country, other times areas with beautiful streams that separated the fields from high woods of different species of trees of various sizes. Had they been planted to please, the trees could not have been better arrayed. The river passed through the middle of these woods, and several streams flowed into it, joining from one side or the other. The soil along this river was very good in appearance, for, although the trees were large, this did not keep beautiful grass from growing beneath them.

From time to time, we found small prairies divided by narrow skirts of woods; some were a league in length, and others were more or less the same in breadth. The most common trees were hornbeams,[13] pecan trees,[14] elms, and a kind of ash. As for oak trees, there were different species of them. We sometimes found very thick woods where we were forced to make a passage by cutting through with our hatchets so our horses could pass. That evening we killed a bison. While some were busy dressing it, others worked at making a barricade in order to spend the night in a motte of trees located near a small prairie. We made the barricade of wood around us beyond arrow-shot range. With lengths of wood entangled one with the other, it was impossible to approach us without making noise. We also cut the grass that deprived us of a view of the prairie so that no one could slip in and conceal himself there. We made our fire outside the enclosure so we would be able to better see around us. These natives are quite cunning and have better eyesight

[12] On January 15, La Salle's party was marching west-northwest upstream along the west bank of the Navidad (the Second Cane River) a few miles above its junction with Sandy Creek, which joins the Navidad from the east side. The party was moving upstream along the route of modern Texas State Highway 111. See USGS *Seguin*, NH14–9.

[13] The American hornbeam is found today in East Texas, but the tree Joutel identified as a hornbeam may have been the more common river birch. See Vines, *Trees of the Southwest*, 142–144. See also Paul W. Cox and Patty Leslie, *Texas Trees: A Friendly Guide* (San Antonio: Corona Publishing Company, 1995), 68, 70.

[14] In the late seventeenth century, neither the Spaniards nor the French made a distinction between walnut trees and pecan trees. The trees Joutel saw could have been either type, but today the pecan is the more prevalent in the area. See Vines, *Trees of the Southwest*, 127, 124; and Cox and Leslie, *Texas Trees*, 278–285. Cheatham and Marshall suggest that the elm was likely *Uimus crassifolia* or *U. americana*; the ash was possibly *Fraxinus pensylvanica*.

than we have. We killed several more bison and then spent the night keeping a close lookout without hearing anything.

On Thursday, the 16th, we proceeded on our way moving alongside the same river,[15] finding almost always the same country. We noticed a kind of slope that dominated one side of the river and, at almost the same distance away, a point of woods. We still found, from time to time, that we had to cut a path with hatchets which tired us. But what was advantageous to us was the abundance of hunting, for we always saw plenty of bison and turkeys. We had a dog that ran after them when she spotted them and forced them to separate. Then we would come to take them. We made about three leagues that day, heading northwest.[16]

On Friday, the 17th, we followed the same course with some difficulty because of the woods we came upon from time to time and the many streams we had to cross. We found a hillside on which there were at least 200 to 300 Indian huts, that is to say the hut poles only as the natives had taken with them the hides, or *apaquois* which are reed mats, with which the huts are covered. The Indians had not long departed, and, judging from the number of these huts, there must have been 1,000 or 1,200 people.[17]

We went on about two leagues. Along this way, Nika found a herd of bison including some cows and killed seven or eight of them. We took only the best and the fattest parts. After this, we continued our course. We returned to the woods where, after going about a league and a half, we crossed a stream with a bed that was very treacherous. After we had passed through another small wood, we found another small stream into which several others emptied. The bed proved to be too poor, and we did not want to endanger the horses and to run the risk of their getting stuck there. We were forced to camp on the creekbanks as night was approaching, and we made a small barricade as usual.

As the rain fell unexpectedly during the night and continued as well the next day, the 18th, we were forced to remain there. We were quite cold because we only had our blankets to protect us from the rain, not having the materials for making shelter. Besides that, our horses were not faring well because there was no grass here. La Salle sent some men to see if they could find some way through and some place where there was more grass. But the rain was so heavy that there was no semblance of camping possible. The ravines were becoming large rivers.

On Sunday, the 19th, the rain having abated a bit, we moved out even though there was a very thick fog and the way was difficult. We had water halfway up our legs and sometimes to our thighs; furthermore, we had to cut through heavy brush

[15] La Salle's party was continuing northwest, following the Navidad upstream along the western or right bank in southeast Lavaca County.

[16] The Navidad flows from a northwest direction in the area La Salle was moving through on January 16; the party was about five miles southeast of modern Hallettsville.

[17] Joutel apparently assumed without being able to count, that there was an average of four to six occupants in each of the Indian huts in this area. About two weeks later, La Salle's party visited a village with apparently larger huts that housed about twelve to fifteen occupants each. In 1690, several Spanish diarists recorded Indian villages in the same area with an estimated population of one to three thousand; De León reported a village of three thousand Indians called Naaman. Bolton (ed.), *Spanish Exploration in the Southwest*, 420, n. 3.

in the way I mentioned before. We found it to be as thick as the densest brushwood in France. We nevertheless continued to climb to the top of the ravines with a great deal of trouble. Some of us had to go ahead to open up the way when some difficulty arose while the others led the horses. We would have had even more difficulty going through if we had not found some bison trails to follow in one direction or the other.

For that reason, it is advisable to beware. When one walks in the woods, one should follow bison trails to avoid obstacles which these animals have an instinct for bypassing. They take less difficult passages on firmer ground, where the woods and cane are less thick, and likewise where there are the best fords on the rivers. Although the trails taken by the bison often detour the route which one would wish to take, one finds other paths that rejoin it or come close to it. When one comes upon these bad stretches, one should take the most recent and widest trail. When the bison find some difficulty, whether it is some fallen tree or other similar thing, they look for another way. Not that the bison trails avoid the difficulties of roadways. They become, in effect, like streams after the rains. Some places are rutted with big holes from one footstep to another. When these kinds of trails are dry, they are quite difficult, being rough and hard. These conditions were not very agreeable for us because we were not shod as we should have been for these kinds of trails. For the most part, our shoes consisted of only a piece of bison or deer skin that we sewed like slippers. If we had had well dressed skins, this would not have been half bad, but we had to use the hides of the bison we had killed. When fresh, they fit well, but when they had dried on our feet, we could not pull them off. We were forced to stand in water a while to soak them. Another inconvenience with these shoes was that they chafed our feet until they were sore.

But to return to our trail, although it was beaten down, we were not spared difficulty. The bison, in spite of the density of the brush, found a means to make a passage through it by force or between two trees. But our loaded horses could not pass unless we made an opening ourselves which we had to do often. We walked thus all day without making much progress and without finding a single suitable place to camp that was not flooded from the previous days' rain although we went from side to side.

While we were hacking some brush to open up a passage, we heard a noise like a waterfall, and we surmised this could be some ravine with high and scarped banks, promising us some suitable place to camp. We headed for the place, camped there, and made a kind of fort as usual. We spent a rather cold night, the ground being so soaked with water that it filled every step we made. What was also vexing was that our horses had almost no grass to eat in that area, and they again had to substitute whatever they could find for hay and oats.

On the 20th, a little rain fell, but this did not stop us from marching. After crossing a half league of woods and the same distance through marsh, we found open country through which there was a wide bison trail going toward the river. We surmised that there must be a ford there. We walked about a league, following the path, after which La Salle sent some men to investigate. The river had overflowed, and its current was so violent that the noise could be heard from far away.

This noise was caused by several overturned trees which had fallen into the water. Not finding any way to cross the river, we had to camp on the river bank. While we waited for the waters to recede, we hunted and killed a few bison and remained there that day.

On the 21st, we advanced upriver about a league to the northwest. After crossing a little river, or a branch of this same river, and finding it narrow and about eight to ten feet deep, La Salle ordered a large tree cut down and made to fall to the other side. Another tree was felled from the other side to lie alongside the first tree. After that was done, we passed our packs from hand to hand, and, after they had been carried across, we had the horses swim across farther down where there was a way out on the other side.[18] We made camp there near the river on a rise protected on one side by a swale and a small stream. On the other side there was very lovely open country.

Surrounding that place were beautiful trees of different kinds. The grass was dry, and very little green grass was to be found during this season unless it was found in certain humid swales where there was always some green grass. Our horses had only what they could find, and we had to find some place for them.

While we were at work at making a small fort with a barricade of wood as usual, La Salle wandered a bit to see if he could find some grass. During that interval, we heard a voice shrieking. Quickly gathering our arms, we went to investigate where we had heard the noise. When we arrived there, we saw a band of Indians coming directly for us. They stopped when they came into view, and they made signs to us to come to them, indicating to us that they came in peace by putting their bows on the ground. In turn, I gave them a sign to approach which they did immediately, and, upon joining us, they caressed us in their customary way, rubbing their hands on their chests and then rubbing ours. They gave evidence of their friendliness by these gestures, either putting their hands over their hearts or by hooking their fingers to indicate the alliance they wished to make with us.[19] At least this was the interpretation I was able to make from it because I did not have the advantage of knowing their language. As La Salle was not in camp, I did not consider it appropriate to take them there. For that reason, I had them stop within a pistol shot range until the gentleman arrived. While someone went to search for him, I offered them a smoke. There were 15 of them.

When La Salle returned, we conducted them to the camp where they noticed the kind of fort we were making in our customary way. We made them understand

[18] Along the upper reaches of the Navidad, the river continues to flow from the north-northwest; La Salle's party crossed the river apparently at a point near the present Colorado County line. Douay estimates that the distance traveled between the Second Cane and the Sablonnière (Sandy Creek) was five leagues, which is the approximate distance between the Navidad and Sandy Creek near the Fayette-Colorado County line. Cox (ed.), *Journeys of La Salle*, I, 239.

[19] This represents one of the few diary or journal comments in which an Indian sign is physically described by either a French or Spanish author. The hooking of fingers was a familiar sign used widely by Indian tribes in the west and is a recognized sign today in American Sign Language as an indication of friendship or alliance. See W. P. Clark, *The Indian Sign Language* (Lincoln: University of Nebraska Press, 1982), 30, 183. The practice of indicating friendship or peaceful intentions to a visitor by rubbing hands over their own chests and then over the chests of the visitors was one followed by Indians from South Texas to the Mississippi River. See Chapter XV.

that this was to protect ourselves from surprise and, further, that we always kept a close lookout. After that we showed them how effective our arms were. We fired a few shots into a tree. They stopped in surprise, admiring the hole that the bullet made. They also admired the holes made in the slaughtered buffalo and their shattered bones. They let us know that they had come to the sounds of gunshots which had surprised them. La Salle in turn made them understand that we were going to the Cenis. He had already been with that tribe during his last journey when he stayed for some time in their village, and he had set several words of their language down in writing. Now there was among this group one man who understood the Cenis language.[20] La Salle repeated to him several of the words that he had written in the Cenis village to check whether these words were correct; they proved to be quite accurate.

They let us know that their tribe was called *Ebahamo*,[21] that their village was not far away, and that they were allies of the Cenis and friends of many of the tribes situated in the region. La Salle gave them a few small presents, and, after they were there a while, they went back, apparently satisfied. They indicated that they would return the next day to see us.

We spent the night without hearing anything; we feared they might rob us of a few horses because we had to lead them to graze a little way off where it was marshy and blooming. Apparently a fire had spread through during the summer and there was a little green grass. There was always someone there to mind the horses, and some of them were hurt because we did not have everything necessary to harness them, nor did we have pack saddles or regular saddles. Therefore, the horses needed a little rest as much as we did.

We had had much hardship in these woods where it had been necessary to hack through to make a passage. Besides this, even though we had five horses, we were forced to carry our own small packs, that is say those of us did who had their own personal belongings. Sieur de La Salle had taken along all of his clothing and papers; Monsieur Cavelier [the Abbé], likewise, had brought several church ornaments, up to a dozen habits, and what there were of his belongings and supplies. As a result, we had difficulty leading the horses which did not help us out to any great extent.

[20] The report that an Indian with the Ebahamo tribe spoke the Cenis (Caddoan) language tends to confirm other reports that the Cenis, a western Caddoan tribe, had a heavy influence on Indians residing as far west as the lower Colorado and Guadalupe rivers. This Tejas or Cenis influence and relationship with tribes in South Texas and northern Mexico was also suggested in Padre Massanet's account of De León's 1689 expedition, in which the padre reported that the first Indians that De León's party met after crossing the Guadalupe in DeWitt County called out "Techas! Techas!" Apparently this meant that the tribes (the Emet and the Cava) were allies of the Caddoan tribes, including the Tejas (the Cenis), and were enemies of the Apache. Bolton (ed.), *Spanish Exploration in the Southwest*, 359. Newcomb notes that "the Caddoan tribes of East Texas exerted considerable influence and perhaps dominance over the natives of Central Texas." See Newcomb, "Historic Indians of Central Texas," 3. Cenis contacts apparently extended west of the Rio Grande; in De León's 1690 expedition, the Spanish party found at the tribe's village in East Texas an Indian visitor (Tomás) from the area near Parral, a Spanish mining community in southern Nueva Vizcaya (modern Chihuahua), over seven hundred miles to the southwest.

[21] See Thomas N. Campbell, "Ebahamo Indians," in Tyler, et al. (eds.), *The New Handbook of Texas*, II, 776. As Campbell mentions, the tribe does not appear to be one of the coastal tribes with which La Salle was at war.

To return to our Indians, they did not fail in their promise. At 9 o'clock the next morning [January 22], a band of 25 arrived, some of whom had round shields[22] which they make with the sturdiest bison hide that they have the skill to process and that they use to protect themselves from arrows. Not all the natives had them. Some had left their shields in the woods, and when they had been with us a while, they went to get them. They made us understand that they were going to war against enemy tribes to the northwest.

Some of the Indians indicated that they had seen men like us and pointed to the west making us understand that they were only a ten days' journey away. This is about 200 leagues. They added that in the time it took to reach these men, there were almost always bison on the way except for a day or so. The natives also indicated to us that there were only four large rivers to cross. We determined that this must be New Spain, judging from the direction they showed us.[23] La Salle wrote down several words from their language which, it appeared, is not very easy because they speak from the throat a great deal. Judging from what I was able to determine later, their language is more difficult than the Cenis' and differs as Flemish does from high German, and there are differences in their customs.[24]

When we told them we were going to visit the Cenis, they informed us that to the northeast we would find plains and to the north, on the other hand, we would experience great hardships because of the forest that was very difficult.[25] This was all in signs, however, and one is often mistaken in the interpretations one makes from these signs, taking things in one way when often they mean another. However, La Salle was persuaded to take the direction they recommended, fearing that the woods would give us as much trouble as the ones before had. As the

[22] Other tribes carrying oval or round leather shields were reported in South Texas a short time later. While traveling through western DeWitt County in 1693, Salinas Varona encountered a hostile band of Jumano who carried round leather shields. See Foster and Jackson (eds.) and Brierley (trans.), "The 1693 Expedition of Governor Salinas Varona," 290.

[23] As it is doubtful that Spaniards in New Spain had visited the area between the Guadalupe and Colorado rivers at this time, it appears that the Ebahamo had visited northern New Spain. The statements that the Spaniards were only a ten-day's journey away (the Rio Grande is about 250 miles to the southwest), that there were four large rivers to cross (perhaps referring to the modern Guadalupe, San Antonio, Nueces, and Rio Grande), and that bison were usually found along the route except for the last few days appear accurate and further suggest that the tribe was very familiar with the route and the area between Central Texas and northern New Spain. The statement also supports the thesis that there was a well-used trade route between northern Mexico and Central Texas.

The comments made later by the Teao and Palaquechare that they had traveled with the Cenis to visit the Jumano also tend to confirm reports that the Cenis and their allies in South Texas traveled southwest to trade with tribes in Coahuila, Nueva Vizcaya, and West Texas. See Chapter IX. The Jumano village near the junction of the Mexican Conchos River and the Rio Grande identified in Major Antonio Retis's 1715 expedition diary was about twenty-three leagues upstream on the Conchos. See Reginald C. Reindorp (trans.), "The Founding of Missions at La Junta de los Rios," *Supplementary Studies of the Texas Catholic Historical Society*, 1 (Apr., 1938), 10–17.

[24] Here we have substituted the manuscript description of the differences because it is more expansive than Margry's version.

[25] The Ebahamo apparently were warning La Salle not to continue traveling north-northwest but to veer northeast toward the customary Colorado River crossing area near modern La Grange and thereby avoid the dense Post Oak Belt. The manuscript includes the northeast or north option, which is not in Margry's account.

Indians spent part of the day with us, the gentleman gave them food and sent them to cut some meat from several haunches of bison we had [killed?] there. This they did, and after they had eaten, La Salle gave them a present of some knives and glass beads with which they were well satisfied at least to all appearances. Some of our people bartered with them for a few dressed deer skins. After they had been with us for a while, they went off, indicating to us that they were going to war.

After the Indians left, we busied ourselves setting our horses' loads right and mending the *panneaux*[26] of sorts that we had fashioned, filled with dried grass. We had the idea to make a kind of Picardy pack saddle[27] because it was necessary to devise something to prevent sores on the horses. We had great difficulty doing this. Even though each one tried to give his opinion, La Salle was not in a mood to follow anyone's advice except his own.

At length, the day was used as I have said; that night rain fell unexpectedly and lasted the next day [January 23], forcing us to not travel at all. On the 24th and the 25th, we did not make much progress either because the rain still fell from time to time. We came upon several streams on our route which caused us difficulty because the waters were high. The country was quite beautiful and abundant in game.

On the 26th, we continued our course and arrived on the banks of a river named La Sablonnière[28] because of an accident that happened to the gentleman of that name during the first journey he made with La Salle when they left the bay-side. As the water had receded a bit, we forded the river. We had to carry the horses' loads in several trips one after another which was rather annoying to us because that happened often. Under orders from La Salle, who feared that the horses would strain their backs, this manner of crossing was not only necessary for rivers but also for most ravines. Thus we were greatly overworked by this without counting the small packs we had to carry on our backs. The horses were loaded with things such as the clothes and linens of these gentlemen with which they could well do without. But it was not their labor and did not cost them.

For me, there were a few days when I became indisposed. I feared falling sick because I had had so much trouble pulling myself from the mud in crossing the rivers. On this last crossing, we endured much more than before in getting our horses across because the bottom was not firm. Therefore we had to find another crossing for them other than the one where we crossed. We made camp about a half-league distance in a woods. There I tried to recover from my indisposition. I made a big fire alongside of which I lay down, and as I was disgusted by meat (the only food we had), I pulled some hardtack from my small pack that I had been

[26] A *panneau* is a small cushion filled with horsehair that is placed like a blanket between the saddle and the horse.

[27] Picardy is a region in northern France bounded on the north by the Strait of Dover and in the west by the English Channel. *Webster's New Geographical Dictionary*, 953. However, I have not determined if a Picardy pack saddle is identified with that region.

[28] The river called La Sablonnière (The Sandy) is present-day Sandy Creek. Although Joutel says the stream was named for the gentleman of that name (the Marquis de la Sablonnière), Douay reported that the name of the stream was derived from the sandy condition of the creek's banks and bed. Cox (ed.), *Journeys of La Salle*, I, 239. Joutel's account also notes that an unusual amount of sand was found near the creek, which helps to confirm the identity and name of the stream as present-day Sandy Creek.

saving for more than a year. I used that to restore my appetite a little. This succeeded and I found I was better.

The country along this last river did not appear to me to be very good. It was sandy, and even the trees were not very pretty. They were different from those we had passed before because there was a great deal of sand. Also, the river apparently overflowed often dragging with it a lot of sand which was left in places according to what I could tell.

On the 27th, we continued on our way and made camp beside another small stream. But this one was much deeper which forced us to go farther upriver more than a league to find a place that could be forded. We crossed it and the water came as high as our thighs.[29] We had to camp in a small motte of trees situated on the bank of the stream because a heavy rain commenced. The stream itself rose in no time. La Salle, having noticed places in the woods where mud and sand remained, realized that the river must have overflowed before and gave orders to cut forked branches and stakes to make a platform upon which to place our clothes and powder in case the rain continued. The precaution was well taken; indeed, the river did rise and overflowed and even threatened some of our men who, to protect themselves from the mosquitos, were camped on a small island where there were no trees around and very little grass. Had they not abandoned their camp, they would have been carried away downstream. They lost some clothing which they did not have time to take with them. We were surprised by such an immediate and violent flood.

Now, we were further at a disadvantage with the necessity to use our covers to protect all the clothing we had put on the platform. That is to say, what covers we had for some of our men only had bison skins which they had obtained in trade with the Indians. Thus we were exposed to the harshness of the weather. Unfortunately for us, the wind and rain came from the north and were very cold, wet, and penetrating so that even the warmest of us could not keep from trembling. Finally, to add to our misfortune, we were very poorly positioned to make a good fire even though we were camped in a woods. Indeed, there were only medium-sized live oaks, and there was no dry wood. In fact, it was just a small motte. We had to make a platform to set our fire upon. We had trouble lighting and maintaining it because it was on the damp [ground]. Hence, we spent a rather unpleasant night; but there was no way to do otherwise.

Once it was daylight, we searched for a higher place to go camp because the water had reached us and was gaining steadily. We camped about a quarter of a league from that place in the middle of the plains, and we left all the gear on the platform we had made. To warm ourselves, we had to go look for wood in that same motte or another one that was not any closer. To get there we had to go

---

[29] Although some writers have suggested that the Sablonnière was the modern Colorado River (E. W. Cole, "La Salle in Texas," *Southwestern Historical Quarterly*, 49 [Apr., 1946], 484), the report that La Salle's party waded across the stream in water only up to their thighs indicates that the stream they crossed was much smaller than the Colorado, which was flooded at the time, as were all other local streams from the constant rains.

through water up to our thighs, and yet it was only green wood. But, the cold forced us to make a virtue of necessity. We, meanwhile, spent the whole day in that location and had trouble staying dry there. Our horses were also suffering, and I noticed that they had gathered themselves next to the woods for shelter from the wind. In this way each of us was suffering in this situation, being deprived of everything. If the weather had overtaken us in another place, we would not have been troubled. Wood would not have failed us, and we would not have suffered.

This country was, however, quite beautiful. There were open fields that extended beyond our view with mottes of trees from place to place. The fields were full of fine grass and normally there were plenty of bison. True, in that season there were not many; but La Salle told us that when he had passed by this way earlier, there had been a great number of the animals which one could well see from the quantity of manure or dung that there was in these fields and from the way the fields had been grazed.

On the 29th, we continued on our way. We traveled about three leagues by the most wretched trails, always having water up to the knees. We proceeded to camp beside a stream that we crossed the next morning and then headed for a woods on the other side. La Salle sent Nika and some other men out hunting, and they killed a few bison. On their return, they told us they had seen some natives' huts and also some horse tracks. Besides that, they had heard dogs barking. We spent the night, however, without hearing anything, always keeping a close lookout. We did not make a fort as we had done before.

On the next day [the 31st], Sieur de La Salle, accompanied by his brother the Abbé, Morenger, the young Cavelier, and a few others headed for the place where the hunters had seen these huts. He told me to watch over the camp, advising me not to wander at all for fear of some surprise. They proceeded toward the huts without the Indians noticing them. The natives had positioned themselves on a rise that was almost surrounded by the stream beside which we were also camped. The rise was covered by woods with openings that provided a view of the wide open country beyond the woods. There were 24 or 25 huts and in each one there were five or six men and many women and children.[30] When they saw our people coming near, they came out to meet them. After this, the Indians conducted them into the chief's hut which was soon filled with people, each one coming to observe us.

The elders who had gathered spread out dressed bison skins upon which they had La Salle and his entourage sit. Then they gave them both smoked and fresh meat. Their huts were shaped like a sort of oven, covered with bison skins, scraped, dried up, and withered, and perhaps soaked with grease so they would not shrink. The natives told La Salle that several of their allies had seen our tracks, and they knew we were going to the Cenis. They understood that we would have to pass by this place and were persuaded to come see us.[31] At least this was the interpretation

[30] Apparently the Indian huts Joutel saw in Fayette County were larger than those he had seen closer to the coast in southern Lavaca County.

[31] It is significant that the Indians said that they had come to that location to meet La Salle because they knew he would cross the Colorado River at the customary ford. A similar incident occurred in 1693

the gentleman made of it, and this was apparently the case, considering the large number of different tribes that we saw afterwards.

La Salle presented them with some knives and some tobacco to which they responded with a few dressed hides. They are skilled at dressing the bison hides retaining the hair and cleaning it well.[32] For each hide they were given a knife with which they were well pleased. But they brought a large number of skins and we were rather encumbered already, for our horses had quite some trouble carrying what they had. Therefore, we let them know we did not want any more, but, that if they had horses to trade, we would give them hatchets and other things in exchange. They indicated that they had only two horses, and they did not want to get rid of them. As for their hides, they were very well worked, but they were not suitable for the rain, because they stiffened once they were wet. We used them to cover ourselves, and our coverings were used for shelter or to cover our packs. I would not have thought that the hides could be so well resistant [to water], considering that they were so thick and spongy, and the hair was long.

La Salle returned to the camp, and we were still there on the 1st of February. Several Indians came to see us, or rather to see if we would give them something, for they knew we had given presents in the village and elsewhere. They hoped for the same. They brought hides with which they tried to persuade us to exchange knives. But, as I have already mentioned, we were rather encumbered.

La Salle sent some men out hunting, and those who went as escort were entertained at the spectacle of an Indian from one of these tribes pursuing a bison that he had wounded. The bison, feeling a little provoked, wanted to take revenge on the Indian. Thus, the animal and the Indian ran one after the other, each in their turn, and this continued for a long time. But the Indian, seeing our people, turned back and headed for the place where the rest of his camp was. This ended the combat and cut short the amusement of our hunters who gave us an account of it on their return. The Indians headed straight north.

On Sunday, February 2nd, we continued on our journey heading directly to the Indians' village where we stopped about an hour. There we traded a few scraped and dried bison skins for some collars that they make from bison skin. They are so called because the Indians use them to carry loads on the back. The collars are about a *quartier* [33] long and four fingers wide, and they fit them over the head with two straps at each end, about two arms length long, with which the Indians tie up and fasten their bundles, whether wood or other things. They make

---

to Salinas Varona, who was told at the Rio Grande crossing that some Indian bands intended to intercept his party near the same Colorado River crossing and, as forecast, the Indians met him there. See Foster, *Spanish Expeditions into Texas*, 81–87.

Both the Abbé Cavelier and Father Douay give the names of some of the tribes and information about the Indians they met near the Colorado crossing. Douay said that the area was occupied by forty large villages of the Quanotinno, who made war on the Spaniards and dominated their Indian neighbors. The Abbé Cavelier said that La Salle's party had been intercepted by a band of 150 mounted Kanoutinoa, who were hunting bison with lances tipped with sharpened bone. Cox (ed.), *Journeys of La Salle*, I, 240, 290.

[32] The carefully dressed hides retained the animal's hair, which was cleaned and combed. Hides dressed with the hair removed also were prepared and are referred to as skins.

[33] A *quartier* equals thirty centimeters.

these collars rather carefully. They comb the hair and decorate them like their bison hides. Also, they make tight compartments in them. This kind of collar was very useful to us for making the horses' loads hold fast and to serve as girths which we did not have. They were much better than the straps that we had to make from recently stripped bison which hardened so much that there was no way to use them once they dried unless they were soaked. That is why we traded for a number of these collars. Besides, they did not cost us much, considering that we obtained them for a needle or two.

They also presented us with a few pieces of smoked meat. We noticed that they had removed the two horses which they had when La Salle was there. The removal may have been made because we had asked if they wanted to trade them, or perhaps they feared that we would take them by force, but the horses were nowhere near them. Thus, after we had been with them for a while, we resumed our journey.

The country along this stream is very beautiful, but it did not seem very fertile to me because it was sandy, either because of the proximity of the river or another reason. This stream was the swiftest one we had seen. It would be easy to construct mills on it.[34] The trees in this region are almost all oak, but they are not very big perhaps because the soil is not very good.

As soon as we left that place, we crossed beautiful open country that was a good league and a half wide[35] and longer than the eye could see. It was level from one side to the other with plenty of grass. After that we came to a very pretty river, named La Maligne, that had been given the name because on the previous journey of La Salle an alligator had seized his chamber valet, named Dumesnil, by the shoulders and dragged him to the bottom.[36] The servant was taken while swimming across the river with Nika to see if the ground on the other side was firm enough for the horses. This was the only one of our people who had this misfortune. I observed, as long as I stayed at the settlement, that these animals fled from men. I noted afterwards on our journey, in places where the natives were bathing, they made the alligators flee.

[34] This large, swiftly running tributary to the Maligne (or Colorado) was probably present-day Buckners Creek, which drains a twenty-five-mile area west of the Colorado crossing and is the only major creek that flows from the west into the Colorado in the area. Douay calls the tributary stream the Robec River, and says that it was seven or eight leagues beyond the Sablonnière. Cox (ed.), *Journeys of La Salle*, I, 239. The distance between the major headwaters of Sandy Creek and Buckners Creek is approximately twenty miles or eight leagues. See USGS *Seguin*, NH14-9. The party was about four miles southwest of La Grange.

[35] This open area is west of Rabb's Prairie. In 1686 Douay said that the large stream he called the Robec (probably Buckners Creek) was crossed one and a half leagues before reaching the Maligne. Cox (ed.), *Journeys of La Salle*, I, 224. This distance report is consistent with that found in the 1693 Spanish expedition diaries of Salinas Varona, who crossed the Colorado near the same location. Foster and Jackson (eds.) and Brierley (trans.), "The 1693 Expedition of Gregorio de Salinas Varona," 293, 294.

[36] As mentioned in the introduction, several recent studies assume that the Maligne was the Brazos rather than the Colorado. See Mardith K. Schuetz, "Commentaries on the Interrogations," in Weddle (ed.), *La Salle, the Mississippi, and the Gulf*, 260. Joutel confirmed that the Maligne was named for the death of Dumesnil, La Salle's servant, who was drowned by an alligator while crossing the river. Maligne means malice or wickedness in French and English. Parkman concurred that Dumesnil was seized by an alligator "on the Colorado" in *La Salle and the Discovery of the Great West*, 415.

La Maligne is wide like the Seine at Rouen,[37] and its current is nearly the same. Thus, it is navigable and not obstructed with wood. It flows through very beautiful country. The open country that we had just crossed goes along one side of the river. On its banks are trees of different species and sizes. In the wet locations and entirely along the banks are willows, linden trees,[38] and the like and a little farther inland there are oak, elm, pecan trees, and several other kinds of trees.

We camped beside the river at about the range of a pistol shot from the edge of a motte of trees. We cut off some bark to make shelter because it was necessary to stay in this same place for several days, time to allow the high waters to recede from the rain and to let our horses rest a bit. They were tired of the poor pasturage we had found along the way, and at this place there was excellent grass even though it was dry and tough because of the season. We killed several bison, turkeys, and some deer, ducks, doves, and other kinds of game.

I noticed a certain animal that is shaped like a rat, but larger, like a medium-sized cat. It has the appearance and color of a rat except it has a longer snout. Beneath one side of its abdomen is a sort of sack in which it carries its young.[39] This seemed to me quite extraordinary. We killed several which we ate. They are quite good when fat and taste like a suckling pig. These animals live on fruit, that is to say on acorns and nuts.

Sieur de La Salle, when he camped at this same place on his previous journey, had hidden some strings of beads in the hollow of a tree, anticipating that he would pass here again. In addition, his horses then had been heavily loaded with maize. These were found again.[40]

While we were in that place, Indians came to see us nearly every day, calling themselves by different tribal names. They made us understand that they came to see us because of what their allies had told them, that we harmed no one. La Salle confirmed to them that we brought peace. There were some who stayed from morning until evening. We had them smoke and eat, and, additionally, the gentleman always gave them some small thing. Without that [gesture], one is not welcome among these people, who have nothing, so to speak, except a few hides.

---

[37] Joutel's comments on the relative size of the Maligne, the Canoe, and the Cenis rivers are further evidence that they were, respectively, the Colorado, the Brazos, and the Trinity. The Seine at Rouen is a large river that drains the area between Paris and the port city of La Havre. Rouen is upriver approximately fifty miles east of La Havre.

[38] The American linden or basswood (*Tilia americana*) and the Carolina basswood (*Tilia caroliniana*) are found today in Central and Northeast Texas and Joutel may have seen them on the lower Colorado. However, they also may have been birch trees (*Betual nigra*), which are common in the area today and have leaves similar to the linden. Vines, *Trees of the Southwest*, 139, 732; Cox and Leslie, *Texas Trees*, 205–207. Cheatham and Marshall observe that the leaves of mulberry (*Morus rubra*) and linden (*Tilia americana, T. caroliniana*) are more similar than birch and linden leaves.

[39] The animal was a opossum, found frequently today in the same area of the Colorado River basin. Davis and Schmidly, *The Mammals of Texas*, 15.

[40] La Salle had left a hidden store of grain or a sign on a tree to mark the location of his 1686 crossings of the Colorado, the Brazos, and the Trinity rivers because he apparently expected that he or some of his party would follow the same route and use the same river crossings on a return trip to the Cenis.

They told us the names of a number of villages or rather a number of tribes, their allies as well as their enemies. I have listed their names below. Those who live to the north of the Maligne[41] are the:

| | | |
|---|---|---|
| Spichehat | Exepiahohe | Ahehouen |
| Kabaye | Ahouergomahe | Meghey[42] |
| Teheaman | Kemahopihein | Telamene |
| Tehauremet | Koienkahe | Ointemarhen |
| Kiabaha | Komkome | Kouyam |
| Chaumene | Omenaosse | Meraquaman |
| Quouan | Keremen | |
| Arhau | Korimen | |

Toward the west and northwest are others as follows:

| | | |
|---|---|---|
| Les Kannehouan[43] | Piechar | Chancre |

[41] As the Maligne, or Colorado River, at the projected crossing location about five miles upriver from present-day La Grange runs from the northwest to the southeast, Joutel's reference to the area north of the Maligne refers to the area on the eastern side of the river, across the river from where La Salle's party was encamped at the time. See USGS *Seguin*, NH14-9. Michel's condensation of Joutel's journal, as translated into English in 1714 and reprinted by Isaac J. Cox, does not place the list of Indian tribal names at this point in Joutel's account (when La Salle was on the west bank of the Maligne River), but rather, in a confusing manner, inserts the list later in the journal narrative when La Salle meets the Teao Indians east of the Colorado River. Cox (ed.), *Journeys of La Salle*, 114–115. Then, in another confusing mistake, Michel and Cox repeat a flawed rendition of the list when the French party is in East Texas. Cox (ed.), *Journeys of La Salle*, 145–146.

A review of the 1713 printing of Michel's French version and its 1714 English translation confirms that the alterations and mistakes in the placement and duplication of the list of Indian tribal names occur first in Michel's French condensed version and were repeated in the 1714 English translation and subsequent reprints. Copies of the 1713 and 1714 original versions of Michel's work in French and English are held in the Rare Books Division of the Library of Congress.

Newcomb cites and perhaps relied on Cox's reprint of the English translation of Michel's condensation of Joutel's journal and E. W. Cole's questionable study of La Salle's 1687 route to project the location of a number of important Central Texas tribes, including some of the tribes named in Joutel's list. See Newcomb, "Historic Indians of Central Texas," 13–14. Robert A. Ricklis and Michael B. Collins also cite Cox in trying to unscramble the location of Central Texas tribes Joutel identified; they write: "Joutel recorded 17 individual groups before reaching the Brazos (Cox, 1905). On the other side of the river, an equally complex situation was noted." See Ricklis and Collins, *Archaic and Late Prehistoric Human Ecology in the Middle Onion Creek Valley, Hays County, Texas*, Texas Archeological Research Laboratory Studies in Archeology 19 (Austin, 1994), 18. My study suggests that Joutel recorded nineteen named tribes that lived west of the lower Colorado and twenty-two tribes on the east side of the Colorado.

[42] Newcomb considers this tribe the same as the Mayeye. "Historic Indians of Central Texas," 24. In 1718 Govenor Alarcón met the Mayeye a few miles east of the Colorado River and other Spanish expeditions encountered the tribe in the same area. See Foster, *Spanish Expeditions into Texas*, 277. This information on the location of the Mayeye supports the contention that the Maligne was the present-day Colorado River.

[43] Joutel does not name the Indians who gave him the list of tribes that lived across the Colorado to the north and that lived on the western side of the Colorado (where La Salle's party was at the time). The only suggestion that one tribe was special may be implied from the fact that according to Joutel's manuscript and in Margry's version, "Les Kannehouan" was the first named western tribe (and the only name that was written with an article). It is particularly significant that Joutel wrote the tribal names down and, several days later, read his understanding of the names back to the Indians, who confirmed Joutel's notes. Joutel does make it clear that the Maligne (unlike other Texas rivers) was considered to be a boundary river by the tribes.

| Peissaquo | Tohaha[44] | Tohau[45] |
| Panequo | Petaro[46] | Pechir |
| Kuasse | Petao | Petsare |
| Coyabegux | Tserabocherete[47] | Serecoutcha |
| Orcan | Onapiem | Tsepcoen[48] |
| Peinhoum | Piohum | |

They also named the Cenis and a few other tribes which I have not written. They told us that their boundary was the Maligne River which normally they do not cross unless they are going to war. They also told us that they were friends and allies of the Cenis, at least from what we could understand. They were surprised when we repeated to them the tribes that they had named for us a few days before when we had written their names down.[49] They saw us looking at the paper. They told us that they sometimes went to war with tribes to the east but that their strongest enemies were from the southwest where they indicated there were a number of tribes against them at war. They also said they were allies of 45 tribes, that few of them were stationary, most were roving, living off only hunting and fishing like those which we had encountered before. For this reason they disperse to different places in order to subsist better, and they drive the bison back and forth to each other. It seemed from this that the woods and the rivers are their boundaries for hunting. There were many Indians in this region, and that was the reason we had not had plenty to hunt.

During the time that we stayed there, La Salle had us work on a canoe or "boat" in our language. We made it with bison hides from which we removed the hair. After that we stretched them out to dry, and, when they were dry, we cut them in squares to fit them together to sew. We placed four together and sewed them end to end with sinew.

The advantage of bison is that their parts can be used as much for subsistence as for clothing. First the meat is very good, much better than the beef in France. Besides that, they have very fine hair which is quite as suitable as anything similar for making cloth. The hide is, to all appearances, capable of being prepared in different ways, and even the jet-black horns are useful for many things even though they are not very long. But some horns of old bison are quite thick. We used their sinews not only to sew their hides but also to mend clothes.

[44] Between 1689 and 1693, the Tohaha were frequently seen on Spanish expeditions in the area indicated by Joutel, west of the Colorado River crossing. See Foster, *Spanish Expeditions into Texas*, 287–288. This association, plus that of the Toho (see following note), supports the contention that what the French called the Maligne was the Colorado River.

[45] This is probably the Toho, a tribe frequently encountered in the area west of the Colorado River, as indicated on Joutel's list. Foster, *Spanish Expeditions into Texas*, 288.

[46] The tribal name Petaro is not found in the manuscript version, which lists nineteen tribes west of the Colorado River, not twenty as found in Margry.

[47] It appears that the tribal name is spelled "Tsesaboehrete" in the Library of Congress manuscript.

[48] It appears that the tribal name is spelled "Tseperen" in the Library of Congress manuscript.

[49] My assertion that Joutel's account is based on contemporaneous notes that he kept during the journey is supported by his account of the natives' reaction to his ability to repeat accurately the names of forty-one tribes that he had written down a few days earlier.

Now I will return to the construction of the canoe. When the skins were sewn, we erected a framework for the boat with two poles that we fastened at the two ends. We next fixed cross bars at intervals and mounted the skins on this. We sewed the skins over the framework passing them through small wooden floor pieces made from pliant sticks. When the boat was built, we turned it upside down to grease the seams with tallow mixed with charcoal in order to plug the holes and to prevent water from entering through the seams. The canoe ready, we had only to wait for the waters to recede to cross the river.

The Indians came to see us every day that we remained there. They told us many things, but it was quite hard to understand them because their language was difficult. Besides, each tribe had its own language or dialect,[50] as it were, or at least there was some variation, which one might expect, since in France we know the language changes from one province to another even though we trade and speak with one another. I would have trouble learning their language without spending a period of time with them. That is why I am surprised that the author, of whom I have spoken before, boasts of having taught them a great many things and speaks of having seen a fine order among these tribes. For my part, I did not notice that nor even that they had any religion. Yet, I was quite often there to smoke with those who came to see us. La Salle, who did not smoke tobacco, told me to keep the natives company for it was necessary to use discretion with them so as not to offend them. In truth, small in number as we were, we had no hope of passing through their area forcibly.

Because the country is not cold, the Indians are all nude except for the women who cover their nudity. But when the sharp north wind blows, the natives put on dressed skins. These skins are quite clean and very soft just like the white ones we have in France. The women use these skins by arranging them like a skirt to cover from the waist to the knees. I also noticed that these Indians had some earthenware pottery [*poteries de terre*][51] in which they cook their meat and roots; they also have some small baskets made of reeds or rushes.[52] I have said that I did not notice any religion among them; however, they sometimes indicated to us that there was something great above, pointing to the sky. Some natives, seeing us read in our prayer book in which there were some pictures, told us that they had seen similar things, pointing out the area west of us. This convinced us that they must mean the Spaniards.

There is not, however, much likelihood that the natives traded much with the Spaniards, not having even a hatchet or a knife or anything else.[53] True, their

---

[50] Spanish explorers also mentioned that natives living between the present San Antonio and Brazos rivers spoke many different languages. See Padre Massanet's observation discussed in Foster, *Spanish Expeditions into Texas*, 58.

[51] The natives in Central and South Texas area in ca. A.D. 1250–1300 regularly used pottery. Perttula, et al., "Prehistoric and Historic Aboriginal Ceramics in Texas," *Bulletin of the Texas Archeological Society*, 66, (1995), 195.

[52] Caddo basketry is described in John R. Swanton, *Source Materials on the History and Ethnology of the Caddo Indians*, Bureau of Ethnology Bulletin 132 (Washington, D.C.: U.S. Government Printing Office, 1942), 156–157, and in Bolton, *The Hasinais*, 121.

[53] The Spanish policy was to restrict trade with the Indians; consequently, the few Spanish metal

horses must have come from the Spaniards, but by what means? Theft or otherwise? Do they steal them directly from the Spaniards or from others who are able to procure them from the Spaniards? I do not know. The Indians have dogs[54] with straight ears and muzzles like foxes, but they do not bark like ours in France. In short, these people, although roving and vagabond, have neither customs nor ways of life that are cruel. It is true one should not trust in that. Indians are acclaimed when they are able to kill men, and there is more glory in killing men armed like us whom they consider almost as spirits. Therefore, we kept a good watch for fear of surprise. These tribes, in reality, are to be feared more than the tribes that are sedentary because these have neither a home nor a place to detain them. They go where the hunt attracts them or the fishing proves to be abundant.

To return to our journey, we stayed at that same place until February 9th when we put our boat in the river to send our bundles across. We swam the horses across, one after the other, but with some difficulty. The waters had been extremely high and had left a great amount of mud. We were fearful that some of our horses would get stuck in the mire from which it would be difficult to pull them out. As a result, we took the precaution of investigating ahead to see if the landing was firm. After we had crossed, we proceeded to camp about a half league from the crossing because the grass was quite good there, although there was not much of it. The bison had almost entirely grazed the area except for a few small spots.

On the 10th, we set off on our way. Having gone about a half league, we found burned fields and smoke all around us. This made us suppose that there were Indians in the vicinity. Consequently, La Salle, seeing that there were also bison in the area, decided it would be opportune to stop there and smoke some meat. He feared that we would not find much game afterwards among such a large number of natives who live only by hunting and who are so much more skillful in this exercise than we are. When Indians wound a bison or a deer, if they want to go to the trouble, they follow it and finally get it. This we were not able to do. Furthermore, the natives have a particular knowledge of the country and the places the bison frequent. The bison were found in rather large numbers, which was surprising, in the middle of several bands of people who roamed in these areas. In addition, the grass was burned and almost none had appeared. But these animals seem to delight in searching for the small sprigs of grass just beginning to sprout. We stayed there for two days; during that time we killed several bison which we smoked for our provisions.

Then on the 12th, about noon, we set off again on our way and proceeded about two leagues. We did not want to hurry the horses at all. We camped beside a

objects that the local Indians possessed likely were acquired through some means other than normal commerce with the Spaniards.

[54] Recent archaeological studies suggest that the ancestors of the Indians who roamed present Texas eight thousand years ago or earlier also had domesticated dogs, the ancestors of which may have made the walk over a dry Bering Sea bottom with their masters fifteen or perhaps thirty thousand years ago. See Leland C. Bement, *Hunter-Gatherer Mortuary Practices During the Central Texas Archaic* (Austin: University of Texas Press, 1994), 44, 45, 52, 56, 57. Joutel noted later that members of his party and local Indians used dogs to hunt bison (Chapter IX), and Governor De León in 1689 reported that the Indians in nearby DeWitt County were seen using dogs to carry or perhaps pull a travois loaded with bison hides. See Bolton (ed.), *Spanish Exploration in the Southwest*, 395.

river which La Salle had named the Dure on his first trip.[55] That night, the wind blowing from the north brought us a great storm with thunder and rain that compelled us to stay there on the 13th although the rain had ceased at noon. Because it was feared that the ravines would be too high, we decided to remain there until the 14th. We then continued on our way; we first crossed four or five swollen streams which fed the river where we had camped before. We found very beautiful country although the ground did not seem to me to be too fertile, being a little sandy. Nonetheless, the area was quite productive judging from the grass growing there. In fact, the soil was sand mixed with clay. There were lovely clumps of woods with small slopes and valleys from one side to the other, quite agreeable, and watered by very pretty streams with good fresh water. In other places, we saw great open fields bordered by tall woods of very beautiful trees of different kinds and where the game was abundant.

We headed about three or four leagues toward the northwest to avoid a great forest which appeared to be impassable.[56] La Salle, who had traveled through the area the previous autumn, had then encountered many difficulties. There was a hill and we wanted to see if the forest continued very far. We saw that it formed a sort of half circle around us so that there was no way to avoid it and it would be necessary to pass through it. We took advantage of a bison trail, and it led us through an area that was less dense. After having gone about a league, we camped in the woods. The wind, which had been blowing cold from the north all day, continued even stronger during the night.

On the 15th, we continued on our same route to the north-northwest and worked to get through the same forest that had obstructed our way. The trail was very poor; we had to use the same method we had used before, opening a passage with hatchets in several places. What was worse, our horses had much trouble getting through. At nine o'clock we passed by one of the encampments where La Salle had stopped the previous autumn. At noon, we arrived at a very pretty prairie where we noticed a great many tracks of men who must have passed through there the same day. We also spotted two smoke plumes that appeared to be very close, one to the northeast and the other to the southwest. We headed on about two leagues farther to the north-northeast.[57]

[55]  The Dure was likely present-day Cummins Creek, which is about fifteen to eighteen miles northeast of La Grange. Douay wrote that the "river" that the party crossed four leagues beyond the Maligne was called the Hiems, that the party turned north-northeast after crossing it, and that large Taraha, Tyakappan, and Palona Indian villages were found near the stream. Cox (ed.), *Journeys of La Salle*, I, 241. Cummins Creek is the only sizeable creek that flows into the Colorado from the east between La Grange (near the crossing) and Columbus. It runs generally north to south about four to five leagues east of the projected crossing area on the Colorado.

[56]  The great impassable forest was the Post Oak Belt, which runs from below San Antonio across northwestern Fayette County and eastward past the Brazos. On the east side of the Colorado, La Salle continued to follow from camp to camp the path he had used the previous year. The route, which also was followed generally by Spanish expeditions to East Texas in the 1690s, crossed central Fayette County along the Oakville Escarpment. The slightly elevated and hilly Oakville Escarpment is noted on the map of the United States prepared by Erwin Raisz, "Landforms of the United States," reprinted in the *Historical Atlas of the United States*.

[57]  La Salle, moving along much the same route that De León marched in 1690, followed a trail that ran

I found the land better in this region than in the former. The soil was rich and black in places and was more than 12 feet in depth. The land was marked by streams fed by very clear springs, some of which issued from rocks beneath the ground. The same rocks and stones would be very suitable for building and for making limestone.[58] Bison were not abundant in this area; the natives who had set fire to the grass had scattered them. Besides, Indians had hunted there for some time. Even though the grass was burned off, we still saw a great many deer, but they took off in the distance. There also were many turkeys and other game. The scenery was very agreeable: mottes of trees from place to place, and, in locations where the grass had been burned some time ago, it was beginning to green and looked like the wheat fields of France in April.

At five o'clock in the evening, we came upon a wide, beaten trail leading toward the east where many tracks of men, women, and horses were imprinted. A little while later, we crossed a trail going northwest. We camped beside a stream that formed a semicircle and was trimmed by thick bushes and thickets. In the crook of the stream we posted a watch for cover from that side. We were protected from the other side by a motte of trees in the shelter of which we posted sentries which we likewise did on the field side from where we could be attacked. The men were ordered to keep watch on the ravines and in the high grass through which the natives could slip. We put our horses out to graze in a small area of the prairie that the fire had spared or rather had not reached. We also saw in the vicinity many tracks of men who had passed by that very day. We concluded that there must be a village not far away and, in fact, we could hear dogs howling during the night. For that reason, we stayed on guard.

---

generally east and northeast from the Colorado crossing near modern La Grange to the Brazos crossing near modern Navasota. See the maps of the routes followed by De León, Terán, and Salinas Varona in Foster, *Spanish Expeditions into Texas*, 35, map 5; 53, map 7; and 79, map 9. Bolton described La Salle's 1687 route between the Colorado and the Brazos as follows: "Crossing the Colorado near Columbus [about ten leagues downriver from La Grange], he made his way to the Brazos, which he passed just above the mouth of the Navasota." Bolton, "The Location of La Salle's Colony on the Gulf of Mexico," 173–174. As subsequently indicated, I project that La Salle crossed the Brazos below the mouth of the Navasota.

[58] Joutel's reference to finding limestone here, about fifteen miles west of Brenham, and again a week later (on February 22) helps confirm that the line of march was along the slightly raised and fractured Oakville Escarpment, which is identified on Texas geological maps as the Oakville Sandstone. The stone formation is depicted as a narrow (usually ten- to twenty-mile) continuous belt that extends from the San Antonio River near Karnes City to the junction of the Brazos and Navasota. See the *Geologic Map of Texas* (4 parts, 1: 500,000), Bureau of Economic Geology, University of Texas at Austin (1992).

# CHAPTER IX

# March to the Brazos

n the morning of February 16, La Salle, his brother [the Abbé], and several others, numbering seven, headed in the direction from which the barking of dogs had been heard to see if there was an Indian village there. He ordered me to take charge and have everything ready to leave upon his return. He also posted a man as sentry on a small rise from where he could see the farthest. He then set off on the mission I mentioned.

They had gone only a quarter of a league when they saw some horses and after that a number of huts. The Indians had not noticed them. The village was situated on the slope of a ridge in the shelter of a motte of trees. There were about 40 huts together and several others were seen set apart on the northeast side. But neither La Salle nor the rest of the group went there. When they entered the village and the natives saw them, they came to meet them and, as was their custom, conducted them to the chief's hut where they were received in the usual manner. Skins were spread out upon which those who entered the hut were asked to sit. La Salle gave his usual order to a few of his men to stand watch and observe the Indians' demeanor and their movements.

When La Salle entered into the hut, the elders along with a number of others presented themselves to him. The gentleman let them know that we were going to the Cenis and that he came in peace everywhere, particularly with them and their friends and allies. He added that afterward we would return to our county to obtain knives and hatchets that we would then give to them along with other things they needed and that we would trade them for bison hides. They demonstrated that they were quite satisfied and content with this. La Salle presented them with some knives and glass beads, as he usually did, and, in return for these gifts, the natives would have gladly loaded our horses with dressed hides; but the gentleman told them that we were hindered enough carrying our packs but, on our return, we would trade for all the hides they had. Likewise he said that we had come upon several tribes along our way with whom we had alliances and his intention was to come in peace everywhere. He named for them the tribes we had seen,

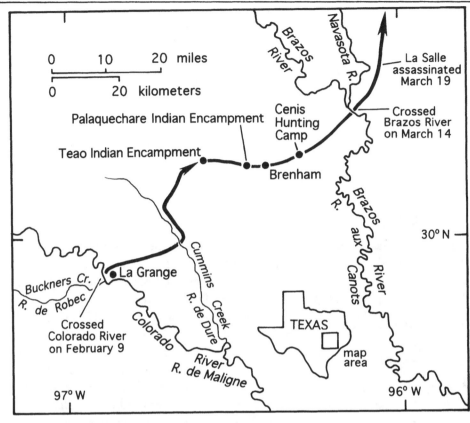

La Salle's journey between the Colorado and Brazos rivers, 1687

those whose names he had written. They also told him their name which was Teao[1] which we had not heard mentioned before. They presented food to those who entered their hut as was their custom.

Their huts were built like those we had seen before except they appeared to have more occupants. They confirmed what those before had said regarding Europeans to the southwest of us, or rather to the west. They said that several of their people had gone there and a band of them had even entered into relations with the Chouman[2] who, they indicated, were friends of these Europeans (who

[1] The Teao was a tribe not previously identified by either Joutel or Douay. Newcomb locates the Teao east of the Brazos, in an area near the Grimes and Montgomery county line in "Historic Indians of Central Texas," 13, 14. According to my projection, the Teao were encountered about fifteen miles west of Brenham near the Fayette-Washington county line, not east of the Brazos.

[2] The Chouman or Jumano from West Texas was a widely ranging tribe that Spanish diarists repeatedly encountered in the late seventeenth and early eighteenth centuries in several areas, including at the crossing of the Rio Grande, on the upper Nueces River, near the San Marcos River, and along the lower Colorado River. See entry "Jumano," in Foster, *Spanish Expeditions into Texas*, 276. While the Jumano visited the Tejas (Cenis) in the seventeenth century, it is also clear that the Tejas journeyed below the Rio Grande during the same period. See Francis B. Steck, "Forerunners of Captain De León's Expedition to Texas, 1670–1675," *Preliminary Studies of the Texas Catholic Historical Society*, 2 (Sept., 1932), 17, 18, n. 32, 19, 31.

must be Spaniards). They also told us the Choumans wanted to join with them and the Cenis to make war against a great nation called the Ayano[3] and Cannohatinno[4] who were at war with the Spaniards and stole their horses whenever they could surprise a band of them. All this, however, is from the interpretation that I could make from their signs. It is very hard to determine the correct meaning from their language and often one thing is mistaken for another. They also made us understand that 100 Spaniards were to have come to the Cenis for this war but, having learned of our march, they had gone back. This made us believe that the Spaniards were not informed of our weakness, for they would hardly have to be very intrepid as their risk was little, having much more knowledge of the country than we did.

La Salle let them know, in turn, that we were at war against these people but that we did not fear them. Finally, he tried to make them understand he had been sent by the greatest *capitaine* in the world who had directed him to treat them well and go to war with them against their enemies. This cajolery, if he made himself clear to them, was in answer to their greatest wish. The gentleman told them that for this reason he wanted to leave some people with the Cenis to learn their language so that when we returned they would serve us as interpreters. But apparently these people conceived from this some jealousy, for they indicated that the Cenis would not allow that. La Salle, who knew the Indian ways, guessed what

---

La Salle's party is apparently moving upstream along Cummins Creek in the vicinity of the prehistoric archeological site called Cummins Creek Mine. The report of the investigations made at the site suggests that the area was used by long-distance bison hunters from the southwest, perhaps from the Nueces River basin, in A.D. 600 to A.D. 750. This interpretation is significant in light of Joutel's report that the Jumano (a cosmopolitan West Texas bison-hunting tribe) were allies of the Teao. See Steven M. Kotter, et al., *Final Report of Cultural Resource Investigations at the Cummins Creek Mine, Fayette County, Texas*, Studies in Archeology 11 (Austin: Texas Archeological Research Laboratory, 1991), 154–161.

[3] The Anao [Ayano?] tribe was included in Fray Francisco Casañas de Jesús María's list of enemies of the Hasinai. See also Newcomb's analysis of Casañas's tribal list in "Historic Indians of Central Texas," 15. See Thomas N. Campbell, "Anao Indians," in Tyler, et al. (eds.), *The New Handbook of Texas*, I, 161. The Abbé Cavelier wrote that soon after crossing the Maligne (the Colorado) the French party visited the Ticapanas, and two days later the Palomas. Before reaching the Canoe (the Brazos), the Abbé said their party also met some Tipoy and Anami. Cox (ed.), *Journeys of La Salle*, I, 292, 296. In 1718, Governor Alarcón met a large tribe in Colorado County that his diarist called Aname, which was about thirty to forty miles south of the Anami village the Abbé mentioned. Francisco Céliz, *Diary of the Alarcón Expedition into Texas, 1718–1719*, ed. and trans. Fritz Leo Hoffman (Los Angeles: Quivira Society, 1935), 67.

[4] According to Douay, the Cannohatinno (Quanotinno) was a tribe that La Salle's party met near the Colorado crossing. Cox (ed.), *Journeys of La Salle*, I, 240. See a discussion of the Cannohatinno in Thomas N. Campbell, "Cantona Indians" in Tyler, et al. (eds.), *The New Handbook of Texas*, I, 962–963. Campbell reaches no conclusion as to whether the usually friendly Cantona (reported frequently by Spanish expedition diarists) and the Cannohatinno were the same people. However, Newcomb concludes that "it seems probable that the Canohatino and the Cantona were a single ethnic group," in "Historic Indians of Central Texas," 24.

I do not agree with Newcomb. It should be noted that in his *Relación*, Fray Casañas listed another tribe called Cantouhaona (possibly the Cantona) as a tribe friendly to the Tejas (Cenis) and the Canabatinu (Kanohatino, Cannohatinno) were listed as enemies of the Tejas. Fray Francisco de Jesús María Casañas, *Relación*, August 15, 1691, AGN, Historia, vol. 394, fols. 3, 12, cited in Bolton, *The Hasinais*, 58, n. 10. This dual listing suggests at least that the Cantouhaona and the Cannohatinno are different tribes. It is also significant that Joutel carefully read back to repeat and confirm his understanding of the correct name of the tribe called "Kannehouan" that he listed as living to the west of the Colorado (where the Cantona were always encountered) and that a few days later he mentions being informed of an enemy tribe of the Cenis that he identified as the Cannohatinno. Joutel apparently believed these were two different tribes.

caused them to speak in this way. They were never happy that things should be given their neighbor which they greatly desired for themselves. La Salle told them he did not believe he would be badly received in the Cenis' country; he had already been there and had promised them he would return.

An old man told us that we should find three of our men among the Cenis, indicating that they looked like us.[5] La Salle was confounded by whom they might be: they could be the men who had deserted on his last expedition, or perhaps they were three of the five he had permitted to return to the settlement, among whom had been Hurié and [Dominique] Duhaut. In their talk, the Indians often mentioned the Ebahamo [Ebahama?], and it seemed they were saying that this tribe had taken the three men in question which made it doubtful that these could be the three men of whom I spoke.

La Salle asked them for a few horses in trade for hatchets, but they indicated that they only had a few and needed them to carry meat. They seemed apprehensive that we might take them by force. In fact, they had let the horses loose except for a large roan whose back was completely flayed. These people are not skilled at making saddles, or pack saddles, or cushions, so it is difficult to protect the horses from sores when they carry a load. This did not keep La Salle from trading for the horse, injured as it was, hoping that it would heal along the way without anything to carry until it was well.

After spending some time with the Indians, La Salle returned to join us and found us ready to depart as he had ordered; we set off on our route. We had proceeded only a quarter of a league when we were stopped by a wide stream in which one of our horses became stuck in the mud and got out only with a great deal of trouble, limping from its efforts. For that reason, we lost the rest of the morning looking for an easier crossing. After having gone a league or a league and a half, we were stopped by a stream across which we had to carry all our packs, the water reaching to just below our waists. After that, we reloaded our horses which were having difficulty because the river had overflowed not long before and soaked the ground, leaving a great deal of mud. Moreover, it was in a forest where the sun seldom penetrated to dry the ground.

La Salle had sent people out to hunt and had ordered the hunters, if they killed anything, to send smoke signals, so some of us could come to bring back the meat. This they did, and, when the smoke was seen, we went to the other side of the woods and searched for the two bison that the hunters had killed. We camped there. During the night a storm blew up which lasted until the next day, and the north wind did not stop blowing. At nine o'clock in the morning, two Indians came to kill a bison very close to our sentry, but, noticing him, they stopped their hunt. We remained there to let the waters run off.

---

[5] It was not unusual for La Salle or for Spanish explorers to be informed by the local Indians about some activity that was transpiring up to a hundred miles away. The notifications were usually accurate, as when the Indian tribes in western Frio County accurately told De León in 1690 that he would find two young Frenchmen near the Colorado, which was over 150 miles to the east. See the discussion of the accuracy of reports Indians gave European expedition leaders along the trail in Foster, *Spanish Expeditions into Texas*, 37.

On the 18th, the wind rose again from the north and it was a bit cold until the sun had risen enough to warm the air. At noon, while we were continuing on our way, one of our horses fell in a ravine. It injured its shoulder which forced us to stop, but after the horse had rested a bit, we loaded it with only a part of its burden that it carried quite well. We went about a league and a half through a forest where the trail was rather good and arrived at the top of a hill. Here we found a very pretty circle of hills, some covered with woods, others half covered, and others bare. They surrounded a wide stretch of bottom land where several streams flowed into a sort of meadow forming ponds here and there, afterwards entering a large forest that was situated on our route. The country was as lovely to the eye as one might wish, crisscrossed as it was with many streams of clear, good water. It appeared that nature took pleasure in forming this country and arranging the woods from place to place. For the most part these woods were oak and walnut, the nuts of which are very good and taste the same as those in France, but the shell is harder. We found many nuts beneath the trees, and they were very good.

On the 19th, we made a circuit about three quarters of a league along the summit of these hills to get across the bottom land at a more narrow spot; but we were not able to approach it because the water was swollen and rocks, steep in places, formed the base of the hills. We found one route although it was quite difficult. Indeed, when we got to the bottom, our horses, even without their loads, sank in the boggy ground, and we had to make them run so they would not have time to bog down. As a result, we had to carry the loads until we found firm ground. This led us to the bank of a small stream; but it was deep and we could not ford it. Therefore, we felled a tree across to the other side at a place where the river was more narrow, and we passed all our packs across from hand to hand. Afterwards, we swam our horses across at another ford. At the moment that we were carrying out this maneuver, we heard dogs chasing bison.[6] Two of the bison came toward us, and we fired a few shots at them. One dropped in place; the second fled although wounded. The dogs which we heard belonged to some Indians who were not accustomed to the noise of gunshots and were uneasy about what this could be. They were not long coming in our direction to investigate. While we were busy rearranging our horses' loads, we saw two Indians slipping from tree to tree until they noticed that we had discovered them. They then stopped short not daring to advance. When they arose, we gave them a sign to approach which they did. Then we gave them a smoke while waiting for La Salle to return. The gentleman had followed some fresh bear tracks which had been seen near the river. Besides, he was glad to explore the lay of the land. Someone went to look for him. The Indians carried neither bows nor arrows. When La Salle returned, he indicated to them that he wanted peace with them and that we had no bad intentions toward anyone. They had an undressed bison hide that they showed us. The hide may have been

---

[6] This is the first reference in Joutel's account indicating that Indians used dogs to hunt bison; no Spanish expedition diarist in Texas in the late seventeenth century made such a report. In earlier hunting trips near the French settlement, Joutel tells that their dogs cut individual bison from the herd to isolate the animal for the kill.

182 from the animal that we had wounded and had fallen near where they were, or it may have been from one they themselves had killed.

La Salle told them that we were going to the Cenis. They indicated that the Cenis were their friends and that their own village was about a half day's journey from where we were. La Salle believed them to be from that [Cenis] tribe[7] because of their accent and even some words, for he had written down several expressions when he was with the Cenis, and he repeated them to these people. As our horses were loaded, we made them understand that we wanted to move on. Consequently, they pointed out a way to us by which we would come upon more open country. They even walked with us to the place where we camped that evening about a league and a half from where we had been. Then they invited us to go to their village, and, after staying with us a while, they went off. They also had their dogs which were not lacking in appetite. When they were preparing to leave, La Salle gave the Indians a few strings of beads and some other trinkets. Then they went off.

On the next day, the 20th, La Salle sent Morenger, Nika, and a few others to their village to see if there they might have a horse they wanted to trade. A short time later we saw two Indians coming, one we had met the preceding day. Upon their arrival, we let them know that some of our men had gone to their village; but they had not met them. They embraced us to show us their friendship. They told us many things, and La Salle gave them the names of some of the tribes we had found on our way. They then told us their name was Palaquechare[8] and that they were allies of the Cenis. Their chief had visited the Spaniards with the Chouman,[9]

---

[7] Campbell notes that La Salle's observation suggests that the "Palaquesson" (Palaquechare) Indians were Caddoan. See Thomas N. Campbell, "Palaquesson Indians," in Tyler, et al. (eds.), *New Handbook of Texas*, V, 21, in which the author uses the tribal name given by Douay rather than the version given by Joutel. Campbell says La Salle probably encountered the tribe between the Brazos and Trinity rivers in the vicinity of Grimes County, rather than between the Colorado and Brazos rivers in western Washington County as my reading of Joutel's account suggests.

This mixup is noted because it illustrates again that many anthropologists, ethnohistorians, biogeographers, and other specialists need to track as precisely as possible the daily line of march of expeditions to locate exactly the subject of their inquiry reported in the expedition account. Historians frequently have failed to demonstrate a sound methodology for accurately identifying expedition routes and have not correlated the names of rivers and creeks used in French and Spanish colonial documents with the modern names for the same streams. This failure may create distortions in the studies made by archaeologists and other specialists who properly look primarily to historians and geographers to provide accurate geographic information on the location of expedition routes, Indian encampments, river crossings, and sightings of plants and animals.

[8] The Library of Congress's manuscript copy of Joutel's journal has been consulted to comment on the correct spelling of the tribe's name given in Margry's version of Joutel's journal. In instances where the proper spelling of the name is in question, I have noted the difference between the spelling found in the manuscript copy and that found in Margry's version. As in other matters where there is a conflict between the Joutel account found in Margry and the Douay account found in Le Clercq, I have assumed that the more reliable rendition of the tribe's name is that found in Margry and confirmed in Joutel's manuscript. Therefore, I refer to the tribe as "Palaquechare," as found in Margry and confirmed in Joutel's manuscript, rather than "Palaquesson," as found in Douay. Cox (ed.), *Journeys of La Salle*, I, 241. As noted earlier, Campbell uses the same spelling of the tribal name as Douay.

[9] Like the Teao Indians, the Palaquechare (accompanied by the West Texas Chouman or Jumano) had visited the Spaniards, presumably in northern New Spain. Joutel's account offers further evidence of the Central Texas Indians' high degree of mobility, and how these tribes and the East Texas Caddo visited their western neighbors several hundred miles to the southwest in West Texas and northern Mexico.

a tribe having some commerce with the Spaniards who had given them horses. Regarding this matter, they told us about the same thing that the last tribe had told us. This made us certain that the Choumans had made some present to their chief to persuade him to lead us to them so that they could talk to us. Thus, the Spaniards could not have been far from this place, and these tribes must have seen them from what one could interpret, particularly La Salle, who had much more experience in this than anyone in the group and who, moreover, had always taken the trouble to put a few of their words down in writing. He also took a few of these people's words down.

The Indians stayed with us about four or five hours in the afternoon, relating all kinds of things to us only a very little of which could we understand. They indicated that they were going to war toward the east, where they pointed out smoke trails, and told us that a part of those tribes had flat heads. This gave La Salle reason to believe that these could be the tribes he had seen on his exploration and the Colbert or Mississippi River must be in that direction. This thought was confirmed when they told us that the other tribes planted corn or maize.[10]

The natives indicated that their tribe did not live in a fixed place, but that this did not keep them from also planting corn and beans when they found themselves in a favorable place where they would like to remain for some time.[11] However, I

[10] On his trip down the lower Mississippi, La Salle encountered Indians who had flat heads and raised corn. See the Sieur de Tonty's account of La Salle's 1682 discovery of the Mississippi in Cox (ed.), *Journeys of La Salle*, I, 18. See also Minet's secondhand account of the trip and his reference to the Flatheads and specifically the Corroa on the lower Mississippi in Minet, "Voyage Made from Canada Inland Going Southward during the Year 1682," 60, 60, n. 72.

Authorities agree that Nicolas de La Salle penned the most comprehensive and reliable firsthand account of La Salle's 1682 discovery expedition of the Mississippi and that Nicolas' original manuscript edited by Margry (*Decouvertes*, I, 570) has since been lost. See Patricia Galloway, "The Minet Relation: Journey by River," in Robert S. Weddle (ed.), *La Salle, the Mississippi, and the Gulf*, 17–27. Recently, a previously unknown transcript copy of Nicolas' original manuscript was discovered in the Archives of the Texas State Library and Archives Commission and is presently being prepared for publication.

The Caddo and Indian tribes residing on the east side of the lower Mississippi were frequently at war during the later part of the seventeenth century and the early eighteenth century. See Smith, *The Caddo Indians*, 116. When Joutel later visited the Caddo on the Red River, he saw a young Caddo warrior whose ears had been cut off apparently by the Chickasaw, who resided on the east side of the Mississippi. See Chapter XIV. The custom of artificially flattening the human head was not limited to natives living in the lower Mississippi region. The Huastec leaders on the northern Mexican Gulf Coast also had flattened or broad, artifically elogated heads. See Donald E. Chipman, *Nuno de Guzman and the Province of Panuco*, 28, citing Fray Barnardino de Sahagun, *Historia general de las cosas de Nueva Espana* (5 vols.; Mexico: 1938), III, 131–132.

[11] The Palaquechare seem to be geographically, and by their lifeways, on the cusp between the Caddo Indians, who lived to the northeast in established villages supported primarily by domestic horticultural production, and the other Indians to the southwest, who hunted, fished, and foraged, moving within a known region but without any settled residential location. In 1716 and again in 1721, Spanish expedition diarists also reported Caddo farmers with fields of corn and melons residing between the Brazos and the Trinity. See Foster, *Spanish Expeditions into Texas*, 119, 153.

Most authorities who write about the Indians in the area between the Trinity and the Colorado rivers declare that the native population in the area did not practice horticulture. For example, Leland W. Patterson, in giving an overview of the archeology of southeast Texas (which includes for his purposes the area between the lower Colorado and Trinity rivers), states that: "Agriculture was not practiced in Southeast Texas by aboriginal groups, even though the Caddo Indians practiced agriculture in adjacent

noticed that they were not likely to have mature corn or they would have brought some with them on leaving their village to come to see us. As the hunting was good in this area, and the fishing was too, it was not necessary to worry much about planting. Moreover, they had enemies who drove them away whenever they had the opportunity. So that when they were in a place of some abundance, they stayed there a while until everything was consumed and they had even eaten their corn if they had planted it.

One of them had a finely dressed deer skin that was white as snow. I asked him by signs if he wanted to exchange it for a few needles; I showed him two and demonstrated the purpose they served. Threading each one, I showed him how to sew. Although the needles would not be of much use to them, he made a sign to me to give him a few more. I gave him two more needles, and the skin provided a means for us to make shoes that would be much more comfortable than those we had made from freshly dressed bison hide. We had suffered sore feet from those shoes chafing us. Finally, after they had spent part of the day with us, we gave them something to eat; afterwards we gave them a few trinkets, and they returned to their village.

A little while later, Morenger arrived with the men he had taken with him and reported what he had seen to La Salle. First, they had difficulty finding the village, but they were very well received there. One of the two Indians whom we had seen the day before had come to them with a few others and then led them to the chief's hut where many other Indians awaited them. They noticed that, on the tip of a long cane, the chief held the leaf of a French book that he seemed to venerate. After they had entered the hut, they were asked to sit down upon dressed skins and were then presented with food as was the custom. Then the chief recounted several things with signs, among others, that they had been conducted to our settlement by a man like us and that they had been fired upon. This could have been when Barbier encountered some Indians at the Cane River where there were a few wounded, or perhaps it occurred on another occasion when I had ordered them fired upon. The man they had with them must have been one of our deserters. This led me to believe that these Indians must be those whom Barbier had fired upon on the Cane River because those Indians had guns and had made a sign to come to them saying: "Vene a qua, seignore." Perhaps this had been the Spaniard who had deserted at the beginning. Perhaps he had promised to bring them together with us; and, as he had not succeeded (we supposed), they could have killed him to avenge those of their band who had been wounded and others killed in that encounter. I am not certain of this account, and, moreover, it makes no difference in things.

After other discussions, Morenger gave them some small presents, as La Salle had ordered him to do. To this they responded with dressed skins, some bison,

---

North East Texas during the Late Prehistoric period." See Leland W. Patterson, "The Archeology of Southeast Texas," *Bulletin of the Texas Archeological Society*, 66 (1995), 245. Joutel's account suggests that in 1687 Cenis or tribes closely related to the Cenis planted corn and beans in Washington County west of the lower Brazos.

some deer, which were their riches. Morenger then asked the Indians for horses, but they said they had hardly any and needed them for hunting.[12] As a result, nothing was achieved and this was all the fruit of their trip. We spent the rest of the night without hearing anything.

On the 21st, we resumed our route; but the horse that had fallen in the ravine had strained its back which it did not feel at first, but it did feel it after resting and could only walk with difficulty. We therefore had to find another means of carrying its pack. In these circumstances, La Salle judged it best to make two trips although, in truth, there was much more risk in being separated as small in number as we were. However, it was thus resolved and executed.

La Salle left on the first trip and ordered me to stay with five men to take charge; they traveled about two leagues at which point they unloaded their horses and sent them back with two men to get the others. The injured horses were led; in fact, the horse that was injured last was not in condition to be useful, its back was rubbed raw almost its entire length. While the horses were returning, La Salle sent someone out to hunt. The country, the entire two leagues, was fine although at that time it was not in its full beauty as the Indians had recently set fire to the countryside, and much of it was black and covered with the ashes of burned grasses. There were small hills and valleys intersected with streams of lovely fine water.

As the wind blew from several different quarters, the bison (which have a very acute sense of smell) were alerted to the hunters' presence. They were not able to shoot because they were unable to get close. I had noticed this several times: wind was the main element to watch on this kind of hunt. We camped near a large forest where we kept a good lookout for fear of surprise.

On the 22nd, we headed north-northeast moving through this forest which was about a league and a half in breadth. It was crossed by several streams and a small river which joined lower downstream with the one we had crossed the day before and we moved away from to return to it a little upstream. The terrain is quite good in the low ground and on some of the rises, but there are other parts that are barren. We made camp on one of these rises, that is to say on a rocky crest at the foot of which passed a small river whose bed was paved with flat rocks, good for building and making limestone.[13] We made two trips, as I said before, and this day I was in the advance party. Thus, when I arrived, I had the horses unloaded and returned to get the remaining baggage. La Salle had stayed behind.

The day after I sent the horses back, Nika went hunting and I put the horses that were not sent back out to pasture. I intended to find a place where the grass was good as the horses only had the grass they could find in the open fields. The grass was not very good at that time of the year, being dry except for a few spots where fire had occurred during the autumn and the grass had sprouted again.

[12] Like the Teao and other tribes that La Salle had met west of the Colorado, the Palaquechare had a few horses. Horses were used primarily as pack animals for bison hunts rather than for personal transportation, but the tribes did not have as large a horse herd as the Cenis.

[13] La Salle's party was moving through the hilly part of central Washington County, which has an abundant supply of limestone construction material. See Darwin Spearing, *Roadside Geology of Texas* (Missoula, Mont.: Mountain Press Publishing, 1991), 80–82.

Upon my return, I saw several bison coming out of the woods near the place where we were camped. As I had my musket, I started to approach them; but then I saw two Indians coming out of the same woods after them. As I did not know how many Indians there might be, I returned to camp, where I had those who were there take arms. I then took the young Cavelier with me to investigate; and we got as far as a ravine in front of the Indians. As Nika had left alone, I feared that he might have been surprised by the two Indians I had seen. But after a closer look, I recognized that one was Nika who had met the second Indian in the field. The second was a Cenis[14] whom Nika had met in the Cenis village on the previous trip with La Salle. Upon meeting, they recognized each other. Nika had asked him to come and see La Salle.

We returned to camp where I gave the Indian tobacco to smoke and afterwards something to eat while awaiting the arrival of La Salle. I knew he would be glad to see the Cenis. The Indian indicated to us that there were several bands of Cenis hunting in this region, dispersed in various places in order to subsist better as was their custom of doing. He told us that the place where they were camped was a half league from where we were.

Nika told me how they had met. The Cenis was busy pursuing a herd of bison. Nika, having seen this from a distance, attempted to get ahead of him without being discovered, even concealing his musket down the length of his body, so that he would surprise him and not find him in a state of flight, so to speak. But when they neared and saw each other, they recognized each other and embraced in their own way.

When La Salle arrived, he was very glad to see the Indian and asked him first if he knew anything about the four men who had deserted on his last trip. The Indian told him that three were in their country, one was with the Cenis and two with the Assoni. The Indian showed his joy at seeing La Salle; we even had with us one of the horses that he had traded to us. As La Salle had promised the Indian that he would return to see him, this proved La Salle to be a man of his word. La Salle asked this Indian several questions regarding the five men to whom he had given permission to go rejoin me at the settlement; but he had not heard a word of them. This made us think they must have been surprised and killed by the Indians as no one had news of them nor of Bihorel who remained lost, having been left behind.

The Indian, after being with us for some time and as evening approached, indicated that he was leaving to return. La Salle gave him some trinkets and let him know that we were going to their [principal] village and that he wanted to live in peace with them. The Indian let us know again that they were 15 people in four or five huts and that their people were in several places around the area.

As I mentioned, when Nika had first come upon him, he was pursuing a herd of bison and, once together, they approached some cows at which the Cenis, before they were near, had shot several arrows. Nika had fired a musket at one of them and had hit and killed it from a distance. This surprised the Cenis who went

---

[14] The presence of the Cenis hunter and his encampment further confirms the use of the area between the lower Brazos and Colorado as a Cenis hunting ground.

to inspect the bullet hole which had passed through the animal. Much astonished, the Indian had remained a while without saying anything, admiring the power of our guns. After he had left, we went to collect the meat from the bison and spent the night as usual.

The next day, the 23rd, we continued along our route to the northeast; we passed the place where the Cenis were camped at a distance of about a league and a half, just as the Indian we had seen had told us. There were only three huts; they had their women and children. La Salle ordered a halt near them and sent some of the men back to collect the rest of the provisions as we had done previously. The Indians had two horses, one was a small, very pretty gray stallion. La Salle asked them if they wanted to trade, but they indicated they needed it to carry their meat, both fresh and smoked, which they smoke in the sun, cut up in small pieces. La Salle gave them presents of a few knives as thanks for giving us meat as well as a few dressed hides. They indicated that a small party of Cenis had gone to war against a nation of their enemies, but a large band of them wanted to join the fight when they returned from the hunt. They were situated in a small woods beside a stream. We stopped in this place until the return of our horses, after which we left again and made camp on the bank of a wide stream that ran at the foot of one of the highest hills that I had seen in this region. The stream formed several small waterfalls between some small crags through which it passed and swelled below where several other streams emptied into it. This one continued on to empty in turn into a valley where it appeared there was plenty of water in the autumn, winter, and spring but was dry in the summer. At least it had very little water according to La Salle who had crossed it dry the summer before. During that period, he had found the terrain quite dry, but now everything was wet with water at least a half-league in breadth.

While we were marching, we noticed that one of our large axes was missing. We only had two of them; they were used when we wanted to cut down some trees to cross a river or for some similar purpose. Therefore, this loss was considerable. Accordingly, La Salle sent Nika back to the huts we had passed to see if they might have seen it and to promise them another. He went as far as the encampment that we had made before but found nothing, and it remained lost. I neglected to say that these Indians had told Nika that if we would wait for three days, they would lead us to their [principal] village. This proposal did not keep La Salle from setting out.

On the 24th, we camped beside the marsh that I mentioned where we found a number of poor trails. We did not travel at all on the 25th because the rain completely soaked us. We were prepared for the rain by the warning taken from the moon which had a reddish circle of ill portent. We meanwhile were rather poorly encamped because the water running off the hills came into our huts in spite of our best efforts to divert it. Besides that, the ground was so soaked that we had trouble extricating ourselves and particularly the horses.

The way was very poor because of the number of depressions and slopes we found. La Salle then saw the difficulty there would be in crossing the marsh that was flooded for a distance of almost a half-league. He also saw several streams across which it would be necessary to locate fords for the horses to cross. For that reason, he decided that it was prudent to send Nika back to see if the other Indians were ready to leave. Soon thereafter, one of the Cenis whose hut Nika was going to arrived at our camp, coming from the hunt. He indicated to La Salle that they were ready to leave but that we must return to the place where we had camped before, near that high hill. Nika, upon his return, repeated the same thing to us, and, on the 27th, we broke camp to do what they told us. But because we found a very poor trail along the marsh, we headed inland toward the right where we found very lovely country crossed by many streams and covered from one end to the other with different trees and beautiful fields.

On the 28th, as we were continuing along our route, we saw Indians advancing toward us at a distance. One came to meet us and told us that he would show us the trail and a passage to cross the marsh. La Salle told him he would give him a few knives and other things if he did this. We headed for camp near this high hill that I have mentioned before as the highest in the region,[15] not that it was very high except in comparison to the entirely flat country we had experienced since we started our march. This hill is naturally fortified, escarped, and inaccessible on one side with a flat top of a little more than one and a half acres[16] of very good terrain like that of the neighboring area. This terrain would be good for everything, whether for grains or for vineyards. One can see a great distance from here and the country is most agreeable, except in the direction of the marsh, although that is not unpleasant. In this place, there would be means for making wine because of the favorable aspect of the slopes. In short, it would be hard to find a country better suited than this one to all things necessary for settlement. There are, in fact, lovely fields and prairies planted from one end to the other with beautiful groves of trees of different species, the majority of which are oak and walnut. The stone is very well suited for building, and it has the convenience of waters so that the people who would inhabit this country could consider themselves fortunate. In addition to this bounty, the country is abundant in game and there would be little difficulty in settling and establishing a community.

On the first day of March, we continued and went to meet the Indians [Cenis] who were camped on the edge of the marsh. The rain stopped us there until the 5th. During this time, we investigated a place where one could cross at a deep ravine that funneled all the waters of this valley and would carry boats part of the year. This ravine went on to empty into the large river which had been named the *Rivière aux Canots* [Canoe River] because La Salle had gone down it in canoes made of skins, as will be noted later. On the banks of this ravine are stones of good quality, suitable for building, of different thicknesses, and which could be moved easily by way of this ravine. A canoe was needed to cross the ravine because it formed a large wide river at that time of year. We started to make one, as we were

---

[15] According to government military maps, the region that La Salle's party was crossing in Washington County is hilly, with summits exceeding five hundred feet in elevation, whereas the maximum elevation in the coastal area is less than 150 feet. See U.S. Defense Mapping Agency map, JNCA–6. The route apparently passed through or near the present-day city of Brenham.

[16] Two *arpents* (Joutel's estimate) is equivalent to approximately 1.7 acres. McDermott, *Mississippi Valley French*, 15, 16.

accustomed, from bison skins. The Indians came to watch us and discover what we were doing. They did not take as many precautions when they crossed a river, for they all swam quite well[17] and did not have much baggage.

On the 6th, we decamped and crossed the ravine, but we did not make much headway beyond. We disassembled our canoe[18] and put it on the back of one of our horses as there were other rivers to cross. The 7th and 8th, we continued along our route and we found quite pretty country in places. The 9th, we did not travel at all because of the rain. The 10th, we made camp beside another stream where we felled a big tree by which we crossed. We found country that could not accommodate the water from its numerous rivers which had overflowed a short while previously, leaving the ground muddy and making progress difficult. Our horses suffered more than we did because they found almost no grass. Settlement in these places would not be advantageous, although it would be good to establish and raise silkworms because mulberry trees which thrive in cool terrain are in abundance here. These mulberry leaves are larger than ours and the trees grow much taller. The Indians use the bark for making huts as well as a kind of rope because it is leathery and fine.[19]

On the 12th, we again crossed a stream by felling two trees, one from one bank and the other from the other bank, and passed our baggage from hand to hand because, as one might well guess, this kind of bridge is not easy going. But one does the best one can. We made camp on the bank of another stream where we had to execute the same maneuver. On the 13th, we camped on the banks of the Canoe River,[20] named as I have said before, because La Salle had gone down

[17] Spanish diarists on expeditions along the Rio Grande and on Matagorda Bay also reported that Texas natives could swim well. See Captain Alonso de León's report of the local Indians swimming across the lower Rio Grande. Alonso de León, et al., *Historia de Nuevo León*, ed. Genaro García (Mexico City: Bouret, 1909), 302, and Francisco Céliz's account of the natives swimming across a wide cove in Matagorda Bay in *Diary of the Alarcón Expedition*, 64, 65. La Salle's route required the crossing of several large creeks, the largest probably New Year Creek, and might have included Jackson Creek and Doe Run Creek as well. USGS *Austin*, NH14–6.

[18] The canoe or boat was constructed in a manner that permitted it to be disassembled, perhaps by removing the internal skeletal wooden supports from the outer skin of the boat. The party was probably near New Year Creek east of Brenham.

[19] This is Joutel's first mention that Indian huts were partly constructed with mulberry tree bark. Joutel mentions the use of tree bark for construction again when he visits the Quapaw (Chapter XV).

[20] Joutel recorded that La Salle's party had traveled northeast approximately twenty-five leagues from the Colorado to the Brazos River crossing area; the straight-line measured distance on USGS *Seguin*, NH14–9, and USGS *Austin*, HY14–6, is about fifty miles or twenty-one French leagues. This direction (northeast) and distance are consistent with that reported by De León in 1690 (approximately twenty-two Spanish leagues northeast) and Salinas Varona in 1693 (twenty-three Spanish leagues northeast), supporting my contention that the river the French called the Maligne was the Colorado and the one they called the Canoe was the Brazos.

Bolton projected that La Salle crossed the Brazos "just above the mouth of the Navasota" in "The Location of La Salle's Colony on the Gulf of Mexico," 173, thus requiring the party to ford two rivers—first the larger Brazos River and then the smaller Navasota. Joutel's narrative suggests otherwise. Joutel writes that a canoe was required to cross a large stream (which Joutel called a ravine) on March 6 and was required again to cross the Canoe River on March 14; the use of the canoe was not mentioned thereafter. Again, the first and smaller stream was described as an intermittent ravine and the second was the very large Canoe River. No other crossing was reported immediately after the crossing of the Canoe River. If

it in skin canoes on his first and second trips.[21]

In that earlier crossing, La Salle had a raft built to cross the river because the river was very rapid. When they found themselves in the middle of the river, they were carried by the current for more than three leagues, unable to land, and they risked being carried away down to the sea.[22] As a result, they were separated from one another with one party on the raft and the rest on land. Now Nika, who had crossed to the other bank and had gone hunting, was bewildered, not finding them along the way according to plan. He did not know where they were and consequently did not meet up with them until a few days later. But those who had remained on land were in even more of a predicament because they could make almost no headway due to the cane which was so thick they had to cut it in places to make an opening, and they feared they would not be able to rejoin the others. Father Anastase was in this latter group.

---

La Salle's party had crossed the Brazos first and then the Navasota, they would have crossed first a larger river (the Brazos) and then the smaller Navasota. This apparently did not occur. I therefore conclude from Joutel's account that the French crossed the Canoe (or Brazos) a short distance below the junction of the Brazos and the Navasota after they had crossed several sizeable tributary creeks of the Brazos, as I have tried to identify above.

[21] Joutel's statement that La Salle had gone down the Canoe (or Brazos River) "on his first and second trips" is unclear unless Joutel was stating that La Salle first visited the Brazos on his trip eastward in the fall of 1685 and then again in 1686. In Douay's account, the Canoe River is called the Rivière des Malheurs, a name intended to reflect the disaster that La Salle narrowly averted. Cox (ed.), *Journeys of La Salle*, I, 229.

[22] Joutel's comment that La Salle's party on the Canoe River risked being carried to the "sea," meaning the present-day Gulf of Mexico, confirms that the river the French called the Canoe was the lower Brazos, which drains directly into the nearby gulf, rather than the upper Trinity, which is over 140 miles north of the gulf.

# CHAPTER X

# Assassination of La Salle[1]

To return to our journey, it was a matter of repairing our canoe to cross the Canoe River which was quite large and wider than the Maligne.[2] Its current was not as agreeable, being rougher; however, it appeared much more navigable. It must be very wide near its mouth in view of the number of other rivers that empty into it. We crossed the river on the 14th [of March] and made camp on the other side where we met the Indians who we had left after we had crossed the marsh and the big ravine. They had remained behind and had taken another route. Some others came to see us who were of the same tribe [Cenis]. In the evening, after they visited for some time, they returned to join their people who were camped about a half-league away; but those who had escorted us camped nearby.

Hunting was beginning to fail because this was along the route used by the Indians moving to and from their village. On the 15th, we continued on our way with our Indians. We found the country more agreeable than any we had seen

---

[1] Margry made numerous editorial changes in this chapter to clarify or to heighten the drama while remaining faithful to Joutel's account. Margry also deleted Joutel's critical references to the "other author" (Douay's account written by Le Clercq).

[2] Joutel's comparison of the size of the Canoe (the lower Brazos) with the Maligne (the lower Colorado) is very helpful in confirming the identity of the two rivers. Although both are recognized as large Texas rivers, the Brazos (or Canoe), at the point where La Salle crossed (below the junction with the Navasota River), is a substantially larger river than the Colorado (or Maligne) at La Grange. It is also likely that the Brazos (or Canoe) would appear to Joutel to be wider and more navigable than the Colorado (or Maligne). Moreover, both the lower Colorado at La Grange and the lower Brazos near Navasota are considerably larger than the upper Trinity (or Cenis) River at the crossing into central Houston County. The relative size and drainage areas serviced by the lower Colorado, the lower Brazos, and the upper Trinity are shown in "Major river basins in Region 3," in Hester, et al., *From the Gulf to the Rio Grande*, 11, fig. 9. It is extremely unlikely that the upper Trinity would appear to Joutel to be wider and more navigable than the lower Brazos, as suggested by those who argue that the Canoe River was the Trinity and that La Salle was shot near the Trinity.

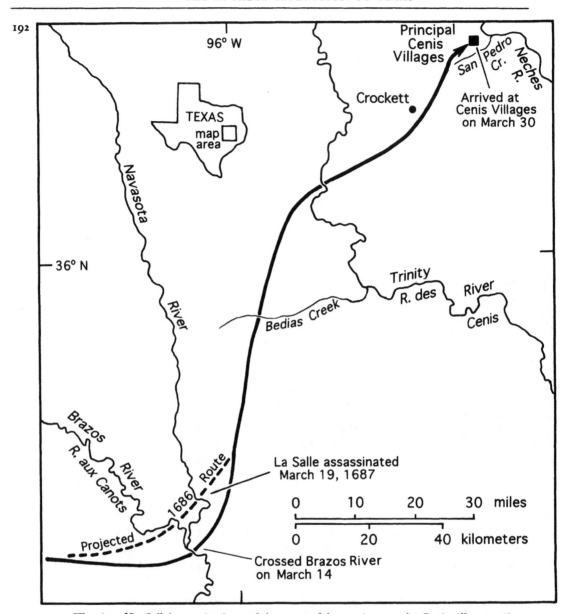

The site of La Salle's assassination and the route of the survivors to the Cenis villages, 1687

before. The land was good although sandy; but it did not seem to be as productive judging from the grass growing there.

We did not go far that day for the following reasons. When La Salle was returning from the Cenis [on his 1686 trip], he was loaded with more corn and beans than his horses could carry. Therefore, he had decided to hide some of it.[3] This he did for two reasons: in the first place, he had difficulty carrying it all. In the second place, he knew there was no hunting between here and the Cenis' village except for turkeys; and now, on the present trip, there would be no reliable hunting. Besides that, we did not have much shot. That is why, seeing that we did not have enough provisions to undertake the trip to the Cenis' village, La Salle decided to send some men to look for the corn that was left in his cache which was about two or three leagues from the place where we were camped. He ordered seven or eight, including [Pierre] Duhaut, his surgeon, the Chaouanon [the Shawnee Nika], Hiems, Tessier, his personal servant, Saget, and others. A few of the Indians who had come with us accompanied them. But when they reached the place, they found all the corn spoiled and rotten. Either the hiding place had been opened, or perhaps it was not well made, but water had penetrated inside. So they prepared to return.

On the return, the Shawnee saw two bison,[4] went after them, and killed them. After that, they designated a man to go back to inform La Salle, so that if he wanted the meat smoked, he could send some horses to carry it. The person delegated was the gentleman's servant [Saget]. He arrived in the evening with one of the Indians who had gone with them. La Salle waited for the next day to send back some men and ordered his nephew, Morenger, to go there with Marle, Mounier [Pierre Meunier?],[5] and his servant to guide them. They were to send a horse back with some of the fresh meat as soon as they arrived, and they should dry the rest in the meantime.

They left on the 17th, but the day passed without hearing any news of them. On the 18th, La Salle appeared to be quite worried when no one returned; he was apprehensive that some misfortune had happened to them. Perhaps they had been surprised by Indians, or they had lost their way. Not knowing what to think, when

[3] La Salle hid a cache of corn at the ford of the Brazos near the camp he used in the fall of 1686, as he had near the Colorado crossing. The ford and campsite that he used in 1686 apparently was above the ford that he used in 1687 and may have been at the customary ford used in the drier months, which De León, Terán, and Salinas Varona used later. See Foster, *Spanish Expeditions into Texas*, 35, map 5; 53, map 7; 79, map 9. It appears that in 1687 La Salle's party crossed five to ten miles south of the city of Navasota.

[4] Joutel's report that La Salle's party killed two bison east of the Canoe River argues against any serious consideration that the Canoe River was the Trinity, as assumed by Parkman, Wood, Weddle, and several other contemporary historians, anthropologists, and archeologists. There was no report of bison east of the Trinity by any seventeenth- or eighteenth-century Spanish expedition diarist. See the entry "Bison or American Buffalo (cíbolo)" in Foster, *Spanish Expeditions into Texas*, 236, 237. Fray Gaspar José de Solís wrote specifically on the issue, stating that some bison were near the Navasota (as Nika discovered) but none were in the woods east of the Trinity. Margaret K. Kress (trans.), "Diary of a Visit of Inspection of the Texas Missions Made by Fray Gaspar José de Solís in the Year 1767–68," *Southwestern Historical Quarterly*, 35 (July, 1931), 59, 60.

[5] "Mounier" was probably Pierre Meunier, who later testified that La Salle was killed near the Brazos; see Appendix A. Here Margry mistakes the manuscript spelling "Mounier" for "Monnier."

evening came, he decided himself to go investigate. As he did not know the exact place, but the Indians who were camped nearby had gone to the location and returned with Saget, La Salle sent word to them that, if they would lead him to the place, he would give them a hatchet. One agreed to go. These people have a much better sense than we do for finding trails and the places that they have been. They are trained for this from their earliest years, the hunt being one of their most important occupations. The Indian promised to lead La Salle, and the gentleman prepared himself for departure the next morning. He ordered me to stand ready to leave with him though preparations were easy to make as we were on the march everyday.

That evening, when we were talking about what could have happened to those who had left, it seemed that La Salle had a premonition of what was to happen. He asked me if I had heard of the men contriving something among themselves or if I had noticed that they had some evil plot. I said that I had not heard anything except in certain encounters when they complained, argumentative as they often were, but that I knew nothing else. Furthermore, as they were convinced that I would defend his interests, they would not have told me if they had some wicked design. The rest of the evening was passed in much disquiet.

Finally, morning came and it was a matter of leaving. This was the 19th, and although La Salle had first decided that I should go with him, he changed his mind in the morning because there would be no one to remain on watch at that camp. He then told Father Anastase to accompany him. After that he told me to give him my musket because it was the best one of our party; I gave it to him with my pistol. Thus, three of them left: La Salle, Father Anastase, and the Indian guide. In leaving the gentleman ordered me to take care of everything and to be sure, from time to time, to make smoke signals on a small rise near our camp, so that if they were lost, that would serve to set them straight and direct them toward the smoke. So they departed. Only five of us remained there[6] which was not much defense in that one was the small son of Talon [Pierre], and another [Pierre Barthélemy?] who was good for little more. In fact, there were only the Abbé, the young Cavelier, and me.

As La Salle, on leaving, had directed me to make smoke signals from hour to hour by setting fire to the small area of dry grass on a rise that would flare for a while, I carried out this maneuver during the day. But toward evening I was greatly surprised, as I was going to the rise, to see one of the men approaching who had left with the first group to collect the corn. When we met, I saw that he was quite stupefied and rather wandering. On approaching me, he began to tell me that there was much news and that a mishap had occurred. I asked him what. He told me that La Salle was dead and so was Morenger, and two others, the Indian [Nika], and the gentleman's servant [Saget].

At this news I stopped, completely disconcerted, not knowing what to say with the knowledge that they were assassinated. The person who brought me this ugly

[6] Joutel's identification of the five members of La Salle's party who remained at base camp confirms that Pierre Meunier was at the hunting camp where La Salle was killed. Weddle agrees that Meunier "witnessed events surrounding the murders that culminated in the death of La Salle." See Weddle, "Meunier, Pierre," 649.

news added that the murderers had at first sworn my death as well. I had no trouble believing that because, as I said before, I had always acted in the interests of La Salle. Having command, it is difficult to satisfy everyone and to prevent there being a few malcontents.[7] At this juncture, I was greatly confounded as to what part I should take, if I should go off into the forest where Providence and God would lead me. But, by good fortune or ill, I did not have a musket, having taken only a pistol, and I had neither powder nor shot except that in my horn. In no matter what direction I should turn, my life was at great risk. Actually, the man who brought word assured me that they had changed their minds and had agreed not to commit any more murder unless they met resistance and I took the defense.

The man who brought me this news was L'Archevêque,[8] a native of the city of Bayonne, whom Duhaut had taken on at Petit Goave where he was enlisted. Although he told me that no harm would come to me, I trusted nothing of the kind. But as I was in no condition to go very far without either arms or powder, as I said, I abandoned myself to Providence and to all that might happen. So I returned to camp where I found that these miserable murderers had taken possession of all the clothes and effects of La Salle and even those that were personally mine. They also had seized all the arms for themselves.

When I arrived, the first words addressed to me by Duhaut, who was the one who had killed La Salle, were that each one commands in his turn to which I replied nothing. In a corner I saw the Abbé, praying to God, and on the other side was Father Anastase who did not dare to approach me, nor did I dare go toward him until I had determined the assassins' plans. They were like raging madmen, at once very agitated as well as confused. I remained for some time without speaking or moving, so to speak, for I did not dare address either the Abbé or Father Anastase for fear of giving some umbrage to our enemies.

As they had put the meat on to cook when they arrived, by evening, it was a matter of having supper; they distributed the meat as they saw fit. They said that formerly someone else had given them their portion but that from now on they would give out portions. Without doubt, they wanted to compel me to say something so as to have cause to bring about some trouble. But I managed, no matter what, to keep my mouth closed. When night had come and there was the question of standing watch, they were perplexed because they could not do it alone. Then they told the Abbé, Father Anastase, me, and those who were not a part of their conspiracy that we had only to stand guard as usual and that it was not necessary to think about what had happened. They said that it was a deed done, that a stroke of despair had driven them to it, that they regretted it, and that they wished no more of the same for anyone else.

The Abbé took his turn to speak and told them that they had killed themselves in killing La Salle, as only he could get us out of this country, and that there was not much likelihood that we would be able to escape. Finally, after many excuses

---

[7] Here we have followed the manuscript more closely than Margry.

[8] L'Archevêque is described as being a paid assistant or servant of Duhaut. Parkman, *La Salle and the Discovery of the Great West*, 421. The Frenchman's fascinating career is described in Weddle, *The French Thorn*, 38, 70, 77, 105.

196    were alleged on one side or the other, they gave us our arms. One of them had taken my musket because it was better than the others; he had grabbed it from La Salle's hands. He had also laid hold of my pack, linen as well as knives, beads, necklaces, and other similar things. But he returned these things to me afterwards.

Accordingly, we stood watch during which time the Abbé recounted to me the way they had arrived and how they had entered La Salle's camp in a fury and seized everything. The Abbé, having learned then of the death of his brother, asked that, if they wanted to do the same to him, they give him a little time to make his peace with God. They replied that they would help him however they could, as they had done until that time, and that he must forget what was done. They added that they were sorry for it but there was no remedy for it now. It was Morenger, they said, who had caused these misfortunes and that he had forced them to commit this ugly deed. The Abbé told them he forgave them although he had every reason for resentment, having lost his brother and his nephew.

During the night, we consulted about what we could do. I made it clear to him that I would not abandon him, or Father Anastase, or the young Cavelier, his nephew. We promised to not abandon each other, except in death no matter what happened, until we reached a secure place. We resolved to do the best we could to get ourselves away from these miserable murderers, meanwhile agreeing to seldom speak to each other in their presence so as to give them no cause for distrust or suspicion. We spent the time thus until the next day without sleep even tempting me, for I did not have confidence in their promises after such an enormous act.

When day had come [March 20], they considered which route they should take, that is to say, if they should return to the settlement or push onward. They decided to move straight on to the villages[9] of the Cenis. To that end, they asked the Indians if they would continue with us for the remaining 40 leagues, more or less, of travel,[10] promising them some knives if they would show us the way. They accepted. We got under way, but, after going about a league and a half, the Indians stopped and, pretending that they had forgotten something, retraced their steps.

[9]   The word "villages," found in the manuscript but not in Margry, refers to the principal Cenis villages along San Pedro Creek in eastern Houston County. Pierre Talon's comment that La Salle was killed about six leagues from the Cenis village refers to the Cenis village or hunting camp near the Canoe (Brazos) River, not the main Cenis villages in eastern Houston County. See Pierre and Jean-Baptiste Talon, "Voyage to the Mississippi through the Gulf of Mexico," 234. This interpretation is clarified in the following sentences in Margry's text, which correctly note that Joutel's party was forty leagues south of the principal Cenis villages, and the party traveled eleven days, from March 20 to March 31 to cover the forty-league distance.

[10]   Joutel's comment that the French party's camp was located approximately forty leagues from the principal Cenis villages is very helpful in confirming their location. I project the French camp to be a few leagues east of the modern-day city of Navasota, which is about a hundred miles (or approximately forty-one French leagues) from the headwaters of San Pedro Creek in Houston County, where the principal villages of the Cenis were. See USGS *Austin*, NH14–6; USGS *Beaumont*, NH15–4; and USGS *Palestine*, NH15–1. Although Douay did not maintain a written daily record of the trip, the priest did prepare an estimate of the distance covered and the general direction followed on major segments of the 1687 trip; he estimated that the party marched about one hundred leagues from the Bay to the Cenis—"sixty leagues north-northeast" (to the Brazos?) and "forty east-northeast to the Cenis." Cox (ed.), *Journeys of La Salle*, 255. These estimates are generally consistent with Joutel's specific daily record and the distances measured on USGS maps.

They made signs to us that we only had to continue along the way and that they would meet up with us.

The Indians saw that we were missing three men in addition to La Salle, and the one who had led them had seen one of the dead men. They knew how many we were because they had traveled with us for some time, and they also saw that Nika was missing. I believed that it was because of this that they returned to see what could have happened. Now that could only produce a bad end. When I pictured the Indians thus, I feared that they might conceive some vicious design against us and plan to stay behind waiting for the opportunity to surprise us. Meanwhile, as there were neither means nor strength to gain the upper hand, we continued our route and traveled straight north[11] to reach a small trail that led to the Cenis Indian village that we were searching for. By this pathway all the Indians come and go in this region,[12] either because the route was better or otherwise.

We found this to be rather lovely country, beautiful fields and woods from place to place. We continued for about five leagues and made camp on the edge of a motte of trees. When we arrived there, one of our people set the grass on fire which spread in short time, so we could see the exposed country for a great distance. Just as we were going to move the horses, so that they could graze more at ease and find the best grass (having nothing else to give them), we saw an Indian coming toward us. When he joined us, he made us understand that he had another man and two women with him about a half-league from there. The sight of the fire had made him come to see what it was. They were of the Cenis tribe and were returning to their village. We let the Indian know that we too were going there and that, if he would lead us, we would give him a few knives and beads. He showed us by signs that he was satisfied and that he was going to tell his comrade to come with their women. Indeed, that evening they came and slept near us, but we spent the night keeping a close watch.

That night L'Archevêque recounted to me the details of La Salle's death. As I had not had the time until then to speak to anyone, I still did not know by what cruel stratagem he was overcome. I will report here the facts just as they were told

[11] From the camp near the Navasota, Joutel's party traveled "straight north" through present Grimes County toward the Trinity crossing in Houston County, where the party turned east. This is the same direction and the general route followed by De León in 1690 and Salinas in 1693 from the Brazos crossing north to the ford on the Trinity and then east to the principal Cenis villages. If the Canoe River had been the Trinity, as suggested by some authors, the party would have traveled east, not due north, and only twelve leagues, not forty, to find the principal Cenis villages.

[12] Joutel here confirms that there was but one common Indian pathway from the Cenis main village (in present eastern Houston County) to the bison hunting areas near the lower Brazos. The Cenis trail extended to the lower Colorado, as Joutel and diarists on Spanish expeditions in the late seventeenth century indicated.

Recent archeological studies indicate that some trade and cultural connections apparently extended from East Texas and central Arkansas to the lower Brazos River area as early as 1500 B.C. See the discussion of mortuary practices and the social complexity of natives in the lower Brazos and Colorado River valleys in the Middle Archaic (3000 B.C.–1500 B.C.) and the Late Archaic (1500 B.C.–A.D. 100) in Patterson, "The Archeology of Southeast Texas," 247–248, citing among other sources, Grant D. Hall, *Allens Creek: A Study in the Cultural Prehistory of the Lower Brazos River Valley, Texas*, Research Report 61 (Austin: Texas Archeological Survey, 1981).

to me by L'Archevêque. You will remember that I spoke before of the two bison that Nika had killed and someone had come to advise La Salle who had then sent Morenger and the others. After the men had worked to smoke the bison meat so that when someone arrived they would only have to load it on the horses to take away, they boiled the marrowbone and other animal perishable parts not suitable to keep to eat among themselves as was the custom. But when Morenger arrived at the place, he seized the meat, including the perishable parts, telling them that he intended to take charge of the meat from then on and they would not eat it as they had done in the past. He took away all the meat they had, treating them in a brusque manner. This aroused their indignation against him. Moreover for a long time, they had been angry with the man because he had mistreated some people, even the surgeon to whom he owed his life for the diligence with which the surgeon had been devoted to him when he had been wounded near the coast. The surgeon, feeling mistreated after many offers of service and friendship, developed a hatred for him. As for Duhaut, something else had happened, namely: when he had become lost on the first trip, he blamed Morenger because he had not waited for him, and he still held a grudge for this. The old grievances against Morenger had risen up in their hearts with this last offense, an evil spirit seized them, and incited them to perform this wretched deed. Duhaut declared that he wished to suffer no longer and that it was necessary to avenge himself.

Five of them then planned together; they were Duhaut, Liotot (the surgeon), Hiems, Tessier (the former master of the *Belle*), and L'Archevêque (the one who came to warn me). After deliberating, they resolved to murder Morenger. They even gave rise to this suspicion by the discussions they held. For that evening after supper, when Morenger only gave them very little meat and reserved for himself what there was, they began to say they were going to make some *casse-têtes* which are clubs of a kind that the Indians make and use in their surprise attacks to split the heads of those who have the misfortune to fall into their hands. The plotters then cut some pieces of wood just as they had planned, and when Morenger was asleep along with Nika and La Salle's servant, Saget, these wretches, seeing their chance, thought only of carrying out their detestable plan. As they were the only ones awake, they hesitated as to how they should proceed. But the surgeon, more cruel than the others, took an ax, stood up, and began with Morenger. He struck him several times on the head; not many are necessary to kill a man. Afterwards, he went after Saget and then the unfortunate Nika who could not help what had occurred between them. Thus, this wretch massacred all three of them in a few instants, without their having time to say one word. Only Morenger, not immediately dead, sat up, without speaking however; and then the murderers forced Marle to finish him even though he was not in their conspiracy.

While the surgeon was executing his plan, the others were in ambush, arms in hand, in the event someone awakened and stood up to defend himself. The murder was committed but that was not all. They had achieved nothing yet because they had no explanation for La Salle. For that reason, they resolved to get rid of him, seeing plainly that they could not cover up their crime with any pretext. Consequently, they decided that they must rejoin us and that, upon their arrival, they would club us both, La Salle and me, and afterwards they would bring the others under control. But because it had rained the previous days, the stream along the way was too high to ford and take their meat across, so they needed to make a kind of raft which delayed the execution of their plans. As a result, La Salle left camp to go in search of them.

Now this is how Father Anastase recounted to me the assassination of La Salle. As I mentioned, the two of them [La Salle and Anastase] had left with an Indian as a guide. When they came near the place without seeing anyone, La Salle was troubled when he saw a large flock of eagles[13] in the air. This sight caused him to believe that those he was seeking were not far away. He then fired a shot so that, if they were nearby, they could hear it and respond. That assured his misfortune because the shot warned the assassins who prepared themselves.

Having heard the shot, they surmised that La Salle must be coming to meet them; they then prepared themselves to take him by surprise. Duhaut crossed the river with L'Archevêque, and when Duhaut caught sight of La Salle in the distance coming straight to them, he hid in the tall grass to wait for the gentleman at the crossing. La Salle, who was expecting nothing, had not even reloaded his musket after he fired it. La Salle first saw L'Archevêque, who appeared a little farther on, and inquired where Morenger was. L'Archevêque replied that he had drifted away. Then a shot was fired by Duhaut who was quite close by, hidden in the deep grass. The shot hit La Salle in the head; he fell dead in place, without uttering a word. This occurred to the great astonishment of Father Anastase who was close to him and thought he would meet with the same. He did not know what to do, go forward or flee. But Duhaut came out, shouting to him that he had nothing to fear, that no one wished him any harm. A stroke of despair had compelled him to do this, he said, and for a long time he had wanted to avenge himself on Morenger who had tried to lose him and who had caused, in part, the loss and death of his brother and several other situations. The Father was very ill at ease.

When the assassins were gathered, they plundered the [body of] Sieur de La Salle as a final cruelty, stripping him of even his shirt. The surgeon particularly treated him with derision, naked as he was, calling him great Pasha. After despoiling him, they dragged his body into the brush where they left it to the discretion of wolves and other wild animals. After they had satisfied their rage, they started back again to join us where they planned to get rid of me if I resisted them. As they wanted to bring their meat along, they offered the Indians some knives to help them cross the stream and they made their way back to us.

To return to our journey, on the 21st, we broke camp and headed out until about noon when the rain forced us to stop for two days beside a large river where one of the [Cenis] Indians who had been with us before arrived with his wife and two horses. We spent the night and the following day there during which sad thoughts passed through my mind.[14] In fact, it was difficult not to be fearful of this

---

[13] In his personal account, Douay reported that the murder scene was about two to four leagues from base camp. Cox (ed.), *Journeys of La Salle*, I, 242–243. As Joutel earlier referred to black and turkey vultures as eagles, this reference to eagles may be to vultures or buzzards. See Chapter VI.

[14] Margry inserted this sentence, which is not found in the manuscript.

kind of people whom we could not think of without great horror. When I reflected upon the cruelty with which they had acted and the danger we were in, I wanted to seek revenge for the evil that they had committed. This would have been
quite easy when they were asleep, but the Abbé deterred us, saying that we must
leave vengeance to God Who reserved it to Himself. And the Abbé had more reason for revenge than I, having lost his brother and his nephew. The young Cavelier
had as much desire as I did to repay the murderers in kind, and the occasion for
this often proved advantageous. But, as the Abbé always dissuaded us, these
notions passed.

On the 23rd, we continued on our route northeast and came to the small trail
I have spoken of, the one that led to the Cenis' [main] village. We made camp
beside a large stream[15] which gave us trouble in crossing because it had overflowed;
and there was no wood nearby suitable for making a raft. Also, we did not have
enough skins to make a canoe, besides that would take too long. The Indians saved
us from our predicament by offering to carry our baggage in exchange for some
knives. This they did. I have mentioned before that they use dried skins which they
fold up at the corners with straps through which they place branches to make them
more sturdy. Then they fill them with whatever they can hold and push them in
front of them while swimming. This was how they took all of our baggage across.

Those of us who knew how to swim crossed to the other bank. But a number
of our company did not know how to swim, and I was among that number. We
were somewhat at a loss when one of the Indians gave me a sign to go get a nearly
dry log which he had seen nearby, and when we had carried it to the water, he told
me to put it in. Then, fastening a strap on each end, he made us understand that
we should hold on to the log with one arm and try to swim with the other arm and
our feet. The Abbé got in the water first and I after him. Father Anastase also got
in, then the Indians swam along each supporting the log with one arm. However,
Father Anastase nearly made us sink because he did not ease up at all; he simply
weighed down on the log. While trying to swim, I stretched out and kicked with
my feet, and I accidentally hit the Father in the stomach. At that moment he
thought he was lost and, I assure you, he invoked the patron saint of his order, St.
Francis, with all his heart. I could not keep from laughing although I could see I
was in peril of drowning. But the Indians on the other side saw all this and came to
our help and got us across to the other bank.

Still there were others to get across including the young Cavelier, the young
Talon boy, and Tessier. We made the Indians understand that they must go help
them, but because they had become disgusted by the last trip, they did not want to
return again. This distressed us greatly; however, patience was necessary. What
was unfortunate was that a rather cold wind was blowing from the north and those
on the other side had sent their clothes ahead and only had their shirts.
Consequently, they had trouble keeping themselves from trembling both from
cold and from fear.[16] But after we begged the Indians and promised them more

[15] By the evening of March 23, Joutel's party had reached the area near modern Bedias Creek.

[16] This sentence has been rewritten as it appears in the manuscript. The Margry revision mistakenly
attributes the cause for their fear to "the cruelty of the Indians in threatening to leave them behind."

beads and other trinkets, they decided to go back. This time they had no intention of taking the log, remembering it had been such trouble. They took one of their skins in which they had carried the clothes across, and they put the young Cavelier with the Talon boy in it. As neither one was very big, they set them together and carried them across just as they had managed with the clothes. As for Tessier, who knew how to swim a little, he risked it and swam over. We rejoiced to find ourselves together again. Our scheme, however, had not been very prudent, for, in separating ourselves from each other, we had in effect abandoned ourselves to the Indians who, had they been ill-intentioned, could have easily gotten rid of us to obtain our booty. We camped the night at that place. The land in that region did not seem very good to me: it flooded occasionally and left sand and mud on the ground. Nevertheless, there were beautiful trees.

On the 24th, we continued our route; that day we crossed nasty swampy country which our horses had much difficulty pulling themselves through. On the 27th and 28th, we kept following the small path I have mentioned which led to the Cenis' village although we often lost the trail because, as it was not constantly traveled, it was not beaten down; but we found it more or less by following the known direction which was northeast.[17] But the Indians, who have a better sense than we have once they have passed through an area, remembered it. That was why we had no trouble when they were with us.

We crossed two wide ravines which caused us uneasiness because of their great depth and also because they had been obstructed with trees when La Salle had crossed them on this last trip.[18] Fortunately, we found them dry. We made camp on the banks of a rather big river that was called the Cenis River[19] although it was about 10 or 12 leagues distant from there [the Cenis' main village].[20] We had hoped to ford [on foot?] it in spite of its width as this is how they had crossed it on the last trip.[21] But now the water was high, and there was no way to cross it

---

[17] On March 27 and 28, Joutel's party continued traveling northeast, probably near the Madison-Leon County line.

[18] Some member of Joutel's party, perhaps Father Douay, must have told Joutel that the Cenis guides were leading them along the same route that La Salle had used the previous year. The two ravines were likely Boggy and Keechi creeks, about ten to twelve miles southeast of Centerville.

[19] This is the Trinity River. Early eighteenth-century French maps identify the Trinity River as *Rivière des Cenis*. See the discussion of early eighteenth-century maps showing Joutel's route in Delanglez (ed.), *The Journal of Jean Cavelier*, 171–172. The Jumano referred to the Trinity River as the River of the Tejas. See Bolton (ed.), *Spanish Exploration in the Southwest*, 339.

[20] The Trinity River, at the traditional crossing used by Salinas and later Spanish expedition leaders, was about twelve leagues from the principal Cenis villages (near San Pedro Creek in eastern Houston County as Joutel accurately noted). On June 7, 1693, Salinas crossed the Trinity River at 8 a.m. and proceeded that day and the next to the Spanish mission located near the principal Cenis (Tejas) village. Salinas traveled about twelve Spanish leagues between the Trinity and the Indian village. Foster and Jackson (eds.) and Brierley (trans.), "The 1693 Expedition of Gregorio de Salinas Varona," 299.

[21] The traditional crossing of the Trinity in central Leon County near the Texas Highway 7 bridge was at a low water ford that had a hard bottom across the full width of the river. One of the best descriptions of the ford is given by Nicolás de Lafora, who wrote in 1767, "We crossed the Trinidad River on a stone ledge which extended across its entire width." Kinnaird (ed. and trans.), *The Frontiers of New Spain*, 165. The following year the Padre José Gaspar de Solís wrote that he also waded across the Trinity on a bed of fine flint. Kress (trans.), "Diary of a Visit of Inspection of the Texas Missions," 59.

without boats. For that reason, we had to wait and build a canoe with a few bison skins we had. We began work on the canoe the 28th.

The Indians, seeing us stopped, crossed the river and proceeded ahead. The country was beautiful in this region along the river although the soil did not appear to me to be the best, being sandy in places. But it was quite agreeable because of the many trees of several species. There was one tree that La Salle had called a *Copal* which is a beautiful tree with leaves similar to those of the maple and the linden. A gum extrudes from it like a pine.[22] This tree gives off a very pleasant odor and so do its leaves. It grows very straight, but the wood is not very hard. We saw a tree in that place where La Salle had cut the King's arms[23] and a few other trees on which individuals had made crosses, all carved into the bark.

[22] The description of the shape of the leaves, the straight trunk, and the soft wood suggests the American sweetgum (*Liquidambar styraciflua*). Vines, *Trees of the Southwest*, 325. It should be noted that the reference to the extrusion of gum appears in the manuscript but Margry omitted it. According to a recent preliminary archeological report on the plant remains in neighboring Cherokee County, evidence of sweetgum was found in the area dating to prehistoric times. Richard I. Ford, "Appendix I: Preliminary Report on the Plant Remains from the George C. Davis Site, Cherokee County, Texas 1968–1970 Excavations," in *Bulletin of the Texas Archeological Association*, 68 (1997), 104–105.

[23] According to Joutel, La Salle had identified the location where he crossed the modern Trinity River by marking a tree, as he had identified the Colorado and Brazos crossings by leaving caches of food.

CHAPTER XI

# The French among
# the Cenis

 e found no more bison after leaving the place where the disaster occurred, but there were plenty of turkeys.[1] If we had had plenty of lead, we could have killed enough turkeys, but we were short of it. Of course, we had two or three thousand bullets, but we had to cut them and it was dangerous to damage the barrels of our muskets. That meant we could not shoot much, and besides, we did not know if we might have to use these bullets in an attack by a band of Indians or some Spaniards whom several tribes had mentioned. Moreover, we did not have adequate food supplies, and we were not assured of finding any in the [Cenis] village.

Therefore, although it was a little late to think of this precaution (it should have been taken right after the calamity), we held counsel, and it was decided to go see if there was any corn in this village and if the Indians would like to trade with us. For this effort, four men from the company were selected, and I was included among them. The second man was Hiems, the buccaneer whom La Salle had enlisted at Petit Goave as a gunner; the third man was the surgeon Liotot, and the fourth was Tessier, the former master of the frigate. All three of them were conspirators, authors of or accomplices in the assassination of La Salle. When this news was announced, I was not very happy and would have preferred to withdraw, but it was necessary, by whatever means, to keep my feelings secret and to not show the hatred I felt because they were, so to speak, the masters. Duhaut had divided all the belongings, saying that the largest portion belonged to him. In truth, all the

---

[1] Spanish expedition diarists reported seeing few bison after crossing the lower Brazos but found numerous turkey. See entries "Bison or American Buffalo (cíbolo)" and "Turkey" in Foster, *Spanish Expeditions into Texas*, 236–237, 244–245. Fray Francisco Casañas wrote that the Tejas (Cenis) customarily traveled four days from their main villages west of the Neches River to find bison. Mattie Austin Hatcher (ed. and trans.), "Descriptions of the Tejas or Asinai Indians, 1691–1722," *Southwestern Historical Quarterly*, 30 (Jan., 1926), 211.

hatchets and knives were his because La Salle had put everything he had on board the *Belle* that had run aground and had lost all his personal belongings.

I was very ill at ease being forced to leave the Abbé and Father Anastase (with whom I had tried to console myself) and to find myself with three wretches whom I distrusted after the crime they had committed. I conferred with the Abbé and Father Anastase about what I should do. We concluded that there was no way to refuse, for that would cause an ill effect; thus I abandoned myself to Providence, as I had done before, putting everything in God's hands. After this, the matter resolved, the canoe was completed and two horses were swum across; we were given a dozen and a half hatchets and three or four dozen knives, a number of beads, and some other trinkets that Duhaut put in my hands, telling me to trade for some horses in case I found any.

We made camp on the other side of the river [the Trinity River] about three leagues from the crossing. We found a country of valleys and hills of medium height on which there were many trees, mostly oak and walnut, which did not grow as large as those we had seen earlier, perhaps because the soil was rocky. In truth, the trees were much more lovely in the low ground and the soil was better, producing very beautiful grass. All we had for food was a turkey when we left camp which served as supper.

The next day, the 30th, which was Easter, we continued our route finding almost the same country except for a few areas where we saw tall pine groves.[2] The pine trees are quite lovely and very straight, but their cones are very small. The land seemed to contain iron ore as the soil and rocks were reddish and heavy. Even the water itself gave that indication in some places and did not taste very good.

At two o'clock in the afternoon, we saw three men, one of whom was horse-back. They were coming from the direction of the Cenis' village and consequently straight to us. When they came closer, I noticed that one was dressed in the Spanish manner, wearing a short jacket or doublet, the body of which was blue with white sleeves as if embroidered on a kind of fustian; he was wearing small, tight breeches, white stockings, woolen garters, and a Spanish hat that was broad and flat in shape. His hair was long, straight, and black, and he had a swarthy face. I therefore did not have much difficulty persuading myself that he was a Spaniard after all that had been told us by the tribes we had passed who had said that the Spaniards would come.[3] I will not lie; I was quite troubled, fearing there was a

---

[2] Several Spanish diarists described the tall pine woods of East Texas as commencing east of the middle Trinity in Houston County. See entry "Pine" in Foster, *Spanish Expeditions into Texas*, 256–257. Cheatham and Marshall suggest the pine was *Pinus echinata*.

[3] Joutel's repeated references to the close relationship between the Cenis or Tejas Indians and tribes in northern Mexico support other reports that the Tejas traded extensively with and visited friendly tribes in Coahuila and Nuevo León in the 1670s and perhaps long before. In describing the beliefs and worship of the Tejas, Fray Francisco Hidalgo reported that the men and women of the tribe got drunk on peyote, an imported product that grows today only in South Texas and northern Mexico. Mattie Austin Hatcher (ed. and trans.), "Descriptions of Tejas or Asinai Indians, 1691–1722," *Southwestern Historical Quarterly*, 31 (Oct., 1927), 55–56.

As Swanton notes, there apparently was trade in turquoise and cotton goods conducted between the Indians in New Mexico and the eastern Caddo (Cenis or Tejas) Indians in the 1540s, when the De Soto-

party of them in the village. Assuredly, I did not want to fall into their hands, persuaded as I was that there was no quarter to hope for from that nation and that the best bargain to expect was slavery in their mines.

I was, however, not disposed to let myself be captured, and I was ready to club this man if I noticed something suspicious or saw another one coming. When they reached us, I spoke to this man in a broken Spanish or Italian to which he responded nothing, except he said several times: "Coussiqua", which is to say in the Cenis language: "I have none of it" or "I don't understand it." The two other men were naked. One had a very pretty gray mare, very strong, although she fed only on grass for in this region they have no oats or barley. Each one had a small basket full of very finely ground, parched [corn] meal, and after we had posed several questions to them, we lit a flame with a pistol in order to give them some tobacco to smoke.

They offered us both of their baskets of cornmeal and indicated to us that their chiefs were waiting for us in their village. They let us know that they had plenty of corn for us if we needed it. We gave them a knife and a few strands of beads. We asked them if there were men like us in their village. They told us there was one and that two others were in another place called Sapony [Nasoni?]. The man dressed like a Spaniard showed me a printed paper which contained indulgences granted by the Pope to missionaries of old and new Mexico, all of it in Spanish. This confirmed for me what the previous tribes had told us and that there was no doubt that there were Spaniards around. The Indian even indicated to us that he had been with them; and he described the Spaniards to us as having black beards. At length, after they had smoked, they made it understood that they were going to the place where our people were; and I took the opportunity to write a short note to be taken to them which I gave to the Indians as proof that we had seen them.

Although we were very hungry and the parched cornmeal they had given us further aroused our hunger, we did not want them to know how much we needed food. As soon as they left us, we continued our route and proceeded about a quarter of a league until we found a stream beside which we stopped for our horses to graze. At the same time, we started a fire to cook some *sagamité* [4] which is a porridge, although one most often eats this parched cornmeal without cooking it further because it is already cooked, the corn having been parched in hot cinders. Hardly had our fire been lit when we saw the three Indians retracing their steps, apparently having changed their minds; they came and posted themselves within pistol shot range of us. We signaled them to approach us when the *sagamité* was prepared and cooked and come to eat with us which they did. After our horses

Moscoso expedition visited the Caddo. Swanton, *Source Materials on the Caddo Indians*, 192. Juan Bautista Chapa's report of the Spaniards meeting an Indian named Tomás from Parral (southern Chihuahua) at the Tejas village in 1690, three years after Joutel departed, also supports the thesis that this long distance overland network stretched over seven hundred miles and involved personal visits, trade, and possibly cultural exchange. In his analysis of the Caddoan mounds found near the Neches, Parker Nunley speculates that some form of exchange may have existed for many centuries. Nunley, *A Field Guide to Archeological Sites in Texas* (Austin: Texas Monthly Press, 1989), 118–127.

[4] The French term *sagamité* refers to a food similar to cornmeal porridge that is prepared by boiling corn in salt water. McDermott, *Mississippi Valley French*, 135.

were well fed, we resumed our route, the Indians with us, and we carried on diverse conversations without understanding much.

We decided not to enter the village that evening as it was late. Having judged it unwise to enter by night, we stopped beside a stream where we camped. Two of the Indians headed off on a small trail which went to the right of the one we were following, and the one who was dressed remained with us and spent the night. We still kept a close watch, for fear of surprise, because we were close to the village, only about a half-league away. Our Indian spent the night rather quietly. He was a most sober man who did not speak much; the two others spoke much more. He told us, as I have already said, that he had been with the Spaniards and that they had given him the suit of clothes, and he indicated that the Spaniards would come to their village. All this quite agreed with everything the other had told us which did not please me. I did not want them to arrive, and I was apprehensive that we might find some of them in the village.

Meanwhile, day dawned, which was the 31st, and we took the path to the village where the Indian conducted us to the chief's hut which was a long league's distance from the entrance of the village. On the way, we passed several huts that were grouped in hamlets; there were seven or eight of them, each with twelve to fifteen huts together with space between each other and fields around the huts. Before arriving at the chief's hut, we met all the elders who came to greet us ceremoniously, dressed in their finery which consisted of some dressed skins in several colors which they wore across their shoulders like scarves and also wore as skirts.[5] On their heads, they wore a few clusters of feathers fashioned like turbans, also painted different colors. Seven or eight of them had sword blades with clusters of feathers on the hilt. These blades were squared like those of the Spaniards; they also had several large bells which made a noise like a mule bell. With regard to arms, some Indians carried their bows with a few arrows, while others carried tomahawks and had smeared their faces, some with black and others with white and red. A few of them also had some piece of blue material which they must have obtained from the Spaniards, and in this attire they came to meet us.

The one who was leading us made a sign for us to stop which we did. There were about a dozen elders or chiefs who marched in the dress that I have described, and the warriors and the youth were in the wings. They had with them one of the Frenchmen who had deserted La Salle on the last journey. When they drew near, the elders all raised their hands above their heads and came straight toward us uttering a certain unanimous howl. When they had joined us, they embraced us, one after the other, demonstrating their affection. After the first salutation, they presented us with tobacco to smoke and brought the Frenchman to us. He was a Provençal;[6] he was naked, as they were, and what surprised me further was that he had almost forgotten his own language and could not put two

---

[5] Bolton gives a similar description of the clothing worn by the Cenis in *The Hasinais*, 128–131; Fray Casañas does the same in his account of the tribe. Hatcher (ed. and trans.), "Descriptions of the Tejas or Asinai Indians," 213–214.

[6] The Provençal was otherwise unnamed, but Parkman wrote that the man was from Provence, in southern France near the Italian border. Parkman, *La Salle and the Discovery of the Great West*, 441; *The*

words together but could only talk gibberish. Finally, having recognized me, he came to embrace me; he did not at first dare to present himself, fearing that La Salle was with us. Although he told me that he had been sick when he left the gentleman, he told us that the Indians had been very solicitous and taken very good care of him during his illness and had shown him friendship. I asked him if there were any Spaniards in the village and if he had seen any. He told me no, but that the Indians often spoke of them, saying they would come in number.

To return to the ceremonies the Indians performed for us, after we had smoked they led us to the chief's hut from which we proceeded quickly to where they were all in a large hut that was about a quarter of a league from there. Here they conducted their festivities and made their preparations for war. Upon our arrival, we found mats spread on the ground on which they made a sign for us to sit, and the elders also sat down themselves around us. After this, they had food brought to us, whatever they had, namely *sagamité* or porridge of beans *de brésil*,[7] boiled corn bread and another bread made of parched cornmeal and some nuts baked in the cinders, and another bread made with nuts and sunflower seeds.[8] They urged us to eat, and, as it had been some time since we had tasted bread, even though this was made of corn, it seemed very good to me, for it had been freshly baked. I was even afraid that it might make me ill because I ate so much. Since the disaster, we had not had much food and only meat for a long time, and we were quite glad to have this change.

After we had eaten, the Indians gave us tobacco[9] to smoke again during which time they told us about their plan to go to war against a great tribe called the Canohatinno. They wanted somehow to excite us to go with them. All of this was

---

*Oxford-Hachette French Dictionary*, ed. Marie-Helene Correard and Valerie Grundy (New York: Oxford University Press, 1994), 656.

[7] Margry rendered Joutel's manuscript *de brésil* as *de Brésil*, but we have followed the original version, which probably means that the beans had a reddish-brown color. Lynn Marshall called to our attention that the term *"brazil"* applies to a reddish-brown wood from which dyers obtain a red color. See entry "Brazil" in *The Oxford English Dictionary* (12 vols.; Oxford: Oxford Unviersity Press, 1993), I, 1066–1067.

[8] Espinosa also described the importance of the sunflower and sunflower seed in the diet of the Cenis. Espinosa, *Crónica de los colegios de propaganda fide de la Nueva España*, 419. Heiser has described domesticated food plants found in eastern North America during the past three thousand years. He notes that the principal food crops at the time of first European contact with the native population were corn (maize), squash, and beans, which apparently came from Mexico, but that "the sunflower . . . [was] domesticated in eastern North America before the arrival of corn and beans from Mexico." Heiser, "Enthnobotany and Economic Botany," 200. A cache of a type of gourd or squash (*Cucurbita pepo* ssp. *ovifera*) and sunflower (*Helianthus anneus* var. *macrocarpus*) dated three thousand years ago were found in northwestern Arkansas. See Gayle J. Fritz, "A Three-Thousand-Year-Old Cache of Crop Seed from Marble Bluff, Arkansas" in Kristen J. Gremillion (ed.), *People, Plants, and Landscapes: Studies in Paleoethnobotany* (Tuscaloosa: University of Alabama Press, 1997), 42–62.

[9] Pierre Talon listed tobacco in his report of the crops the Cenis raised. Pierre and Jean-Baptiste Talon, "Voyage to the Mississippi through the Gulf of Mexico," 232. In 1716, Fray Espinosa confirmed that the Tejas (Cenis) cultivated tobacco. Gabriel Tous (ed. and trans.), "Ramón Expedition: Espinosa's Diary of 1716," *Preliminary Studies of the Texas Catholic Historical Society*, 1 (Apr., 1930), 20. Specialists report that the lower Rio Grande is the only place where wild tobacco grows in Texas today. Alfred Richardson, *Plants of the Rio Grande Delta* (Austin: University of Texas Press, 1995), 234–235. Cheatham and Marshall observe that the tobacco grown as a crop might have been *Nicotina tabacum* but that other species of *Nicotina* grow in Central and West Texas.

in signs. I wanted next to make some present to them to thank them for their welcome. With this intention, I drew out a dozen knives and a few glass beads to give to the women, but we made them understand that it would be necessary to give us some provisions and that we would give them something else in exchange. They gave us a sign that they would do this.

I noticed that many young people served the elders. They performed drills in shooting the bow and running. After we had been there for some time, the Provençal told us that he lived in another hut and in another hamlet. He invited us to go there; and we suggested this to the elders who said that they would come with us. Accordingly, we reloaded our horses and got under way with a party of elders and some young men. I thought it would not be very far, but it was almost five leagues.

About halfway we arrived at a river[10] that we crossed over on the trees which La Salle had felled across it on his earlier trip.[11] Along the way, we saw huts from place to place that were in hamlets according to where the land was good and fit for cultivating, for they kept their fields around their huts. But there were large stretches of country where there was no one for more than a league.

Finally we arrived at the Frenchman's dwelling which was in a chief's hut. There another band of elders came to receive us with a ceremony and to conduct us to their assembly hut. They called them such because, when they were preparing to go to war, they constructed these huts for their feasts to stir up the young men to go fight. We found mats spread out on which they asked us to sit and presented us with tobacco to smoke, but they did not make as much ceremony for us as the first ones had.

After we had been with them for a while, we indicated to them that we were tired and that we would like to rest. The Provençal told us that we should go to sleep in his hut which we did. He lived in a chief's hut, not having one himself. There are normally eight or ten families in these huts, which are very large; some are 60 feet in diameter. The huts are made in a different method from those we had seen earlier. These are round, in the shape of beehives, or rather like large haystacks, being composed of the same except they are higher. They are covered with grass from the ground to the top. They make a fire in the center,[12] the smoke going out through the top through the grass. These Indians make them in a different way than the other tribes: they cut full-length trees as thick around as a thigh and plant them in the ground upright in a circle, joining them at the top. Then they lath the huts and thatch them from the ground to the top.[13]

[10] This river was the Neches. Fray Casañas says that the distance from the Trinity River crossing to the main Cenis villages was about ten leagues (about the same distance as that Joutel gave) and that the distance from the main village to the Neches was east about three leagues, again matching the distance Joutel gave. Hatcher (ed. and trans.), "Descriptions of the Tejas or Asinai Indians," 209.

[11] The bridge over the Neches La Salle constructed with large logs is mentioned again when Joutel prepares to leave the Cenis and visit the Nasonis. The party was west of Alto. See Chapter XIV.

[12] The fire in the center of the Cenis's hut was symbolically maintained on a continuous basis in the same manner as religious perpetual fires were maintained by the Natchez, Taenas, and other tribes that La Salle encountered on the middle Mississippi in 1682. See Minet, "Voyage Made from Canada Inland Going Southward during the Year 1682," 60, n. 73.

[13] See Bolton's discussion of Cenis building arts and architecture in *The Hasinais*, 111–118. The

Once we were in the hut, which was one of the largest in the area, we were shown a place to put our packs and to sleep. These huts were much more comfortable than those we had seen before. The Indians raise their beds three feet high. They fashion them neatly with long reeds, making each bed separate with matting that forms a cradle.[14] We laid down our baggage and put our horses out to pasture where there was very fine grass at that time, for the Indians had set fire during the fall. The grass had grown again very beautiful and green. The women had made *sagamité* which they offered to us. After we had eaten, because we were tired and needed to rest, I asked the Provençal if we were safe. He told us there was nothing to fear. So we lay down but I did not sleep deeply because I did not know these people.

About half past 3 o'clock in the morning, I heard people walking around the hut muttering something. I went out to see what it was and saw five Indians, the elders whom we had seen on arrival. They were circling around the hut. I learned from the Provençal that they did this from time to time because the chief of the hut had died not long before. I was not able to learn the purpose of these ceremonies, not knowing their language. The rest of the night passed without my hearing anything.

The next day, after the sun had risen a little, that is between 8 and 9 o'clock, the elders came to find us and took us to the hut where they were gathered. There we found mats upon which they asked us to sit. As I had the evening before, I told them the reason that we were there was to see if they would exchange food supplies for some other things and particularly to see if they had some horses to trade for hatchets as La Salle had done on his previous journey. After we had been there a while and they had given us a smoke, they gave us something to eat. To thank them, we made a present to them of a few knives and beads for the women.

The elders asked the women to bring us food provisions, as we had requested, and a little while later, several of them came, some bringing us corn, some meal and beans and similar things, and I gave them beads, copper rings, needles, and other trinkets in exchange. One Indian brought a very fine stallion to us. I gave him a hatchet and a knife. At first I believed that there was some flaw with this horse that was very handsome and would have been worth fifteen to twenty *pistoles* in France, and cheap for that. But there was nothing wrong with him. Thus, if the Indian felt content with the exchange, I felt the same way. The rest of the day passed in trading food supplies with the women and girls who brought them to us for beads and other things. I learned from the Provençal that the Indians had not entered their huts at all since they had built the assembly hut and that the women took care of bringing them food and the young people served them.

Because it was necessary to return with the news and provisions to our people who had remained beside the river [the Trinity River], we decided that, as there were more provisions than our people needed to come, that one of us should stay

---

Marqués de Rubí wrote in his diary account that the Tejas (Cenis) huts "are divided inside with partitions made of woven reeds, which they also use to make the bedrooms, furnished with beds that are elevated, decent, and comfortable." Jackson (ed.), and Foster (annot.), *Imaginary Kingdom*, 126.

[14] The raised beds of the Cenis caught the attention of a number of Spanish expedition visitors, such as Espinosa, who described them. Tous (ed. and trans.), "Ramón Expedition: Espinosa's Diary of 1716," 24.

in the village to trade and that the three others should return with the three horses to bring what there was. In that way, upon their arrival, we could determine in what direction we should head.

The lot fell to me to stay, not that we drew by chance. This was by common accord. Although I did not feel too secure among these people whom I could not understand at all, in some way I was content to stay there with the hope I had of seeing the two other Frenchmen who the Indians indicated were not far away. Perhaps they could give me some means to extricate ourselves from these miserable murderers whom I could not look at without horror. The matter thus resolved, the three others headed off with the three horses and provisions. The Provençal accompanied them as he wanted to see the Abbé, and a few Indians also went with them. When they departed, the wife whom the Indians had given the Provençal when he had recovered, seeing him go, believed that he would not return. This put her in an ugly mood, according to what I observed because she was in the same hut, and I saw her take something that belonged to the Provençal and throw it after him as if she wanted to say she wanted nothing further to do with him.

At length, after their departure, which was on April 2nd, I gave a knife to a young Indian so he would inform the two Frenchmen and tell them that if they would come, I would be very glad to speak with them. I had, it is true, reason to believe that, having deserted La Salle, they would find some difficulty with this proposal, thinking that I could be the gentleman. Nevertheless, the Indian performed my errand.

During the time I was at that place, I did not want for visitors: the women and girls brought me corn, beans, and meal, nutbread, and sunflower seed bread for which I gave something in exchange. Also the elders often visited to exhort me to go to war with them, telling me that they would secure some horses which the nation they planned to fight had in large numbers. They told me many other things to which I did not respond as I was unable to understand them. When they recounted their victories over their enemies, I did not fail to say yes, that was good. What I understood quite well was their appreciation of knives and hatchets which they liked very much and which they needed, not having any, even though they had been among the Spaniards. This was proof that the Spaniards had not given them much. Only the women had a few pieces of thick blue cloth[15] that they used to make small tunics of a sort that they wore in front and behind, but there was little of it.

These Indians have a certain custom of pricking their bodies, making all sorts of figures that stay imprinted forever because, after they prick themselves, they press finely powdered charcoal into the cut to make it last. The men make figures of birds and animals; others prick most of their bodies with zigzags; the women prick their breasts in small, exact divisions, and on their shoulders they have large

---

[15] According to Bolton, Padre Massanet wrote that the Tejas (Cenis) were fond of blue cloth because Sister María Jesús de Agreda had visited the tribe wearing a blue garment. Bolton adds that Padre Casañas, after living several years with the tribe, explained that the Tejas simply liked blue because it matched the color of the sky. Bolton, *The Hasinais*, 133–134.

florets which we call *point d'Espagne*. I do not doubt that they suffer much pain when they do this kind of thing, but it is only once and for always. The Provençal had pricked himself like the other men.

Among these visits that I received without fail, not gaining much from conversing only by signs, I had one from an Indian who told me that he had been with the Spaniards. Because I still did not understand their signs well, this one demonstrated that he wanted to take me to the Spaniards. For this purpose, he drew several figures which did not please me much as he indicated that he would take me by the arm. This suggested to me that he wanted to conduct me by force. To this I would not freely surrender myself. At that time, I told myself that if I had it to do over again, I would not have remained thus alone; but it was too late to think about that. It was necessary that I make the best of my situation. While he was engaging me in these discussions, I noticed that he was distracting my attention away from a hatchet. But, seeing this, I secured it with about a dozen others I had. In the evening he left. As I was alone, I was quite disconcerted because I dared not leave for fear of being robbed of something.

I had another, more curious visit which affected me acutely. One night, about one o'clock in the morning, after I had gone to bed, I became aware of a naked man with a bow and some arrows in his hand who came to sit near me without speaking to me. As I had on my mind the Indian who had wanted to trick me out of the hatchet, I believed that this one too wanted to sneak something away, thinking I was asleep. Besides, I had heard La Salle say several times that the Indians were skillful at stealing and that it was necessary to beware of their feet as well as their hands. I can make assurances, however, that these people must not be confused with those whom La Salle spoke of because they are not thieves. Whatever the case, with regard to the one who had come to sit near me, I did not know who he might be and I thought of the accounts I had heard regarding the Spaniards. These accounts caused me to be uneasy. Therefore, I asked this man what he wanted. As he made no reply, I took my pistol and freshly primed it, and my musket as well, to avenge my death, before it was dealt that is, in case I was attacked. This man, seeing me take arms, stood up and went off near the fire which, as was the custom, never died in these huts because the Indians laid them with thick logs which sustained the fire for a long time. When the logs are cut, the Indians start a fire at the two ends, one near the other, and put small wood around it.[16] I saw these logs, which took eight or nine men to carry, set in a way that, with little kindling, a good fire was lit.

But to return to my man, when he was alone near the fire, I got up, took my arms, and approached him. Looking at him in the glow projected by the flame, I noticed that his face was marked like the people of this tribe. For his part, he saw that I was looking at him and he recognized me. He began to speak and threw his arms around my neck. He was one of the Frenchmen who had abandoned La Salle and to whom I had sent word. After the first greetings, he asked me how I had

---

[16] Margry apparently misread the manuscript here; his version reads "same" (*même*) not "small" (*menu*) wood.

arrived there, how many we were, and where La Salle was. He told me that he had not dared come by day for fear of being met by the gentleman who would know that he had abandoned him. I told him of the disaster that had occurred which news caught him by surprise and apparently distressed him. After several other questions, I asked him if his companion was with him and why he had not come. He told me that he had not dared, fearing to find La Salle. They were both sailors: this one was a Breton named Ruter[17] and the other one from the La Rochelle area was named Grollet.[18] He told me that the third who had deserted with them had died,[19] that they had been sick, and that the Indians had been of much help to them, taking good care of them and giving them everything they needed. I asked him if he had heard any mention that there might be Europeans in this region. He told me no, but that a few spoke of their existence, indicating however that they were quite far away, except for the Spaniards who they said were closer. He told me that he and his companion were together in a hut where they were cherished by the Indians because they had gone to war with them. They had killed one of their enemies with a rather opportune gunshot, which had won them trust and a reputation among the Indians, although they only had one musket between them. They had no more than about two charges of powder left, not being able to take any when they fled, and they had only a few bullets, so their musket had become almost useless.

I asked him if he knew anything about the Colbert, or Mississippi River, but he told me he did not except that there was an Indian nation to the northeast on a great river and their village was about forty leagues away. These Indians, Ruter told me, said that there were many nations on that river and that their village was friendly to them. This information gave me some satisfaction that this village was on the route we should take if we were able to push ahead. I had told him that I did not want to remain with these wretched murderers; I would rather live with the Indians. Thus, after several questions, I gave him what I had to eat; after that, we went to sleep.

The next day [April 4?], several elders came to see us. Ruter told them he had been at war which they well knew as they were almost the same tribe and they were all allies. The elders told me I should be like him and go with them to war, so we could bring back horses. To please them, I often said "amen;" but I tried to make them understand that we were going to gather more men and that when we returned we would go with them. Ruter made them understand that I was a chief in our nation, or a captain, which they called *cadi*, and when they wanted to express the name of chief or commander in speaking to me, they addressed me as *cady capita*. The word *cadi* is pronounced with a double "a." Besides the word *capita*, they

---

[17] Parkman calls Ruter a French savage and reported that sometime after Joutel's party departed the Cenis settlements, Ruter killed Hiems the buccaneer. Parkman, *La Salle and the Discovery of the Great West,* 448, 472.

[18] Jacques Grollet was later captured and interrogated by Governor Alonso de León. An English translation of this interrogation, which occurred at De León's Guadalupe River camp in DeWitt County, is found in O'Donnell, "La Salle's Occupation of Texas," 15–20.

[19] The third man was not otherwise identified by name.

had another word for their horses which they call *cahouaille*, which may come from the Spanish word *cavaille*.[20]

During my conversation with Ruter, as soon as it was daylight, I was amazed by his ways. It would have appeared that he had lived with the Indians for ten years; he was naked and barefoot; for clothing he had only a paltry covering that the Indians of the area make with turkey feathers, joined together very neatly with small strings. But what amazed me above all was that he had pricked and marked his face like them. As a result, there was almost nothing about him that was unlike them except that he was not as agile. As for religion, I believe that was what bothered him the least: this libertine life quite pleased him.

I asked him to go look for his companion and decide together whether, unless he were afraid of something else, he would be disposed to pursue our journey with us, in case we should proceed with it some day. He asked me for some strands of glass beads to make a present of them to the women of the hut. I gave them to him and even added some knives and rings. After that he left and I remained alone, to my great vexation, although I often had company, the elders coming often to visit to converse with me about their war plans. They thought that their enemies, seeing the effect of our arms, would flee, and in this way they would be their masters and would carry off scalps. That, indeed, is their way of conducting war (in the Turkish manner, without quarter) bringing back these scalps for trophies. One can distinguish the warriors' huts and the braves' by the number of scalps that are there. They dress them very cleanly and display them in the most visible place in the hut.[21] When there are several Indians sharing a scalp, they take it and separate the hairs, that is to say, when the hair is long. They make small tresses of them which they fasten along a reed, and this is placed in a row with the scalps.

These men had a large assembly hut where they prepared for war with feasts and rejoicing, and they did not return to their customary huts at all. The women brought food to them at that place, the young people served them, and then ate after they did. When they had eaten and smoked, they made the young people practice running. I had the pleasure of seeing them doing their exercises several times because the hut where I was lodged was situated very close to the one where they were. As a result, I saw everything they did. Two of the more active chiefs lined up the young people one after the other and, when they were all in order, they were off at a given signal which happened all in an instant. They vied with each other to gain the lead. Afterwards, they planted two stakes some distance from each other, and a number of them would take off at a run to see who could more or less make the circuit the fastest. After this, they were made to practice with the bow. They spent their days in this way.

---

[20] The Spanish word for horse is *caballo* rather than *cavaille*, as Joutel stated. *Cavaille* is not a Spanish word.

[21] Captain Alonso de León (the elder) described how the Indians of Nuevo León in the early 1600s stripped the scalp from the top of the head of a dead warrior: they placed a hot rock in the fleshy part of the scalp to dry it, and they then would put the scalps on a stick about half a lance long. See Carl L. Duaine (ed.), *Caverns of Oblivion* (Corpus Christi: Carl L. Duaine, 1971), 41.

There was one elder who came often to see me. He was one of the Indians most respected; he always urged me to go to war with them. After Ruter's departure, he came one morning when I was at work sewing some shoes from an antelope skin for which I had traded. He brought me a girl whom he made sit near me and told me to give her the shoes to sew. At length, he indicated to me in some way that he was giving her to me as a wife. But because I had many concerns to think of other than women, I did not converse much with her although she was shapely. Eventually, after she had been near me for awhile, she realized that I was not recognizing her presence and went away.

The night passed without my noticing anything out of the ordinary. I did not sleep deeply because of my constant fear. When I saw someone out of the ordinary arrive, I was perplexed because I was not at all familiar with their ways. As the elder of whom I spoke before came often, I made him understand that it troubled me that I did not understand their language at all. He pointed out that I must live with them and they would whisper their language in my ears. Everyday people would come to see me. The one who had spoken to me about the Spaniards, or rather said that he had seen men like me but with longer beards, saw me reading my Book of Hours and told me that these people also had books. He made me understand that he still wanted to take me to these men, but I always indicated I did not at all want to go, telling him that they were not our friends. All these kinds of discussions continued to worry me because I did not want to be in the vicinity of these Spaniards even though in all likelihood they must have been at least 200 leagues away.

I remained thus, without news, until Sunday, April 6th, when the two Frenchman (of whom I spoke before) arrived, dressed alike, each one having only a cloak of turkey feathers on his shoulders, his head and feet bare. The second man was not marked in the Indian manner, as was the first one, nor was his hair cut as most of the Indians did theirs with the hair clipped off except for a few tresses which they fasten to or coil around a small piece of wood that they hang to one side.[22] They all have a small tuft of hair on top of their heads to the rear like the Turks. However a few keep all their hair and do not cut it; it is always straight, thick, and black like jet.

The second Frenchman [Grollet] seemed a little more sensible than the first [Ruter], apparently being more religious. I recounted all that had happened during our journey, the disaster that had occurred, the manner in which the murderers had made themselves masters of all the belongings, and the plan we had to detach ourselves from them even if we were obliged to stay with the Indians, considering that only misfortune could happen to us with them. He told me, in his turn, all of their adventures since they left La Salle, how they had joined a war party with the Indians and killed one of their enemies and, furthermore, had routed them and put them to flight with the good result for them that the Indians held them in high esteem and entreated them to return to war shortly. After much discussion, I asked him what he had learned about this village to the northeast that

[22] Different tribes had identifiable manners of hair dressing. Bolton discussed this under the heading "Coiffure" in *The Hasinais*, 131–132. See Swanton, *Source Materials on the Caddo Indians*, 141–142.

his comrade mentioned to me. He replied that he had heard the Indians say that there were people like him to the northeast, but that they were very far, and the Indians had even shown him a few beads which they said came from there. He said that in the village to the northeast, the people were their friends and allies.[23]

This information gave me considerable hope and confirmed my inclination to go ahead, if the Abbé would trust me. I asked him if he would like to undertake the journey with us; in case he would, we would share with him as well as his comrade a portion of what we had. He stated that he would be most glad and his comrade also; that they could not ask for more than to be with us if the Abbé would receive them well. I told them that I would help them as I could; and, because they wanted to see the Abbé, I added that they could go meet him and the others who were coming. I also requested that they not speak to the others of the plan I had, nor even let them know of the village to the northeast; in a word, that they not speak of anything to anyone except to the Abbé. They headed off.

I remained alone again with the Indians. I knew that the Indians soon intended to continue their revelry, then to leave the region where they were after setting fire to their assembly hut to destroy it which apparently had only been constructed and dedicated to serve this occasion. Unfortunately I did not know their language and could not fathom the reason they were taking this action. All I was able to learn was that these kinds of gatherings were brought about only to deliberate on a plan of war which they eventually executed as will be seen.

[23] The allies to the northeast were the other Caddoan tribes, the Cahinno or Cahaynohoua Indians, and the Quapaws, whom the French had met earlier near the mouth of the Arkansas River.

# CHAPTER XII

# The Assassins' Plan

On Tuesday, April 8th, three men arrived, namely the Provençal, one of the two deserters, and one of our company, each with a horse, to collect the provisions that I had acquired in trade. I learned then of the plan of the murderers to return to the settlement where they would construct a shallop by which means they would go to the Islands [modern Haiti]. But I suspected this was just an idea. To effect it was another matter: none among them could even produce a model. There were neither carpenters nor caulkers, and, furthermore, they did not have the necessities, scarcely any tools or nails. Everything had been left behind with the ship [the *Belle*]; besides, in the beginning when we had the tools and the workers, nothing had been made. That was why I did not believe they could succeed. Be that as it may, such seemed to be their plan.

Meanwhile, if the provisions that I had sent to them could have sufficed until they reached the Canoe River crossing, a little beyond where they had committed their assassination, they would have gone on and left me in the village for pawn. To that end, they had remained near the entrance of the village in order to return to the settlement as soon as we had sufficient provisions for them to manage it. I was not angry about their plan as it provided an easy way for me to leave them by maintaining that I could not bear the fatigue of the trip. I had only to consult the Abbé regarding this. Therefore we proposed to meet them. As I had traded for all kinds of dry foods, namely corn, beans, meal, and other similar things, it was necessary to make sacks to put each thing in separately which we did with deer skins which I traded for with the Indians.

The next day, which was the 9th, we departed, but we could not make much headway because the rain stopped us. We were forced to stay in a hut so our provisions would not get wet, and we spent the rest of the day and the night there. Our horses, grazing on very fine grass which had grown a half foot in height, were compensated for the lost time. All the terrain of this region is almost of the same kind, all hills and valleys, in which the bottom land is quite good; but the hills seemed arid and rocky to me although they still had beautiful grass and trees everywhere.

For the most part, these trees are oak and walnut. There are a number of places which seemed, from what I could tell, to be iron ore deposits, and this seemed so to the others as well.

On Thursday, the 10th, we rejoined the others. There I learned from the Abbé and Father Anastase of the decision these wretches had made and of the manner in which they had acted with respect to the Abbé and Father Anastase regarding food even though they had sufficient amount to give them some. But they were playing the masters and alleged that others had deprived them of food in the past, so they claimed it was their turn. As no one wanted to dispute them, they had a very easy excuse. At length, after we arrived, I returned to Duhaut the rest of the hatchets and knives, beads, and other things he had given me. The five of the conspiracy then concluded that they should eat together and that we four would eat together, namely: the Abbé, Father Anastase, the young Cavelier, and me. I was delighted with the decision which permitted us to talk freely without giving them umbrage. As a few bands of Indians had passed on their return from a hunt, the others had traded with them for some meat and fat which they reserved for themselves without offering the Abbé or Father Anastase even a morsel. They gave us only corn that we had to have the Indians pound, giving them a few needles. Fortunately, I had a good number of them in my personal possession.

On Friday the 11th, as the murderers' plan was to return, they decided that a few of them should return to the Cenis' village to try to procure a few horses so that each one could have his own. With this intention, four men left, namely, three of them and one of those who had lived with the Indians. On the next day, the 12th, the two others left too to join the third one, so that six of them were away, the strongest ones at that. As a result, it would have been easy for us to get rid of those who remained if we had wanted to; but the Abbé, as always, squelched that desire telling us that revenge was not for us, that God would know revenge Himself. So we were patient; but, because it would be better if they knew that we did not plan to return to the settlement, I told the Abbé that it would be advisable if he informed them of this and asked them for a few hatchets, some knives, and some powder, and shot which we were due as our share, for they belonged to the King. As for the hatchets and knives, I did not find it strange that Duhaut had taken possession of them as they were his; but it was necessary to find a subterfuge so that they would not take a stand against us. This the Abbé did, telling them that we were tired and that we could not bear the fatigue of the trip that we had made before; that, consequently, we were resolved to stay in this village with the Indians. They were surprised, not expecting this proposition. So Duhaut told the Abbé, when he proposed this to him, that he would respond to him the next day. The Abbé had said that if he gave him a few hatchets, knives, and other things, he would make him a promissory note. Thus we were awaiting the favor of a response from Duhaut which we found quite unnerving.

The next day [the 13th], after they had consulted (he and the surgeon, his companion in wrongdoing), they told the Abbé that they wanted to do right by us in this matter and that they would leave us half of the munitions and more, and almost all the hatchets and other utensils. They told us that they intended to go with speed, so they could succeed with their plan which was to construct a shallop. They added that if they were not able to succeed, they would return to join us and that they would bring Father Zénobe who had been with La Salle on the discovery journey, and he would know some of the tribes and be familiar with their ways. Likewise, if they succeeded, they would find some way to send us word so that we could join them. They also added that, during their absence, we must stock plenty of provisions so that when they came back to join us, we only had to proceed with the route. The Abbé told them that that would be fine. But it was not my intention to wait for them; to the contrary, my idea was still to gain territory and distance ourselves from them and try to reach the village that the two Frenchmen had earlier mentioned to me. But we did not want to reveal our plan to them, so we told them that we would stay in the village, stock many food supplies, and even plant seeds, like the Indians.

We remained at this place for a good length of time. Those who had gone to the village did not return because the river in the village had overflowed and prevented them from crossing back. Furthermore, they got along well with the Indians as much for their carefree and idle way of life, in which they took pleasure, as for the wantonness of the women who had little difficulty giving in if they were urged in the least bit. However the Indian women do not publicly prostitute themselves;[1] at least I noticed nothing unchaste while I was living with these people. If they practice prostitution, they at least have the reserve to hide it. The women are quite well shaped in the bust, and their facial characteristics are rather handsome; but they disfigure themselves in different ways. Some make a stripe from the tops of their foreheads to their chins; others make a sort of triangle at the corners of their eyes, along with the marks they make on their breasts and shoulders. They also prick their lips, and once they are pricked, it is for the rest of their lives. I do not doubt that they are in pain when they do these things to themselves for the blood must gush in order for the coal to penetrate. The breast of course is a very sensitive part.

It is the women who do almost all the work around the hut whether to collect wood, pound corn, or almost everything there is to do. They even hunt. When the men have killed some animals, usually it is the women who go to collect the meat. Even when they cultivate the soil, again it is the women who do most of it although I noticed afterwards a rather clever practice of this tribe. When they wish to dig the ground around a hut, they form a sort of assembly, sometimes including more than a 100 people of both sexes, as in France, particularly in the Caux region when they want to harvest some field of turnips each one works, and the owner of the field feeds the workers. They operate in the same way. On the given day, all who have been given the word come to work with some sort of pickax which they make, some from a bison paddle[2] and others from pieces of sharp wood secured

---

[1] Bolton describes the casual and formal relationships between Cenis women and men in more detail in *The Hasinais*, 86–89. Apparently, women were relatively free, after their first marriage, to relate to any man as the two of them wished.

[2] The bison bone used as a pickax was probably made from the animal's shoulder blade. Cenis agricultural implements are described in Bolton, *The Hasinais*, 122, and in Swanton, *Source Materials on the Caddo Indians*, 127, 131.

with cords made from tree bark.[3] While all these workers toil, the women of the hut for which the work is being done are responsible for preparing food. When they have worked a length of time, that is to say until about noon, they stop and are served the best of what there is to eat. When someone returns from a hunt with meat, it is used for the feast; if they do not have any meat, they bake corn in the cinders or boil it, putting beans *de brésil* [4] in it, which is not too good a dish, but that is their way. They wrap the mixture in corn shucks and boil it.[5] After the meal, most of them amuse themselves for the rest of the day; then, when they have worked for one hut, they go to another one on another day.

The women of the hut are also responsible for planting corn, beans, and other things; the men do not plant at all.[6] These Indians do not have one iron tool; also they only scrape the ground, not being able to dig into the earth very deeply; however, things grow marvelously. It was the planting season when we were there, and I observed their ways. When I let them know that we wanted to stay with them, they told me they would make us a hut and give us women; but their most frequent solicitations were to tell me we must go to war with them. Not one day passed without a few Indian men or women coming to our camp; we were about a quarter league distant from their huts. The young people even spent entire days with us. Also, I often went to their huts to trade, whether for corn, beans, fat, or some similar thing which the women handed over for beads, needles, pins, rings, or other objects which we might have.

As Duhaut knew I had a few necklaces of imitation amber, copper rings, needles, pins, and other trinkets, he told me that I could buy food supplies with these, for he did not intend to furnish me any. Not to quarrel with them, I did not contest this. For his part, Father Anastase had a number of red and white rosaries; we unstrung them to make bracelets and necklaces which we exchanged for corn and meal. Thus we did the best we could to maintain a friendship with the Indians with whom we had decided to remain for some time. For this reason, I promised to go to war with them which it would have been necessary to do if matters had developed as we planned. But a change occurred when one of the deserters told Duhaut of the

---

[3] Espinosa described the construction of wooden sticks the Cenis used in cultivation in *Crónica de los colegios de propaganda fide de la Nueva Espana*, 432, 435.

[4] Padre Casañas referred to five or six kinds of beans the Tejas (Cenis) grew. He added that the Tejas gathered an edible wild root, like a sweet potato. Hatcher (ed. and trans.), "Descriptions of the Tejas or Asinai Indians," 211.

[5] De León refers to an Indian food wrapped in corn shucks that the Tejas (Cenis) called *tamales*. Bolton (ed.), *Spanish Explorations in the Southwest*, 415. Casañas also mentions that the Tejas made *tamales* by mixing the seeds of watermelons, sunflowers, and calabashes with corn. Hatcher (ed. and trans.), "Descriptions of the Tejas or Asinai Indians," 211.

[6] Cenis men helped clear fields and stir the soil, but the women stored the seeds and planted the crops. Bolton, *The Hasinais*, 98; Swanton, *Source Materials on the Caddo Indians*, 162–163. This suggests that the horticultural work of selecting, drying, storing, and planting seeds and the domestication of improved varieties of seeds and plants, with the consequent expanded tribal production of food, may be credited primarily to Indian women. Specialists have argued that increased agricultural production was one of the key factors that permitted the restructuring of Indian communal life from small roving units dependent principally on hunting, fishing, and gathering to more densely populated and politically organized permanent settlements dependent principally on horticulture.

plan we had according to what I had told him when he came to meet me. He told
Duhaut that there was a village to the northeast about 40 or 50 leagues distance and
that the distant tribe were friends of those with whom we were living. He added
that, according to what he had heard from the Indians, there was a great river in
this village. Now Duhaut communicated this to his companion in crime, the surgeon, and added that we intended to go to the village. With this information,
Duhaut and Liotot, having reflected upon my plan, changed their minds, realizing
that their scheme to return to the settlement to construct a craft or shallop was not
well conceived and did not appear likely to succeed. Therefore, they told us one day
that, according to what they had learned, they wished to proceed with us.

No news could have provoked me more, because my greatest desire was to be
separated from these wretches whom I could not envision without horror, remembering the cruelty with which they had acted. Besides I felt that we would always
be threatened with the same treatment as they must realize that, if we arrived in
safety in some country, it would be difficult not to reveal their crime. I was consequently most disconcerted, or rather we were most disconcerted. Indeed, the
Abbé, Father Anastase, and the young Cavalier saw the same danger and with good
sense admitted that, sooner or later, they would get rid of us. What was unfortunate was that there was almost no recourse.

We consulted often on what we should do; the Abbé always insisted that we
must not avenge ourselves. Although I posed it to him that if we were fortunate
enough to find some European nationality, English or otherwise, the murderers
could not doubt that someone would accuse them of their crime. Nevertheless the
Abbé repeated to us that we must have patience, try to place ourselves in the care
of God, and resign ourselves to His will.

We remained camped at that place for the rest of the month [April] during
which time we pounded corn to take along on the journey, and so it was I left
almost every day to go to the Indians' huts to pound our corn and to trade with
them when there was trade to be found. The women parched the corn and then
pounded it and made very fine flour of it. If these Indians had mills, their work
would be much easier as this is an ordeal. They have large mortars[7] that they make
from the trunk of a tree hollowed by fire to a certain depth after which they scrape
and clean it. There are up to four women together pounding the corn: each one
takes a thick pestle about five feet in length and they keep time, as blacksmiths do
when they strike their anvils. When they have pounded for a certain time, they
extract the meal and other women pass it through small sieves which they fabricate
very neatly from large reeds. When they want it very fine, they use small winnow-
ing baskets through which they shake the meal where the finest remains in the bottom. The grit and bran rise to the top. In this manner, they have flour as fine as
could be made and as fine as I have seen in France or elsewhere. We paid them for
their trouble with beads, needles, rings, and other things.

[7] Espinosa also describes how the Tejas (Cenis) used mortars to grind corn into a meal or flour in
*Crónica de los colegios de propaganda fide de la Nueva Espana*, 435–436. According to Alonso de León (the
elder), Indians in Nuevo León in the 1600s used mortars to grind mesquite beans into flour. Duaine,
*Caverns of Oblivion*, 30.

As I have already said, the river [the Neches River] in the middle of the village where we were was high and over its banks, and those who had gone to the other side [east of the Neches] could not cross back over with the horses and the supplies that they had acquired. Duhaut, whose plan now was to follow the route with us, told us that it would be best to get nearer the river so that when it subsided we would be close by to cross it. The river was about three leagues distance from where we were. We concluded, consequently, to camp on the river bank, but we did not have enough horses to carry all the packs and the food supplies that we had gathered because the others had taken the horses. For this reason, it was decided to make two trips to the river so that, when it was low enough, we could cross over on the trees that had been felled before and join the others.

This was done the first day of May. As at that location we were not far from the huts where we had been previously, the Indians continued to come and visit at intervals but less frequently than before. In these circumstances, some of those who were on the other side, and among them L'Archevêque, protégé of Duhaut, informed Duhaut that Hiems was aware of his plan to push ahead but did not approve of it because of the dangers he perceived in it. The Indians had dissuaded them, making them believe we would not be able to get through because of their enemies [along the way]. But the report of these Indians was designed more to attract the others to stay with them than to warn of any real threat from their enemies. Furthermore, these Frenchmen had become addicted to the wantonness of the women who already displayed toward them a certain attachment, and the Indians had managed to engage them to go on a war party they had planned.

So we remained at that camp until the 8th of the month, the day of the Ascension of Our Lord. On that day, several of our men were at practice shooting with blanks to clean their arms when, around 10 o'clock in the morning, Hiems arrived with 20 Indians accompanied by the two who had been living with the Indians, Ruter and Grollet. They had been with those who were on the other [east] side of the river. Hiems greeted us all rather coldly and went off to join Duhaut, his companion in crime. They continued talking together for some time, but I was unable to gather anything because I was too far from them. I know only that Hiems told Duhaut that he had learned of his plan to continue on the route with us and that it was not his intention. Consequently, he demanded his part of the spoils, that is to say the belongings and apparel of the late Sieur de La Salle which they had seized, to which Duhaut answered that everything belonged to him because he had made several advances of funds to the deceased La Salle. The dispute became prolonged and heated; Hiems finished by telling Duhaut that he then must pay him his wages as he had killed his leader. And, at the same moment, I heard a pistol shot; Hiems had shot Duhaut who fell four steps from there. At the same instant, Ruter fired his musket at Liotot and shot three bullets through his body.[8]

[8] Pierre Talon gave a different and rather ambiguous account of this incident. He testified that Duhaut was shot by Hiems (James), who in turn was killed later by the French sailor Ruter, who was subsequently killed by the surgeon Liotot. The surgeon, Talon claimed, was later killed in a battle between an enemy coastal tribe and the Toho (with whom both Talon and the surgeon were living). Pierre and Jean-Baptiste

In the middle of this slaughter, not knowing if the same was going to happen to me, I ran as fast as possible for my musket to stand on my defense, but Hiems, having seen me, shouted to me to lower my arms. He said that he did not have the same intention toward me, that the deed was done, that he had punished Duhaut who was not content to have killed his leader but also wanted to appropriate everything for himself. I was not any the less constrained, for I had not had much conversation with Hiems since the disaster occurred nor in fact ever as he was German by nationality and a Lutheran. However, after I regathered my senses a bit, I observed that the Abbé and Father Anastase were no more assured than I who had grabbed a musket without reflection. As it was, I had taken the young Cavelier's musket that was unloaded because he had just been shooting blanks with the other men. Hiems then came toward us and said that we were only making ourselves frightened, that he wished us no harm, and that, although he had been a part of the conspiracy, the act had been against his best judgment and that, if he had been close to La Salle when Duhaut killed him, he would certainly have prevented it. He apologized to the Abbé.

But to return to the shooting, Duhaut who had received a pistol shot on the mark had fallen dead stiff without saying anything, and when we came up to him, we found his shirt on fire, burnt from the strike. Liotot although he had taken three bullets through his body did not cease breathing for a few hours during which he had the advantage of confession. Ruter, who had fired the gunshot, wanted to finish him with a pistol shot which he did after the surgeon had confessed. In spite of the repeated objections of the Abbé that this was too cruel and inhumane, Ruter carried out his intention, alleging that Liotot had in confessing himself the good fortune that the gentlemen whom he had massacred had not. Thus, the wretches received retribution for their crime. I meanwhile reflected upon what the Abbé had told us before, that God Himself would know revenge, and I was very glad not to be soaked in their blood. They had been paid back with almost exactly their own coin. But all of this did not place us outside danger and did not rid me of the fear I had.

Twenty Indians had been spectators to the events, and that could only produce ill will among these peoples who could conjecture, and with good reason, that we were a wicked people to kill each other in this way. So after the first reaction, it became a matter of finding a subterfuge and a pretext to convince the Indians that one had reason to act as one had and, as Hiems had promised the Indians that he would go to war with them, we made it understood that the ones who had been killed had not wanted to give them powder and shot to go to war. That was the explanation we gave for the way they had acted. The Indians, seeing that it was in their interest, accepted this as truth, at least in appearances, and then a grave was dug into which we placed the dead, an advantage that La Salle and Morenger, who had been left to the discretion of the wild animals, had not had. They had not had

Talon, "Voyage to the Mississippi through the Gulf of Mexico," 235–236. Apparently Duhaut's burial site was a few miles east of the customary Neches crossing, where the Cenis (Tejas) in 1690 showed De León the graves of unidentified Frenchmen. Bolton (ed.), *Spanish Exploration in the Southwest*, 417.

the charity to bury them,[9] and had stripped them of everything, even their shirts. I heard this wretched surgeon, although he had three bullet holes in his body, pray to leave him to live, hoping that the Indians could heal him. His prayer was in vain.

When all was somewhat calm, one of the group was missing, namely L'Archevêque, Duhaut's protégé, being from the same place. Hiems took umbrage at this and he proposed to kill him upon his arrival to prevent his attack. We pointed out to him however that that would be too cruel and that we could manage to bring peace between the two of them. With this intention, I took my musket and headed in the direction in which L'Archevêque would return. He had gone hunting for turkeys. When I saw him, I told him of what had happened and the way he should behave, and that we had managed to calm Hiems, by assuring him that nothing harmful would befall him for his part. With that, I returned the service he had rendered me when he came to tell me the bad news of La Salle and the ill will the others bore me. I told him he must not think of the past and I gave to him, as an example, the Abbé and the way in which he had acted. He promised me he would not offend Hiems and so we headed back. When we arrived, I made him talk to Hiems who told him that he wished him no harm; L'Archevêque replied that neither did he wish harm for him.

Thus, after all these deadly strikes, it became a matter of determining what should become of us and in what direction we should set our course. Hiems told us that he had promised the Indians he would go to war with them and he wanted to keep his word. He said that if we would await his return, his and those who would go with him, we would then see what we should do. While waiting, we could stay with the Indians in their villages.

---

[9] The manner in which Duhaut treated La Salle's body was described in the Abbé Cavelier's account in an altogether different and fictitious way in order to make it appear that the Abbé's brother had been able to receive sacraments. Delanglez (ed.), *The Journal of Jean Cavelier*, 109–111. The same fictitious story is in the Douay account. Cox (ed.), *Journeys of La Salle*, I, 243, 244. This is noted to suggest that full confidence should not be given to the accounts of Jean Cavelier and Douay, at least with respect to religious matters.

# CHAPTER XIII

# Hiems Accompanies a Cenis War Party

n view of the circumstances, it was deemed wise to return to the place we had left, that is to the hut of one of the chiefs who had always been friendly to us. When we arrived at his hut, the chief made a sign to us to take half of it showing us one side, and we put all our belongings together in one place. As I had noticed that the natives, who were seven or eight to a hut, would make separate beds with matting shaped like staves, we likewise divided off the ground area that the chief had given us. Afterwards, we gave food to the Indians who had been present at the murder of Duhaut and Liotot; then they went off to sleep somewhere or another.

That evening, after the Indians had gone, Hiems told the Abbé and me that we could stay in this place until they had returned from war as he had promised the Indians that he would go and did not want to fail them in his word. He said he would leave all the goods and other belongings in my hands; and when they returned, we would determine what course to take. This resolved, we promised to await his return. In any case, there was no likelihood of doing otherwise or attempting anything as they had on their side the Indians who could have done us harm. So we again left everything to Providence.

The next day, six of our Frenchmen left, namely four of our company and the two who had lived in this area among the Indians and who had gone with Hiems. They each took a horse and went off to join the Indians who had taken another trail. Likewise, six of us remained in our hut: the Abbé, Father Anastase, the young Cavelier, a small son of this Talon I have mentioned [Pierre], whom La Salle had brought along with the intention of leaving him in this country to learn the language, a young boy from Paris [Barthélemy], and me. Two others stayed on the other side [west] of the river [the Neches], one of whom was Tessier and the other the Provençal.

We remained in that place with the women and several old men who were not able to go to war. On Saturday, the 10th, the two men on the other side of the river came to join us. The Provençal was to have gone to war with the others but was prevented from going by a splinter of wood that had injured his leg. During the men's absence, we only saw the old men who came to see us from time to time and related news which we had much difficulty understanding. Being able to communicate only by signs, I often found myself quite distraught. What made me most uneasy was that the women sometimes broke out crying and I was unable to guess the cause. I had learned from La Salle that they cried when they wanted to perform some ill deed as if they were crying for the death of those they wanted to kill. That is why this upset me, as I often saw this kind of performance. I have since learned that their tears were caused by the memory of some of their friends or relatives who had been killed in war parties such as the one that had gone out. As I was ignorant of this, I was given often to alarm.

Meanwhile, we spent a length of time without hearing anything; only the old men continued their visits. As we said our prayers in common everyday, evening as well as morning, they came to watch us. We tried then to make them understand the magnitude of He Who had given us life, making the corn and other plants grow; but we did not know their language, and it was very difficult to make them understand God. That is why I am surprised that the author of whom I have spoken several times dares to allege that he preached to them and catechized them; this he could not have done without having spent several years with them to learn their language.

We were all uneasy until the 18th of that month when, to our great surprise, we saw one morning at daybreak a troop of women enter our hut who were painted and smeared. When they had all entered, they began to sing various songs in their language at the top of their voices; after which, they began a kind of circle dance holding each other's hands. For what purpose were they performing this ceremony that lasted a good two or three hours? We learned that it was because their people had come back victorious over their enemies. As soon as the village had heard it, they all gathered in the way that I have told. Their dance ended with a few presents of tobacco that those in the hut made to the women who had come. I noticed during their dance that, from time to time, some of them took one of the scalps that was in the hut and made a show of it, presenting it first from one side, then the other, as if to jeer at the tribe from which the scalp had come. At noon, one of the warriors also arrived at our hut, apparently the one who had brought the news of the enemies' defeat.

This Indian told us that the people of his village had indeed killed 40 of the enemy and that the others had taken flight; at this news, everyone displayed great joy. But what disturbed me then was to see that, as joyful as these women were, they broke out crying. I was fearful, as always, of some malicious plan against us according to what I had heard in the past. After all these ceremonies, the women went to work: pounding corn, some parching it and others making bread. They were preparing to bring the food to the warriors.

The women left the next day, the 19th, to go and meet the warriors. As it was necessary to use a bit of diplomacy in regard to Hiems and the other Frenchmen who had gone to war, I decided it was wise to send them some food too. I told the Abbé this and he approved; and as the Provençal, who had lived a length of time among these Indians, was familiar with their way of speaking, I told him to go with the women. This he did, and in the evening they all returned.

We learned then of the way they had proceeded: they had met, surprised and struck terror into their enemies with a few gunshots fired by our men who, having killed a few of them, drove the others to flee. Indeed, before any of them had been killed, the enemy was waiting staunchly, not demonstrating any fear. But hearing the shots from the guns, of which they had no understanding, they ran as fast as possible. In this way, our Indians killed or captured 48 individuals, men as well as women and children. They killed several women who had climbed trees to hide as they could not escape by running, not having enough time to follow along with the others.

Few men found themselves thus defeated, but the women were left for victims because it was not the Indians' custom to give any mercy except to children. They cut off the scalp of a woman still alive, after which they asked our people for a charge of powder and a bullet which they gave the woman and sent her back to her tribe telling her to give that to her people as a warning that they should expect the same treatment in the future.

I believe I have spoken elsewhere of this practice of taking scalps. It involves cutting the skin all around the head down to the ears and the forehead. They then lift the entire skin which they take care to clean and taw to preserve and display in their huts. They thus leave the sufferer with an exposed skull, as they did with this woman whom they sent back with word to her tribe.

The warriors brought another woman to the women and girls who came to meet them with food. Then they gave to the women and girls this unfortunate captured woman to be sacrificed to their rage and passion according to the account of our men who were witnesses.[1] When these women arrived and learned that there was a captive, they armed themselves, some with short heavy sticks, others with wooden skewers they had sharpened, and each one struck her as caprice seized her, vying with each other. The unfortunate woman could do nothing but await the finishing stroke, suffering as it were the martyr's role, for one tore away a handful of hair, another cut off a finger, another dug out an eye. Each one made a point of torturing her in some way; and in the end there was one who struck a hard blow to her head and another who drove a skewer into her body. After that she died. They then cut her up into several pieces which the victors carried with them, and they forced several other slaves taken earlier to eat the pieces. Thus the Indians returned triumphant from their war. Of the 48 persons whom they took, they gave mercy only to the young children. All their scalps were brought back, and several women who had gone to war with the others even carried some heads they brought back.

[1] Bolton describes the role of Cenis women in torturing captives in more detail in *The Hasinais*, 175–177.

Hiems and his comrades, those who were with him on this war party, also participated in the glory of this victory. They told me how they had approached their enemies. They had left their horses behind two days before reaching the enemy for fear that the horses would make noise neighing. They went two or three days without making a fire. In a word, they had done so well that they came upon their enemy who, not realizing they were so powerful, were waiting for them. Had it not been for the gunshot that our men fired, the enemy perhaps would not have run away. That is what was said to the Indians when the warriors sent that woman back to tell her people that the warriors no longer feared them because they had firearms which were of more value than their bows. The whole evening was spent talking about this battle after which each one went to lie down and rest.

On the next day, the 20th, the Indians assembled and went to the chief's hut where all the scalps were carried as trophies along with the heads. Then they began to rejoice which continued all day in that hut, and the ceremony continued for three more days. After that, they proceeded to the huts belonging to the most eminent among them whom they called *cadis* which means chiefs or captains. They invited the six Frenchmen who had accompanied them to participate in their festivities just as they had participated in their victory. As we were staying in one of the most important chief's huts, they came there after concluding their celebration at the hut of the head chief.

I was astonished at the way they conducted themselves. After all had arrived, the elders and the *cadis* took their places on the mats upon which they sat down. Then one of these elders, who had not been with them but who seemed to be an orator, began to speak as master of ceremonies. He delivered a kind of eulogy or oration of which I understood nothing. A short time later, each warrior who had killed in battle and had scalps marched forward preceded by a woman carrying a tall cane and a deer skin. Then came the wife of the warrior carrying the scalp; the warrior followed with his bow and two arrows. When they arrived before the orator or master of ceremonies, the warrior took the scalp and placed it in the hands of the orator who, on receiving it, presented it to the four quarters of the compass, saying many things that I did not understand. After this he placed the scalp on the ground on a mat spread for this purpose. Another warrior approached in the same manner until each one had brought his scalp as a trophy. When all this was done, the orator gave a kind of address, and they were served food. The women of the hut had cooked *sagamité* in several large pots knowing the assembly would come. After they had eaten and smoked, they began to dance in an unclosed circle formation. They set a sort of rhythm that they stamped with their feet and waved with fans made from turkey feathers; in this way they adapted all this to their songs which seemed too long to me because I could not understand anything.

Their ceremony ended with a few presents of tobacco which those from the hut gave to the elders and the warriors. I must mention too that the master of ceremonies brought food and tobacco to the scalps as if they were in condition to eat or smoke. They also had two young boys whom they had captured and given mercy. One was wounded and could not walk; therefore they had put him on a horse. They brought pieces of flesh of the woman they had tortured, and they made these two young boys eat some of it. They made a few other slaves, whom they had captured another time, eat pieces of her flesh as well. As for them, I did not notice whether they ate any themselves. After they had finished, they went off to a few other huts, and this ceremony lasted there for three days.

We decided that we should let our six people who had been at war with them rest before speaking of our departure plans. I was still inclined to push ahead, that is, to go to the village I mentioned before to gain some knowledge of the great river that La Salle called the Mississippi or the Colbert in which I still had considerable hope. Therefore, I did all I could to encourage the others to proceed. Tessier, although an accomplice to the assassination of La Salle, proposed to the Abbé that, if he would promise to do him no wrong and accuse him of nothing, he would pursue the route with us. L'Archevêque said the same. The Abbé promised them not to speak of it at all, adding that, for himself, he pardoned them and he would manage to have them pardoned. Thus, we thought only of preparing ourselves for when the occasion presented itself.

On the 22nd of May, one of the [Cenis] warriors arrived at the Indians' village. They thought he had been killed because he had been left wounded on the field of combat and abandoned for dead. He told how for six days he had eaten only a few small roots without cooking them; he had five or six arrow wounds, three of which were in his abdomen and had caused a heavy loss of blood. Abstinence, fatigue, along with the fear he had (which could not have been slight finding himself abandoned), all this had contributed to weaken him. Thus a small private hut was made for him, so he would be more at rest where they tended him in their way which was to clean the wounds well. Some people among them suck the wounds, spitting out the blood and pus they withdraw. They also use a medicinal plant to stanch the wounds. As this warrior had gone a long time without food, they made him a very thin *sagamité* and gave him a little at a time. The other Indians were very joyful at his return. He recounted of the way he had retreated from the field of battle and how, after he had revived from his wounds, he had seen a band of enemy who, happily for him, had not seen him. It is to be presumed that they would have given him no mercy.

After that we spent the 23rd and 24th without anything extraordinary happening. On the 25th, those of our people who had been at war with the Indians came to our hut; since their return, they had spent the whole time with the chiefs and warriors amusing themselves. After several discussions, one among them to whom I had spoken about pursuing the course objected, saying that there was no likelihood of success for such an enterprise in which there was so much risk, knowing neither the way nor understanding these people's language. He added that the Indians had told them that there were enemies all around them, that it was impossible to avoid these enemies from whom there was no hope for mercy.

After this man had finished his speech, Hiems began speaking and said that he was not a man to cut off his own head, that the Indians had assured him that we would not get through. He concluded by saying that we must divide the spoils to which no one responded. He had claimed everything for himself after killing Duhaut, and they had represented themselves as masters since the death of La Salle which no one of us had wanted to dispute. After he had finished, we watched him take the hatchets, putting 30 aside with four or five dozen knives and about 30 pounds of powder and some shot. That was the portion he set aside for us four, namely: the Abbé and his nephew, Father Anastase and me. He gave each of the others a couple of hatchets and as many knives and two or three pounds of powder and kept the rest for himself, associating himself with the men who had lived among the Indians. After this they went off to another hut about a league and a half distance from the one where we were. They also took the best horses. Then, those four men who were linked together went off. The Abbé told Hiems that he should give him a few beads although he had four or five pounds of them which Duhaut had given him when he was determined to return to the settlement. But we did not want to let them know we had the beads. So we asked them for some more.

Hiems seized all of La Salle's clothing and the rest of his belongings as well as the 1,000 *livres* or thereabouts in gold belonging to the deceased Le Gros which La Salle had taken after his death along with some other effects. There were many of La Salle's papers, and the Abbé, having examined a few of the essential ones, took them. He had the rest burned so that, if some Indians went to the Spanish, they would have no certain proof of us to give them.

Meanwhile, I was surprised when I saw this sudden change because I feared that it would discourage the Abbé and the others of whom there were not a great many. I perceived that the Abbé was inclined to return to the settlement which I felt no inclination to do. I was however very glad to be parted from Hiems and the few others who had taken to debauchery with the Indians and there was no reason to hope that they would readily abandon their ways. Moreover, there was always some bad end to fear from them. For another thing, my principal desire was to send some news to France whether by Canada or somewhere else. These motives caused me always to urge for pushing ahead so that we could help those at the settlement, a plan that would have succeeded if we had not encountered obstacles which were to follow.

After Hiems and his cohorts had arrived at their hut and inspected all the goods, not finding as many beads as they had hoped, they believed that I must have taken some, or perhaps someone among them had taken some. This compelled them to return the next day. They told us that they had not found all the beads that they should have and that we must have taken them. I showed them my pack, knowing full well that there were none in it, and the Abbé, who had the box of beads in question, being forewarned, had put it in his pocket. Although the beads were not of great value, they were nevertheless of great use for obtaining food provisions from the Indian women who considered them as the women of France do pearls and other similar things. Eventually after they had searched, they went back. After they had departed, I told the Abbé and Father Anastase that it was necessary to remove ourselves from these people as soon as possible as they would not be long in wasting what they had, and then it would be necessary to give them ours, not to mention that we could be running the risk of our lives.

To this end, we arranged the loads on each of our horses and prepared to leave the next day, the 26th. This move surprised many of the Indians, particularly the chiefs who had demonstrated so much affection for us and did not cease to urge us to live with them, telling us they would give us wives and build us a hut. But their words and offers did not prevent us from leaving. We had hoped to be nine in our company, but two, having heard the Indians say that their enemies would cut off our heads and we would would not get through, withdrew at the moment of departure. These two were [Pierre] Meunier, who called himself the son of a treasurer of France,[2] and the other called L'Archevêque. Just the same, this did not stop us from leaving to the great regret of the Indians who did what they could to dissuade us.

We took the route that went by the others' hut, that is to say, that of Hiems and his comrades, and we said goodbye to them. Hiems was surprised to see us leaving and told us that he did not believe we would go far, that he hoped to see us soon, and that if we would wait until they had returned from a hunting party they were planning with the Indians, they would consider proceeding ahead or returning to the settlement. I told him that we were going to the Assoni which was the place where Grollet and Ruter had lived and that we could wait for them at that location which was about 15 to 18 leagues from his hut. After we had been with them for some time, we took our leave.

I had some expectation that Grollet would come. He was a good and wise fellow who had not done as his comrade Ruter had, following the lifestyle of the Indians, without thinking of God or religion, enjoying only the libertine and idle life. We again asked Hiems for a horse which he gave to us; but what pained me greatly was that this wretch had acquired for himself the clothes and apparel of the late La Salle, one item was scarlet and the other of a blue cloth with gold braid that was as wide as two or three fingers. It was bitter for us to see this scoundrel flaunt the spoils of him he had betrayed. Hiems asked the Abbé to give him a letter to the effect that he was innocent of the assassination of La Salle so that if he returned to the settlement he could show Chefdeville and Barbier and the others that he was not guilty. The Abbé gave him a note in Latin as he had demanded because this man [Hiems] spoke good Latin. He also had a good understanding of mathematics. That is why he boasted that there was no one in the group capable of getting us out of this country except himself and that he intended to search for Fort Caroline where he hoped to find some English, having served for that nation and whose language he knew quite well. At length, we parted company after embracing and making farewells as are made upon such an occasion.

We left numbering seven, namely: we four, Tessier, Marle (who claimed to be descended from a noble family), and a young boy named Barthélemy who was from Paris. We had six horses upon which we put the few things that we had. These did not consist of much but would be quite useful for our journey.

[2] Pierre Meunier testified before Spanish authorities in Mexico City that he was from Paris. See Appendix A.

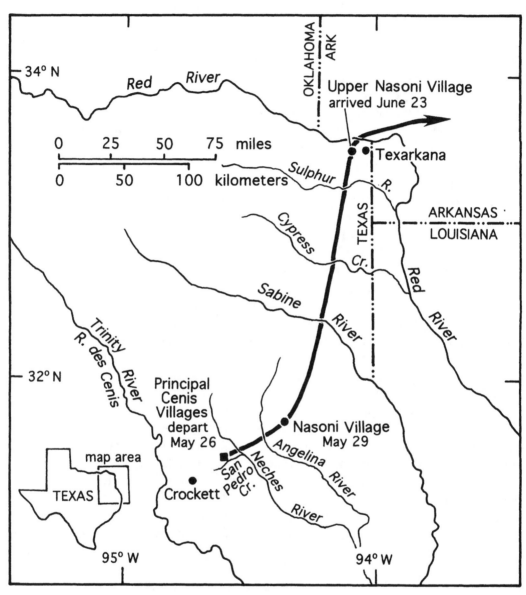

Joutel's route from the Cenis villages to the Red River, 1687

# CHAPTER XIV

# The Assoni and Cadodaquis

e began our journey, abandoning ourselves to Divine Providence. We camped on the bank of a river [the Neches] where we had been before and spent the night there.[1] The next day we cut down a few trees which we placed alongside the other logs which had been cut down the summer before when La Salle had crossed the river there.[2] Upon these we crossed the river handing our baggage from hand to hand, not without difficulty. Each one did his best however and mishap was avoided. We had our horses cross at another spot where the banks were lower because this riverbed was obstructed with fallen timber and moreover the edges were quite high when the water was low. Consequently, when I realized that we had crossed this river, I was hopeful that we could cross other rivers.

We followed our route toward the east and traveled about five leagues,[3] from time to time finding huts in hamlets or in open areas, but sometimes we traveled a

[1] The camp was on the Neches River, which runs generally north to south about three leagues east of the principal Cenis villages located near present San Pedro Creek in northeastern Houston County. The precise itinerary is uncertain because the manuscript uses *lendemain* (next day) at both the close of this sentence and the introduction of the following sentence. Although the Margry edition reads simply: "We spent the night and the next day there," our interpretation of the manuscript is that they cut trees the next day.

[2] See the reference in Chapter XI to the log bridge over the Neches that La Salle constructed. In 1690, when he visited the Tejas (Cenis) in the same area, De León mentioned the same log bridge. Bolton (ed.), *Spanish Exploration in the Southwest*, 417.

[3] When the Marqués de Rubí passed along this same route on September 5, 1767, his engineer and diarist Nicolás de Lafora wrote that he saw on the summit of a hill a mound that appeared to be man-made. Kinnaird (ed. and trans.), *The Frontiers of New Spain*, 165. Although Joutel refers to seeing numerous hills and rises, he does not suggest that any were man-made. The Caddo and the mound builders along the Mississippi built ceremonial and other mounds. Swanton notes that De Mézières wrote about the temple of the Nebedache, which was built on a mound their ancestors constructed in the same area of East Texas. Swanton, *Source Materials on the Caddo Indians*, 154. See also Roger G. Kennedy, *Hidden Cities: The Discovery and Loss of Ancient North American Civilization* (New York: Maxwell Macmillan International,

league and a half without passing one. The terrain appeared to me to be almost the same as before, that is to say: hills and valleys covered with woods that were a short distance one from the other; but the oak and the walnut trees that made up these woods were not as large as those I had seen elsewhere. The hillsides, which were rocky, generally resembled iron ore. The bottom lands between these hills were quite favorable; the land that the Indians cultivated produced very fine corn, beans and other similar crops, and very lovely grass grew elsewhere. We found here and there very beautiful places, and beside water there were elms, aspen, and other trees that thrive near water. We camped[4] near a hamlet where we traded with the women for corn and meal. I always took care to procure food supplies whenever I had the chance.

On the 28th, we continued following the same line of march [toward the Assoni] village, and found almost the same kind of country. We marched about four leagues and again camped close to a large number of huts. On the 29th, following the same way, we passed by a village where the Indians told us that they were called Naodiche[5] and were allies of the Cenis whose customs they shared. We stopped there to feed our horses and trade for more corn and meal. The village chief said he would accompany us to the Assoni[6] about three leagues farther.

After staying a while in this place, we reloaded our horses and the chief led us on. However, it then began to rain. We were not too well received by the Assoni who had not been alerted that we were coming as the Cenis had been. In due course, we were taken to the chief's hut. The elders appeared there afterwards, having been advised of our arrival; in the meantime we unloaded our horses. We placed our baggage in an area of the hut that the chief showed us, then we pastured our horses. When all the elders had gathered that evening, we made it understood that we had come to visit them and to make peace with them, and that we wished to go to our own country to collect goods to give them and their allies, and that then we would bring men to settle and live among them. With this they all seemed content although all had been in signs.

That evening they presented us with smoked meat to eat that had been brought to the hut for that reason. A short while later they served us a porridge

---

1994), 201–202. The mound Lafora referred to along Joutel's route is protected today within the Caddoan Mounds State Historic Site on the bottomland of the Neches River. Nunley argues that one interpretation of the various excavations at Caddoan Mounds suggests that there were remarkable similarities between the East Texas mounds and the culture evidenced during the Classical Period in Mexico, and he adds that about A.D. 700–900 the Mesoamerican culture was spreading throughout North America. Nunley, *Archeological Sites of Texas*, 116–127.

[4] Here Margry misread *campames* (camp) in the manuscript as *coupames* (cut).

[5] Swanton refers to the Naodiche, a western Caddo tribe, as the Namidish in *Source Materials on the Caddo Indians*, 40.

[6] The Assoni were a Caddoan tribe Joutel listed later as Nasoni or Nassoni and the Spaniards called Nasoni. See "Nasoni" entry in Foster, *Spanish Expeditions into Texas*, 279. Swanton covers the history of the Nasoni, including Joutel's visit, in *Source Materials on the Caddo Indians*, 40, 123, 128, 148, 214. Douay rather accurately estimated the distance and direction from the Cenis to the Nasoni at twenty-five leagues, east-northeast, Cox (ed.), *Journeys of La Salle*, I, 255. The party was at a village located near present-day Cushing.

made with acorn meal[7] that they had cooked in the broth from the meat, but this did not seem very palatable to me. I may even assert that one must be very hungry to eat it. The elders spent a part of the evening with us in the hut, and I saw them make certain faces, looking in the direction of our baggage, which did not please me. Under the circumstances, I did not feel sleepy at all, so we decided to keep watch, one after the other, without letting them know that we were suspicious of them. The chief appeared to us to have an imperious and stern disposition and always kept his gravity. However, the night passed without anything extraordinary happening.

On the next day, the 30th, the elders assembled. They prepared mats and seats outside the hut where they indicated that we should go sit. As our baggage was in the hut, I was not comfortable about leaving it. Therefore we decided to always leave someone to keep watch over our belongings. For this reason, only five of us went to their gathering where, as soon as we arrived, we made a present to them of two hatchets, six knives, a few beads, some rings, needles, and other similar things, indicating to them that when we returned, we would give them more. They showed their contentment; but when we indicated our intention to continue traveling farther, they gave us evidence of their regret, letting us know that they had enemies all around them from whom it would be difficult to escape and that it would be much better if we remained with them. We promised that we would return with goods and men to go to war against their enemies; we also made them understand that if the women would bring us food supplies, we would give them beads and other things in exchange which was done.

During this exchange, the young Cavelier came to tell us that the Indians had come to look at our baggage and that, from their expressions, they seemed to have some mischievous intention. They had lit some dry canes[8] to see better because they do not have knowledge of candle-making nor of burning oil (although they make oil with nuts). I was perplexed because what was more annoying in this instance was that we did not understand them. Meanwhile, I went into the hut and, while making an appearance of securing the meal the women had brought us, I put my pistols in my shirt in case I observed some mischievous attempt on their part, but nothing unusual happened.

I attempted to satisfy the native leaders with promises that we were going to our country and our plan was to return, that we would bring many people with us to defend them from all enemies, and also that we would bring hatchets and knives and pickaxes for working the ground. At length, they showed some satisfaction; nevertheless they still alleged that their enemies would present us with difficulties as would the poor trails where our horses would sink in and not be able to get out. They continued to exhort us to stay with them and entreated us to accompany them to war. What prompted them the most on this issue was that the two Frenchmen, Ruter and Grollet, had been to war with them and had killed, as I

---

[7] This is Joutel's only reference to how Indians prepared acorns to eat. Swanton discusses acorn dishes served by the Caddo in *Source Materials on the Caddo Indians*, 133.

[8] This is Joutel's first reference to the native population's use of dried cane as candles or torches. Swanton discusses the Caddos' use of cane torches. Ibid., 156.

236

have said, one of their enemy quite opportunely with one shot of a pistol or musket. We made use of the rest of the day trading for meal and corn which we received in exchange for other things. We were never lacking for company, and I always tried to trade for food supplies to continue the journey. On the 31st, we likewise had visits, but then it began to rain.

On the first of June, some Indians who came to see us repeated everything that the Assoni had told us. But as I had heard La Salle say several times that the Indians' practice was to discourage visitors from going to their neighbors, we did not give their warning credence. Nevertheless, as there were rainstorms every day, we were not in a hurry to leave. Moreover, I had promised Grollet, who was to come and meet us, that we would wait eight days for him. Therefore, we asked where the hut in which the Frenchmen had lived was located, the one in which the Indians[9] had so well cared for them.

We did not much care for the chief[10] with whom we were staying; he was harsh looking and did not seem honest. This was the reason we tried to move away from him. The chief of Grollet's hut, informed of our request, came to see us and invited us to go to his hut. We promised to do so, and the next day we did; but before leaving the hut where we were, we gave the chief a few knives and the women some beads and rings. The one who had invited us then came to conduct us to his hut about a quarter league away.

Along the way to our new location, we passed various other huts and saw men and women cultivating their fields of corn, beans, and pumpkins. The corn was well along, almost ready to eat, and there were plenty of beans which they were gathering. Then when we came to the hut, the chief showed us an area to put our baggage and showed us the rest of the hut. Those living there received us very well. After unloading our horses, we put them to pasture which was plentiful in this region. However it was necessary to tie the horses so they would not eat the corn. We tied them using hide straps that we had braided. However the dogs chewed at our horses' straps. The dogs were always hungry because the Indians did not feed them too well, particularly in this season when they were in the height of corn production (unless they were hunting). As we were concerned about what we could do about this, the Indians showed us some small walnut trees from which they told us to take bark that came off in strips and was a good replacement for our straps. We did this and the dogs did not eat these.

As soon as we were situated in the hut, the chief showed us much friendship. The mistress of women, who appeared to be the chief's mother because she was older, was responsible for providing the food. That was the custom and ordinary practice in each hut. One woman had supremacy over the provision and distribution of food to each person even though there were several families in one hut. In the preparation of *sagamité* too, one of them made it for everyone according to what I saw; some furnish the corn, others the meal, but when all was cooked, the mistress or matron was responsible for serving a portion to each person. We were always served our share first.

[9] Here Margry mistakenly has "masters" for what is "Savages" [Indians] in the manuscript.
[10] The French word used for the chief was "le chef."

I took care to always give her something as well, sometimes this was a knife, another time beads or some rings and needles, and also some necklaces of false amber of which I had a number. I also promised to give her a hatchet in order to encourage her to treat us well; thus, we were much better situated in this hut than we were in the hut where we were before and even elsewhere. Indeed, it was much cleaner.

These Indians' huts are made like those of the Cenis except they are not as high. There is a large platform above the door that is made with pieces of wood placed standing up with other pieces across, and canes are arranged and pressed close together upon which they place their ears of corn. There is another platform opposite upon which they place their barrels or casks (which are made with canes and bark) in which they put their shelled corn, beans, nuts, acorns, and other things. Under this they put their pottery.[11] Each family has their own personal barrels; and they have their beds to the right and the left in the manner that I described earlier. These Indians also have another large platform in front of their huts that is elevated about 10 or 12 feet upon which they place their ears of corn to dry after gathering them. This they are careful to sweep every day.

We stayed at this place for a length of time waiting until the rains had passed. During this time, we managed to subsist on what we were able to get from the Indians. I did not want to use our food supplies in order to save them to proceed with our journey and to reach the next territory. This required me to take care of our good old woman so that she would supply us with a share of their food. It is true that this consisted usually of only some fresh beans which the Indians produced in a large number because they grow very well in this area. However they do not make much of an effort in preparing them; for them it suffices to put them in a large pot, without even removing the strings, then they cover the beans with vine leaves until they are almost cooked.

They have a certain type of sand that they collect near the village where we last were. This place is called *Naouidiche* which means salt, and, from what I noted, the residents of this village have taken the name of this sand. They take a handful or two, more or less, depending on whatever they have to salt, and they put it in water for a length of time to steep.[12] After this, they pour the water into the beans

[11] Joutel is describing the food storage and cabinet area in Nasoni huts. Fray Massanet also described the interior food storage area of a typical Caddoan hut, writing that over the door on the inside there was a structure of rafters, very prettily arranged to hold jars or sacks of food items. Bolton (ed.), *Spanish Exploration in the Southwest*, 378. For an overview of the distinctive Caddoan pottery in Northeast Texas see Perttula, et al., "Prehistoric and Historic Aboriginal Ceramics in Texas," 176–183.

[12] Joutel's party is in an area that was visited by the De Soto-Moscoso expedition in 1641–1643. The narrative of the Gentleman of Elvas (who was on the expedition) tells that the Indians encountered near the Ouachita Mountains in Arkansas prepared salt from sand. See "The Account by a Gentleman from Elvas," 141, 212, n. 255. The most detailed description of the method used by Tanico Indians to prepare small salt blocks from salt and sand in the middle 1500s is found in Luys Hernández de Biedma, "Relation of the Island of Florida," ed. and trans. John E. Worth, in *The De Soto Chronicles*, I, 305. Later Joutel refers to this trade in small salt blocks produced by the Tanico near the Ouachita and Saline rivers in Arkansas. See Chapter XV. In contrast to the production of salt blocks by the Tanico, the Cenis produced salt in the form of a salt-sand procured from the salt marshes in the northwestern part of the Cenis territory. Bolton, *The Hasinais*, 106–107.

238

or meat that they want to salt, and this gives it taste. That was the only seasoning we had in eating these beans. When the beans were cooked, the good old woman took care to give us each our portion in a reed[13] basket, and we would then peel and eat them. We were obliged to subsist part of the time on this kind of food.

The Indians held feasts rather often to which they invited us. As this was the season when they worked their fields, feasts were common, and they invited one another and celebrated. However, I was not of a mind to leave our baggage and did not attend any. Only the Abbé [Cavelier] and I stayed to keep guard. The others went more often to eat and particularly the young Cavelier, Marle, and the Parisian [Barthélemy] because these Indians very much liked young people. Our good old woman took care, when there was a feast of meat, to bring us some sometimes, and she often asked us if our stomachs were full and if we were hungry.

I had heard from the two Frenchmen who had lived in this place that a young man in the hut had offered to guide them to the Cadodaquis[14] village. The Indian had also told them that there were people like them in that direction but that it was quite far. I, therefore, saw to it that I talked to him. The Frenchmen had given the Indian the name of Marquis to which he answered. Every day that I was with him and the chief of this hut, I made it understood that if they would lead us to the village of which I have spoken, we would give them each a hatchet and a knife. When they told me that they had enemies who would not let us pass, I told them that we never slept all at the same time and there was always someone on watch, that was why we were not fearful. Besides we did not harm anyone, and this allowed us to pass everywhere. Eventually one day he told me that he would lead us and that the chief would come as well. They indicated to me that when the sun had made five turns around the world, which meant as many days, they would leave; so we promised to give them many things. We were only awaiting Grollet who had said that he wanted to proceed with us which would have pleased me. Therefore I gave one of the two Indians a knife so he would go see if the two Frenchmen were still at the place we had left them.

While with the Indians every day, I tried to learn some words of their language which I put in writing. But I noticed that they were often mischievous and what they told me for the things I asked was foolishness because when I repeated a name that they had given to me, they would burst into laughter at certain words. I then realized they had said one word instead of another. Meanwhile they were quite surprised when they saw me writing on paper what they had told me.[15] This perplexed them; they likewise were surprised when we read aloud from our Book of Hours. I tried to make them understand that we prayed to a great Master Whom I showed to them above and told them that it was He Who made all things grow and

---

[13] In describing the basket, Margry mistakenly says bark instead of reed as found in the manuscript.

[14] The Cadodaquis was an Eastern or Northern Caddoan tribe that the Spaniards called the Kadohadacho. Smith, *The Caddo Indians*, 8. Cox notes that the name of the tribe Cadodaquis (or "Cado Daquio") was a combination of the name of the tribal group "Caddo," and the name of the river "Daquico" mentioned by De Soto's chroniclers in their travels west of the Mississippi. Cox (ed.), *Journeys of La Salle*, I, 249, n. 1.

[15] Joutel confirms here that he was taking written notes on the journey.

who gave us light and all other things. But this was not easy to make them comprehend without knowing their language.[16]

When the five days that our Indian [Marquis] promised had passed, and he saw that we were preparing to leave, he came to tell us he was sick. Showing us his side as if it was bothering him, he told us he could not walk and that, if we would wait a few days until he was well, he would come with us. We agreed to this because we very much wanted them to guide us although he was just pretending to be sick, from what I saw later, because he knew very well how to lie.

On the next day, several Indians came to our hut to see us, and, after they had visited with us for a length of time, they told us that there were people like us who were coming in large numbers from the east and that they were moving toward the west as if they wanted to reach the Spaniards. We did not know and could only guess who these people might be, and this made us uneasy. I did not want to fall into the hands of the Spaniards who are very jealous of the country they possess in this region. We wondered if these were Spaniards who might have gone ashore near Caroline,[17] coming from Havana, and who were attempting to cross America toward the mines of Saint Barbara.[18] Meanwhile, although we were very disconcerted, we could not let the Indians know this nor let them see that we were fearful. Therefore when they spoke of them, I told them that if these were their enemies, we would defend them. They detained us with this kind of news and came often to repeat the same thing to us. As we believed it was true, it was a matter of our determining how we should proceed.

The Abbé and Father Anastase were almost decided on going to meet these people because they knew that the Spanish respected ecclesiastics and monks; therefore that did not disconcert them too much. But I was not so minded because the greatest mercy I could hope for from the Spaniards was to work in the mines which would not agree with me at all. Therefore, I would have chosen to head for the woods in case they came. However when the Indians saw that we did not appear to be very troubled by this and that the Abbé and Father Anastase asked them to guide them to these people,[19] they began to laugh and said there was no one and that they were not coming. Meanwhile I did not know what to think about this; indeed I found it difficult to imagine where they had conceived of these kinds

[16] The following is Joutel's note: "Therefore, I am surprised that the author I have mentioned before [Chrétien Le Clercq] could assert that Father Anastase preached to them and made the mysteries of our religion understood. This could not have occurred unless he knew their language perfectly, which I did not notice that the Father did, and he did not bother to write down a single word."

[17] In the 1680s the British controlled the coastal area of present-day North Carolina and South Carolina. An excellent study of the British in the Carolinas in the 1600s is found in Verner W. Crane, *The Southern Frontier, 1670–1732* (New York: W. W. Norton and Company, 1981), 22–47. For a more recent study of the English settlement and trade patterns in South Carolina in the 1670s, see Martin, "Southeastern Indians and the English Trade in Skins and Slaves," 304–324.

[18] Santa Bárbara was an important mining community in what is now southern Chihuahua. Peter Gerhard, *The North Frontier of New Spain*, rev. ed. (Norman: University of Oklahoma Press, 1993), 236–238.

[19] As a former soldier, Joutel continued to display an open fear of being captured by the Spanish military, but the Abbé Cavelier and Father Douay seemed to think that their personal fortunes might improve if they were discovered by their Spanish Catholic brethren.

of lies, if they were of their own invention to prevent us from leaving or if they had heard them from those we had left who might have told them these things to intimidate us.

Whatever the case, when I saw that the one who had feigned illness was healed, I told him again that we were ready to leave and that if he wanted to show us the way, we would give him what we had promised him. He again told us, laughing, that if we wanted to wait five more days, he would come. Seeing then that he was making fun of us, I told the Abbé and Father Anastase that it was necessary to make a decision and that time was passing and nothing was being accomplished. The Abbé held that there was too much risk in undertaking a journey of this importance without knowing the way; moreover we did not have adequate food supplies, and we ran the risk of perishing from hunger if not being killed by Indians who might surprise and attack us as their enemies were those with whom we were staying. He added that there would not be as much risk in returning to the settlement because hunting was more abundant there. But, as I saw it, the way to the settlement was not the best or the surest, and even if we had the good fortune to reach it, we would not be any more advanced; to the contrary, we would still have to return. Besides I foresaw more difficulties and risks in returning to the settlement than in pursuing our course because the tribe against whom the Cenis and six of our people had gone to war lived in that direction. According to the report of the woman who had been tortured, they were the same tribe who had killed the five men whom La Salle had given leave to join me at the settlement. Furthermore, we would be obliged to rejoin the men from whom I praised God everyday for having delivered us. Therefore, I insisted on going ahead.

Father Anastase was somewhat inclined in my direction. We told the Abbé that we would be at less risk and, regarding food, that we had meal, corn, and beans for fifteen days during which we would make headway. Furthermore, we had six horses which we could use one after the other, and by this means we could move quickly. Besides the villages which the Indians had mentioned were only about 40 to 50 leagues away,[20] and when we arrived there, if we found no means to go farther, we could stay there a while where we could learn something, whether from them or some other tribe, about the river [the Mississippi River] or New England or Canada.

As the corn was beginning to ripen, I watched a ceremony being conducted by one of the elders who had come to the hut. After his arrival, the women went to gather a great many ears of corn. They prepared it by parching and put it in a small basket which they carried on a ceremonial stool which is used only for that purpose and upon which no one sits. (One day I wanted to sit on it and the good old woman told me that I must get up or I would die.) To return to the ceremony, when all was ready, the elder approached the stool accompanied by the chief of the hut, and they were there for an hour, or an hour and a half, mumbling over the ears of corn, after which they distributed them to the women who gave them to the youth and

---

[20] The anticipated distance of about forty to fifty leagues from the Nasoni to the Red River was accurate.

also presented some to us. When the elder or the chief of the hut did not eat any, I asked him the reason. He told me that he would eat some when the sun had circled the world eight times. As I did not know their language at all, I could not find any other explanations for it. I noticed that after this ceremony the women went every day to gather corn to eat. We also ate this food. Now the corn was not yet at the stage for making flour to make bread. Therefore the ears were parched in order to eat them, and the Indians gave us plenty. I also noticed their precautions with the dogs at this time, fearing they would go eat the new corn. They tied up the mouths of the dogs and fastened a forepaw under the throat so they could not get to the stalks of corn.

Thus we spent a few days; then we prepared ourselves for the departure. I had finally convinced the Abbé and the others to take up the journey to the Cadodaquis although the gentleman still found difficulties with this. But we went ahead, abandoning ourselves to the grace of God in Whom we placed all our confidence. So when we were ready, realizing that Grollet[21] was not coming, I told the chief of our hut one night that we were planning to leave the next day. He let the elders know this, and they appeared as soon as morning came to see us depart. We gave the good old woman a hatchet in recognition of her good care and a few rings and beads to the other women. I then renewed the offers we had made to those who had promised to guide us. Next we made the elders understand, as best we could, our plan to go to our country to collect the things they needed and our wish to come and establish ourselves among them, with which they seemed satisfied, all the while showing their regret to see us leave. I then told them that when the leaves fell they would see us back.

With our horses loaded, we took our leave from the tribe embracing some of the Indians, particularly those who had shown us their friendship. We got under-way on Friday, the 13th of June, about noon. The two Indians who had promised to guide us came to lead us about a half-league along a small path that did not last long, and this troubled us. Then they left us. One of them however indicated to me that when the sun had made its round and was where it was then, which I believed must be the next day, they would come to join us. In reiterating our promises, I told them that would be good. We pursued our journey alone toward the north-east, the direction that they had indicated or shown us, at any rate, was [toward] the village. We guided ourselves principally by the sun; but we found this trouble-some when the sun was high and we were in the forest and it was necessary to walk to the right and the left. But I also had a small compass[22] which guided us.

[21] When he surrendered to De León and was interrogated near Vado del Gobernador in DeWitt County in 1689, Grollet testified (along with L'Archevêque) that Hiems rather than Duhaut had killed La Salle. O'Donnell, "La Salle's Occupation of Texas," 17, 20. It appears that L'Archevêque, who was a wit-ness and probable accomplice to the assassination, may have been trying to protect the reputation of Duhaut, who had hired him. Perhaps Grollet wished to support the testimony of his companion. This illustrates the difficulty in assessing the situation when faced with such conflicting reports.

[22] Joutel used a compass to record (very accurately) the direction taken each day on the journey. The fact that magnetic north and true north may vary up to six degrees does not seriously diminish the value of his readings. The degree of accuracy of his readings of the compass can be measured in Joutel's earlier account in which he was following the west bank of the Navidad River upstream in a generally north-northwest

We[23] proceeded on our route to the northeast about three leagues. On the 14th, we continued four to five leagues, and on the 15th, we covered five to six leagues and camped beside a stream. Crossing ravines fatigued us because it was necessary to unload the horses to let them cross and to prevent them from sinking in the mud and slimy ground from which we would have to pull them out. Because of that, we had to carry all of our packs on our shoulders. At noon, stopping to let our horses graze as we customarily did, we saw our two Assoni Indians returning. This pleased us because they had gone to the village [where we were going] and they knew well the route that must be taken, having followed it since they were young.

We asked them to eat and smoke and then got underway again. On the 16th, we crossed a river about as wide as that of the Cenis[24] and continued to move and covered about four leagues. We found very poor trails. On the 17th, we traveled about three leagues. One of our men, feeling ill, caused us to postpone our departure until noon. On the 18th, we crossed a deep river[25] and covered about five leagues. The 19th, we continued on the same course and crossed yet another river. On the 20th, we traveled four or five leagues, heading in the same northeast direction. We found several swamps from which we had some difficulty getting ourselves out. On the 21st, we crossed a river that was not deep.[26] We traveled about three leagues.

As one of our Indians was feeling ill, we rested beside the river we had crossed. The other guide, seeing his comrade ill, went hunting and killed a deer which were numerous in that country. They are, in truth, difficult to approach, but the Indians are skillful at this. They fit tanned deer heads on themselves and imitate them so well that they often make the animals come within range. They do the same thing with regard to turkeys.[27] There were many reeds on the banks of this river.

---

direction for nine days (January 15 to 24). Current government maps confirm that the Navidad flows toward the bay generally from north-northwest in Lavaca and Jackson counties from the point that La Salle's party began its ascent up the right bank of the river. See USGS *Seguin*, NY14-9.

Most seventeenth-century Spanish diarists also gave accurate daily compass readings, despite frequent statements by Texas historians that the directions given by Spanish diarists were unreliable. In referring to Alonso de León's 1689 diary, Carlos E. Castañeda wrote: "As usual, we cannot place any dependence on the direction of travel as recorded in the comprehensive diary." Castañeda, *Our Catholic Heritage in Texas*, I, 333. Unfortunately, Moscoso had no compass when marching through Texas and Arkansas. See "The Account by a Gentleman from Elvas," 139. However, most European explorers had compasses and the instrument had been in use for several hundred years before De León and La Salle initiated their explorations into Texas in the 1680s.

[23] Margry prepared the account from June 13 to July 9, 1687 from Delisle's extracts of Joutel's manuscript and from Michel's published summary of Joutel's journal.

[24] This river was probably the Sabine, which originates in East Texas, runs east and southeast and then southward to the Gulf forming the Texas-Louisiana boundary. The camp was about eight miles south of Marshall.

[25] This is probably Cypress Creek.

[26] Probably the Sulphur River.

[27] The Cenis means and methods of hunting bison, deer, and turkey, including the use of deer antlers, paint, and deerskin covers, are described in interesting detail in Bolton, *The Hasinais*, 104–106. Oviedo gives a fascinating description of West Indies natives hunting geese underwater, with only their heads above water covered by a gourd with holes through which the natives could see their prey. Oviedo, *Natural History of the West Indies*, 22, 23.

On the 22nd, our Indian felt better, and we packed off through country that was more agreeable and beautiful than that we left behind. We traveled that day five or six leagues. Our Indians named several Indian nations to the right and left, and farther on—that of the Cadodaquis, among others, the Cappa who, they made us understand, were on the same route that we were taking but beyond the village that we were seeking.[28] The Abbé clearly remembered that these same Indian nations had been named by La Salle[29] which made us happy. On the 23rd, we traveled about four or five leagues. We crossed lovely fields and prairies bordered by tall woods of very fine trees where the grass was so tall and so cumbersome that it was necessary to cut a path to get through.

When we found ourselves within a half-league of the Cadodaquis,[30] one of our Indians went to inform them. They then came to meet us, the chief mounted on a fine gray mare. Upon his arrival, this chief professed to us great friendship. We indicated to him that we intended harm to no one unless they attacked us first; we offered him a smoke after which he made a sign to us to follow him. We reached the bank of a river[31] with him where this Indian chief gave us a sign to wait while he went to inform the elders.

A short time later, a band of natives came to join us, and they made us understand that they had come to carry us to their village. Our Indians made us a sign that this was the custom of the country and that we must submit and let them carry us. Although we were embarrassed by this ceremony, seven of the most hardy ones offered us their backs or their shoulders. The Abbé, as the leader, was the first to be carried, and the others were likewise.

As for me, being rather large and who furthermore was carrying clothes, a musket, two pistols, shot, powder, a kettle, and various other items, I assuredly

[28] Joutel confirms here the existence of an identifiable, well-used, and well-known route from East Texas to the Mississippi River.

[29] La Salle had visited the area on the Mississippi and the Cappa on his 1682 trip down the river, which accounts for his brother's knowledge of the names of the tribes.

[30] Douay, who did not keep a daily itinerary, estimated the distance and direction followed from the Nasoni to the Cadodaquis as forty leagues north-northeast. Cox (ed.), *The Journeys of La Salle*, I, 255. This projection was slightly less than that Joutel recorded, which was forty-four to forty-nine leagues. The straight-line measured distance from the projected area location of the Nasoni village to the Cadodaquis village near the Red River is approximately one hundred miles or about forty-one and a half French leagues.

[31] This "river" is not the Red River, but rather a slough or former tributary of the Red. In his study of the Kadohadachos, F. Todd Smith includes a map showing the location of the "Old Kadohadacho Village" near (but not directly on) the right side of the Red River about twenty miles west of the Texas-Louisiana state line. See F. Todd Smith, "The Kadohadacho Indians and the Louisiana-Texas Frontier, 1803–1815," *Southwestern Historical Quarterly*, 95 (Oct., 1991), 181. Smith's map is consistent with Joutel's information on the location of the first Caddo village the French party visited near the Red River.

Frank F. Schamback identifies with a map (Figure 1-2, "Important archeological sites in the Great Bend area") and a description a cluster of Caddo sites in the area of the Red River Joutel visited, a short distance north-northwest of Texarkana. These sites include Roseborough Lake (41 BW 5) and the Hatchel-Mitchell-Moore's complex. Frank F. Schamback and Frank Rackerby (eds.), *Contributions to the Archeology of the Great Bend Region of the Red River Valley, Southwest Arkansas* (Fayetteville, Ark.: Arkansas Archeological Survey, 1982), 9–10.

In their study of the route of the De Soto Expedition in Texas, James E. Bruseth and Nancy A. Kenmotsu also identified the Hatchel-Mitchell-Moore site complex as probably the first village Joutel visited near the Red River. See "From Naguatex to the River Daycao," 212.

weighed more than my one bearer could support. As I was taller than he was (and my legs would have touched the ground), two other Indians had to carry me. Thus I had three bearers. Other Indians took our horses to lead them and we arrived in the village in this ridiculous fashion. Our bearers, who had gone a good quarter league, needed rest; and we, delivered from our mounts, laughed privately, for we had to guard ourselves from doing so in front of our hosts.

As soon as we arrived at the chief's hut, where we found more than 200 people had come to see us, and when our horses had been unloaded, the elders let us know that it was the custom to wash strangers on their arrival, but as we were dressed, they would wash only our faces. This an elder did with fresh water that he had in a kind of earthen jug,[32] and he washed only our brows. After this second ceremony, the chief gave us a sign to sit down on a kind of "platform that was raised about four feet off the ground and made with wood and cane. Here the four village chiefs came to address us, one after the other. We listened to them with patience, although we could understand nothing of what they were saying, and we became very tired of their lengthiness and, what was more, from the intense heat of the sun which beat vertically down on us.

These harangues finished, being nothing other than assurances that we were most welcome, we let them know that we were going to our country with the plan to return soon and bring them goods and all they might need. We then made the usual presents to them of hatchets, knives, beads, needles and pins, telling them that when we returned, we would give them more. We again made it understood that, if they would give us corn or meal, we would give them something else in exchange to which they agreed. Afterwards, they gave us some *sagamité*, bread, beans, pumpkins, and other things to eat which we needed, having eaten almost nothing during the day. Some of us had not eaten by necessity, and others by devotion; the Abbé wanted to observe a fast on the eve of St. John's feast day, whose name he bore.

On the 24th, the elders gathered in our hut. We made it understood that we would be pleased if they gave us guides to conduct us to the Cappas' village which was on our way; but instead of agreeing to this, they asked us earnestly to stay with them and go to war against their enemies, having heard of the wonders of our guns. This we promised to do upon our return which would be soon, and they appeared content.

Thus our hope grew; but the joy we expressed was interrupted by a disastrous accident that happened to us. The Sieur de Marle, one of the finest of our company, having finished breakfast, wanted to go bathe in the river that we had crossed the previous day. He did not know how to swim, and he ventured too far in the water to a point from which he was unable to get back, and unfortunately he drowned. The young Cavelier, who heard that Marle was going to bathe, ran after him. When he got near the river, he saw him go under. Cavelier returned running

---

[32] Archeologists say that the Caddoan ceramics can be traced back to about A.D. 800 to 900, but prehistoric ceramics had been produced in Northeast Texas about a thousand years earlier. See an overview of Caddoan ceramics from Northeast Texas in Perttula, et al., "Prehistoric and Historic Aboriginal Ceramics in Texas," 175–183.

swiftly to tell us. We went quickly with a number of Indians who arrived sooner than we did, but it was too late. A few of the Indians plunged into the water and pulled him dead from the bottom of the river—with difficulty because of the many fallen trees in it.

We carried Marle's body to the hut and shed many tears. The Indians were companions in our grief, and we paid him the last respects and said the customary prayers after which we buried him in a small field behind the hut.[33] During this sad ceremony, we prayed to God, reading from our books particularly the Abbé and Father Anastase. The Indians regarded us in wonder: how we spoke while looking at the pages of our books. We tried to make them understand that we were praying to God for the deceased, pointing to the sky.

We must bear witness to these good people whose humanity seemed remarkable in this sad accident, by the sensitive gestures they made, by their actions in all they could do to take part in our grief. The like of this we would not have found in many places in Europe. During our short stay, we witnessed a ceremony that the chief's wife conducted: every morning she carried a small basket of roasted ears of corn to the grave of the late Marle. We could not fathom the reason for this.

In our conversations, the chief identified the four villages that made up their district[34] and their tribe. The first one was called Assoni (the tribe that we had left); the second was the Nastchez; the third was the Natschitas;[35] and the fourth was the Cadodaquis, each of which, he indicated to me, was not too distant from the others. [Representatives from] all these villages had come to greet us on the day of our arrival.

On the 27th, having heard the Indians say that we would find some canoes to cross the river on our way, Father Anastase and I went to see if what they told us was true. We walked a league and a half. I was quite surprised to see another river, one other than the one we had seen. This one was even more lovely and free of obstruction, as wide as the Seine at Rouen, but its current a little swifter.[36] From what we could determine, the one we had seen first must be a branch of this one

[33] Kathleen Gilmore (with the collaboration of H. Gill-King) has postulated with a high degree of confidence that Marle's grave has been identified at the Eli Moore site in Bowie County. The skeletal analysis strongly suggests that the individual was a muscular European male in his middle years, forty to fifty at the time of death. The cause and manner of his death remains a question, however, because the body was buried with two lead balls just below the rib cage. Gilmore and Gill-King, "An Archeological Footnote to History," *Bulletin of the Texas Archeological Society*, 60 (1989), 303–324.

[34] See Thomas N. Campbell's description of the Lower and Upper Nasoni in the entry "Nasoni Indians" in Tyler, et al. (eds.), *The New Handbook of Texas*, IV, 938–939.

[35] Swanton considers the Natschitas the same as the Natchittas Joutel listed and further identified as the Natchitoches in *Source Materials on the Caddo Indians*, 8. Cox notes that the tribe's name is similar to the Naquiscoza Moscoso chroniclers referred to in the same area. Cox (ed.), *Journeys of La Salle*, I, 249, n. 1.

[36] This is the present-day Red River. Joutel's party arrived at the river after crossing the bayou or slough at a point northwest of Texarkana. Weddle describes Governor Domingo Terán's visit to the Kadohadachos on the Red River in 1691, but Weddle projects that Terán marched across the shallow part of Caddo Lake near Mooringsport, Louisiana, and found the Kadohadacho village after crossing the Sulphur River in southern Miller County, Arkansas. Weddle, *The French Thorn*, 91–92. Perttula disagrees; he projects that in 1691–1692 Governor Terán visited the Kadohadachos (or the upper Nasoni community) in extreme Northeast Texas near the Red River about forty miles upstream from the location Weddle identified. Perttula, *The Caddo Nation*, 254, 156, fig. 23.

when it was high and overflowing because the first river had almost no current, even though it was wide, unless it was another river which came from another direction. We indeed saw the canoes and we reconnoitered a good place to cross the horses. A young man returned who had had his nose and ears cut off in the territory of their enemies, the Chepoussa,[37] but he had escaped.

Now the chief often named the nations for me, their enemies as well as their allies, and he named some that I had heard formerly from La Salle, and this pleased me. I took the names of these nations and wrote them down so I could recall them.[38]

These tribes are their enemies:

| | | |
|---|---|---|
| Cannaha | Caiasban | Nardichia |
| Nasitti | Tahiannihouq | Nacoho |
| Houaneiha | Natsshostanno | Cadaquis |
| Catouinayos | Cannahios | Nacassa |
| Souanetto[39] | Hianagouy | Tchanhe |
| Quiouaha[39] | Hiantatsi | Datcho |
| Taneaho | Nadaho | Aquis |
| Canoatinno[40] | Nadeicha | Nahacassi |
| Cantey | Chaye | |
| Caitsodammo[39] | Nadatcho | |

These tribes are their allies:

| | | |
|---|---|---|
| Cenis[41] | Nondaco | Douesdonqua |
| Nassoni[41] | Cahaynohoua[42] | Dotchetonne |
| Natsohos[41] | Tanico[42] | Tanquinno |
| Cadodaquis[41] | Cappa[42] | Cassia |
| Natchittas[41] | Catcho | Neihahat |

---

Bruseth and Kenmotsu also conclude that Moscoso (1542), Joutel (1687), and Terán (1691) visited the same Caddo village in northeast Texas, a few miles south of the Red River. Bruseth and Kenmotsu, "From Naguatex to the River Daycao," 212. I concur.

[37] Swanton suggests that the Chepoussa were the Chickasaws in *Source Materials on the Caddo Indians,* 187.

[38] Again Joutel emphasizes that he is maintaining a written contemporaneous record of events. In Cox's reprint of the English translation of Michel's condensation, this list of Indian tribes is omitted. See Cox (ed.), *Journeys of La Salle,* II, 178–179. This omission occurs first in Michel's 1713 condensed French version of Joutel's journal; it was carried forward in the original 1714 English translation and in Cox's reprint. As Margry prepared the list from Delisle's extracts rather than from Joutel's original journal, we were unable to check the spelling of tribal names against the manuscript copy in the Library of Congress as was done in Chapter VIII.

[39] Newcomb writes that these three tribes were also identified as enemies of the Cenis by Padre Casañas, who referred to them as the Zauanito (Souanetto), Quiguaya (Quiouaha), and Sadammo (Caitsodammo). Newcomb, "Historic Indians of Central Texas," 15.

[40] Most likely this is the tribe that the Cenis went to war against during the French party's visit.

[41] Joutel probably visited or met with leaders of these five Caddoan tribes—the Cenis, Nasoni (Asoni), Natsohos (Nastchez), Cadodaquis, and Natchittas (Natschitas).

[42] Joutel met these three tribes on the trip from the Red River to the Mississippi. Although Joutel wrote down the name "Cahaynohoua," modern ethnographers and ethnohistorians most often use the name Cahinno, the variant of the tribal name Douay used, to identify the tribe. Carter, *Caddo Indians: Where We Come From,* 52.

| Nadaco | Daquio | Annaho |
| Nacodissy | Daquinatinno | Enoqua |
| Haychis | Nadamin | Choumay[43] |
| Sacahaye | Nouista | |

Most of their enemies live to the east of their village and have no horses; only those who live toward the west have horses. We guessed from this that they had gotten them from the Spaniards. We noticed that among the horses that we had, some had been branded on the hind quarter, which must have been done by farriers, and there were even two geldings.[44]

We found a very good camp location that we reported to the Abbé upon our return. He had developed a sudden soreness in his feet, and we had to remain there until the 30th. Meanwhile we had many visits from the Indians, young as well as old, and women as well as men. Even the chiefs of the nation called Taniquoe[45] came to visit. We often had mute conversations with them, by gestures only, and the women, accompanied by a few warriors with their bows and arrows, always came into our hut singing doleful tunes. Tears accompanied the songs which would have troubled us if we had not witnessed this same ceremony before and learned that these women came into the chief's hut this way to beg him to bring vengeance on those who had killed their husbands or relatives in former wars. As the habits and customs of this nation were more or less the same as those of the Cenis, I leave that subject without saying more.

On the 29th, in the evening, we informed the chief that we were leaving the next day; we gave a few personal presents to him and also to his wife because she had taken care of us, and we set off on our way. On the 30th, the chief, followed by several other Indians we came upon in huts along our route, came to lead us to the river which we crossed in canoes, and our horses swam across. That done, we took leave of our guides to whom we gave a few handfuls of beads for their wives; but the chief wanted to conduct us on as far as the first village. On our way, we found a hut where our guide made us stop. We were given food; afterward we carried on with our journey.

We set course for east-southeast always following the river [the Red River] even though we would leave it; but we would often rejoin it. We continued always

[43] This tribe was most likely the West Texas Jumano, who frequently visited the Cenis. Swanton, *Source Materials on the Caddo Indians*, 9.

[44] Joutel's comments seem to imply that the horses that they acquired from the Cenis had been secured earlier from the Spaniards and were not raised locally by the Indians. The native population in south and west Texas and in New Mexico and other locations in northern New Spain had acquired horses from the Spaniards. Some of these horses were then traded to the Caddoan tribes in East Texas and may have been further exchanged to tribes near the Red River and in southwestern Arkansas.

[45] The Taniquoe cannot be identified with certainty based only on the spelling of the tribal name Joutel gave, but they may have been the Tanico. Joutel included the Tanico in his list of tribes who were friends of the Cadodaquis, and he later mentioned the tribe as salt traders. It should be noted, however, that the salt trade was conducted by a number of tribes on the lower Mississippi. The Tanico were also included in the list of tribes known to the Tejas (Cenis) that Fray Francisco Casañas, who lived with the Tejas for a few years in the early 1690s, prepared. Newcomb observes that the Tanico "appear to be a non-Caddoan people Moscoso [De Soto] encountered near Hot Springs, Arkansas," in "Historic Indians of Central Texas," 15.

on our journey toward the northeast, and we arrived at a Cadadoquis village, one of four which comprised the nation, about two leagues distant from the place where we crossed the river. We were led to the hut of the chief who received us kindly and who was a friend of the other chief who had guided us. We had to unload our horses to stay. We made the chief understand that we needed food supplies; he spoke of this to the women who brought us some meal which we paid for in beads, and the chief who had led us took his leave of us.

Because our plan was not to linger long in this place, we asked the chief for someone to guide us to the village named Cahaynohoua[46] which was on the way to the Cappa. Fortunately, it happened that two men from that village were there who had come to the Cadodaquis to procure bows. They would travel 50 to 60 leagues round trip for that purpose because they had excellent wood for making bows.[47] We made them understand our wish; and they indicated that they would be glad to guide us; and as they were leaving in only two days, we decided to wait for them.

These Indians had been to the Cappa, and they indicated that they had seen there people like us who had muskets with which they killed bison. They had seen houses and had seen wood sawed, or so we were able to interpret from their signs. In addition, I noticed that their language was quite different from that of the nations we had come across earlier and that they pronounced several words which I had often heard said by Nika, such as *Nicana* which means "my brother" or "my comrade" among the Indian tribes La Salle had visited.[48]

The natives at the place where we were showed us some old hatchets which they indicated had been procured from the people who lived to the northeast and to the east-northeast of their village where, they showed us, there were people like us, but they were quite far away. They also told us that there were some people to the east who were not as far away, and we suspected these latter were the Spaniards from Carolina.

---

[46] Many authors presently consider the Cahaynohoua or Cahinno a Caddoan tribe. See Swanton, *Source Materials on the Caddo Indians*, 8; Smith, *The Caddo Indians*, 25; and Perttula, *The Caddo Nation*, 30, 32. Although Joutel consistently refers to the tribe as the Cahaynohoua, both Douay (or Le Clercq) and the Abbé Jean Cavelier refer to the tribe as the Cahinno or Cahinio. Cox (ed.), *Journeys of La Salle*, I, 254–255, and Delanglez (ed.), *The Journal of Jean Cavelier*, 123. As Joutel said that the Cahaynohoua spoke a different language than the Indians he had just visited and were different in several other respects, his observations do not support the current view that the tribe the French visited on the Ouachita River was Caddoan.

[47] The bow wood was probably the Bois d'Arc (meaning bow-wood), or Osage-orange (*Maclura pomifera*), which the Osage and other Indians used to make bows. Vines, *Trees of the Southwest*, 220.

[48] According to Perttula, the eastern boundary of the Caddoan archeological area was east of the Ouachita River. Perttula, *The Caddo Nation*, 6–9. However, Joutel stresses that words the Cahaynohoua used were the same as words the Shawnee Nika and the Indians La Salle had known near the Great Lakes region used. This would not be expected if the Cahaynohoua were Caddoan Indians, with whom Joutel had been living for several months, during which time he had attempted to learn the Caddo language.

This is mentioned primarily to suggest that Joutel's rich, unabridged account may be helpful to specialists interested in native languages and ethnology. Swanton, who repeatedly cites and personally translates small parts of Margry's version of Joutel's account, curiously fails to mention the fact that Joutel says that the language of the Cahaynohoua (Cahinno) was very different from the Caddo. In reference to the Cahinno, Swanton writes that in the sixteenth century they were "known to the followers of De Soto as the Tula Indians," in *Source Materials on the Caddo Indians*, 7.

The women of this country are well shaped, but they mar their breasts and faces with marks as I have already said. Their hair is tied behind and they take quite some pains to part it in the front. The men cut their hair like the Capuchins; they grease it, and when they have some gathering or feast, they put swan or goose down tinted red in it. They love their children, but do not have many of them[49] perhaps because the women do not always stay with the same husband. They leave one another at the least annoyance they have with each other. The women lodge and eat separately when they have their ordinary menses and have no dealings with anyone, not wanting anyone to share their hearth.

[49]  It is difficult to understand the significance of the observation made by Joutel that the tribe did not have many children. However, it should be observed that most losses in native communities from European diseases were probably of children rather than adults and that infertility was one of the effects of smallpox, to which the Caddo had been subjected. Henry F. Dobyns, *Their Number Become Thinned: Native American Population Dynamics in Eastern North America* (Knoxville, Tenn.: University of Tennessee Press, 1983), 16. The demographics of deaths from smallpox, which the French brought to the Caddo's neighbors, the Quapaw or Acanseas, is described in Ann M. Early (ed.), *Caddoan Saltmakers in the Ouachita Valley: The Hardman Site*, Arkansas Archeological Survey Research Series 43 (Fayetteville, Ark.: Arkansas Archeological Survey, 1993), 204–206. Perttula covers the subject well for the Caddo in *The Caddo Nation*, 11–45.

# CHAPTER XV

# Journey to the Arkansas[1]

The Cahaynohoua Indians who were to conduct us to their village were not ready on Wednesday, July 2, as they had promised. In their stead, a young Indian presented himself and said he would lead us there; so we left with him, continuing to make our way northeast. We continued most of the time along the same river[2] [the Red River] we had earlier crossed which was lovely and navigable for it was not obstructed with fallen trees. We had gone only about one league when our Indian guide said that he had forgotten and was going to return to get a piece of tough skin to make himself some shoes. He added that he would come back and find us and pointed in the general direction that we should take, telling us that we would soon find a river.

The sudden change of this Indian surprised and confounded us; but we continued our course to the northeast and found a river[3] [the Little River] where we camped. We traveled four or five leagues that day. This river was at least as pretty as the one we had just left, but its current was slower. It was flowing southeast from what I could determine; this was the one that the Indian had mentioned to us.

With respect to this, several times I had heard La Salle say that the Indians were great liars, and I also experienced this. When they hear something from someone, Indians assert that they have seen it before and that they have been there.

The river was deep, and we crossed it on a raft that was a great effort to construct. Our horses swam across. Some time after we had crossed, we saw the Indians coming toward us who had promised to conduct us. The natives were

---

[1] Margry continues based on Michel's published condensation and Delisle's extracts from Joutel's manuscript journal.

[2] Joutel's party is moving east downstream along the left bank of the Red River near the Texas-Arkansas state line near Ogden. Joutel's route from the Red River across the present-day state of Arkansas to the Cappa villages near the mouth of the Arkansas River is along a line of march similar to that projected in the map, "French Exploration, 1673–1740," in Hanson and Moneyhon, *Historical Atlas of Arkansas*, 22, map 22.

[3] This is the Little River, a large stream that drains parts of southwestern Arkansas and southeastern Oklahoma. It runs generally from west to east and enters the left bank of the Red River about five miles east of the Texas-Arkansas state border. The party crossed the river to camp near Sheppard.

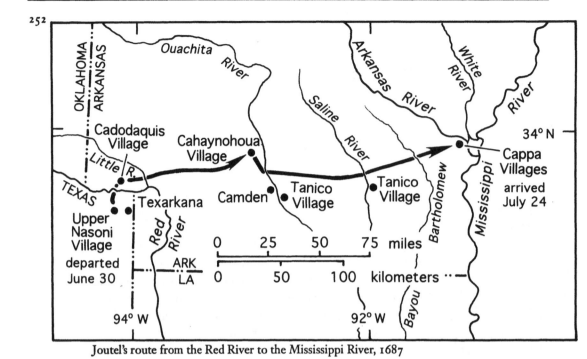

Joutel's route from the Red River to the Mississippi River, 1687

pleased to find our raft, which they used for crossing the river, and we continued on our way together. We traveled about five or six leagues [on the 4th] following almost the same line of march. The country is very beautiful, even more than that of the Cenis, beautiful plains producing fine grass, interspersed with numerous streams lined with lovely trees.

On the 5th, we covered about five or six leagues, always following the common path[4] and forded a river. On the 6th, we forded another river[5] which had been at seven or eight feet five or six days earlier when our Indian guides had crossed it. We crossed another small stream at 2 o'clock. When we had stopped on the bank of a river to eat, we heard the sound of bells which caused us to look around. We saw an Indian who had in his hand an unsheathed sword blade that was adorned with plumage of various colors and two small bells that made the noise we had heard.

[4] Joutel's comment confirms that his party was following the customary Indian pathway and trade route from the Great Bend of the Red River east-northeast, probably following (east of the community of Hope, Arkansas) the Terre Rouge Creek basin toward an area a few miles west of the Ouachita River about fifteen to twenty miles north-northwest of Camden, Arkansas. Joutel's description that the Indian pathway crossed beautiful plains that produced fine grass and were interspersed with numerous streams lined with trees suggests that his party was moving through the more open valley along the left side of Terre Rouge Creek and was not moving directly to the Camden area through the heavily wooded and hilly Poison Springs State Forest. See USGS *El Dorado*, NI15–8. Douay estimated rather accurately that the distance from the Cadodaquis to the Cahinno (or Cahaynohoua) was about twenty-five leagues, east-northeast. According to Joutel's daily count, it was approximately twenty to twenty-four leagues.

[5] This was probably the Little Missouri River.

He signaled us to approach and let us know that he had been delegated by the elders of the village where we were going to come to meet us. He greeted us with many caresses. I noticed that this blade was Spanish and that it pleased him to make the bells ring.

Having traveled about a half league with him, we saw a dozen other Indians coming to meet us. They caressed us many times and conducted us to their village.[6] At the chief's hut, we found dressed bear skins which had been spread out for us to sit upon. They served us food, and the elders, who were waiting for us, were served afterwards. A crowd of women came to see us. The huts of this village were all assembled together, about 100 of them, unlike those of the Cenis, the Assonis, and others we had seen which were [spread out] in hamlets.

On the 7th, the elders came to visit and brought us two bison skins, four otter skins, a white deer skin, all well dressed, and four bows. This was in recognition of the present we had made previously to them. The chief and another leader came back some time later and brought us two loaves of bread, the finest and best we had yet seen. The bread seemed to have been baked in an oven even though we had not noticed that the natives had ovens. The chief stayed with us a few hours. He gestured with much spirit and great care and easily understood our signs which were our common language. He retired after ordering a small boy to bring us everything we needed.

[6] Joutel identified this village as the Cahaynohoua but Douay and Jean Cavelier called it the Cahinno. Perttula refers to the tribe as the Ouachita Caddo and adds that they were living in the vicinity of Camden, Arkansas, when Joutel encountered them. Perttula, *The Caddo Nation*, 164–165, 218, 255. Swanton incorrectly (according to my projection) places the village about thirty-eight miles north of Camden, near Arkadelphia, in *Source Materials on the Caddo Indians*, 41.

The information given in Joutel's full journal account as to the number of leagues traveled and the direction marched conflict sharply with Swanton's projection that the village was located near Arkadelphia on the upper Ouachita River. If Swanton were correct, Joutel's line of march from Arkadelphia to the mouth of the Arkansas River would have been toward the east-southeast (see USGS *Little Rock*, NI15–5 and USGS *Greenwood*, NI15–9), whereas Joutel recorded marching northeast and north-northeast to the Arkansas River. My projection places the Cahaynohoua village near the junction of Terre Noire Creek and the Little Missouri River, about three to five miles west of the Ouachita river and about fifteen to twenty miles north-northwest of Camden. This projection is consistent with Joutel's report of traveling one and a half leagues (or about four miles) from the village to the large river (the Ouachita River).

The location of the Cahaynohoua village was eight to ten miles northwest of the archeological site Georgia Lake, which is on the east side of the Ouachita River. The Handman site is located near Arkadelphia, about twenty miles north of the Georgia Lake site and also on the east side of the Ouachita River. Early comments on Joutel's visit to the Cahinno village and mentions her difficulty in using Swanton's "confusing and contradictory" references to Margry's version of Joutel's journal. Early (ed.), *Caddoan Saltmakers*, 5, 6, 12. This is noted to suggest again that this translation and study may benefit Arkansas archeologists as well as other scholars interested in Texas and Arkansas history.

Although Smith, *The Caddo Indians*, 25, and Pertulla, *The Caddo Nation*, 133, state that the Cahaynohoua or Cahinno were Caddo, Joutel insists that the Cahaynohoua were different from the Cenis or the Cadodaquis. According to Joutel, they looked quite different and spoke a different language; unlike the Cenis, their huts were assembled together, not scattered into farms with their own fields; and they, unlike the Caddo, offered the Frenchmen the calumet, as did the Quapaws. Hopefully, the type of ethnographic information Joutel gives in his full journal will be helpful to ethnohistorians and others interested in sorting out the location and relationships between tribes in Texas and Arkansas. This is the type of detailed ethnographic information that Michel deleted from his condensed version; as mentioned by Early, some of it is also missing from Swanton's study, even though he used selected parts of Margry's version.

In the evening, we attended a ceremony that we had not seen before. A group of elders followed by a few young men and some women came as a group singing at the top of their voices near our hut. The first one carried a calumet [or pipe] decorated with various feathers. Having sung for some time before our hut, they entered the hut and continued their songs for about a quarter of an hour. After that they took the Abbé, as our chief, and led him outside the hut ceremoniously, holding him up under his arms. When they reached a place that they had prepared, one of them put a large handful of grass under his feet, and two others brought clear water in an earthen dish with which they washed his face. After this they made him sit on a skin prepared for him.

Once the Abbé was seated, the elders took their places seated around him, and the master of ceremonies planted two small forked pieces of wood and placed another piece across them. All the pieces had been dyed red. He stretched a dressed bison skin and then a white deer skin upon the sticks and then placed the calumet on top.

The singing began again. The women blended in with the music and the concert was enhanced by noise made with hollow calabash gourds inside which were large gravel stones.[7] The Indians shook them in time to harmonize with the cadence of the choir. The most amusing thing was that one Indian went behind the Abbé to support him and made him rock and swing from side to side in rhythm with the choir.

The concert was not yet finished when the master of ceremonies led two girls out, one carrying a necklace of sorts and the other an otter skin which they placed on the forks beside the calumet. After that, he made them sit on each side of the Abbé facing each other with their legs stretched out and intertwined. The master of ceremonies arranged the Abbé's legs in such a way that his legs were on top and crossed over those of the two girls.

While they were busy with this performance, an elder fastened a dyed feather at the back of the Abbé's head, tying it up in his hair. Meanwhile the singing continued on and on, and finally the Abbé tired with the length of the ceremony. Moreover he was embarrassed to see himself in this position between two girls, not knowing for what design, and he signaled us to advise the chief that he was not feeling well. Two of them immediately took him under his arms, brought him back to the hut, and made a sign for him to rest. This was about nine o'clock in the evening, and the Indians spent the whole night singing; eventually some became completely exhausted.

At daybreak, the Indians came for the Abbé again, brought him outside the hut with the same ceremony, and made him sit down, singing still. Next the master of ceremonies took the calumet which he refilled with tobacco, lit, and presented to the Abbé. He drew back and advanced, without giving it to the Abbé, until this was repeated ten times. When he finally put it in the Abbé's hands, he pretended to smoke it and returned it to them. Next, the Indians made us all smoke, and they also all smoked in turn, the music always continuing.

[7] According to Alonso de León (the elder), Indians on the lower Rio Grande also used gourds filled with pebbles as musical instruments. See Duaine (ed.), *Caverns of Oblivion*, 32.

By nine o'clock in the morning, the sun had become quite hot, and the Abbé, who was bareheaded, indicated that he was very uncomfortable. At last, they ceased singing, led him back to the hut, took the calumet, put it in a deer skin sack with the two forked sticks and the crosspiece of red wood, and one of the elders offered it to the Abbé assuring him that he could go to all the tribes who were their allies with this token of peace and that we would be well received everywhere. This was where we saw the peace calumet for the first time,[8] having had no experience with it as others had written. This tribe is called Cahaynohoua. Neither the men nor the women of this tribe are as handsome as those we had seen previously.

As ceremonies of the type in which we had just taken part are performed by the Indians only in expectation of some presents, and, as we had observed a few of them retire, apparently not pleased that we had interrupted the ceremony, we decided it was prudent to give them something more. I was charged to bring them a hatchet, four knives, and a few strands of beads which pleased them. Then we showed them what our weapons could do, but the noise and fire from the weapons frightened them.

[9]An Indian told us that he had been to the Cappa[10] and, in order to make us better understand the location of the village, he took a stick and traced the river [the Arkansas River] on which it was situated, showing us that it emptied into a much larger river [the Mississippi River]. He indicated however, that the Cappa's river was quite large; he showed us too that he had seen a house built by people like us who had bark canoes.

I had several times heard La Salle say that there was a very large river below that of the Illinois that also emptied into the Colbert or Mississippi River, which he declared would be a good route for trade in beaver skins, and that this river was no farther than about five or six leagues from the Illinois. Therefore, I supposed it could have been on this river that the Indian had seen some Frenchmen, sent probably by Tonty to trade, who could have built themselves a house to serve as a

[8] The calumet or peace pipe was a significant feature in reception ceremonies performed by Indian tribes along the Mississippi, as Joutel later relates, but he says that the calumet was not used in meetings earlier with Caddoan tribes. Diarists did not report that the calumet was smoked when De León and later Terán visited the Tejas (Cenis) in East Texas in 1690 and 1691; however, fifteen years later, when Captain Ramón arrived at the same Tejas villages to reestablish the Spanish presence in East Texas, a ceremonial pipe, adorned with white feathers, was smoked. See Foster, *Spanish Expeditions into Texas*, 120.

Perttula writes that "the Caddo Trace described in 1713 in more detail by Joutel (1906) . . . ran from the Ouachita River to the Red River, and from the Ouachita River to the lower Arkansas and the Quapaw people living there." See Perttula, *The Caddo Nation*, 24. Apparently the description of Joutel's route that Perttula dubs "The Caddo Trace" was based on Michel's 1713 French condensation of Joutel's journal and the English translation Cox republished in 1906 and not on Margry's full version, which gives information such as the number of leagues traveled daily, which is necessary to project the route with accuracy.

[9] Margry notes that Joutel's journal text is resumed here. Joutel's manuscript copy contains no mention of Indians tracing the rivers. Instead, the sentence fragment refers to people who came to trade and built a house (presumably the French).

[10] The Cappas also were called the Quapaws. See W. David Baird, *The Quapaw Indians: A History of the Downstream People* (Norman: University of Oklahoma Press, 1980), 1. Baird adds that there is some evidence from their traditions that the Quapaws were descended from earlier Sioux stock who lived in the Ohio Valley, implying a participation in the Hopewellian culture that flourished in the Ohio basin area centuries earlier.

store. Still I was sure of nothing, but I was convinced that it must be the great river from what the Indian depicted to me. When I returned, I gave an account of what I had learned to the Abbé. He was very pleased, as was Father Anastase, with my observation that the river must be the Colbert. In addition, the name Cappa gave us further proof, for I had several times heard La Salle mention the name. I believed it must have been one of the villages he had visited on his discovery exploration. What further assured me of this was that this Indian said that these men had bark canoes. I therefore had hardly any doubt that these were Tonty's men.[11] La Salle had left Tonty as the commander in the Illinois with a number of men. We spent that day entertaining hopes inspired by this news.

On the 10th, the chief came to see us with several elders who, as always, had something to tell us. I told this chief that we planned to leave, and, as they had indicated that the way was quite difficult, I told him it would be good if they would give us someone among their people to guide us. He invited us, as always, to remain with them, offering us wives, as others had done, and proposing to build us a hut. But I explained that there were not enough of us and that upon our return we would settle among them. I reiterated my request for a few guides as the way was difficult and we would take a much longer time going and returning if we traveled to the right and the left instead of proceeding straight ahead with a guide. I added that we would give each guide a hatchet, a knife, and other things. We went further: we had a saber which the Indians had indicated they very much wanted. They often looked at it, particularly the chief, who was named Hinma Kiapémiché[12] which means in their language "Big Knife." The Abbé told this chief that if he gave us a few guides, we would give them this saber. At this offer, the chief, after thinking about it for awhile, went off without saying anything. At noon when someone brought us food, he returned to us with a few elders. After they had eaten, they drew a little to the side speaking together for a while as if they were taking counsel. Then the chief rejoined us and embraced us and pointed out one of the men who was with him, letting me understand that he and the other man were as one, showing me that his heart and the other's were as one. All of this however was in signs although he was also speaking his language; but I did not understand it, nor he mine. Eventually he told us that he and some other person would lead us to the Cappa, and he said that when we reached the place, the men would return

---

[11] Henri de Tonty, an Italian officer who had lost a hand in the Sicilian wars, was with La Salle and Membré on the 1682 discovery voyage down the Mississippi, including their visit to the Cappas at the mouth of the present-day Arkansas River. Tonty was later left in charge of Fort Saint Louis on the Illinois River. In early 1686 he descended the Mississippi to the Gulf of Mexico with twenty-five Frenchmen and eleven Indians but, after searching the coastline thirty leagues in both directions, found no trace of La Salle's party. On his return trip upriver, Tonty left Couture, De Launay, and several other men at the mouth of the Arkansas River to establish a post in the vicinity. It was this post that Joutel was seeking. See Parkman, *La Salle and the Discovery of the Great West*, 127–128, 300, 326, 453–455.

In early 1690, about two and a half years after Joutel and his party had departed from the Arkansas, Tonty traveled down the Mississippi and visited East Texas to investigate the condition of La Salle's settlement on Matagorda Bay. For a review of Tonty's trip, see Smith, *The Caddo Indians*, 25–26.

[12] In Joutel's manuscript the name appears to be "hinmahy a peniché."

and we would pursue our way. He then urged us to return and bring them what we had promised. We declared that we would do this and further that we would bring women to settle ourselves with them. They appeared to accept this and showed much affection for us.

We fired several shots from our muskets and pistols to please them. I fired too, and a few grains of powder flew out from the touch-hole of my pistol, which was rather large, and hit the ear or near the ear of the man who was to guide us. He was beside me at the time. There was no great harm. However he believed he was very badly wounded. This was not strange because they were not accustomed to these sorts of accidents. I was also very distressed about it, fearing that our guide would change his mind as nothing much was needed to intimidate these Indians. Therefore I made an effort to console him, and, although he said that his head hurt, I indicated to him that it was nothing significant. Nonetheless, for two or three hours he was quite disconcerted. When his pain had passed, he composed himself, and I said again that we would give him what we had promised. The rest of the day passed without further event.

That night, the youth in the village came to our hut at about one o'clock and began to sing various songs in their usual manner. This lasted a good three hours. It appeared that they had come to entertain us, knowing we must leave the next day. After they finished singing, they withdrew, uttering a few cries.

On Friday, the 11th, we loaded our horses to begin our journey, and the chief and the elders gathered to watch us depart. We fired several musket shots to bid them adieu. They appeared sad to see us leave. I can say that this tribe gave us a very fine welcome, and I noticed nothing mischievous about them. I must not omit that they had two very handsome horses which would have made a very good pair of carriage horses.[13] They were grays and very well formed. If we had truly wanted them, they would have accommodated us; but we anticipated that if we found the Colbert River, we would embark upon it and would not be able to take the horses. Consequently, we did not even ask for them. Moreover, we wanted to conserve the few goods we had, not knowing how long our journey would take us.

At last, we departed at about eight o'clock in the morning. We changed directions several times because of poor trails which were swampy and entangled by woods. We would have had great difficulty in getting out if we had not had good guides, principally because of our horses, for we often encountered very difficult ravines. About a league and a half from the village, we found a rather lovely river[14] that formed several channels. We forded it, water up to our waists. It was very clear and the current quite rapid, and it must have been larger lower where the branches reunited. But it was not easy to determine the general course as the branches meander. There were also very lovely woods along its banks. Our Indians explained that there was a village a day's distance on the lower stretch of the river;

---

[13] Apparently the Cahaynohoua also received horses in trade.

[14] This is the Ouachita River; the crossing occurred probably fifteen to twenty miles north of modern Camden, Arkansas. Douay mentioned meeting both the Tanico and the Analso after leaving the Cahinno. See Cox (ed.), *Journeys of La Salle*, 251–252.

they called it Tonicas.[15] This village was a friend and ally to them. The guides wanted to persuade us to go there, but we said the trip would take too long.

We continued on our way through terrible country and very rough trails, encumbered by woods and ravines as well as by swamps. We traveled about five or six leagues. Our route approximated east by north, but as we were making a great many turns, it was difficult to judge. Two other Indians of the same tribe came to join us who told us they were also going to the Cappas. They were taking bows and arrows to trade for other things; they were also taking salt in small cakes, weighing about two or three pounds each. They made it understood that the salt[16] came from the Tonicas, the tribe we had passed by. That day we traveled until sundown as we found no grass for our horses; they were thus forced to do without. There was no grass in these woods which were too shaded and thick.

On the 12th, we continued on our way until about eight o'clock when one of our Indians became ill, and this forced us to stop even though there was little grass for the horses. They had already spent a poor night, their stomachs empty, which troubled us. However, it was necessary not to let it seem so troubling to the Indians, one of whom had already turned back. As soon as it was morning, we lit a fire to cook some *sagamité*. After it was cooked, we presented it to them. The Indian whom the chief had assigned to us was the one who was sick or pretending to be. He signed to us that he could not walk and that he wanted to go back. I told him that he was at liberty to do as he pleased and that if the others wanted to continue with us and show us the way, we would give them what we had promised the chief and him. He spent a period of time thinking about what he should do after which they spoke together without saying anything to us. Meanwhile we were rather troubled about what we would do if they left us because the trails were very

[15] Perttula writes that the Tanico were living in the Ouachita River valley or along the Red River during the seventeenth century in *The Caddo Nation*, 133, 141. Newcomb identifies the Tanico as a non-Caddoan people Moscoso encountered in southern Arkansas in *The Indians of Texas*, 284. A 1997 study of the route of the De Soto-Moscoso expedition suggests that the Spaniards in September 1541 found Tanico (also identified with salt production), a town of Cayas, west-southwest of Batesville, Arkansas on the Arkansas River. See Hudson, *Knights of Spain, Warriors of the Sun*, 315–320. These conflicting references illustrate the current confusion among authorities as to where Tanico Indians were in the sixteenth and seventeenth centuries.

[16] In his account of the De Soto-Moscoso expedition (republished with new annotatons in 1993), the Gentleman from Elvas recorded that near the settlement of Tanico: "The Indians carry it [salt] thence to other regions to exchange it for skins and blankets. They gather it [salt] along the river, which leaves it on top of the sand when the water falls." "The Account by a Gentleman from Elvas," 124. Although Hudson (*Knights of Spain, Warriors of the Sun*, 316) has suggested that in the 1540s the settlement called Tanico and their salt operation was on the Arkansas River approximately sixty miles northwest of Little Rock, Joutel's account indicates that in 1687 the salt operations and the Tanico were on the Ouachita River. See Early (ed.), *Caddoan Saltmakers*, 204–206. Authorities refer to the 130 undocumented years from the departure of the Spaniards on the De Soto-Moscoso expedition to the arrival of the French on the lower Mississippi in the 1670s and 1680s as the "Protohistoric Dark Ages" because little is known of it.

The prospect of salt operations on the Ouachita River in the early 1800s is supported in a 1991 study that reported: "As early as 1811, John Hemphill found a salt evaporation plant near the Ouachita River after acquiring the rights to a spring by bartering with Indians." Milton D. Rafferty and John C. Catau, *The Ouachita Mountains: A Guide for Fishermen, Hunters, and Travelers* (Norman: University of Oklahoma Press, 1991), 191.

difficult. But it was necessary to conceal our concern; that is why I appeared indifferent so they would not take advantage of our need of them. Indeed, they swaggered when they believe themselves to be indispensable. Eventually, after they had muttered for a time and saw that we were preparing to depart, the Indian got up and came to tell us that his illness had passed and that he would come with us. We were very glad about this although I pretended to be not at all worried. At length, I gave them some tobacco to smoke and food to eat and repeated the promises I had made them. Thus we resumed our journey. After having traveled for some time, the Indian let us know that we would soon find bison and that he would kill some and so would his companions. We continued to move along and find poor country, that is, poor trails through dense woods and difficult ravines. We traveled about four leagues that day and saw bison along our way.[17]

On the 13th, continuing to move, we found the same kind of country obstructed by very thick woods which caused us much trouble because of our horses; we had to unload them to cross two large and very difficult ravines. Even without their loads, the horses had difficulty crossing. We traveled about four and a half leagues, only approximately toward the east because of the many detours.

On Monday, the 14th, we continued on our same route, and after traveling about a league and a half, our Indians found some bison tracks. When they saw some fresh dung, the Indians signed to us to unload our horses and wait for them. They indicated that they wanted to go kill some bison for meat, so we did as they said and remained at the same place. We spent a good three hours without any news, when one of them returned and told us he had followed five bison but had not killed any although he had shot many arrows. About two hours later, the other two arrived each with a load of meat. As we had the *sagamité* cooked by the time the other Indian arrived, we offered them some food. They then made a sign for us to cook some of the meat. Each one did his best at this task, but after going a few days without eating meat, it seems fine the moment you get it. So, after grilling the meat, we resumed our journey. We traveled about a league and a half or two leagues and came to a small river[18] which we crossed, and we camped near its banks.

One of our Indians, the one assigned to us by the chief of their tribe, saw some more fresh tracks and, with his bow and a few arrows, went off after the bison herd. He was not long in returning. He let us know that he had killed two cows and invited us to go collect the meat. As we did not know how to follow tracks as the Indians did, I made signs for the other two to come and to lead us there which they

[17] When the De Soto-Moscoso expedition reached central Arkansas in the late summer and fall of 1541, the Gentleman from Elvas reported that bison were to be found nearby, to the north, but that his party had not seen any along the route. "The Account by a Gentleman from Elvas," 126. Another account by Rodrigo Rangel, De Soto's secretary, states that De Soto's men found and killed bison. Rangel wrote that in early September 1541 (when the party was apparently in central Arkansas): "They (De Soto's men) went at midday to kill cows (buffalo), since there are many wild ones." Rodrigo Rangel, "Account of the Northern Conquest and Discovery of Hernando de Soto," trans. John E. Worth, in Clayton, Knight, and Moore (eds.), *The De Soto Chronicles*, I, 304. Luys Hernández de Biedma (who accompanied De Soto as a factor of the Crown), like the Gentleman from Elvas, made no mention of actually seeing bison in 1541 when the De Soto party was visiting the Cayas (or Tanico). Biedma, "Relation of the Island of Florida," 241, 242.

[18] This small river is probably Moro Creek, south-southeast of Forcyce.

did. Four of us headed there, and the others remained to watch over our small collection of goods. The hunter also came with us. We found the two cows he had killed, and we dressed them, and then each of us brought back a load of meat. We covered the meat we were leaving with the hides and returned to camp. Once we had arrived, I told the Abbé that we would have to smoke a little of the meat in order to make our supply of meal last longer. I also made this understood to the Indians who agreed. Therefore we remained at that same place, and the next day we again went to collect a few quarters of the meat which we had covered. The others meanwhile worked at making a pit for smoking the meat. The country was almost everywhere thick with woods, with many large fallen trees that we were forced to go around as our horses were not able to step over them. In addition, there were many ravines and swamps which we had to cross from time to time.

On the 16th, we continued to travel and encountered almost the same country, unaccommodating for our horses, for not much grass was to be found there. We marched about five leagues covering almost all points of the compass because of the winding route. On the 17th, we encountered the same difficulties, and I can assert that if we had not had the Indians for guides, we would have had great difficulty pursuing the route ourselves. We traveled about five or six leagues, and it seemed to me that we moved toward a lower rather than higher latitude. On the 18th, pursuing our course, we came upon a rather large river[19] which appeared to me to run to the southeast. Our Indians found a place for us to ford where the water was almost waist high. It would have been impossible to cross this river in winter because there were wide ravines from one end to the other which, if they had been full, would not have even permitted our approach.

Once we were on the other side, we found another kind of country, much more agreeable to the sight, with a great many clusters of woods of various species, but not as beautiful as those we had seen before. Between the clusters of woods are small prairies full of grass but not as tall as in many other places we had passed. Even though this country was very pretty and most agreeable to the sight, the land did not seem very good to me because the soil was sandy and dry and, as a result, grass and trees did not grow too well.

After we had gone about a league and a half, we saw a herd of bison grazing. One of our Indians, the one who had killed the bison before, told me that it was my turn to go off and kill some. We stopped our horses, and I freshly primed my musket and headed off toward the bison into the shelter of a cluster of woods close to them. This served me well as the wind was blowing from their direction. As I was within range, I took aim at one that fell the moment it was shot. I reloaded my musket and fired at and hit another animal, the herd having hardly strayed. The second one fell about 20 steps from where I shot it. The Indian who had followed me was amazed to see the two bison drop. He was also surprised that the bison had not sensed me at all, for they seemed inured to the noise and became disturbed only after several shots. So the Indian signed to me to fire again at a third one that

[19] This river was probably the modern-day Saline River, several miles north of Warren. The river originates in central Arkansas and runs south to join the Ouachita River a few miles north of the Arkansas-Louisiana state border.

he indicated was a large one. To please him, I did so, but it was not the necessity for meat that compelled us to kill another. I approached the herd and shot the one the Indian had pointed out to me and shattered his shoulder. Then the herd took flight because they either saw or smelled us. We followed the wounded bison for a short time, but, as we did not need meat, I signed to the Indian for us to leave it and return to the others.

When we returned to the bison I had killed, he looked at the holes where the bullet had hit them and he marveled at the shattered bones. Overcome, he came to me and threw down his bow, telling me I must give him a musket because his bow was worth nothing and that he had too much trouble running when he killed bison. He had been amazed that both had fallen, each time with only one shot. This does not always happen; at other times I have fired eight or ten shots at the same bison without it falling although the blows were all mortal. They sometimes go off to die one or two leagues from the spot, or perhaps closer. I admit I was very glad that these had fallen as they did, for I had boasted to the Indians of the virtues of our weapons. They would have had contempt for us if I had not killed any, as he had killed some with his bow and arrows. This success had its disadvantage: the Indian did not cease to press me to give him a musket; but I told him that having still a long way to go and a great many tribes to pass whom we did not know, we needed our weapons. As I was evasive regarding my musket, he indicated to me that I should give him one of the two pistols in my belt, suggesting that when he wanted to make a fire, he had to rub his stick for a long time which hurt his hands.[20] The natives made fire by rubbing wood against wood, whereas we lit one every day with our pistols by means of a handful of dry grass and some powder which was quicker and easier. Again I tried to content him with promises, telling him that upon our return we would give him some and that we would bring a large quantity of them, as we had promised them before.

This was not the end: when the other Indians arrived, they went off together to inspect the place where I had hit the animals, putting their fingers in the holes. Seeing the effect produced by the bullets, they all stood in wonder. I noticed they put their hands over their mouths, according to the Indian custom when they see something extraordinary, as I had noticed in other places. These Indians then made the same request of me as had the first one, but I contented them in the same way, reconciling them to wait until our return which I said would be soon. At length, we began to dress the animals; one was a bull and the other a cow. The Indians next signed to me that we must smoke the meat. I indicated to them that we had enough, but they made it understood that they planned to hide some for their return trip. As we needed them, we did not want to contradict them.

They indicated to us that nearby there was a village of the Tonica which I have mentioned before. Two of the Indians expressed to us the desire to go there and

[20] Alonso de León (the elder) wrote that Indians in Nuevo León in the 1600s started fires very quickly and easily by rubbing sticks. Duaine (ed.), *Caverns of Oblivion*, 30. Swanton discusses the use of a fire stick as the common native American way to start a fire in *Source Materials on the Caddo Indians*, 155–156. Oviedo describes, and illustrates with a sketch, how Indians built fires using a fire stick in *Natural History of the West Indies*, 93.

asked us for two of our horses; but I told them they had to graze because they had been without food until then. The Indians promised me that they would be back at two o'clock in the afternoon, pointing to the position of the sun. I told the Abbé we must not trust them, that they could very well go off with our horses and leave us there. They appeared to be displeased with this, but they nevertheless went off on their wandering while the meat was smoking and drying. About two o'clock by the sun they returned. Then we reloaded our horses and got underway. We walked about a league and a half and eventually made the trip of about three leagues with ease through almost the same, rather agreeable country.

On the 19th, we continued to travel. We came again upon woods, but they did not prove to be as difficult as those we had passed through before. We traveled about five leagues on the same course.

On Sunday, the 20th, we continued although we lost one of our horses during the night; I do not know how because we always tied them. I believe it was or must have been a trick of the Indians who left him there for their return. I signed to them to search for him, but we found no sign of him. Whether they let him stray themselves, or otherwise, he remained lost to us. That caused us some annoyance but we did not tarry in departing and pursuing our course. We came upon rather pretty country with quite lovely plains. The Indians indicated that it stretched very far and that there were many bison there. We marched about five or six leagues toward the northeast that day.

On the 21st, we had rain part of the morning which prevented us from leaving, but at noon we proceeded on our course, finding rather beautiful country with quite pretty plains from time to time and very fine trees. We marched about three leagues that day generally toward the northeast.

On the 22nd, we did not leave until 10 o'clock because of the rain. We had gone about one league when we arrived on the bank of a river[21] that was very deep and seemed to be navigable. We had to make a raft to carry us and our belongings across. I noticed that there were many *caimans* or crocodiles which made us doubt that we were as far up [north] as we had believed. According to the Indians' report of men like us whom they had seen, we believed they must have been near the *Missouris* River. La Salle had told us several times that there were not any crocodiles above the Acansas which is below [south] a good 200 leagues.[22] Besides that, we found a species of beans in the woods which grew there naturally,[23] and I had heard La Salle say likewise that there were many of them growing near the Acansas. After we completed our raft, we crossed the river and made our horses swim across.

On the 23rd, we continued our course hoping to reach the village of the Cappa according to what the Indians had led us to understand. However, access to

---

[21] This river was probably modern-day Bayou Bartholomew, which originates near Pine Bluff and runs south to join the Ouachita River near Monroe, Louisiana.

[22] The comment suggests that Joutel thought he was much farther north than he actually was.

[23] Cheatham and Marshall suggest that the wild bean was possibly *Phaseolus polystachios*, *Apios americana*, *Amphicarpaea americana*, *Strophostyles helvola*, or *Dioclea sp.* See entries "*Apios*" and "*Amphicarpaea*" in Cheatham, et al., *Useful Wild Plants of Texas*, 384–389; 324–328.

the river was difficult because flooding had made a great many ravines which were difficult to cross. We camped near the river after traveling five or six leagues to the east-northeast. The country was mixed with some fine and some poor land although that which seemed poor to me was only so because the approach to the rivers and the ravines was difficult. In the evening, two of our Indians went toward the village to advise them of our arrival, but when they returned, we learned, from what we were given to understand, that they had not been as far as the village. They brought back some ears of corn and a few pumpkins they had taken from their fields.

We spent the night and Thursday, the 24th, we took up our journey again but found that we were very mistaken for we had expected to be very near the village, having heard noise in the night that sounded like a drum. The Indians cover a pot with a dressed skin stretched over the top, and they beat it as a drum or rather a kettledrum.[24] After having gone three leagues by roundabout ways, we met a band of Indians. Several had hatchets and were going to strip bark to cover their huts from what we could understand. They were surprised to see us, or at least they seemed so. We gave them a sign to approach, indicating to them that we did not wish them any harm. Once they had joined us, they gave us many embraces, one after the other, in their manner; they made a present to us of a few watermelons and went back to the village with us, leaving the bark for another day.

Two of our men, who had left us that morning to give notice of our arrival, had not however met this party. A short time before arriving at their fields, or clearings as they were called there, we encountered several bands and troops of Indians who, having heard of our arrival, came to meet us. When they met us, they expressed their great joy at seeing us. They placed their hands on our chests and arms, as other tribes had previously done to us, to demonstrate the friendship they felt for us.[25] I noticed that they said the word *frère* [brother] in all the tribes along the upper part of the river according to what I had heard La Salle say. This is true according to what I have heard since. They led us to a hut in the middle of their field where they had corn, beans, watermelon, pumpkins, and other things in abundance.

On arriving at the hut, we found a crowd of people gathered, men as well as women and girls, who were waiting for us. When we were inside, they made us sit down on the bison and bear skin robes which they had prepared. As the Abbé was our leader and chief of our small band, we noticed that they called him *Panchougua*. We had also heard this word mentioned by La Salle; it meant "chief" or "captain" to this tribe. From this we concluded that we were near that gentleman's great river. At length, as soon as we were seated, the women brought us a large number of watermelons which they grow in quantities in this region. We had not yet seen watermelon, at least not in fruit, because the Cenis and the Assoni had planted them

[24] Seventeenth- or eighteenth-century Spanish expedition diarists did not mention that South Texas Indians used drums as musical instruments. See Swanton's comments on the Caddoan tribes' use of drums in *Source Materials on the Caddo Indians*, 156.

[25] South Texas Indians used these same gestures to greet La Salle's party earlier. See Chapter VIII.

while we were with them. This melon is well named "water melon."[26] The pulp is, so to speak, only water. There are many species of them. Those with red pulp and many seeds, of which there are many, have a sugary taste and are quite sweet. They are refreshing and good for quenching the thirst, but not very nourishing. The Indians also gave us a kind of bread that they prepare in a particular way: they mix with it beans which they leave whole and wrap the bread in corn shucks which they then boil. While we were eating, I noticed that the women took ears of corn to our horses and took pleasure in feeding them. After we had eaten, they offered us tobacco to smoke. After we had been for a period of time in that place, we set out again on the trail to the village and all the Indians joined us. They told us that they had two men like us in their village, which worried me, not knowing who they might be. If they were not the English who inhabit Virginia and the Carolinas, then who? As the Indians said there were only two men, we were not so troubled about them. Besides there was no occasion to pull back elsewhere. Furthermore, these words in languages we understood gave us reason to be hopeful.

We continued to walk the length of their fields which extended a good league along the banks of a river[27] that I believed to be the one that had been mentioned to us. But it did not have much current. The water was quite clear and, according to what I observed later, this must have been the bed and the course of the river in another time. We passed through another wooded area where we found quite lovely cedars similar to those one calls cedars of Lebanon which are very suitable for building and making whatever one would wish. We again encountered several bands of Indians who came to meet us, whose faces were blackened and painted in various fashions. Finally after passing through these woods, we arrived at the banks of the river[28] which was very beautiful, wide at least like the Seine at Rouen but

[26] In Chapter VI Joutel wrote that he had planted watermelon seed at the settlement, but here he comments that he had not seen a ripe watermelon of the species the Cappa grew. He adds that there were many species; one had red pulp and many seeds. In Chapter XVI Joutel repeats that he had not seen watermelon in Europe. Cheatham and Marshall note that watermelon (*Citrullus lanatus*) was native to Africa. Accordingly, the question is raised as to when and by what route this African plant reached the Caddo Indians in East Texas and the Cappa in Arkansas. It appears that the watermelon seed Joutel planted at the post came from the Caddo, although he acquired some seeds on the stop in Hispaniola. Although Swanton does not suggest the specific route that watermelon seed followed in reaching the Mississippi, he postulates that the route crossed Texas in *Source Material on the Caddo Indians*, 131.

[27] Joutel's party was on a tributary or small slough of the Arkansas River near Dumas, several leagues southwest of the principal riverbed. Geographers and anthropologists have noted, and complained, that expedition journalists and diarists usually failed to give specific information about the size of the fields under cultivation by native tribes. See Denevan, "The Pristine Myth," 375. Joutel was an exception; he estimated that this field extended for "a good league" (perhaps two and a half to three miles). In Chapter XVI Joutel gives further specific information on the size of an agricultural field he passed.

[28] This is the Arkansas River, which originates in eastern New Mexico and Colorado and moves eastward through parts of Texas, Oklahoma, and Kansas to the Mississippi River. Douay estimated rather accurately that the distance traveled from the Cahinno village to the Arkansas River was about sixty leagues, east-northeast. Cox (ed.), *Journeys of La Salle*, I, 255. Joutel's daily record reflects a total distance of approximately fifty-five and a half leagues. The straight-line measured distance from the projected crossing of the Ouachita River to the French post on the Arkansas River is approximately one hundred miles or about forty-one and a half French leagues. A map depicting the location of the 1686–1699 French post (later moved and called Arkansas Post) and the first Quapaw (Cappa) village at the time of Joutel's

with a more rapid current. On the other side of the river, on the bank, we saw a large cross standing like those erected by missionaries in France and elsewhere wherever they go. By the cross was a house of the French style, and below that the Indians' village was located. As soon as we saw the cross, we determined that these must not be Englishmen. Besides the bands of Indians who came to meet us, we perceived others crossing the river in boats. They were painted and smeared with various colors: some of them in red, white and black with swan and Canada goose down on their heads dyed red. Others had outfitted themselves with bison horns according to their whim. They resembled more demons than men. But this was their custom, although quite a ridiculous one.

When we had been on the river bank a while, gazing at the village and the boats coming and going, we saw two clothed men come out of the house; each fired a musket shot to greet us. In the village, an Indian also fired a shot; the Indian, who must have been the chief, actually shot first. We responded to their shots with several volleys to the great pleasure of the Indians who were with us who expressed their delight and urged us to fire. While we were firing, boats came and went loaded with people. One of the men from the house embarked on a boat to come and identify us, as they were as concerned about who we were as we were to learn from him who they were. As soon as he was close to us, we asked him what country he was from. He responded that he was French and of the people with Tonty, commander of Fort Saint Louis of the Illinois for La Salle, and that this tribe was that of the Acansas.[29]

When we told him, for our part, that we were some of La Salle's people, he landed as fast as he could. I have difficulty expressing the joy one and the other of us felt, he to learn the news, and us above all to find ourselves having arrived safely in the midst of our people. There were plenty of other difficulties to surmount as we were still quite far from our destination which still greatly worried us. Too, our success made us more sensitive to the death of La Salle, mingling our joy with our pain, for if he had been with us, everything would have succeeded. The Frenchman, learning of the death of the gentleman, was deeply grieved. When he

---

visit is in Morris S. Arnold, *Colonial Arkansas, 1686–1804: A Social and Cultural History* (Fayetteville, Ark.: University of Arkansas Press, 1991), 13, fig. 4.

[29] The Acansas Indians (as sometimes called in Joutel's text) were the same as the Quapaw or Cappa. See Swanton, *Source Materials on the Caddo Indians*, 9. Arnold writes that in 1686 Tonty established the first location of the French post near the Quapaw village of Osotouy, located "near the little community called Nady and the oxbow lake named Dumond." Arnold, *Colonial Arkansas*, 5, 6. According to Joutel's account in Chapter XVI, Osotouy was "about five or six leagues" (twelve to fourteen and a half miles) from the second village (called Thoriman), which was itself only "a gun shot or two" (perhaps one quarter mile) from the Mississippi. According to USGS *Greenwood*, NI15–9, Joutel's information places the Osotouy village and the French post as Arnold suggested. USGS *Greenwood*, NI15–9, identifies an oxbow lake named Dumond on the left side of the Arkansas River approximately thirty-five miles upstream from the mouth of the Arkansas.

A review of the Quapaw from 1673 to 1860 is found in George Sabo III, et al., *Human Adaptation in the Ozark and Ouachita Mountains*, Arkansas Archeological Survey Research Series 31 (Fayetteville, Ark.: Arkansas Archeological Survey, 1990), 122–124. Marquette describes the "Arkansa" whom he and Jolliet met near the mouth of the Arkansas River in July 1673. See Donnelly, *Jacques Marquette*, 224–226.

had landed, he came and threw himself at the feet of Father Anastase, not recognizing the Abbé who, as the case was, was not dressed correctly, having only a small brown cassock according to what was available. However, the Abbé did have an old black jerkin of the late La Salle, who had it for the mourning of the Queen, which he was keeping for his arrival in Canada. Only Father Anastase was distinguishable in his robe of the clergy which had lasted although it was rather threadbare and greasy.

# CHAPTER XVI

# On the Mississippi

nce the embraces were exchanged as upon such occasions, we proceeded to cross the river. We placed all our packs into canoes and suffered no lack of busy helpers to carry everything although I did not entirely trust them. However, the Frenchman told us that we had nothing to fear because the people of this tribe were not thieves like those in Canada, the truth of which judgment I later appreciated. There was also the matter of getting our horses across, and it was necessary for them to swim. I asked if the landing was good because at the place where we were it would not have been possible. The whole bank was quite difficult to descend. I could see that the opposite bank was flat, but I feared it might be very muddy, which was only too true. But the Indians showed us that only a half pistol shot farther downstream the landing was good. So we led the horses there, and they crossed over. Even then, one had great difficulty extricating himself, having landed a little above the others.

After we had crossed, we were taken to the house where a great many Indians came to see us, and those who had put our scant baggage on board brought all of it to the house. After we had rested a while, and the crowd of Indians had diminished a bit, we informed the two Frenchmen of a part of what had happened on our journey, the period of time we had been in the country, and the tragic death of the late La Salle and the others. They seemed much saddened by the news. In their turn, they told us how they had come to be stationed at this post and who they were: one was named Couture,[1] a carpenter, and the other Delaunay. Both were from Rouen. They told us that six of them had been sent by the Sieur de Tonty, on his return from the exploration he had made, on orders from La Salle which had been brought to him by the Sieur de La Forest[2] who served as commander for the gentleman at Fort Frontenac or Catorokoui. La Forest, who left France with us, had

[1] Henri de Tonty later directed Jean Couture to contact the French survivors in Texas, and Couture sketched a map that included information on the route of Joutel's party. See Jack Jackson, *Manuscript Maps Concerning the Gulf Coast, Texas, and the Southwest, 1519–1836* (Chicago: Newberry Library, 1995), 8.

[2] La Forest was one of La Salle's lieutenants. Soon after La Salle returned to Canada in 1675, La Forest joined in a partnership with La Salle and others to conduct the trading operations at Fort

268

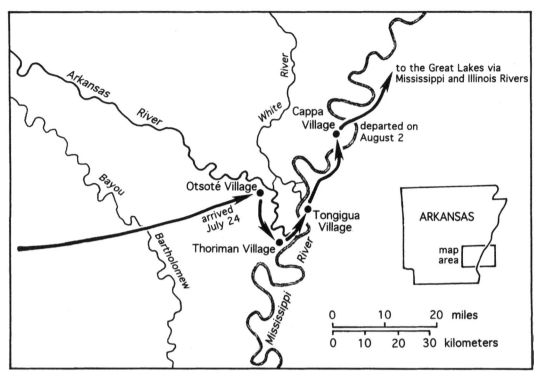

Joutel's movements near the junction of the Arkansas and Mississippi rivers

set course for Canada with the other vessels as I stated in the beginning. Tonty had orders to descend the Illinois River and afterward to the mouth of the Colbert River so he could join us and act on any orders La Salle would have for him relating to the purpose he had in mind. Accordingly, Tonty had descended the river with a number of Frenchmen as well as some Indians. However, receiving no news of us, he had returned up to the Illinois fort. Afterward he sent six men (of whom I spoke) to construct a house among this tribe, the Acansas, alleging that La Salle had promised him this post when he had made the discovery of the river. After the six men had been at this place for a period of time and had received no news, four of them decided to return to the Fort of Saint Louis of the Illinois for instructions, and the two others remained at this post.

At length and after much discourse from each side, we told them that we must manage to reach the Illinois as soon as possible in order then to arrive in Canada before the departure of the ships. By this means, we could send word to France about what had happened regarding the enterprise so that, if the King deemed it proper, he would send relief. This was why it was necessary that the Indians be given no knowledge of La Salle's death as these tribes had seen him on his discovery

Frontenac. In 1684, after being ejected from the fort by Governor La Barre, La Forest sailed for France, where he was directed to return to Canada and in La Salle's name reestablish his position at both Fort Frontenac and Fort Saint Louis on the Illinois River. See Parkman, *La Salle and the Discovery of the Great West*, 101, 351.

expedition and he had given presents to them. If they learned of his death, they might conjecture something and not be inclined to help us. Therefore, it was necessary to take measures and determine the most prompt course of action.

The chief of the village came to invite us to eat. We went and Couture with us. He knew the Illinois language rather well, and the chief understood him well too, so he interpreted everything we asked.[3] At length, when we arrived at the chief's hut, we found skins and mats spread out for us to sit upon and almost the entire village assembled. The elders seated themselves too, forming a kind of semi-circle. We told them that we had come with La Salle who had settled at the seacoast in the direction from which we came; that we had passed through a great many tribes with whom we had made peace; that we were going to Canada and from there to France to collect goods to bring them, as they had been promised; and that we would return from the lower part of the river. We said that we would bring along many people to settle among them and defend them from their enemies, that we had met with many tribes who had given us guides and they also must give us guides along with a canoe and a few men, and finally that we would give each of our guides a musket, six knives, two hatchets, powder and bullets, a few bracelets, and some glass beads for their trouble. After the chief and the elders had heard this proposition, which we could much more easily make understood now we had an interpreter, this chief said that he was going to send people to the other villages of the tribe to inform them of our arrival and to deliberate with them on what they should do.[4] They were quite surprised that we had passed through so many tribes without being captured or killed, considering our small number.

After the chief's speech and several other speeches were over, he had food served to us: smoked meat, several kinds of cornbread, watermelons, pumpkins, and other similar things according to what was available to them. After this, they offered us some tobacco to smoke. After we had been there for a time, we returned to the house with several young people. We spent the night there rather peacefully, conversing at leisure about all that had happened and how they had settled in this place. We learned that the people were docile and that they desired La Salle's return from the lower part of the river as he had promised them at the time of his exploration. We also learned that four villages comprised this Acansas tribe[5] and

[3] Couture apparently learned the language of the Illinois Indians while he was living in Canada and near the Great Lakes. The Acansas (Quapaw) were apparently familiar with the Caddoan and Iroquoian languages, which show similarities according to linguistic studies. See Michael K. Foster, "Language and the Cultural History of North America," in Ives Goddard (ed.), *Languages*, vol. 17 of William C. Sturtevant (ed.), *Handbook of North American Indians* (Washington, D.C.: Smithsonian Institution, 1996), 102, 107–109. The close cultural and linguistic ties of the two groups living near the middle Mississippi may be traced at least to about 3800 B.C., according to Smith, *The Caddo Indians*, 5. For a recent overview of the tradition of the Dhegiha-speaking Kansa (Acansas) and Quapaw along the Mississippi and Missouri rivers, see W. Raymond Wood, "Historic Indians," in Wood, et al., *Holocene Human Adaptations in the Missouri Prairie-Timberlands*, 78–88. Apparently in the 1600s, the Iroquoian language or dialects similar to it were spoken in a broad area of the Northeast. See Grumet, *Historic Contact*, 330–331.

[4] This sentence has been translated from the manuscript, which is clearer than Margry's version.

[5] The Acansas was the name Joutel used for the four tribes living near the junction of the Arkansas River and the Mississippi; the same tribe was identified later as the Quapaws. See Baird, *The Quapaw Indians*, 5–6.

270  bore different names. Two of these villages are located on the banks of the Colbert River and two others on the river called Acansas.[6]

This one where we were was on a small rise where the river [the Arkansas River] does not overflow. The house was located about a half pistol shot from the village on a slightly elevated site. It was built of large pieces of timber jointed with each other, forming a dovetail, up to the roof. It was of beautiful cedar wood and covered with bark which was not bad for roofing. The Indian village was built in a way that was different from those we had seen before in that the huts were constructed length-wise in a dome fashion. They frame them with long logs which they erect, putting the large end in the ground, and they make the logs join together in a semi-circular vault; they are quite large. They cover them with bark. Each hut contains several families who form their own individual households. These huts were quite a bit cleaner than many we had seen. However in one respect they were less orderly than the Cenis and the Assonis and others: that is, most Acansas sleep on the ground like dogs, having only some animal hide under themselves. These people are quite well shaped and alert; the women here are more shapely than those in the last village we passed through. The Acansas are skilled in making very fine canoes, all of one piece, from a tree that they hollow out and finish very well. Of all those I had come upon in the past, I had not seen any better made than theirs. They are also adept at making these dishes which I have already spoken of; they trade them with their neighboring tribes who bring them bows and arrows in exchange, which they are more skilled at making, and others bring them salt. Each tribe trades according to their skill.

They are settled in very fine country. According to the report of the two Frenchman, behind the houses there are prairies, not very distant, in which there are many bison and deer, both bucks and doe. The woods shelter bears and other animals. As for feathered game, they have every sort of species. They also have abundant fish in the rivers. They are very skillful in catching fish by spears as well as by nets which they make. Thus they live better than many other tribes who do not have as many resources. Besides this, they move about on the two rivers by means of their canoes which are very useful to them for transporting their necessities. Furthermore, they grow a much larger quantity of corn, beans, and other vegetables than other tribes. Lastly, they are warriors and call themselves brave as do all Indians. They seemed to take pleasure in seeing our horses eat corn: indeed they untied them from the places we had put them to graze and led them to some nearby fields of corn they had on the opposite side of the river where the largest amount of corn was grown.

They also have several kinds of good fruit including very good peaches. Although the peaches were not quite ripe, they boiled them to eat. They also have a large number of plum trees; in France I have seen many places where the plums were not as good. Their nuts, several kinds, are very good. There is, among others, one kind that is smaller; it is shaped almost like an acorn with a rather tender shell. The others are good as well, but their shells are much harder. They have besides a

---

[6] Acansas was the name Joutel used for the present Arkansas River.

fruit that they call *piaquiminia*[7] which resembles the French medlar in shape, but it is much better, with a very pretty color and more delicate. They make a kind of bread with it that is similar to gingerbread in appearance, but it does not taste the same. They have a great many mulberry trees whose fruit are very good in season, as well as grapes and many other sorts of fruit in quite some abundance whose names are unknown to me.

The villages of this tribe are called: the first one Otsoté,[8] the second is Thoriman, the third Tongigua, and the fourth Cappa which we spoke of at first. Although this tribe is called Acansas in general, not one of the said villages bears the name. The first two are situated on the river called Acansas and the two others on the Colbert River, one on one bank and the other on the other side. We were very hopeful now of getting through because we had the river to guide us, but traveling upstream would be difficult, and it was necessary to avoid surprises which was no small matter.

On Friday, the 25th, the elders gathered and came to explain to Couture, our interpreter, that they planned to have a calumet dance as the other villages had performed it for La Salle and Tonty on their expedition. They said that only their tribe had not danced it because they were a little inland and La Salle's party had seen only those who lived on the Colbert River. The chief's proposal undoubtedly had no object other than to obtain a few muskets because they indicated that they alone had no muskets. When Couture relayed this, the Abbé yielded to their request as we needed them to give us a few men and a canoe to conduct us.

After they heard our response, the Indians assembled and came to the house with several bison robes which they spread out, and then they came for the Abbé. They led him ceremonially to the site and made him sit down. Next they made us sit as well, and they began to sing in their way. The women also came there; they positioned themselves behind the men and sang in time with the others. They set the calumet on two forks in the way that I described with the other tribe. A few of them wore otter skins to honor the calumet which was decorated with feathers of different colors. Finally, they sang at the top of their voices. Fortunately, the Abbé was not as embarrassed as he had been in the other village where the man had rocked him from behind, and, moreover, the two girls had been placed on either side of him. Nonetheless in the afternoon, weary of hearing them shriek and being exposed to the intense heat of the sun (although they had put a few skins in front of him), he informed them that he was placing his nephew, the young Sieur Cavelier, in his place. They said that was fine and continued to sing until the next day. Some of them could almost no longer speak, they were so hoarse.

When the sun had risen a little, they brought a stake that they planted in the ground. Couture told us that their plan was to strike the stake while recounting exploits of their bravery in battle. After that, they threw a few pelts down at the

---

[7] The *piaquiminia* is probably the persimmon tree. See entry "piacminiar" in McDermott, *Mississippi Valley French*, 115–116. Cheatham and Marshall suggest that the fruit tree might have been the Virginia persimmon (*Diospyros virginiana*).

[8] The Otsoté was referred to as the Osotchave in Joutel's August 2 reference. Parkman refers to them as the Osotouy or the Sauthouis in *La Salle and the Discovery of the Great West*, 300, n. 2.

foot of the stake. Whereupon, those of the tribe to whom they were presenting the calumet responded by taking what the former had put there and placing some goods at the foot of the stake. This was, so to speak, a kind of disguised random exchange. I had heard it described by the late Sieur de La Salle. As we were not carrying many goods and we had not much use for their pelts, because we had no convenient way to carry them, we sent word to them that it must wait until our return when we would have goods in large quantity and that at that time we would strike the stake. Their ceremony finished, the Indians took the calumet pipe, put tobacco in it, and presented the pipe to the Abbé. Someone had gone to seek him, and he was reinstalled in his place. After that, they made us smoke, one after the other (that is those who smoked). I then gave them a few pieces of tobacco from France, or rather the Islands, in order to honor the calumet, and they smoked it. The Indians took the calumet, put it in a deer skin sack with the utensils for supporting it, and presented it to the Abbé with a few other pelts and some porcelain necklaces made from shells they obtain from tribes said to be near New England.[9] They brought it all to us at the house. We gave them a musket, two hatchets, six knives, one hundred charges of powder and as many bullets, and some beads and rings for the women. They withdrew quite contented.

The other villages had been notified of our arrival, so our request might be proposed, and on the same day, their chiefs or agents came to the house where they were quite well received. They were given food and tobacco to smoke during which time we gave a recital of our journey by means of the interpreter. They were astonished that we had passed among so many tribes without any of them attacking us or doing us harm. We told them that the other tribes had given us guides, and, at the same time, we advised them of our plan and repeated to them the offers which I mentioned before. We added that, as we did not have any large present, considering the journey we had made and the great many tribes we had passed through, we would give each village as a present a pistol, one hundred charges of powder, as many bullets, two hatchets, six knives, and a few beads and rings, and that, when we returned, we would reward them by giving them goods. Further, we would make war against their enemies and would settle among them. Thus, they only had to deliberate on what they would like to do. They spent some time reflecting without speaking, and after that they consulted among themselves and agreed to give us what we asked, that is to say, one man per village, and we would get a canoe at the Cappas which was the last village. For provisions, we must procure them where we found them, although they told us that they would also give us some in the last village, alleging that the Cappas had more than they had.

As the Indians who had served as guides as far as the Acansas were still with us at the house, we took care to feed them well. To the guide whom the chief had

---

[9] The comment that the Cappa or Quapaw were engaged in trade involving coastal shells from New England confirms the extensive trade network that Native Americans enjoyed in the late seventeenth century. For a summary review of the Indian tribes on the middle Mississippi in the late seventeenth century, see John A. Walthall and Thomas E. Emerson, "Indians and French in the Midcontinent," in Walthall and Emerson (eds.), *Calumet and Fleur-de-Lys: Archaeology of Indian and French Contact in the Midcontinent* (Washington, D.C.: Smithsonian Institution Press, 1992), 1–16.

given us, we gave what we had promised, namely, the saber, a hatchet, and a few knives. But, as Couture wanted the saber, he proposed to the Indian that he take a hatchet in its place which he did. I was not too pleased with this exchange as I had observed that the chief of the village from where the Indian came had very much wanted the saber and we had promised it to him. We gave him a few trinkets with which he seemed satisfied, and he went off with the others. But I suspect that they were nothing but a hindrance to him because, Couture told us, they proposed to dance the calumet for him, scheming to lay hold of his hatchets. However, I do not believe they wanted to take him by surprise because they seemed quite astonished by what had happened to us, and they thought we still had many men in those regions. This gave them reason to fear the consequences of an ill deed.

On Sunday, the 27th, the chiefs and the elders gathered again to deliberate on what they should do, for the length of the journey upriver frightened them: it was close to 300 leagues.[10] Furthermore, they had enemies along the way. Although no settled tribe was on the banks of the great river going upstream, their enemies did often frequent the river. We told them that we had no fear of being surprised because we always kept a close watch; that we had no enemies and we made peace with everyone; and that, with regard to their return, they could go downstream and travel only by night. Couture told us that they considered themselves safe enough when they have a few Frenchmen with them when they sometimes go hunting. After they had weighed the matter a bit, or rather reflected on it, they decided to give us a man as they had promised. The chief came to present him to us, telling us he would come with us. We then made them a present of what we had promised the village with the assurance of reward for each of our guides according to what we had told them. As they knew that we had kept our word to the guides whom we had brought along with us to their country, they had reason to believe that we would act the same in their regard. We told them that if there was material at Fort Saint Louis, we would also give each of them a cloak.

Everything having been resolved, it was now only a matter of considering departure. Now, of the six of us, some were not strong enough to stand the fatigue and difficulties of the journey, for strong arms would be required to handle the oars going up the river. There was also the young boy from Paris, named Barthélemy,[11] who was unconcerned about staying at that place where he would live well without any trouble. We were not displeased to see him remain for several reasons. The first was that the Abbé was determined to conceal the death of La Salle in Canada as well as in the Illinois. The fewer people there were, the easier it would be to hide, besides this young man did not keep much secret. Secondly, we made the Indians understand that we left this young man as a pledge for the men they were giving us, to show them that our plan was to return. As for the death of

[10] According to current maps, the distance from the mouth of the Arkansas to the upper Illinois River is approximately six hundred miles. *Webster's New Geographical Dictionary*, maps "Mississippi," 771, and "Missouri," 775.

[11] Barthélemy later severely criticized La Salle and alleged, in some detail, that La Salle had committed numerous acts of cruelty against members of his party. His assertions are not supported by any other writer. See Parkman, *La Salle and the Discovery of the Great West*, 432 n1.

La Salle, it was concluded that we would not speak of it to anyone, the Indians or anyone else; we would say that he had come with us and led us to a certain place where he had left us which was, in part, true. Indeed, he left us at the place that I have mentioned before. Since the time of the parting, neither the Abbé nor I had seen him. We charged those remaining in the village to keep the secret so that if we were fortunate enough to make the crossing to France this year, we could send help in the spring, provided the court deemed it appropriate. We believed that if the death of the gentleman were known, we would be presented with obstacles, particularly on the part of the Indians who had not readily given us men, for they indicated affection for the gentleman although they had only seen him on his discovery expedition when he had made them a few presents. The Abbé also promised those who remained in that place, namely Couture and Delaunay, that he would do what he could for them as far as help being sent back which he expected would occur and I did as well.

As we realized we would be able to find a part of what we would need in the Illinois, specifically ammunition, we left for the above-named people 15 to 16 pounds of powder, 800 charges of bullets, 300 flints, three dozen knives, 10 hatchets, a few pounds of beads, and a few rings, pins, needles, and other trinkets and utensils. The Abbé also gave them some of his linen. He had taken much more than he could easily carry so that I had had to carry it part of the way even though I had a horse to lead. Likewise, each one left them something, telling them to take courage and that if we were fortunate enough to make the crossing that year, we would be, or at least would hope to be, at the lower part of the river by early spring, the month when there would be some ships there. They received the sacrament of penance before our departure. As we no longer needed horses, they benefited from them also.[12] They would be very useful for hunting and made us more valuable yet to the Indians, making them realize that we were leaving them the best of everything we had.

With everything concluded and arranged, we took our leave and embarked at ten o'clock in the morning on that day [the 27th] in a canoe belonging to the chief from the nearest village who had come to see us. There were at least 20 of us in the canoe, men as well as women. We were saluted on our departure as on our arrival; several shots were fired. The Indians took us by canoe, without great difficulty, for they were punting, and they did not tire a great deal because we had a favorable river current. I noticed that there was a lower part of the river that we rejoined which led us to conclude that the village we had just left must be on an island.

As we needed to have things properly interpreted in the other villages that we had to pass so they would not change their minds, we had Couture come with us as far as the Cappa, which is the last village, in order to make them understand what

---

[12] From Joutel's description it appears that the horses the French party left were perhaps the first among the Quapaws. However, these were not the first horses that Europeans bought to Arkansas. In 1543, the DeSoto-Moscoso expedition abandoned several hundred horses on its trip down the Mississippi, and Garcelano de la Vega reports that Indians directed their anger and arrows at the animals and killed them all. See the account of Garcelano de la Vega, the Inca, "La Florida," trans. Charmion Shelby, in Clayton, Knight, and Moore (eds.), *The De Soto Chronicles*, II, 512.

we needed. We arrived at six o'clock in the evening at the first village, or rather the second, named Thoriman, which was about five or six leagues from the first village.[13] A few individuals there had muskets which either Tonty had given to them or they had gotten from some area farther north. They greeted our arrival with several shots to which we responded. Then we landed and were conducted to the chief's hut where everyone was assembled, that is to say, a large part of the village. They were expecting us and received us very warmly. They had spread out mats of bison and bear skins upon which they made us sit, and then they brought us food. After we had eaten, we made to them the same proposition that we had made to the first village where their chief had been and was party to the agreement. But they obey their chiefs only partially and only as it pleases them. Chiefs are not accepted as such until they have performed glorious deeds and then on the condition that they are generous with what they have and prove themselves trustworthy in some way so as to win the youth over. This is the reason that when a present is made to a chief, he is the one who gets the least because he distributes it to the young people and the warriors whom I would call the most favored.

Be that as it may, regarding the proposition that we made to them, they told us they would deliberate the next day. I observed that among these people, although savages, when they consider undertaking or doing something, they hold counsel together. In short, the rest of the evening was spent going to several huts where they invited us to go eat because it was their custom to ask visitors one after another to go eat at their places. In truth, we would have needed several stomachs because sometimes there were as many as four or five of them waiting to conduct us to each of their huts. Although we were not hungry, we did not hesitate to go, so as not to counter them and indeed to please them. We separated, some going in one direction, others in another. Besides, their feasts did not consist of much: for the most part they were watermelons which served almost as a drink. Now, the season was changing, it was hot, but we feared they would make us sick considering that we were not accustomed to them.

We had taken a few sacks of corn from the house in the previous village. The Frenchmen had given it to us, but we had not had time to grind it. It was from last year's crop and consequently better to keep because it would not ferment as new corn does. We told the chief of this village that if the women would pound it for us, we would give them some beads, and instantly he dispatched two or three lackeys and squires. I had never seen any village where the chief was more obeyed than this one. At the least signal from him, they left one in one direction and the other in

[13] According to USGS *Greenwood*, NI15-9, the Arkansas River near its junction with the Mississippi River turns sharply toward the east and back to the west as it moves generally southward. Although the report of Joutel's five-to-six league canoe trip on the river from the first to the second Quapaw village (which was about one quarter to one half mile from the Mississippi River) cannot be measured with precision using current maps, the information is very valuable to geographers. Baird notes: "The French counted four of these [Quapaw villages]: Tourima [Touriman] and Osotouy on the north side of the Arkansas River, the former near the river's mouth and the latter sixteen miles west." Joutel's account supports Baird's narrative assessment of the location of the two villages. However, Joutel's account does not support the location of the Tourima village found in Baird's map, "Mississippi and Ohio River valleys, showing location of Quapaw villages" in 1682. Baird, *The Quapaw Indians*, 10, 16, map.

another, according to where he wished to send them, with the chief saying but one word. But what I found most entertaining was to see the figures they made, completely nude, some painted, each one having three or four gourds or calabashes tied to his belt in which there were small pebbles or kernels of corn to make noise, with some horse or bison tail hanging behind them. Wherever they went, this made a rather amusing rattle, and we had difficulty keeping ourselves from laughing at seeing these figures; we must not appear to be laughing. Thus we spent the rest of the day.

I went to see the Colbert River which was only about a musket shot or two from there.[14] It proved to be a great river indeed and very swift. I learned from Couture that this village was on an island to which we had come downstream by way of a fork the river forms about a league above it. The river is nonetheless still immense passing in front of the village. Couture also told me that another branch passed behind the first village but it was smaller. The soil there is very good, and very fine corn grows there, producing two or three crops a year, at least two. Indeed, I noticed fields where they had harvested corn that year and had already replanted. In other fields, they had it at all stages of growth, as well as beans and other kinds of vegetables.

Their huts are constructed like those in the previous village; but here they make an elevated platform 15 or 20 feet high on which they sleep to get more air and to protect themselves from the mosquitoes which are the most annoying creatures that I have found in America. Although small, they prevent one from sleeping. But, thanks to this kind of raised platform, when there is some small breeze, these creatures are carried away. I will say no more as I have spoken of them elsewhere.

With regard to the Indians of this village, they have the same hunting advantage as the others, having the convenience of the river, or rather the rivers, with the help of their canoes of which they have a good many and very well made. They also catch fish which they shoot with arrows; they are quite skillful at this. They presented us with fish to eat at several places where we were invited.

On the 28th, the chief and the elders assembled at the chief's hut where we were, and they decided to give us a man, as those in the previous village had done, and to further encourage them, we told them that we were leaving one of our men to live among them, as a pledge in place of those they gave us, to indicate to them that we wanted to return. They declared that they were very well pleased with this. After they had deliberated and shown us the man they were giving to us, we gave

[14] Joutel's report that the Colbert or Mississippi was only "a musket shot or two" from the Thoriman village helps to locate not only Thoriman but also Otsoté, where the French post was situated five or six leagues to the northwest. According to Joutel and USGS *Greenwood*, NI15-9, the Otsoté village and French post was near the Menard-Hodges archeological site. James A. Ford of the American Museum of Natural History concluded that the Menard-Hodges site was the site of the village Otsoté Tonty located in 1686 and Joutel's party visited in 1687. Joutel records that the distance between the first village and the second was five to six leagues, not suggesting that he was estimating the distance traveled on the winding river. This would place the location of Otsoté at or near the Menard-Hodge site as Arnold and Baird suggested. See comments on the 1991 designation of the site as a National Historic Landmark in "Field Notes," the newsletter of the Arkansas Archeological Society no. 276 (Fayetteville, Ark.: Mar./Apr. 1997), 3–5.

them the present as we had done in the previous village. We also gave what we had promised to the women when they brought us the corn that they had come to collect in the morning. The rest of the day was spent in feasts; we went to them to please them rather than to eat.

These Indians have a different method of serving food from those we had previously encountered, particularly the Cenis. The Cenis serve each individual his own plate, but this tribe normally only serves two large plates which they pass around from one to the other. In such a way, while the first ones eat, the others are spectators which is not pleasant for those who find themselves last, particularly if they are hungry. They are a little more tidy in eating than the Cenis in that they have a spoon that they make from the bison horn for eating *sagamité* or boiled corn, whereas the others eat with their fingers. The two dishes, or four, depending on the number of people at the gathering, are served first to the two most important people and afterwards to the others. The host does not eat at all with the others. He is a spectator and assists in the meal only with his presence and even has another to serve the food as a chief-of-service. The host carefully paints himself with different colors and squats like a monkey, maintaining his gravity all the while. I had difficulty keeping myself from laughing at seeing these sorts of poses.

As this was the season when we needed refreshments, we did quite well in this area because there were many watermelons which they all served us. They grow very well there. This is a fruit that I had never eaten and which I have only seen in this country.[15] They are only good to quench the thirst as they are only water and therefore very well named. All the feasts consisted almost solely of these fruits, with bread made in their own way; others gave us peaches which they boiled because they were not ripe yet. They also had many plums and nuts of several kinds including one that is shaped like an acorn that has a very thin shell and its fruit is very good. They have four sections like those in Europe; only their shape is different. There are a number of other fruits whose names I do not know.

On the 29th, we departed this village and embarked in the canoes. The chief of this village came to guide us with 20 of his young people. We entered the Colbert River or the Mississippi as we had so much desired to do. We crossed to the other side where I admired the beauty of the river which was nearly a quarter of a league across with a very rapid current. The Indians punted one after the other, along the margins of the river near the bank, with large poles 15 or 20 feet in length.[16] We arrived at 11 o'clock in the morning at the other village which was

---

[15] See comments about watermelons in Chapter XV.

[16] The Indians on the Mississippi (like those on Matagorda Bay) punted canoes with long poles. In 1992 Richard S. Fuller prepared a study of an archeological recovery of a twenty-five-foot, shallow draft, platform style Indian dugout cypress canoe, probably dating ca. A.D. 1500 to 1600, located about two leagues east of the Mississippi River, on a lake or bayou about eighteen leagues south of the Thoriman village near the mouth of the Arkansas River. Fuller notes that similar canoes were in use by the Mississippi culture from about A.D. 1250. Richard S. Fuller, *Archaeological Recovery and Analysis of an Indian Dugout Canoe (site 22 WS 776) Discovered in the Bank of Steele Bayou, Swan Lake, Washington County, Mississippi* (Baton Rouge, La.: Coastal Environments, Inc., 1992), 40. Dan F. Morse concludes that people living on the middle Mississippi in Arkansas in about 8500 B.C. (whom archeologists refer to as Dalton people)

only two leagues from the one we had left. We were received as at the previous villages. Those who had muskets fired several shots upon our arrival, and we responded to them. Not many people happened to be there because some of them had gone to dance the calumet at the village where we were supposed to go. We were conducted to the chief's hut where we found things prepared in the same manner as elsewhere, that is to say, some pelts were spread out upon which they made us sit, and then they brought us food. We made them the same proposal that we had made to the others, to which they agreed, and we gave them a similar present. Afterwards we had to go to several places where we were invited just as we were in the two other villages.

This village was built in the same manner as the others except that it was not quite as large which was why it bore the name Tongigua which means little village according to Couture. It is situated beside the Colbert River on the right going upriver. The river is quite wide in the location of this village although it is not so everywhere. The trees along its banks are aspen, willows, linden, and *cotonnier*[17] [cottonwood], called such because of a sort of cotton that falls on the water like a kind of down. Some of these grow very large. Besides the trees, there are also canebrakes that would be very difficult if one had to walk through them. Inland even a little way, one finds many other beautiful trees of many species, extremely thick and tall in proportion, as well as many mulberry trees and other kinds of trees. We spent the rest of the day nearly as we had done in the other village.

On the 30th, we left this village to go to that of the Cappa, the last village of this tribe. We had been told that it was about eight leagues away. Because the river had such rapid currents, we had to cross it often to avoid the strongest ones which we could not overcome in view of the depth of the water and the speed of its current. For this reason, we sought the shallow side where the current was not as rough. Ordinarily on most rivers, when the current is moving on one side, it is not the same on the other side unless the river is between mountains. But this area was quite flat.[18] When we encountered river banks where the water was extremely deep and their poles could not reach the bottom, the natives used narrow oars which did not have much pull as they were no wider than a medium-sized plate.[19]

At about 10 or 11 o'clock, we saw 20 to 25 canoes coming down the river. They were the men from the village we had left who had gone to dance the calumet. Because they did not see us from the distance, only six of them came to meet us for the river could not be crossed in a direct manner; one drifted downstream for a

made dugout canoes. Dan F. Morse, *Sloan: A Paleoindian Dalton Cemetery in Arkansas* (Washington, D.C.: Smithsonian Institution Press, 1997), xv.

[17] Although McDermott translated the word *cotonnier* as sycamore (*Mississippi Valley French*, 58), the description of the tree indicates that it is more likely a cottonwood. Cheatham and Marshall suggest that the tree was possibly *Populus deltoides*.

[18] Margry's version is translated "But this area was well placed." The manuscript version is "But this area was quite flat."

[19] Margry notes a gap in the Joutel text as follows: "Here the absence of the 12th notebook of the original text again interrupts the account from July 30 to September 17. Fortunately, the excerpt from the geographer Delisle, which is rather extensive, aids us in filling the gap almost entirely. We have only a little bit to borrow from Michel's summary."

distance about equal to the river's breadth. Those who came to join us gave us food from what they had, but we hardly diminished their provisions for it was only boiled corn. After this, we each went our way; but they went much faster than we did. That day a few storms delayed us and drenched us. Part of the way we went by land, when one could walk, so that only those who were punting the canoe remained in it. The poor weather caused us to arrive late at the Cappa village, for it was at least one o'clock in the morning. Many youth came for the landing, and some conducted us to the chief's hut while others carried our packs. Indeed, it was their custom to unload the canoes when strangers arrived at their place, and I admired the great integrity of these people who, in spite of their need of everything so to speak, carried all of our small bags and did not take anything that I noticed.

We found the elders in the hut and many other people, women as well as men, who had come to see us. As we were wet, they made a fire to dry us, and we were given a light by some young people who held torches made of dried cane. These serve as candles. It is not their practice to do otherwise as easy as it would be for them to use the fat they take from bison, and also tallow from bears and from nuts, which they use to oil themselves. However, I did not observe that they use oil for illumination. They use cane and break off the charred ends from their cane torches as they burn down.

After we had looked around a bit and recovered ourselves somewhat, we told them something of our journey and the number of tribes that we had encountered on our way. They were very surprised at this. We spent some time speaking of one thing and another and were able to make ourselves better understood than in the past with the help of Couture who served us as interpreter. Then they brought us food and spent a part of the evening with us. After that each of them went home and left us to rest.

On Thursday, the 31st, they gathered and told us many things, particularly about their enemies among whom they often cited a tribe called Machigamea[20] who, they said, had killed some of their people recently. Therefore, they expressed the desire to go to war against them, and to have guns, powder, and bullets. We explained that we were going to our country, and our plan was to bring these things back to them, and we would even bring men to go to war with them; that then we would destroy all their enemies and bring peace everywhere. They said all that was good and showed their joy with a few shrieks. They said at the same time that we must not delay in returning. We made the same proposal to them that we had made to the other tribes to which they responded positively. But they feared that we would be surprised by their enemies along the great river. We answered that we never all slept at once and that one of us always stood guard and stayed awake for fear of being surprised. They said that was good and that the Indians

---

[20] When Marquette and Jolliet made their initial exploration of the Mississippi, they met the "Mitchigamea" about eight leagues upriver from the mouth of the present Arkansas. One elderly tribal member spoke a little Illinois and served as an interpreter for their party. Donnelly, *Jacques Marquette*, 224; Parkman, *La Salle and the Discovery of the Great West*, 72. For a recent study of the Michigamea in Arkansas, see Dan F. Morse, "The Seventeenth-Century Michigamea Village Location in Arkansas," in Walthall and Emerson (eds.), *Calumet and Fleur-de-Lys*, 55–74.

who had come with us had told them as much. After several speeches, we gave them the same presents that we had given the other tribes. Sometime later they introduced to us a man and said he was the one who would come with us, and they said they would give us a good canoe and some provisions. Then they brought us food. The feast proceeded as in the previous villages. Each one invited us, vying with the others, and we were obliged to go to please them, but not to eat except for a few watermelons which served us as drink. In short, they gave us what they had.

These people had more peach trees in their fields[21] than the other villages. They also showed us a few pelts, namely, some otter and a few beaver. We told them that we had no goods to give them as a present but that if they would take heart and go hunting, we would buy all their furs on our return and would bring to them what they needed; and that if they would carry what they had to the Illinois country, goods would be delivered to them. They replied that they would be well able to go up there. We encouraged them to hunt, telling them that we would take everything they had of bison, deer, and bear skins, and generally all skins, and that these would be transported through the lower part of the river. They seemed altogether quite content.

This village is located on the left side of the river, going up, on a river bluff or height at least 30 feet in elevation. The village is larger than the others. They have their clearings or fields behind the village, extending about a league in breadth and approximately a league and a half in length. From this field they reap a large quantity of corn, pumpkins, melons, sunflowers, beans, and other similar things, as well as an abundance of fruit from peach and plum trees. They have the same hunting advantage as the others, but they are not as favored in fishing because the water of this great river is almost always disturbed and muddy. According to what I could learn, 400 warriors would go out from this village and at least 300 from the other villages. These are very fine youth, well formed, quite alert, and skilled at hunting, fishing, and also handling canoes at which they take turns with each other because the labor is arduous and one cannot endure it continuously. We spent the rest of the day feasting as usual.

On Friday, the first day of August, the chief came to find us to say that we could not leave yet because the women had not yet pounded the corn for us. At 10 o'clock in the morning, the warriors and the youth gathered to perform a kind of dance. For this they were dressed in all their finery which consisted of some plumage which they had painted and with which several of them adorned their heads; others donned bison horns. Wearing these horns and plumage, and painted black, white, and red, they look like monsters and demons rather than humans.

In the evening the women brought us some flour, beans, and green corn for our journey. They told us that they were going to make bread. They boil it wrapped in shucks of the corn and often mixed with beans.[22] Although this is not

---

[21] The Cappa as well as the other Quapaw tribes had fruit orchards as well as corn and bean fields, but no reference is made to cotton, which at the time, and perhaps for decades or centuries earlier, was grown in central Mexico (including the coastal areas of Huasteca), near Las Juntas de las Rios, and New Mexico.

[22] The Cappa as well as the Caddo prepared a dish similar to tamales made of corn flour and beans wrapped in corn shucks and boiled.

too tasty, if one is hungry, one is not nearly so particular. With regard to the green corn, I believe I have said that it is prepared when the corn is in milk. The ears are boiled or roasted, next they are dried in the sun to preserve them to be eaten later in meat broth or to grind and make into a meal for *sagamité*. One way or the other, it is more delicate than ripe corn, being sweeter, but it is not as nourishing. We gave these women a few copper rings and some beads for their effort, and the day passed in this way.

On Saturday, August 2nd, we prepared ourselves for departure, but there proved to be an obstacle to this in that one of our Indians, that is to say one of those who had been given to us in the other villages, refused to travel either because some panic had seized him or otherwise. He was the one from the first village called Otsotchaué [Otsoté]. He had not adjusted to us; but fortunately, there happened to be a certain man who passed among these tribes as a *hermaphrodite* [homosexual][23] according to what Couture told me. This man, who had come from the Illinois where he was taken prisoner, said that he would come willingly with us, being very glad to go to see the Illinois. We were agreeable to this, so that it was only further a matter of leaving. Accordingly, we informed the chief of this for fear that the other man might become disheartened which would have delayed us. The chief then showed us the canoe that he wished to give to us and we had our packs, which were all ready, loaded in it.

The Abbé bade Couture to take courage, to live on good terms with the Indians and the two Frenchmen who stayed with him, and finally not to speak of La Salle to the Indians, or to anyone. He told him that if we could cross to France this year, there was reason to hope that we would bring help the following spring. The Abbé advised him to instruct the others in the same way; after which we took leave of the chief and all the others who had assembled. They fired several musket shots on our departure and we responded.

[23] This is Joutel's only reference to Indian homosexuals, who both French and Spanish writers referred to at the time as hermaphrodites. See Fray Solís's report of "hermaphrodites" among the Indians at La Bahía mission on the San Antonio River in 1768. Kress (ed. and trans.), "Diary of a Visit of Inspection of the Texas Missions," 44. Later French writers referred to them as berdaches, a term that is used today. See William B. Griffen, "Southern Periphery: East," in Ortiz (ed.), *Southwest*, vol. 10 of Sturtevant (ed.), *Handbook of North American Indians*, 335. There appears to be no reason either to stress or to ignore that among the numerous allegations against La Salle, the engineer Minet accused La Salle of making his "young and handsome valets . . . sleep with him." Minet, "Journal of Our Voyage to the Gulf of Mexico," 123.

# *Appendix A*

## The 1690 Interrogation of Captain Gregorio de Salinas Varona and Pierre Meunier in Mexico City regarding La Salle's 1684–1687 Expedition to Texas

*Archivo General de Indias (AGI), Seville, Mexico, 61-6-21*

In Mexico City, on August 17, 1690, after the Licenciado Don Francisco Fernández Marmolejo, member of His Majesty's Council, judge of this Royal Court and Auditor General of War in this kingdom, had seen the diary, letters, and other papers related to the entrada that General Alonso de León made from Coahuila to the Province of the Texas, by order of His Excellency Conde de Galve, Viceroy, Governor, and Captain-General of this New Spain—[said documents having been] sent by His Excellency to the aforesaid Auditor—he said that (for His Excellency to resolve in this matter that which what would be most to the service of both Majesties) he was ordering that testimonies be taken from Captain Don Gregorio de Salinas Varona, who had been present with General Alonso de León and who is present in this court, concerning some points which are lacking in the records; and from a Frenchman who came along in his company and who was in those regions. These should be asked whatever questions might be suitable. Captain Don Gregorio de Salinas, knowledgeable in the French language, was appointed to interrogate the Frenchman.

Authorized and signed—Licenciado Don Francisco Fernández Marmolejo.

Before me, Sebastián Sánchez de las Fraguas, Military Clerk.

In Mexico City, on August 19, 1690, the Licenciado Don Francisco Fernández Marmolejo, member of His Majesty's Council, Judge of this Royal Court, and Auditor General of War of this Kingdom, had Captain Don Gregorio de Salinas Varona appear before him; from him he received an oath, by God our Lord and the sign of the Cross—as provided by law—by which he promised to tell the truth in what might be asked of him. After the letters of Father Commissary Damián Mazanet, the Journal of General Alonso de León, the efforts made by General De León for the discovery of the Texa [sic] nation, and the Report concerning this, were read to him, and he had heard and understood it, he said that everything is as mentioned in the records and letters, as he was there personally.

*Question:* While at the fort that was burned on April 26 in the old town, which is more or less three leagues from the San Marcos [Lavaca] River that flows into the Bay of Espíritu Santo [Matagorda Bay], where they saw two buoys, why didn't they remove the buoys?

He answered that on that day, after burning the fort, they went down to inspect the Espíritu Santo Bay, which is a little more than two leagues from said town. They saw the bay where they found two buoys with their flag, one of them like a bucket; this was to the north at the mouth of the San Marcos River. The other one had no flag and was to the south. Those seem to be marks to indicate the entrance to the river. They did not take them away because [the buoys] were seen by twenty-three people, who went for that purpose to a distance of two leagues approximately, [but] they did not have a canoe nor any type of raft with which to do it. They tried to do it by swimming, but they were too distant.

*Question:* What is the width of the entrance to the mouth of the river? If you were able to examine it, what is the depth, and what is the least distance from the land to the buoys?

*Answer:* The entrance to the mouth of the river seems to be a little less than half a league [in width], as seen from buoy to buoy; if the depth is not sounded one doesn't know what it is; and there were about three quarters of a league from the closest land to the buoys.

*Question:* What is the distance from the entrance of that River to the sea? What is the circumference of said bay? Do other rivers flow out into it?

*Answer:* The distance from the mouth of the San Marcos to the sea is approximately ten to twelve leagues.[1] As to the circumference, it's very big, from what we could see, and very soundable, as indicated by different people. The San Marcos River flows into said bay from the north, and from the west is the so-called Frenchmen Creek.[2] From the south three small creeks flow in, one of them called Canoes[3] because many broken canoes were found there; farther down, near the entrance to the port of the bay, the river called Nuestra Señora de Guadalupe flows in.[4] All of this the witness inspected, and he saw it with his own eyes, together with the other persons who went there.

*Question:* In what degree [of latitude] is the bay located, and what is the width of its entrance?

*Answer:* It is at 29 long degrees.[5] But he is not certain of the width because they only came to a distance of approximately six leagues from it, where they had the meeting with the Indians of the *Cauquesi* nation to rescue the two Frenchmen and the French girl on June 21.[6]

---

[1] According to USGS map *Beeville*, NH14–12, the distance is approximately thirty miles or twelve Spanish leagues.

[2] Frenchmen Creek is today Garcitas Creek, Victoria County, where Fort Saint Louis was located.

[3] Canoes Creek is probably present-day Placedo Creek, a stream that drains an area of Victoria County fifteen miles to the northwest of Lavaca Bay.

[4] Salinas is describing accurately (for his time) the larger coastal bay area complex that since 1690 has been subdivided into smaller bays and thus renamed. On contemporary maps, the Lavaca River, which Salinas called the San Marcos, runs into Lavaca Bay and the Guadalupe runs into San Antonio Bay. See USGS map *Beeville*, NH14–12.

[5] According to USGS *Beeville*, NH14–12, the latitude reading at the entrance of Matagorda Bay is approximately 28° 20', as Joutel reported (see Chapter II).

[6] The Cauquesi Indians are the same as the coastal tribe called Caucosi by Governor Alonso de León when the Governor, Salinas Varona, and their small party rescued the two young Talon boys and their sister Marie-Madeleine on June 21, 1690. See, Bolton (ed.), *Spanish Exploration in the Southwest*, 420–421; Foster, *Spanish Expeditions into Texas*, 43, 44; and Pierre and Jean-Baptiste Talon, "Voyage to the Mississippi through the Gulf of Mexico," 229.

*Question:* If they had news that a courier had come from the east on behalf of four Frenchmen requesting friendship of the Tejas governor and permission to settle in his province, and if they knew that the Tejas were three days away, why didn't they check the area to see if they were settled, and where, and how many of them were there—since they had Tomás, the Indian,[7] who could help with the language, and since the Governor of the Tejas had told them that they were set-tled, and in what location?

*Answer:* What the Governor said was included in the question. They didn't inspect the place because they were 100 leagues away, and a very large river was sixty leagues away, which couldn't be forded nor crossed without a vessel. They call that river the Caddodachos River,[8] and it is settled on both sides by different Indian nations; and on the other side of the river, forty leagues distant, the French are settled.[9] He doesn't know how many of them, and this is the reason, as he has said, that he did not inspect the area.

*Question:* About the sowing seasons, when are they in those regions? And are they twice a year, and in what season?

*Answer:* What he knows and saw is that the climate and land are much better than in our Spain. Their goodness is proved by a planting of corn being sown and picked in three months. At one time he saw three fields of corn: one had ears ready to be picked, another one had ears of green corn, and the other one was about a fourth of a yard tall. There were plenty of beans, which are picked with-in 45 days. He saw crops of watermelons, pumpkins, and tobacco; so he con-cludes that there could be two harvests per year. The Frenchmen indicated they would come to see the Governor of the Texas for the sowing season, meaning the following year's, which is April or May. What he said is the truth, as promised under the oath that he took, in which he verified and confirmed himself. He said he was forty years old, and he signed it, attested by the said Auditor:

Don Gerónimo [sic] de Salinas Varona.

Before me, Sebastián Sánchez de las Fraguas, Royal and Military Clerk.

On the same day, month, and year, the Auditor General caused to appear before him a Frenchman who had come in the company of Captain Don Gregorio de Salinas y Varona—a well-known interpreter, and one knowledge-able in the French language, who swore by God and the Cross to do [the job] well and faithfully according to his loyal knowledge and understanding—he was asked the following questions:

[7] Juan Bautista Chapa identified Tomás the Indian as being among the Tejas Indians when Governor De León visited the central village area in June 1690. See Juan Bautista Chapa, *Texas and Northeastern Mexico, 1630–1690*, ed. William C. Foster (Austin: University of Texas Press, 1997), 151. According to Chapa, Tomás spoke "Mexican" (Aztec?) and was from Parral, a Spanish mining community in modern-day southern Chihuahua, approximately seven hundred miles southwest of where the Tejas lived.

[8] This was the Red River.

[9] Salinas probably was referring to the small French post on the lower Arkansas River that Joutel vis-ited. It was approximately 180 miles or seventy Spanish leagues from the Caddo villages on the Red River. It later was called Arkansas Post.

He was asked: What is his name? Where is he from? What religion? Age? What kind of work does he have?

*Answer:* His name is Pedro Muñi [Pierre Meunier], Lord of Preouila; he is French; from the city of Paris; son of Luis Muñi, Lord of Preouila; a Christian Roman Catholic; single; with no specific work. From him, through the Interpreter [Don Gregorio de Salinas Varona], I received an oath, by God our Lord and the sign of the Cross, and under this he promised to tell the truth in whatever he might be asked.

*Question:* How long ago did he leave Paris and with whom?

*Answer:* He left the city of Paris to go to la Rochela [La Rochelle] as a comrade of Monsieur de Salas [La Salle], with whom he embarked in a two-hundred-ton storeship called la Ymable [the *Aimable*]. From there they set out for the island of Santo Domingo, in order to continue their journey thenceforth to Monsieur La Salle's settlement; he [Meunier] does not know where it is. La Salle had with him an escort ship of the King, called Laxoli [the *Joly*], with four hundred men, gunpowder, ammunition, supplies, and tools, and fifty officers with all kinds of skills. And when they reached the island of Santo Domingo, four galleys came out and captured a smack that was part of their company and was loaded with wine, brandy, and flour. At that location [Santo Domingo] a storm hit them, and they sailed with it until they arrived at Pitiguao [Petit Goave], where they remained twenty-two days and secured some firewood. One of the pirates who was in that port with a large ship and many very-well-armed men, invited Monsieur La Salle to come to Kingdom, to which La Salle replied that he had no such orders from his King of France. When the frigate left that port, along with another storeship that came with them carrying supplies, and the escort ship, they went looking for the settlement.

After sailing fifteen days, they saw the coast of the Gulf of Mexico, but they lost many days looking for the entrance thereof [the Mississippi]. The pilots told Monsieur La Salle that he had passed the entrance, to which he replied that he had not. However, they were wandering about to the north and to the south looking for a marker that Monsieur La Salle said he had left at the mouth of the entrance to the aforesaid old settlement. When they found the mouth of the entrance to the Espíritu Santo Bay, they measured the latitude. Monsieur La Salle indicated that that was the entrance, as it was at the same latitude; to which the King's captain [Taneguy le Gallois de Beaujeu] objected, saying that he didn't want to go on from there [where they were]. So at the request of Monsieur La Salle, he and the King's captain went by sloop to sound the entrance, which was found to have nine to ten feet of water. It was decided that the vessel called La Vele [the *Belle*] should be brought in. This was done, after placing buoys in the channel first. In order to bring in the storeship [the *Aimable*] with its supplies and tools, they lightened it, using the sloops and launches. When it tried to enter the bay the vessel moved too close to the north side, leaving the buoy in deep water, and ran aground on a sandbar, and the wind heaved it over. That night it was lightened, and everything was unloaded that could be, together with the men; and the vessel was torn open and lost.

And some Indians known as the *Cauquesi*, who were settled on the coast on the southern side of the bay, came together, and Monsieur La Salle—through an Indian[10] from the old settlement who had remained with him, one of two whom he had taken [from Canada] to France—showed them kindness and made friends with them. But these Indians got some men together, and the Indians started taking the barrels of wine and brandy that [La Salle's men] had not been able to take out of the lost vessel. To save [the barrels], La Salle sent a few sailors and five soldiers in a sloop, and they recovered them from the Indians. That night the watchman fell asleep and the Indians found [the party]. They killed two soldiers and injured another two. With this news, La Salle with his people took up arms against the Indians, who abandoned their houses and moved inland. The King's captain [Beaujeu] and La Salle went to bury the dead. There was some controversy over this event, and the captain insulted La Salle, telling him how he had deceived the King by taking so much of his money, only to lose those men. And telling him "Goodbye," he embarked for his ship; he took with him some sailors of the lost vessel and set sail. At this, La Salle built a wooden fort on the southern side of the coast, where he kept the tools and supplies, and he stayed there with three hundred men, including the fifty officers.

With the flour they had, La Salle ordered them to bake some hard bread. With three canoes that the Indians had given him when they were friendly, he went to inspect the Bay. La Salle arrived at a creek called Canoes and disembarked with his Indian to inspect it. The Indian found a bison and killed it, and they took out its heart and tongue. They returned to the fort and told the soldiers that they had found a land with plenty of meat. The following day he sent some soldiers to pick up the bison, and from the same area he sent out eight soldiers to go and explore by land. At the bay, he [La Salle] with another twenty-four soldiers went ashore between the so-called Frenchmen Creek and the San Marcos [Lavaca] River; he set up camp on a small hill and ordered others to go search for the eight soldiers. When they found them, he ordered some men to cut wood to build houses and make a settlement, which they did. They used the three canoes to bring the tools and supplies from the other fort, abandoning it.

With the planking of the broken ship, they built a storehouse (which was taken to be a fort by those who came to discover it in the place where it was located), next to the creek called the Frenchmen Creek. Their houses were covered with bison skin, and they lived there for about a year and a half. Here they built other houses and the residents learned how to handle weapons.

He [La Salle] retrieved from the neighboring Indians four canoes in addition to the three that he had, and with them he decided to go with twenty-five men and make war against the Caucosi Indians and those on the banks of the Guadalupe River who had passed by with their canoes. They found four Indian encampments and fought with them. They killed four of them and returned to their camp.

[10] Although Joutel refers only to Nika as the Shawnee whom La Salle brought with him to Texas, Meunier reports correctly that La Salle took two Indians from Canada back to France with him.

La Salle spent all of that winter [1685–1686] sounding and inspecting the whole of the surrounding bay, trying to bring the eight-piece frigate[11] closer inside. He succeeded in bringing her into the bay up to where the buoys were located—as was seen by the present witness—in the mouth of the San Marcos River. The frigate was broken into pieces on the north shore[12] by a wind that threw her onto the coast.

La Salle left with fifteen men and a priest, who was his brother, carrying supplies on their shoulders. They traveled by land to the northeast looking for their settlement. After six months, he returned (less one man [Pierre Duhaut], who returned a few days after they had left because he didn't want to follow La Salle), without having found the settlement.

La Salle, with twenty men and a Recollet Franciscan priest, set out again by land, traveling to the north [Spring 1686], and arrived at the Province of the Tejas. They traded to the Indians the axes they had with them in exchange for five horse-loads of corn and beans. After six months they returned to the settlement with only five men because the others had died or run away. Later on it was learned that they had eaten each other.

La Salle left for the third time [January 1687] for the Province of the Tejas with the same priest [Anastase Douay], his brother the clergyman [the Abbé Jean Cavelier], and thirteen other men [including Joutel], with the purpose of traveling beyond the Tejas in search of the other settlement. When they were near Espíritu Santo River [the Brazos River],[13] one of his company called Monsieur de V. [Pierre Duhaut], upset at being cheated and having lost a brother [Dominique], shot and killed La Salle. The previous night, a surgeon [Liotot], who accompanied La Salle, had killed the Indian interpreter [Nika], one of La Salle's servants [Saget], and a lieutenant [Crevel Morenger]. The clergyman [the Abbé Cavelier] and the rest of the people, including this witness, arrived at the Province of the Tejas, where he [the witness, Meunier] was left because he was sick. Another three [Pierre Talon, Jacques Grollet, and Jean L'Archevêque] stayed there, and the rest, with the clergyman [the Abbé Jean Cavelier] and the priest [Douay], continued their journey towards the nation of the Caddodachos. To date no news has been received from them. The Indians took a liking to this witness and the other three Frenchmen, and they lived among them until the Spaniards last year captured one named Juan de Arrebec [Jean L'Archevêque] and Xaque Grole [Jacques Grollet], and now on this trip they have recovered this witness and another one [Pierre Talon] who comes behind.

*Question:* Do you know what happened to those who stayed in the settlement burned down by the Spaniards?

*Answer:* He said that while he was lying ill at the settlement of the Tejas, Arxabec [L'Archevêque] set out from there for their settlement, as did Grolec [Grollet] and two more besides the Indians, with the intention of taking them

---

[11]   The frigate (the *Belle*) had six not eight cannon.

[12]   This is the north shore of Matagorda Peninsula, where the *Belle* was discovered in the summer of 1995.

[13]   Meunier identifies the Brazos River area as the place where La Salle was killed, and this study supports his statement.

with the Tejas, to get them out of that misery. They said that when they arrived at the camp, they found it uninhabited, as the people had died of the pest,[14] and some by Indians' arrows, and by 150 barrels of gunpowder that were set on fire, destroying everything within half a league's distance. These had given him news of the aforesaid.

*Question:* Do you have notice of another French settlement in those areas?

*Answer:* When the witness went with some Tejas Indians to the nation of the Caddodachos, with whom they are at peace, they told him that to the east there was a nation of white people. These people had given beads and other things to the surrounding Indians of the Caddodachos, who live on the other side of the Cuchillos River, and he does not know what nation they are or if there is another village.

*Question:* When they left La Rochella [La Rochelle], what priests or clergymen did they bring on the ships?

*Answer:* He said five, three priests of the order mentioned and two clergymen.

He was asked other questions that seemed relevant, to all of which he answered that he did not know more than what he had answered, which is the truth under the oath that he has taken, in which he verified and confirmed himself when it was read to him through the interpreter. He indicated that he was twenty-one years old, more or less, and signed it, with the interpreter.

His Grace attested it.

Pierre Meunier, Sieur de Preuille.

Don Gregorio de Salinas Varona.

Before me, Sebastián Sánchez de las Fraguas, Royal and Military Clerk.

---

[14] The pest may refer to smallpox, which Governor De León reported had struck the French settlement. Bolton (ed.), *Spanish Exploration in the Southwest*, 395. However, the Spanish word *peste* is used to refer to a wide range of ailments and does not necessarily confirm De León's report.

# *Appendix B*

This appendix alphabetically lists the names of Indian tribes or bands reported in Henri Joutel's account of La Salle's expedition to Texas. As the reliability of the accounts by Douay and the Abbé Cavelier is questionable, the names of tribes recorded in those two accounts are not included in the listing of tribal names. As mentioned in the introduction, Jean Delanglez, who translated the Abbé's account, concludes that the Abbé invented the names of some Indian tribes. The names of tribes living in the greater expedition area are included; these names are marked with an asterisk to indicate that Joutel did not refer to the tribe by that name. With each entry in which the tribe or a member of the tribe is encountered, the date of the meeting is mentioned, and the location of the meeting is noted by reporting the county area and in some instances a city near the location where the meeting occurred.

In addition to reporting the names of tribes met en route, Joutel prepared four lists of tribal names that also are included in this appendix. Unidentified Indians recited the first two lists. Joutel encountered the Indians in early February 1687 on the west side of the Colorado (the Maligne) River near the customary crossing area in Fayette County. The Indians told Joutel that their tribe was allied with forty-five tribes including the Cenis (also known as the Hasinais or Tejas), and that the Maligne was a boundary river his tribe crossed to the east only to go to war. The first list named the tribes that lived across the lower Colorado River to the north and east of the river crossing area. The second list named the tribes west and northwest of the river. The Indians said that in some instances these tribes were stationary, but most tribes moved frequently to hunt and fish. The Indians added that they hunted by driving bison herds back and forth between tribes.

The Indians on the west side of the Colorado indicated that they occasionally went to war with Indians living "to the east" across the Colorado but that their strongest enemies lived to the southwest. An identification of the enemies living "to the east" and to the southwest is unclear, but Joutel's record suggests that the eastern enemy might have been the "Flatheads" and the southwestern enemy might have been the coastal tribes of Karankawa. Joutel added that each tribe that visited La Salle's camp near the Colorado had its own language or dialect; that they were nude (except the women covered their nudity); that they had well-worked, clean, soft, tanned animal skins; and that they used earthenware pottery to cook meat and roots. Joutel was describing principally the tribes living to the west of the lower Colorado River (more specifically in the area between the lower Colorado and the San Antonio rivers).

The tribes named in the first list lived north across the lower Colorado River, on the east side of the river, probably primarily between the lower Colorado River and the lower Trinity River basin area, but some tribes may have lived farther east. Joutel does not give any general description of these tribes, and the two tribes (the Teao and the Palaquechare) that he encountered later between the Colorado and the Brazos rivers were not included in Joutel's list. It should be noted that in Michel's condensation the first and second lists are misplaced and are found at a point in the narrative when La Salle's party was closer to the Canoe (Brazos) River than to the Maligne (Colorado) crossing, and the mistake is compounded when Michel repeats a faulty copy of the two lists when Joutel's party reaches the Cenis (Trinity) River.

The chieftain of the Upper Nasoni village near the Red River in northeast Texas recited the third and fourth lists of tribal names to Joutel. The third list names tribes who were enemies of the Caddo; the fourth names Caddo allies. Michel does not include the third or fourth list of tribal names in his condensation. The chieftain said that most of his enemies lived "to the east" of his villages and had no horses. As the tribes living immediately east of his village in southern Arkansas were friends, whom Joutel visited, the enemies "to the east" probably are the Chickasaw and other tribes east of the Mississippi River sometimes referred to as "Flatheads." The chieftain said that only the Indians who lived to their west had horses.

1. Acansas (Acansea, Acancea, Ackansa, Accansea, Quapaw)

Between July 24 and August 2, 1687, Joutel visited the four Acansas villages (Otsoté, Thoriman, Tongingua, and Cappa) near the junction of the Arkansas and Mississippi rivers before proceeding up the Mississippi River to Canada and returning to France. W. David Baird reports that the Acansas were known later as the Quapaws, and, according to their own tradition, were of Siouan stock from the Ohio River basin. Dickinson adds that the tribe was forced west to the Mississippi by the Iroquois and downstream to the area near the mouth of the Arkansas River. Thus, their name means "Downstream People." See Baird, *The Quapaw Indians*, 3–9. Contemporary authorities also consider the Quapaw a Siouan tribe; see Schlesier (ed.), *Plains Indians*, 335. In 1673 Jolliet and Marquette visited the tribe near the mouth of the Arkansas River. See Donnelly, *Jacques Marquette*, 225.

2. Ahehouen

Joutel included the Ahehouen in his list of tribes that lived to the northeast and east of the lower Colorado River. Thomas N. Campbell, "Ahehouen Indians," in Tyler, et al. (eds.), *New Handbook of Texas*, I, 72, 73.

3. Ahouergomahe

Joutel included the Ahouergomahe in his list of tribes that lived to the northeast and east of the lower Colorado River. Thomas N. Campbell, "Ahouerhopiheim Indians," in Tyler, et al. (eds.), *New Handbook of Texas*, I, 73, cites the tribal name found in Michel's condensed version of Joutel's journal and

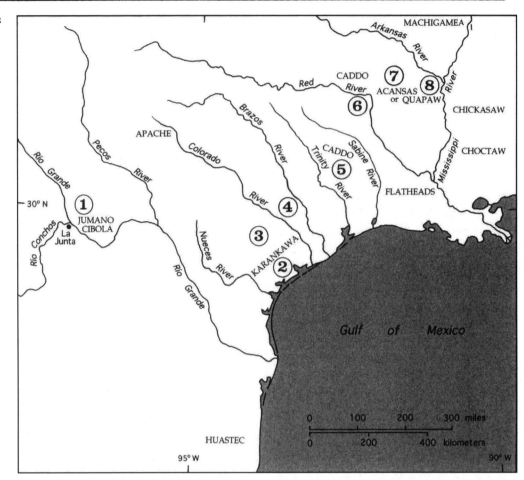

Indians tribes included in Appendix B

says that a printer's error manufactured the hybrid name Ahouerhopiheim. As mentioned in the introduction, Michel's condensation is replete with errors regarding Indian names and cannot be relied upon for the correct or preferred spelling of a tribal name. Margry's version of the spelling of the name Ahouergomahe and that found in the Joutel manuscript copy in the Library of Congress are identical. The name Ahouergomahe does not appear to be a hybrid name or to have arisen from a printer's error.

4. Aquis

Joutel included the Aquis in his list of tribes that were enemies of the Caddo.

5. Annaho

Joutel recorded that the Annaho were friends of the Caddo. Swanton questions whether the Annaho were the same as the Osage in *Source Materials on the Caddo Indians*, 9. Thomas N. Campbell, "Annaho Indians," in Tyler, et al. (eds.), *New Handbook of Texas*, I, 192, says that the tribe mentioned in the 1687 documents of La Salle's expedition was an enemy rather than an ally of the Caddo as Joutel listed.

The geographic area in which Indian tribes were encountered or reported in French expedition journals is indicated either by a circled number (representing several tribes) or by the name of a single tribe. The names of other tribes living in the greater expedition area but unnamed by French diarists are marked with an asterisk next to the appendix entry to indicate that the tribe was significant at the time of the expeditions but was not named.

1. Roving tribes from Chihuahua and the Big Bend. Tribes principally from the Las Juntas area that annually traveled to south Central Texas to hunt and trade: Choumay (Jumano), Cibola
2. Matagorda Bay tribes. Local Central Texas coastal tribes: Bracamo, Cascosi (Clamcoeh)
3. South Central Texas tribes: Local inland tribes living west of the Colorado River: Temerlouan, Ebahamo, Kannehouan, Peissaquo, Panequo, Kuasse, Coyabegux, Orcan, Peinhoum, Piechar, Tohaha, Petao, Tserabocherete, Onapiem, Chancre, Tohau (Toho), Pechir, Petsare, Serecoutcha, Tsepcoen.
4. Trans-Brazos Tribes. Local tribes encountered or reported between the lower Brazos and Colorado rivers: Teao, Palaquechare, Spichehat, Kiabaha, Teheaman, Tehauremet, Kiabahe, Chaumene, Quouan, Arhau, Exepiahohe, Ahouergomahe, Kemahopihein, Koienkahe, Komkome, Omenaosse, Keremen, Ahehouen, Meghey (Mayeye), Telamene, Ointemarhen, Kouyam, Meraquaman
5. Western Caddoan tribes. Local tribes found principally between the Trinity and Red rivers: Cenis, Nasoni, Ayenny, Naodiche
6. Northern Caddoan tribes. Local tribes near the Red River: Upper Nasoni, Cadodaquis, Nastchez, Nastchitos
7. Southern Arkansas tribes. Local tribes encountered or reported on the Ouachita and Saline rivers: Cahaynohoua (Cahinno), Tanico
8. Acansas tribes: Local tribes living on the lower Arkansas River and the Middle Mississippi: Cappa, Otsoté, Thoriman, Tongingua

6. Apache*

Although Joutel does not mention the tribe, the Apache Indians were a significant Texas native group at the time of La Salle's expedition and exerted an influence on many of the tribes that La Salle encountered. The Cenis and their allies in Central and South Texas and the Jumano and other highly mobile bison hunters from West Texas were enemies of the Apache who, in the late 1600s, controlled the Hill Country north and west of San Antonio and much of the area along the middle and upper Colorado River. See Foster, *Spanish Expeditions into Texas*, 276. See also Donald E. Chipman, "Apache Indians" in Tyler, et al. (eds.), *New Handbook of Texas*, I, 210, 211 and Richard J. Perry, *Western Apache Heritage: People of the Mountain Corridor* (Austin: University of Texas Press, 1991), 136–154.

7. Arhau

The Arhau resided east of the lower Colorado River, according to Joutel's list of tribal names.

8. Cadaquis

Joutel listed the Cadaquis among the enemies of the Caddo.

9. Caddo*

The Caddo or Caddoan confederation was composed of a number of tribes culturally and lingustically associated and located at the time of La Salle's expedition in East Texas, southwestern Arkansas, southeastern Oklahoma, and northwestern Louisiana. Joutel visited and described several Caddoan tribes including the Cenis, who were the dominant Western Caddoan tribe; the Nasoni, who had one village north of Nacogdoches and a second near the Red River northwest of Texarkana; and the Red River Cadodaquis. Traditionally, the Caddoan tribes are considered woodland horticulturalists and mound builders as were some of the related tribes that La Salle encountered along the Mississippi. See Cadodaquis.

10. Cadodaquis (Kadohadacho, Caddodacho, Caddodacchos)

Joutel's party visited the Cadodaquis (a Northern Caddoan tribe) from June 30 to July 2, 1687, at their village on the Red River slightly east of present-day Texarkana. A few days earlier, the chieftain of the Upper Nasoni had told Joutel the names of twenty-eight enemy tribes and twenty-six allied tribes including the Cadodaquis. The Nasoni chief also told Joutel that there were four villages in their tribe: the Assoni or Nasoni (whom Joutel said his party had left), the Nastchez, the Nastchitos, and the Cadodaquis; each, Joutel was told, was not too distant from the others.

After visiting the Upper Nasoni village on the north side of a large slough or former tributary one and one-half leagues south of the Red River, Joutel's party crossed the Red River and traveled downstream along the left or north bank for about two leagues to the Cadodaquis village. This village was four or five leagues west or upriver from the junction of the Little River and the Red River. Swanton considers the Cadodaquis the same tribe as the Kadohadacho. *Source Materials on the Caddo Indians*, 8. See Timothy K. Perttula, "Caddo Indians," in Tyler, et al. (eds.), *New Handbook of Texas*, I, 887–888.

11. Cahaynohoua (Cahaynihoua, Cahinno, Cahinio)

Between July 6 and 11, 1687, on their march across Arkansas to the Mississippi, Joutel's party visited the village of the Cahaynohoua, about ten to fifteen miles north of Camden, Arkansas and one and one-half leagues west of the Ouachita River. Two members of the Cahaynohoua tribe guided Joutel from the Red River to the Cahaynohoua village. Joutel reported that the Cahaynohoua spoke a language quite different from the Caddo, and used words also spoken by the Shawnee Nika. Joutel, who was a close observer and had a good ear for different Indian languages, stressed that the Cahaynohoua spoke a language akin to that spoken by the tribes La Salle had visited earlier rather than that spoken by the Caddo, with whom Jouel had lived during the previous four months. For a comparison of the historic Siouan language family and the Northern or Plains Caddoan (Wichita) language, see Karl H. Schlesier, "Commentary: A History of Ethnic Groups in the Great Plains, A.D. 150–1550" in Schlesier (ed.), *Plains Indians*, 335–361. Moreover, Joutel reported that the

Cahaynohoua looked different than the Caddo or Cenis, and that the Cahaynohoua settlement was all in one location, not spread out into farmsteads like the Cenis. Nevertheless, Swanton and contemporary writers including Pertulla and Hudson consider the Cahaynohoua (or Cahinno) to be Caddoan. Dickinson, however, suggests that they were Wichita, another tribe within the Caddoan linguistic group, according to Wallace L. Chafe, "Indian Signs on the Land," 145. See Chafe's extensive analysis of the Caddoan, Iroquian, and Siouan languages in Sebeok (ed.), *Native Languages of the Americas*, I, 527–572.

12. Caiasban

The Caiasban were included in Joutel's list of enemies of the Caddo. Thomas N. Campbell notes that the Caai (cited according to Campbell in a 1691 Spanish missionary report) may be the same tribe as the Caiasban, and the Caisquetebanas, whom De León reported in 1690 a short distance north of Matagorda Bay, may be the same tribe also. However, Campbell adds that these identifications cannot be proved in "Caai Indians," in Tyler, et al. (eds.), *New Handbook of Texas*, I, 879.

13. Caitsodammo

The Caitsodammo were enemies of the Caddo, according to Joutel.

14. Cannaha

Joutel wrote that the Cannaha were enemies of the Caddo. Thomas N. Campbell, "Cannaha and Cannahio Indians," in Tyler, et al. (eds.), *New Handbook of Texas*, I, 960.

15. Cannahios

The Cannahios were on Joutel's list of tribes that were enemies of the Caddo. Ibid.

16. Cannohatinno (Canohatinno, Canotino, Canoatinno, Kanoutinoa, Kanoatino, Quanotinno, Kanohatino)

In mid February 1687, Joutel reported visiting a village or camp of Teao Indians between the lower Colorado and the lower Brazos rivers. The Teao said that the Jumano had asked them and the Cenis to join them in war against the Ayano and the Cannohatinno, who were at war with the Spaniards and stole their horses. Joutel reported on March 31 that the Cenis were going to war with the Cannohatinno. The Nasoni chief on the Red River informed Joutel that the Cannohatinno were one of the twenty-eight tribes that were enemies of the Caddo. Swanton reports that "'Canabatinu' meant Wichita." *Source Materials on the Caddo Indians*, 10. Bolton notes that Fray Francisco Casañas also identified the "Canabatinu" as an enemy of the Caddo. Bolton, *The Hasinais*, 58, n. 10. The Talon brothers described the "Canotino" as being the most wicked tribe, at war against all others, in "Voyage to the Mississippi through the Gulf of Mexico," 257.

Campbell writes that serious consideration should be given to the question of whether the Cannohatinno mentioned in documents of the La Salle expedition was the same tribe as the Cantona Indians the Spaniards frequently encountered near the lower Colorado River. Campbell concludes that the question requires further archival research. See Thomas N. Campbell, "Cantona Indians," in

Tyler, et al. (eds.), *New Handbook of Texas*, I, 962. Newcomb suggests that it seems probable that the two tribes were the same ethnic group. See "Historic Indians of Central Texas," in *Bulletin of the Texas Archeological Society*, 64 (1993), 24.

As indicated, Joutel considers the Kannehouan and the Cannohatinno as separate tribes. The Kannehouan was a friendly tribe and Joutel lists them as living west of the Colorado, where Spanish expedition diarists frequently reported the Cantona's presence. Joutel identified the Cannohatinnos as enemies of the Cenis and other Caddoan tribes. It therefore appears that the Kannehouan and Cantona may have been the same tribe rather than that the Cannohatinno and the Cantona were the same tribe.

In his list of tribes who are neighbors of the Caddo, Fray Francisco Casañas (1691) also considered the tribes he called the Cantouhaona and the Canabatinu as different. The padre listed the Cantouhaona (Cantona?) next to the Toaha (Tohaha) as friendly tribes who lived to the southwest of the Caddo; the padre listed the Canabatinu as an enemy of the Caddo. See Bolton's rendition and analysis of Casañas's list in *The Hasinais*, 56–59. Again it appears that the friendly Kannehouans Joutel listed as living west of the Colorado River were the same as the friendly Cantona, whom the Spaniards repeatedly met (sometimes in company with the Caddo) in the same area west of the Colorado River. As indicated in the text, Joutel considered the Kannehouan and the Cannohatinno as separate tribes; Casañas listed separately in the same document the Cantouhaona as friends and the Canabatinu as enemies of the Caddo.

17. Cantey

According to Joutel, the Cantey were enemies of the Caddo. Thomas N. Campbell, "Cantey Indians," in Tyler, et al. (eds.), *New Handbook of Texas*, I, 961, 962.

18. Cappa (Kappa)

The Cappa village was the largest and last of the four villages Joutel visited before he departed on August 2, 1687, from the area above the mouth of the Arkansas River up the Mississippi to Canada. The village was on the west side of the Mississippi River, approximately ten leagues upriver from the mouth of the Arkansas River. Swanton considers the Cappa the same as the Quapaw. *Source Materials on the Caddo Indians*, 9.

19. Cascosi (Caucosi, Caocosi, Cauquesi, Clamcoeh)*

The Cascosi Indians were members of the coastal tribe living in the Matagorda and San Antonio bay areas when La Salle established Fort Saint Louis. La Salle was at war with the tribe during most of the time that he was at the French settlement, and the Cascosi, which the Talon boys called Clamcoeh, were among the tribes that massacred the remaining adult members of the French settlement. Although Spanish diarists in the seventeenth century referred to the tribe with several renditions of their name, such as Cascosi, Caocosi, and Cauquesi, Spaniards later referred to the coastal tribe as the Karankawa, the name most frequently used by contemporary writers. See Ricklis, *The Karankawa Indians of Texas*; 4, 5; Foster (ed.), *Texas and Northeastern Mexico*, 177, 178.

20. Cassia

Joutel included the Cassia in his list of tribes friendly to the Caddo. Thomas N. Campbell, "Cassia Indians," in Tyler, et al. (eds.), *New Handbook of Texas*, I, 1015.

21. Catcho

Joutel recorded the Catcho as friends of the Caddo.

22. Catouinayos

The Catouinayos were on Joutel's list of enemies of the Caddo.

23. Cenis (Hasinais, Tejas)

On February 19, 1687, La Salle met some Palaquechare Indians whom La Salle believed to be Cenis because of their accent and their use of some Cenis words that La Salle knew. Bolton also notes that Joutel's report suggests that the tribe was Caddoan. *The Hasinais*, 691. The tribe's encampment was in western Washington County between the lower Colorado and Brazos rivers. Joutel also met Cenis hunters between the Colorado and the Brazos and was led along the trail from the Brazos to the Trinity by Cenis guides. This western Caddo tribe was the same as the Hasinais, according to Swanton. *Source Materials on the Caddo Indians*, 8.

Although the principal villages of the Cenis were near San Pedro Creek in eastern Houston County, members or bands of the tribe apparently had farms and hunting camps west of the Trinity and west of the lower Brazos. The Tejas also were reported visiting allied tribes between the San Antonio River and the Colorado on several occasions as well as tribes south of the Rio Grande. See Foster, *Spanish Expeditions into Texas*, 274, 275.

24. Chancre

Joutel reported that the Chancre lived west of the lower Colorado River.

25. Chaumene

The Chaumene lived on the north and east side of the lower Colorado River, according to Joutel's list.

26. Chaye

The Chaye were an enemy of the Caddo, according to Joutel. Swanton considers them to be the same as the Choye, and according to Tonty, the tribe was identified with the Yatasi. *Source Materials on the Caddo Indians*, 9.

27. Chepoussa

Joutel identified the Chepoussa as enemies of the Caddo. While Joutel was visiting the Cadodaquis near the Red River in Bowie County in late June 1687, a young man whose nose and ears had been cut off by the Chepoussa returned to the Caddo village, having escaped the Chepoussa. Swanton notes that the Chepoussa were perhaps the Chickasaw (*Source Materials on the Caddo Indians*, 40); his interpretation is consistent with Joutel's report in Chapter IX that the Palaquechare, allies of the Cenis, were going to war in the east against a tribe that had flat heads and planted corn. Tonty wrote that La Salle's party on the lower Mississippi in 1682 met some "Chikasas" who had flat heads and that a number of tribes along the lower Mississippi had flat heads. Cox (ed.), *Journeys of La Salle*, I, 18.

28. Chickasaw*

The Chickasaw was a significant tribe of horticulturalists that La Salle's 1682 expedition party met in present-day northern Mississippi. They were known, as were some of their neighbors, for having flat heads and were enemies of the Cappa and Caddoan tribes west of the Mississippi. La Salle's chroniclers make several direct and indirect reference to tribes characterized as having flat heads, such as the Chickasaw and other tribes living east of the south Texas tribes.

The engineer Minet reported that an elderly Texas coastal native (a Cascosi or Karankawa), said he knew and had fought some Flatheads. In his note, Weddle writes that the old Indian may have been referring to any one of several tribes known for their custom of flattening the human head, but Weddle adds without explanation that the Flatheads were not a tribe "with which the Karankawa might have come in contact." According to Joutel's account, this observation is questionable, as a number of South Texas tribes referred to the Flatheads as enemies. Weddle adds that Minet, in his account of La Salle's 1682 exploration of the Mississippi, wrote that the Coroa also had flat heads. Minet, "Journal of Our Voyage to the Gulf of Mexico," 110, 110, n. 52.

Joutel refers to enemies of the Caddo called Chepoussa, whom Swanton identifies as the Chickasaw in *Source Materials on the Caddo Indians*, 187. The Palaquechare, whom La Salle identified with the Cenis, lived west of the lower Brazos and told Joutel's party that they were going to war with tribes to the east who had flat heads. See also Stubbs, "The Chickasaw Contact with the La Salle Expedition in 1682," 41–48.

As some scholars of the prehistoric Mississippi Valley have suggested that there may have been Mayan or Huastecan influence on the central and lower Mississippian cultures (McNutt, *Prehistory of the Central Mississippi Valley*, 222–224), it is significant that early sixteenth-century Spanish chronicles reported that Huastec leaders, like their counterparts on the Mississippi, had "broad artificially elongated (or flat) heads." See Chipman, *Nuno De Guzmán and the Province of Pánuco*, 28, citing Fray Bernardino de Sahagun, *Historia general de las cosas de Nueva España*, III, 131–132.

29. Choumay (Chouman, Jumano)

The Choumay were friendly to the Caddo, according to Joutel's list. Swanton considers them to be the same as the Jumano. *Source Materials on the Caddo Indians*, 9. Two tribes (the Teao and the Palaquechare) informed Joutel about this widely roving tribe from West Texas when he met them between the Colorado and the Brazos in February 1687. It should be noted that the Caddo living on the Red River near the Oklahoma and Arkansas state lines named as an ally a tribe that resided in the Big Bend, more than six hundred miles to the southwest. The Talon brothers described the Choumay as not being at war with anyone, and stated that many of the Choumay could speak Spanish. "Voyage to the Mississippi through the Gulf of Mexico," 257. See Foster, *Spanish Expeditions into Texas*, 276; and Nancy P. Hickerson, "Jumano Indians," in Tyler, et al. (eds.), *New Handbook of Texas*, III, 1016–1018.

30. Cibola (Cibolo)*

The Cibola were highly mobile bison hunters who resided principally in West Texas near the Big Bend. Several Cibola leaders in early 1689 testified to Spanish authorities in Chihuahua that they had on several occasions met and traded on the middle Rio Grande with strangers (Frenchmen) who were dressed with armor, carried muskets like the Spaniards, and inquired about the silver mines in Parral. Cibola witnesses were the first to report the destruction of Fort Saint Louis on Matagorda Bay, which they had visited several weeks earlier. The Spaniards later met the Cibola near the Colorado on one of their annual trade missions and bison hunting trips. See Foster, *Spanish Expeditions into Texas*, 272.

31. Coyabegux

The Coyabegux lived west or northwest of the lower Colorado, according to Joutel. Margery H. Krieger states in "Coyabegux Indians," in Tyler, et al. (eds.), *New Handbook of Texas*, II, 384 that the area Joutel refers to was mainly Tonkawan territory, although that seems unlikely at the time of Joutel's visit since the first report of Tonkawa Indians in Central Texas was not made until 1768 by the Spanish expedition diarist Fray Gaspar José de Solís. See Foster, *Spanish Expeditions into Texas*, 288.

32. Daquinatinno

Joutel wrote that the Daquinatinno were friends of the Caddo. See Margery H. Krieger, "Daquinatino Indians" in Tyler, et al. (eds.), *New Handbook of Texas*, II, 509.

33. Daquio

The Daquio were friends of the Caddo, according to Joutel. Margery H. Krieger, "Daquio Indians," in Tyler, et al. (eds.), *New Handbook of Texas*, II, 509.

34. Datcho

The Datcho were enemies of the Caddo, according to Joutel's list. Margery H. Krieger, "Datcho Indians," in Tyler, et al. (eds.), *New Handbook of Texas*, II, 515.

35. Dotchetonne

According to Joutel's list, the Dotchetonne were friendly to the Caddo.

36. Douesdonqua

The Douesdonqua were allies of the Caddo, according to Joutel's list.

37. Ebahamo

Joutel reported that La Salle's party encountered a friendly band of Ebahamo on January 21 and 22, 1687, approximately sixty miles north of Matagorda Bay in eastern Lavaca County. The Indians were allies of the Cenis, and one Indian in the group spoke the Caddoan language. They also knew the route to the Spaniards who, the Indians said, lived ten days to the west. Although Douay refers to the Bahamo (Bracamo) as living near the French settlement [Cox (ed.), *Journeys of La Salle*, I, 237], it appears from Joutel's account that the two tribes— the Ebahamo and the Bracamo—are different. Campbell concludes that the Bracamo and Bahamo Douay mentioned are variants of the same name but expresses doubt as to whether the Bahamo and the Ebahamo are the same people in "Ebahamo Indians," in Tyler, et al. (eds.), *New Handbook of Texas*, II, 776.

38. Enoqua

According to Joutel's list, the Enoqua were allies of the Caddo.

39. Exepiahohe

Joutel reported that the Exepiahohe lived on the east side of the lower Colorado. See Thomas N. Campbell, "Enepiahe Indians," in Tyler, et al. (eds.), *New Handbook of Texas*, II, 868.

40. Flatheads

Joutel and Central Texas Indians used the term Flatheads to identify tribes that resided east of La Salle's immediate exploration area, probably principally on the east side of the central and lower Mississippi River. As the name suggests, the tribes artifically flattened the heads of the young, giving their faces a broad and elongated shape and appearance. See Chickasaw.

41. Haychis

The Haychis were allied with the Caddo, according to Joutel. Swanton considers them the same as the Eyeish. *Source Materials on the Caddo Indians*, 8. See also Thomas N. Campbell, "Haqui Indians," in Tyler, et al. (eds.), *New Handbook of Texas*, III, 446.

42. Hianagouy

The Hianagouy were enemies of the Caddo, according to Joutel's list. Margery H. Krieger, "Hianagouy Indians," in Tyler, et al. (eds.), *New Handbook of Texas*, III, 585.

43. Hiantatsi

Joutel included the Hiantatsi in his list of enemies of the Caddo. Margery H. Krieger, "Hiantatsi Indians," in Tyler, et al. (eds.), *New Handbook of Texas*, III, 585.

44. Houaneiha

The Houaneiha were enemies of the Caddo, according to Joutel's list. Thomas N. Campbell, "Houaneiha Indians," in Tyler, et al. (eds.), *New Handbook of Texas*, III, 710.

45. Huastec*

The Huastec Indians lived on the western Gulf north of the Mayan Penninsula in the area between Pánuco (near present-day Tampico) and the Palmas River (present-day Soto la Marina), about 180 miles south of the lower Rio Grande. Contemporary authorities suggest that during the period ca. A.D. 700 to 1000, and perhaps earlier, Native American cultures on the middle and lower Mississippi may have been influenced by the Huastecs (and Mayans), who by 1500, and probably centuries earlier, cultivated corn, beans, and cotton, domesticated ducks and turkey, made pottery, used the bow and arrow, had both sailing and rowing ships, and (some) artifically flattened the heads of infants. See Chickasaw and Flatheads. See also Weddle, *Spanish Sea*, 78, which mentions native vessels under sail and cites Díaz del Castillo, *Historia Verdadera*, I, 45–46 and Fernández de Oviedo y Valdés, *Historia general y natural de las Indias*, III, 301.

46. Jumano (Choumay, Chouman)*

The Jumano were residents of the La Junta area near the junction of the Rio Grande and the Mexican Conchos River. Along with several other West Texas tribes including the Cibola, the Jumano annually visited the area west of the

the lower Colorado to hunt bison and to trade with local tribes. Both La Salle's chroniclers and later seventeenth-century Spanish diarists (Terán, Massanet, and Salinas Varona) reported meeting the Jumano in Central and South Texas during the summer months. See Foster, *Spanish Expeditions into Texas*, 272, 276. Also see Choumay.

47. Kabaye

The Kabaye lived to the east of the lower Colorado. Campbell notes that they may be the same as the Cava in his entry "Kabaye Indians," in Tyler, et al. (eds.), *New Handbook of Texas*, III, 1025. However, Spanish diarists reported the Cava on the west rather than the east side of the Colorado. See Foster, *Spanish Expeditions into Texas*, 271.

48. Kannehouan

The Kannehouan lived to the west of the lower Colorado and was the first tribe that Joutel listed living in that area. Late seventeenth-century Spanish expedition diarists frequently referred to meeting the Cantona Indians in the same area, and there is a similarity in the two names. Campbell mislocates the tribe when he states that the Kannehouan probably lived near the Brazos rather than west of the Colorado in "Kannehouan Indians," in Tyler, et al. (eds.), *New Handbook of Texas*, III, 1029.

In his assessment of the 1691 list of tribes prepared by Fray Francisco Casañas, Bolton notes that the Cantouhaonas were named as friends of the Caddo and the Canabatinu were named as enemies. *The Hasinais*, 58. It seems likely that the Kannehouan, who Joutel listed as living west of the Colorado, were the same tribe as the Cantouhaonas, who Casañas named as friends of the Caddo, and that these two tribes were distinct from the Canabatinu or Cannohatinno that Joutel and Casañas named as enemies of the Caddo. See Foster (ed.), *Texas and Northeastern Mexico*, 177.

49. Karankawa

The Karankawa was the name of the coastal group of natives who lived in the Matagorda and San Antonio Bay area during the time of La Salle's expedition and who held the surviving French children captive. As mentioned, Karankawa was not the name used by either the French or the Spaniards, who used Cascosi or Clamcoeh in the seventeenth century, but is the name used most commonly today. See Cascosi.

50. Kemahopihein

Joutel reported that the Kemahopihein lived on the east side of the lower Colorado.

51. Keremen (Korimen)

Joutel reported that the Keremen lived to the north and east of the lower Colorado. Margery H. Krieger, "Keremen Indians," in Tyler, et al. (eds.), *New Handbook of Texas*, III, 1075.

52. Kiabaha

The Kiabaha lived on the east side of the lower Colorado, according to Joutel's list. Campbell places the tribe near the Brazos in "Kiabaha Indians," in Tyler, et al. (eds.), *New Handbook of Texas*, III, 1084.

53. Koienkahe

Joutel includes the Koienkahe in his list of tribes that resided in the area east of the lower Colorado River.

54. Komkome

The Komkome were included in Joutel's list of tribes that lived on the east side of the lower Colorado. Campbell suggests that they probably lived near the Brazos River in "Konkone Indians," in Tyler, et al. (eds.), *New Handbook of Texas*, III, 1155.

55. Kouyam

Joutel lists the Kouyam as one of the tribes that lived on the east side of the lower Colorado. Thomas N. Campbell, "Kouyam Indians," in Tyler, et al. (eds.), *New Handbook of Texas*, III, 1159.

56. Kuasse

The Kuasse lived on the west side of the lower Colorado River, according to Joutel. See Margery H. Krieger, "Kuasse Village" in Tyler, et al. (eds.), *New Handbook of Texas*, III, 1164.

57. Machigamea (Mitchegama, Michigamea)

While visiting the Cappa in late July 1687, Joutel mentioned the Machigamea who lived on the middle Mississippi. The Cappa considered the Machigamea an enemy. Dickinson reports that the name Machigamea means "Great Waters," and that the tribe belonged to the Illinois confederacy in "Indian Signs on the Land," 154. See also Morse, "The Seventeenth-Century Michigamea Village Location," 55–74.

58. Meghey (Mayeye)

Joutel included the Meghey in his list of tribes that lived on the east side of the lower Colorado River. Campbell writes that it is generally agreed that the Meghey and the Mayeye (later identified by the Spaniards), were the same tribe and that both were said to live between the Colorado and the Brazos in "Mayeye Indians," in Tyler, et al. (eds.), *New Handbook of Texas*, IV, 586. On Alarcón's 1718 expedition, the Mayeye were reported about thirty miles northeast of Columbus in Colorado County, and in 1727 Rivera also saw them between the Colorado and Brazos rivers. See Foster, *Spanish Expeditions into Texas*, 277.

59. Meraquaman

The Meraquaman lived on the east side of the lower Colorado, according to Joutel's list. Thomas N. Campbell, "Meracouman Indians," in Tyler, et al. (eds.), *New Handbook of Texas*, IV, 627.

60. Nacassa

Joutel listed the Nacassa tribe as enemies of the Caddo.

61. Nacodissy

The Nacodissy were friends of the Caddo, according to Joutel's list.

62. Nacoho

The Nacoho were enemies of the Caddo, according to Joutel's list.

63. Nadaho (Nadaco)

Joutel listed the Nadaho as enemies of the Caddo. Swanton considered the Nadaco to be the same as the Anadarko. See *Source Materials on the Caddo Indians*, 11.

64. Nadamin

The Nadamin were friends of the Caddo, according to Joutel's list. Thomas N. Campbell, "Nadamin Indians," in Tyler, et al. (eds.), *New Handbook of Texas*, IV, 931.

65. Nadeicha

Joutel wrote that the Nadeicha were enemies of the Caddo.

66. Nahacassi

The Nahacassi were enemies of the Caddo, according to Joutel. Swanton considered the tribe the same as the Yatasi. *Source Materials on the Caddo Indians*, 9.

67. Naodiche

Joutel's party visited the Naodiche on May 29, 1687, when the expedition was about ten leagues northeast of the Neches River crossing in southern Cherokee County on the way to visit the Nasoni, who lived three leagues to the northeast of the Naodiche in northern Nacogdoches County.

68. Nardichia

The Nardichia were enemies of the Caddo, according to Joutel's list.

69. Nasitti

Joutel wrote that the Nasitti were enemies of the Caddo.

70. Nasoni (Assoni)

Joutel's party visited the Nasoni from May 29 to June 13, 1687, at their village in north-central Nacogdoches County, and, according to Swanton, Joutel visited the Upper Nasoni on the Red River with the Cadodaquis. *Source Materials on the Caddo Indians*, 8, fig. 1. Thomas N. Campbell, "Nasoni Indians," in Tyler, et al. (eds.), *New Handbook of Texas*, IV, 938, 939.

71. Nastchez

The Nastchez visited Joutel and the others during the French party's stay with the Upper Nasoni and Cadodaquis (June 23–30, 1687).

72. Nastchitos (Natchittas, Natschitas)

The Nastchitos were allies of the Caddo who visited Joutel's party during their June 23 to 30, 1687, visit with the Upper Nasoni. Swanton considers the Natchittas the same as the Natchitoches. *Source Materials on the Caddo Indians*, 8.

73. Natsohos

The Natsohos were allies of the Caddo, according to Joutel. Swanton considers the tribe the same as the Nanatsoho. *Source Materials on the Caddo Indians*, 8.

74. Natsshostanno

The Natsshostanno were included in Joutel's list of tribes who were enemies of the Caddo.

75. Neihahat

The Neihahat were allies of the Caddo, according to Joutel

76. Nondaco

The Nondaco were allies of the Caddo, according to Joutel.

77. Nouista

The Nouista were allies of the Caddo, according to Joutel.

78. Ointemarhen

According to Joutel's list, the Ointemarhen lived on the northeast and east side of the lower Colorado River. Margery H. Krieger, "Ointemarhen Indians," in Tyler, et al. (eds.), *New Handbook of Texas*, IV, 1129.

79. Omenaosse

Joutel wrote that the Omenaosse lived to the east of the lower Colorado River. Margery H. Krieger, "Omenaosse Indians," in Tyler, et al. (eds.), *New Handbook of Texas*, IV, 1151.

80. Onapiem

The Onapiem lived on the east side of the lower Colorado River, according to Joutel. Margery H. Krieger, "Onapiem Indians," in Tyler, et al. (eds.), *New Handbook of Texas*, IV, 1151.

81. Orcan

The Orcan lived on the west side of the lower Colorado, according to Joutel's list. However, Campbell locates the tribe near the Brazos or between the Brazos and the Trinity rather than west of the Colorado in "Orcan Indians," in Tyler, et al. (eds.), *New Handbook of Texas*, IV, 1165.

82. Otsoté (Osotouy)

Joutel visited the Otsoté village on July 24, 1687. The village was on the Arkansas River about five or six leagues northwest of the junction of the Arkansas and Mississippi rivers, according to Joutel. This location is apparently the same as that projected by Morris S. Arnold, who writes that the Osotouy village was about twenty-five miles upstream from the mouth of the Arkansas River. Arnold, *Colonial Arkansas*, 5, 6. Dickinson reports that the name Otsoté means "dwelling(s) in the bottom lands." See "Indian Signs on the Land," 144. The village had extensive fields of corn, beans, watermelon, and squash as well as orchards of fruit trees that extended for over five miles near the lower Arkansas River.

83. Palaquechare (Palaquesson)

Joutel met the Palaquechare on February 20, 1687, between the Colorado and the Brazos rivers about six to eight miles west of present-day Brenham. Joutel reported that they spoke a language and had an accent similar to the Cenis, and thus La Salle thought they were from the Cenis. According to Joutel, this tribe grew corn and beans. Campbell writes: "La Salle thought that their language resembled that of the Hasinais, whom he had previously visited, and this suggests that the Palaquesson [Palaquechare] Indians were Caddoans" in "Palaquesson Indians," in Tyler, et al. (eds.), *New Handbook of Texas*, V, 21. If this is correct, the report is further evidence that the Cenis or Tejas occupied an area considerably farther west than described by most Caddoan authorities such as Perttula. See *The Caddo Nation*, 8, fig. 1. The report also indicates that horticulture was practiced in the area between the Colorado and Brazos rivers, farther west than many geographers have projected.

84. Panequo

The Panequo lived west of the Colorado River crossing, according to Joutel's list. Margery H. Krieger, "Panequo Village," in Tyler, et al. (eds.), *New Handbook of Texas*, V, 35–36; and Thomas N. Campbell, "Panequo Indians," in Tyler, et al. (eds.), *New Handbook of Texas*, V, 35.

85. Pechir

The Pechir lived on the west side of the lower Colorado, according to Joutel.

86. Peinhoum

According to Joutel's list, the Peinhoum lived on the west side of the lower Colorado River. Margery H. Krieger, "Peinhoum Village," in Tyler, et al. (eds.), *New Handbook of Texas*, V, 129.

87. Peissaquo

The Peissaquo lived west of the lower Colorado River, according to Joutel. Margery H. Krieger, "Peissaquo Village," in Tyler, et al. (eds.), *New Handbook of Texas*, V, 130.

88. Petaro

The Petaro lived west of the lower Colorado River, according to Margry's version of Joutel's list. Citing unidentified records of the La Salle expedition, Campbell writes that the Petaro did not live west of the Colorado but rather well to the north and northeast of Matagorda Bay, "possibly between the Brazos and Trinity River," in "Petaro Indians," in Tyler, et al. (eds.), *New Handbook of Texas*, V, 166.

It should be noted that the tribal name is likely a mistake and there possibly was no such tribe. The manuscript copy of Joutel's journal in the Library of Congress does not include the name Petaro. The manuscript lists only nineteen tribes west of the Maligne or Colorado, whereas Margry (probably by mistake) gives the names of twenty tribes including the name Petaro. His apparent mistake has led to confusion and apparently mistaken reports of a tribe named Petaro, which Margry or a typesetter seems to have inadvertently inserted next to Petao.

89. Petao

The Petao lived west of the lower Colorado River, according to Joutel's list. Thomas N. Campbell, "Petao Indians," in Tyler, et al. (eds.), *New Handbook of Texas*, V, 165, 166.

90. Petsare

According to Joutel, the Petsare lived west of the lower Colorado River.

91. Piechar

According to Joutel, the Piechar lived on the west side of the lower Colorado River. Margery H. Krieger, "Piechar Village," in Tyler, et al. (eds.), *New Handbook of Texas*, V, 192.

92. Piohum

The Piohum lived on the west side of the lower Colorado, according to Joutel.

93. Quiouaha

The Quiouaha were enemies of the Caddo, according to Joutel. Thomas N. Campbell, "Quiouaha Indians," in Tyler, et al. (eds.), *New Handbook of Texas*, V, 394.

94. Quouan

According to Joutel's list, the Quouan lived east of the lower Colorado River.

95. Sacahaye

According to Joutel, the Sacahaye were allies of the Caddo. Swanton considered the tribe the same as the Soacatino. See *Source Materials on the Caddo Indians*, 9.

96. Serecoutcha

The Serecoutcha lived west of the lower Colorado River, according to Joutel. Margery H. Krieger, "Serecoutcha Indians," in Tyler, et al. (eds.), *New Handbook of Texas*, V, 977.

97. Shawnee*

The Shawnee Indians lived near the Great Lakes and the Ohio River valley and were allies of the French when La Salle explored the area during the 1670s and early 1680s. La Salle's native hunter and guide Nika, whom La Salle took with him from Canada to France and then to Texas, was a Shawnee. See the discussion of the Shawnee on the Ohio in Thomas E. Emerson and James A. Brown, "The Late Prehistory and Protohistory of Illinois," in J. Walthall and Thomas E. Emerson (eds.), *Calumet and Fleur-de-Lys*, 77–128.

98. Souanetto

The Souanetto were enemies of the Caddo, according to Joutel. Thomas N. Campbell, "Souanetto Indians," in Tyler, et al. (eds.), *New Handbook of Texas*, V, 1150.

99. Spichehat

According to Joutel's list, the Spichehat lived north and east of the lower Colorado River. Margery H. Krieger, "Spichehat Indians," in Tyler, et al. (eds.), *New Handbook of Texas*, VI, 27.

100. Tahiannihouq

The Tahiannihouq were enemies of the Caddo, according to Joutel's list. Thomas N. Campbell, "Tahiannihouq Indians," in Tyler, et al. (eds.), *New Handbook of Texas*, VI, 193.

101. Taneaho

The Taheaho were enemies of the Caddo, according to Joutel.

102. Tanico (Tonico, Tonica, Tonniqua?)

According to Joutel's list, the Tanico were allies of the Caddo. Joutel's Cahaynohoua guides informed him on July 11, 1687, that the Tanico had a village downstream on the lower Ouachita River and on July 18 Joutel's guides informed him that a Tanico village was downstream on the lower Saline River. Swanton notes that the Tanico may have been the same tribe as the Tunica, the tribe De Soto's chroniclers called the Cayas. *Source Materials on the Caddo Indians*, 9. Dickinson discusses the Tunica salt makers and traders on the Ouachita River in the late 1600s. See "Indian Signs on the Land," 156.

103. Tanquinno

The Tanquinno were allies of the Caddo, according to Joutel's list.

104. Tchanhe

The Tchanhe were enemies of the Caddo, according to Joutel. Thomas N. Campbell, "Tchanhié Indians," in Tyler, et al. (eds.), *New Handbook of Texas*, VI, 226.

105. Teao

La Salle met the friendly Teao tribe on February 16, 1687, near the north-eastern Fayette County boundary with Washington County. The Teao indicated with signs that they were allies of the Cenis and had visited the Jumano, who were their allies in West Texas.

106. Tehauremet

This tribe lived on the east side of the lower Colorado, according to Joutel. W. E. S. Dickerson, "Tehauremet Indians," in Tyler, et al. (eds.), *New Handbook of Texas*, VI, 235.

107. Teheaman

According to Joutel's list, the Teheaman lived on the east side of the lower Colorado River.

108. Tejas*

The Tejas Indians were the same tribe the French called the Cenis and the Spaniards referred to as the Hasinais. They were the Western Caddoan tribe whose principal residential area was eastern Houston County along San Pedro Creek but who also occupied the areas east of the lower Colorado and along the middle Brazos with farming communities and year-round hunting camps and parties. See Foster (ed.), *Texas and Northeastern Mexico*, 189. See also Cenis.

109. Telamene

The Telamene lived on the east side of the lower Colorado River, according to Joutel. "Telamene Indians," in Tyler, et al. (eds.), *New Handbook of Texas*, VI, 243.

110. Temerlouan

The Temerlouan were mentioned only in the testimony of the Talon brothers, who describe the tribe as living "farther up," perhaps in the northern part of Matagorda Bay, because the brothers mentioned that La Salle had taken some of the Temerlouan's canoes. The tribe was an enemy of the Toho, who were allies of the Cenis. "Voyage to the Mississippi through the Gulf of Mexico," 257.

111. Thoriman (Tourima)

Joutel visited the Thoriman village on the lower Arkansas River on July 27, 1687. Joutel says the village was about one or two gunshots (probably about one hundred to two hundred yards) from the Mississippi River. Dickinson discusses the uncertain translation of the tribal name in "Indian Signs on the Land," 144.

112. Tohaha

Joutel reported that the Tohaha lived to the west of the Maligne (or lower Colorado) River. Swanton considers them to be the same as the Toaa. *Source Materials on the Caddo Indians*, 29. Spanish expedition diarists recorded the Tohaha in the same location (between the lower Colorado and the Guadalupe) as Joutel. See Foster, *Spanish Expeditions into Texas*, 287, 288. Joutel's list placing the Tohaha on the west side of the Maligne River and Spanish reports of visiting Tohaha villages on the west side of the Colorado River support the contention that the Maligne was the present-day Colorado River. See also Thomas N. Campbell, "Tohaha Indians," in Tyler, et al. (eds.), *New Handbook of Texas*, VI, 516, 517.

113. Tohau (Toho)

According to Joutel's list, the Tohau lived west of the Maligne (or Colorado) River. The Talon brothers described them as close neighbors of the Cenis and like the Cenis, enemies of the tribes at the bay. "Voyage to the Mississippi through the Gulf of Mexico," 235–236. Spaniards later repeatedly reported encountering Toho west of the Colorado as well. This pattern also supports the contention that what the French called the Maligne River is the present-day Colorado. See Foster, *Spanish Expeditions into Texas*, 288. Thomas N. Campbell, "Toho Indians," in Tyler, et al. (eds.), *New Handbook of Texas*, VI, 517.

114. Tongigua (Tongingua)

Joutel visited the Tongigua, a Quapaw village, on the east side of the Mississippi on July 29, 1687. The village was about two leagues upriver from the mouth of the Arkansas River and on the opposite side. Dickinson reports that the name has been translated to mean "Little Town," which Joutel also suggested. See "Indian Signs on the Land," 144.

115. Tsepcoen (Tsepehoen)

The Tsepcoen lived on the west side of the lower Colorado River, according to Joutel's list. Campbell writes that records of La Salle's expedition indicate that the Tsepehoen (Tsepcoen) lived "well to the north or northeast of Matagorda Bay, probably near the Brazos River" rather than west of the Colorado River in "Tsepehoen Indians," in Tyler, et al. (eds.), *New Handbook of Texas*, VI, 581.

116. Tserabocherete

The Tserabocherete lived on the west side of the lower Colorado River, according to Joutel's list.

# *Appendix C*

Henri Joutel sailed with René-Robert Cavelier, Sieur de La Salle, from the
west coast of France to the island of Hispaniola and on to Matagorda Bay on the
Central Texas Gulf Coast, arriving in early January 1685. During the next two
years, Joutel remained as post commander at La Salle's settlement, Fort Saint
Louis, on a stream flowing into the bay, today called Garcitas Creek, while La
Salle and his men were engaged in expeditions to the southwest and northeast.
This itinerary commences on January 12, 1687, the date Joutel departed the
post with La Salle and a party of seventeen men to search for the Mississippi
River; the itinerary closes on August 2, the date Joutel's party of five departed
the Cappa Indian village on the middle Mississippi to go to Canada and return
to France.

Joutel, who was an experienced military man, estimated very accurately in
French leagues the distance traveled each day and also recorded compass readings of the direction followed. Route and other information from Anastase
Douay's account of the trip are used to check and supplement Joutel's itinerary
account. Although Douay did not keep daily notes of the journey, at the close of
his account he does give reasonably accurate estimates of the directions and distances traveled along major segments of the trip—between the bay and the
Cenis; from the Cenis to the Nasoni; from the Nasoni to the Cadodaquis; and
on to the Cahaynohoua and the Cappa.

The eleven detailed expedition route studies I conducted in preparing material for *Spanish Expeditions into Texas, 1689–1768* convinced me that diary or daily
itinerary information on the distance and direction traveled recorded by a careful and knowledgeable chronicler such as Joutel can form the basis of very reliable route projections. These projections need to be corrected and refined with
relevant information from other sources, such as accounts made by other expedition members, and need to be verified using information on the terrain; the
known location of native tribes, flora, and fauna along the route; and by employing aerial photographs, USGS maps, and on-site inspections of the expedition
area. All these supplemental sources were available and used for the route projection made in this study. I consider the location of the campsites to be accurate
generally to within three to five miles of the site given in the table and the map.

A comment is warranted regarding the correct conversion of French leagues
Joutel used into miles. In his exhaustive study of the linear league in North
America, Roland Chardon concludes that the customary French land league
(*lieue de poste*) was 2.422 miles and the customary Spanish land league (legua
legal) was 2.6160. For the purpose of this study, I have used the rounded figures
of 2.4 and 2.6 respectively. See Chardon, "The Linear League in North

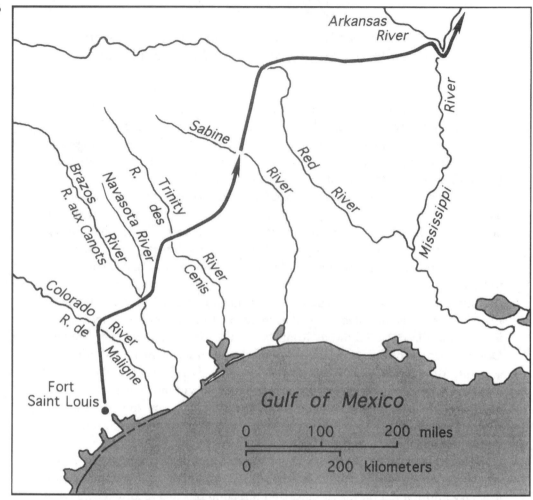

The La Salle expedition's route from Matagorda Bay to the Mississippi River

America," *Annals of the Association of American Geographers*, 70 (June, 1980), 129–153. In addition, McDermott, *Mississippi Valley French*, which was consulted in the translation of the text of Joutel's journal, offers the same conversion of a French post league as 2.4229 English miles (93).

As mentioned, heavier moisture was a principal hallmark of the Little Ice Age at latitudes as far south as the Gulf of Mexico, and its presence is fully supported by Joutel's commentary. The heavy winter rains and flooded conditions in the coastal prairies affected the selection of La Salle's route and forced his party to travel first directly north to the higher and drier elevations rather than travel directly northeast across the low wetland coastal prairie between the lower

Colorado and Brazos. In addition, Joutel reports that grass was plentiful for the large bison herds, that rivers and creeks were frequently flooded, and that heavy rains forced the delay of La Salle's party on five days of their twenty-two-day trip between the bay and the Colorado River crossing and on seven days of their thirty-three-day trip between the Colorado and the Brazos. Cibola hunters and traders from West Texas, who visited the area annually, confirmed Joutel's reports of heavy precipitation and flooding, especially during the winter months, in the river basin area between the Guadalupe and the Colorado. Charles W. Hackett (ed.), *Historical Documents relating to New Mexico, Nueva Vizcaya, and Approaches Thereto*, 251–281.

| Date | Distance in French leagues [Miles] | Direction | Summary of Movement [County] |
|------|-----------------------------------|-----------|------------------------------|
| Jan. 12 | 1.5 [3.6] | NNE | Camped near the location where meat was smoked called Le Boucan [Jackson]. |
| Jan. 13 | 3 [7.2] | Same | Crossed First Cane River (Lavaca) by raft, five leagues above the mouth of the river and one to two leagues above the junction of the Lavaca and the Second Cane River (the Navidad). Killed bison [Jackson]. |
| Jan. 14 | 3.5 [8.4] | N | Marched to west bank of Navidad (Second Cane River) at prior camp site. Met unidentified local Indians about five miles south of Edna [Jackson]. |
| Jan. 15 | 2–3 (est.) [4.8–7.2] | WNW | Moved slowly upriver along the west bank of the Navidad; killed bison [northern Jackson]. |
| Jan. 16 | 3 [7.2] | NW | Moved upriver [southern Lavaca]. |
| Jan. 17 | 3.5 [8.4] | Same | Moved upriver; saw vacant Indian huts [Lavaca]. |
| Jan. 18 | —— | —— | Rain delay. |
| Jan. 19 | 3 (est.) [7.2] | Upriver | Walked all day, but not much progress because of rain [Lavaca]. |

| Date | Distance in French leagues [Miles] | Direction | Summary of Movement [County] |
|------|------------------------------------|-----------|------------------------------|
| Jan. 20 | 2 [4.8] | Same | Continued slowly over wet terrain about four miles east of Hallettsville; killed bison [Lavaca]. |
| Jan. 21 | 1–2 [2.4–4.8] | NW | Crossed Second Cane River (Navidad), met Ebahamo Indians (friends of the East Texas Cenis and West Texas Jumano), and camped near river [Lavaca]. |
| Jan. 22 | —— | —— | Rain delay; killed bison. |
| Jan. 23 | —— | —— | Continued rain delay. |
| Jan. 24 | 1 (est.) [2.4] | N (est.) | Made slow progress [northern Lavaca]. |
| Jan. 25 | 1 (est.) [2.4] | Same | Continued with little progress because of rain [western Colorado]. |
| Jan. 26 | 1 (est.) [2.4] | Same | Crossed La Sablonnière (West Sandy Creek) and camped nearby. Douay reported that the party traveled about five leagues from the Second Cane River to the Sandy River [western Colorado]. |
| Jan. 27 | 3 (est.) [7.2] | Same | Moved upstream to the headwaters of Sandy Creek, a few miles northwest of Weimer. Douay reported that they traveled about eight leagues from Sandy Creek to the Robec River (Buckner's Creek) [southern Fayette]. |
| Jan. 28 | .5 [1.2] | Same | Moved to higher ground; rain delay [Fayette]. |
| Jan. 29 | 3 [7.2] | Same | Camped on right side of the Robec (Buckners Creek) about four miles southwest of La Grange [Fayette]. |
| Jan. 30 | —— | —— | Visited a nearby Indian camp to trade for horses; killed bison [Fayette]. |

| Date | Distance in French leagues [Miles] | Direction | Summary of Movement [County] |
|------|------------------------------------|-----------|------------------------------|
| Jan. 31 | ——— | ——— | Remained to visit unidentified friendly Indian camp [Fayette]. |
| Feb. 1 | ——— | ——— | Remained to hunt and trade with the Indians [Fayette]. |
| Feb. 2 | 1.5 [3.6] | N (est.) | Moved along and then crossed the Robec, which Joutel said was swift and would be good for mills, and moved across a wide prairie (possibly Rabb's Prairie) to the same crossing the Spanish later used on the Maligne (Colorado) River. Douay and Joutel, independently, reported traveling one and a half leagues from the Robec to the Maligne River crossing, about five miles north of La Grange [Fayette]. |

According to Joutel's account, from January 12 through February 2, La Salle's party traveled approximately thirty-five leagues or about eighty-three miles north from Fort Saint Louis to the higher, hillier, and drier ground near the crossing of the Maligne (Colorado) River. The straight-line measured distance from Matagorda Bay near Garcitas Creek to the customary crossing of the Colorado River about five miles north of La Grange is about eighty-three miles. See USGS *Beeville*, NH14-12, and USGS *Seguin*, NH14-9. La Salle's party remained on the west bank of the Colorado River for a week, until February 9, meeting and hunting with numerous Indian tribes, receiving information about local tribes, and constructing a canoe or boat for the crossing of the first large river encountered after leaving the bay area. The projected location of the Colorado crossing is at Rabb's Prairie near the shallow water, rock ledge fording area locally called the Ripples, which the Indians used as the customary ford on the lower Colorado and the Spaniards subsequently used as the Colorado crossing on the Camino Real.

| Date | Distance in French leagues [Miles] | Direction | Summary of Movement [County] |
|------|------------------------------------|-----------|------------------------------|
| Feb. 9 | .5–1 [1.2–2.4] | E (est.) | Crossed the Maligne (Colorado); camped about half a league beyond the river [Fayette]. |

| Date | Distance in French leagues [Miles] | Direction | Summary of Movement [County] |
|------|-----------------------------------|-----------|------------------------------|
| Feb. 10 | .5–1 [1.2–2.4] | Same | Traveled short distance [Fayette]. |
| Feb. 11 | ——— | ——— | Remained to hunt bison and smoke meat [Fayette]. |
| Feb. 12 | 2–3 [4.8–7.2] | E (est.) | Marched to a large creek named the Dure (Cummins Creek) about fifteen to eighteen miles northeast of La Grange [Fayette]. |
| Feb. 13 | ——— | ——— | Rain and storm delay [Fayette]. |
| Feb. 14 | 4 [9.6] | NW | Moved along the pathway La Salle previously used, probably following the left bank of Cummins Creek upstream [Fayette]. |
| Feb. 15 | 2–3 [4.8–7.2] | NNW, NNE, and E | Moved along a poor trail; passed the campsite La Salle used the previous autumn; camped near an Indian village [Fayette]. |
| Feb. 16 | 1.5 [3.6] | E | Continued through hilly woods to a Teao village about fifteen miles west of Brenham; traded for a horse [Washington]. |
| Feb. 17 | ——— | ——— | Delay for bison hunting [Washington]. |
| Feb. 18 | 1.5 (est.) [3.6] | ——— | Marched along a hilly pathway; good trail, probably along present-day Indian Creek [Washington]. |
| Feb. 19 | 1 [2.4] | ——— | Camped near the Palaquechare Indians, hunted bison with dogs [Washington]. |
| Feb. 20 | ——— | ——— | Visited the Palaquechare village where the Indians planted corn and beans, the first location with |

| Date | Distance in French leagues [Miles] | Direction | Summary of Movement [County] |
|------|-----------------------------------|-----------|------------------------------|
| | | | horticulture northeast of the bay area [Washington]. |
| Feb. 21 | 2 [4.8] | —— | Injured pack horse slowed trip [Washington]. |
| Feb. 22 | 1.5 [3.6] | NNE | Met a Cenis hunter whom La Salle recognized from his 1686 visit to the Cenis and confirmed Cenis occupation of the area for hunting [Washington]. |
| Feb. 23 | 1.5 [3.6] | NE | Passed the highest hill seen on the trip, moved to another campsite La Salle had used in 1686; near Brenham [Washington]. |
| Feb. 24 | —— | —— | Poor trails; remained nearby [Washington]. |
| Feb. 25 | —— | —— | Rain delay [Washington]. |
| Feb. 26 | —— | —— | Rain delay [Washington]. |
| Feb. 27 | —— | —— | Returned to Feb. 23 campsite [Washington]. |
| Feb. 28 | 1 (est.) [2.4] | —— | Met Cenis guide on pathway and camped again near highest hill [Washington]. |
| March 1 | 1 (est.) [2.4] | —— | Stopped at nearby Cenis camp; constructed canoe to cross a large ravine (perhaps New Year Creek) east of Brenham, a tributary of the Canoe (Brazos) River [Washington]. |

Between March 2 and March 5, La Salle's party, delayed by rain, completed the construction of a canoe.

| Date | Distance in French leagues [Miles] | Direction | Summary of Movement [County] |
|------|-----------------------------------|-----------|------------------------------|
| March 6 | 2 (est.) [4.8] | E (est.) | Crossed a ravine with the canoe and then |

| Date | Distance in French leagues [Miles] | Direction | Summary of Movement [County] |
|------|------------------------------------|-----------|------------------------------|
|  |  |  | disassembled it to use crossing the Canoe River; not much headway made [Washington]. |
| March 7 | 2 (est.) [4.6] | ——— | Continued slowly along route [Washington]. |
| March 8 | 2 (est.) [4.6] | ——— | Continued along route [Washington]. |
| March 9 | ——— | ——— | Rain delay. |
| March 10 | 1 (est.) [2.4] | ——— | Crossed creeks on felled trees [Washington]. |
| March 11 | ——— | ——— | Unaccounted. |
| March 12 | 1 (est.) [2.4] | ——— | Crossed creeks on felled trees [Washington]. |
| March 13 | 1 (est.) [2.4] | ——— | Camped on the west bank of the Canoe (Brazos) River, which Joutel described as wider and swifter than the Maligne (Colorado) [Washington]. |
| March 14 | 1 (est.) [2.4] | ——— | Crossed the Canoe River five to ten miles south of the city of Navasota and camped nearby [Grimes]. |
| March 15 | 1 (est.) [2.4] | ——— | Continued on the way with Cenis guides, but "not far" to new campsite [Grimes]. |
| March 16 | ——— | ——— | Remained near camp for return of the men La Salle sent "2 or 3 leagues" to recover a cache of corn La Salle left in storage near his 1686 river crossing area [Grimes]. |
| March 17 | ——— | ——— | Remained in camp waiting for men to return with bison meat [Grimes]. |
| March 18 | ——— | ——— | Remained in camp waiting for news [Grimes]. |

| Date | Distance in French leagues [Miles] | Direction | Summary of Movement [County] |
|------|-----------------------------------|-----------|------------------------------|
| March 19 | ——— | ——— | Joutel remained in camp; La Salle departed for the hunters' camp two to three leagues away near the crossing he had used in 1686, probably two to four miles north-north-east of Navasota; La Salle was shot and killed enroute [Grimes]. |
| March 20 | 5 [12] | N | Moved along the pathway with the Cenis guides, who accurately estimated that the principal Cenis village was about forty leagues away [Grimes]. |
| March 21 | 3 (est.) [7.2] | Same | Marched until noon; camped near a stream about fifteen to eighteen miles east of Bryan [Grimes]. |
| March 22 | ——— | ——— | Rain delay. |
| March 23 | 6 (est.) [14.4] | NE | Moved along the trail most of the day to a large unnamed creek (probably Bedias Creek); used a log to cross the creek and camped nearby [near the corner of Walker, Grimes, and Madison]. |
| March 24 | 4 (est.) [9.6] | NE | Marched through swampy country along a narrow trail [Madison]. |
| March 25 | ——— | ——— | Unrecorded. |
| March 26 | ——— | ——— | Unrecorded. |
| March 27 | 5 (est.) [12] | NE | Followed a dim trail and crossed two wide, deep, and dry ravines (probably Boggy and Keechi creeks) about ten to twelve miles southeast of Centerville [Leon]. |

| Date | Distance in French leagues [Miles] | Direction | Summary of Movement [County] |
|------|-----------------------------------|-----------|------------------------------|
| March 28 | 5 (est.) [12] | NE | Arrived at the customary crossing of the Cenis (Trinity) River [Leon]. Began constructing a canoe to use to cross the river and found the tree on which La Salle had carved the king's arms on his 1686 trip. |
| March 29 | 3 [7.2] | E (est.) | Crossed the Cenis (Trinity) River by canoe, probably near the Texas Highway 7 bridge, and camped nearby [Houston]. |
| March 30 | 6 (est.) [14.4] | —— | Met a Cenis on horseback who escorted Joutel's party to camp near the Cenis settlements about six to eight miles west of Weches [Houston]. |
| March 31 | 6 [14.4] | —— | Greeted by residents of the main Cenis village and then moved to the village a short distance east of the Neches River west of Alto [Cherokee]. |

According to Joutel, from February 9 through March 13, La Salle's party traveled between twenty-nine and thirty-two leagues or between 69.2 and 76.8 miles from the crossing of the Maligne (Colorado) to the Canoe (Brazos) River crossing. According to USGS *Seguin*, NH14-9, and USGS *Austin*, NH14-6, the straight-line measured distance between the Colorado crossing north of La Grange and the Brazos River crossing below its junction with the Navasota River is about sixty-two miles.

From March 14 through March 28, Joutel recorded that his party and their Cenis guides traveled about thirty leagues or seventy-two miles from the crossing of the Canoe (Brazos) River to the Cenis (Trinity) River crossing. According to USGS *Austin*, NH14-6, USGS *Beaumont*, NH15-4, and USGS *Palestine*, NH15-1, the straight-line distance between the two points is approximately sixty-two miles.

Between March 29 and March 31, Joutel marched with a Cenis escort about fifteen leagues or thirty-six miles from the Cenis (Trinity) River crossing to the Cenis village on present-day San Pedro Creek and then about two to three leagues beyond the Neches River. The distance is about thirty-six miles, according to USGS *Palestine*, NH15-1.

Although Douay did not keep a daily account of the distance and direction that La Salle's party traveled, he did estimate rather accurately that the party marched a total of one hundred leagues north-northeast and then east-northeast from the bay to the Cenis. Joutel recorded an accumulated total of 110 leagues for the same trip.

Joutel's party remained with the Cenis near the Neches River until May 26, when the small French party and their guides left the Cenis village area west of the Neches to visit the Nasoni. Joutel said members of his party estimated the distance from the Cenis to the Nasoni to be fifteen to eighteen leagues, which proved to be accurate.

| Date | Distance in French leagues [Miles] | Direction | Summary of Movement [County] |
|------|-----------------------------------|-----------|------------------------------|
| May 26 | 3 [7.2] | NE (est.) | Camped near the Neches River, near a log bridge La Salle built in 1686 [Houston]. |
| May 27 | 5 [12] | E | Continued with guides along the Caddo trail, camped about five miles east of Alto [Cherokee]. |
| May 28 | 4 [9.6] | NE | Continued along the trail [Nacogdoches]. |
| May 29 | 4 [9.6] | Same | Passed a Naodiche Indian village, received a guide, and camped at a Nasoni village near Cushing [Nacogdoches]. |

Between May 26 and May 29, Joutel recorded traveling about sixteen leagues or 38.4 miles from the Cenis village area near San Pedro Creek west of the Neches to the Nasoni village south of the Nacogdoches-Rush country line. The measured direct distance is approximately thirty-eight miles. Douay estimated the distance to be twenty-five leagues and the direction to be east-northeast.

Joutel and his party remained with the Nasoni from May 29 to June 13, when they departed with Nasoni guides to visit the Cadodaquis. The Nasoni accurately told Joutel that the Cadodaquis were forty to fifty leagues away.

| Date | Distance in French leagues [Miles] | Direction | Summary of Movement [County] |
|---|---|---|---|
| June 13 | 3 [7.2] | NE | Departed along a small pathway that the Nasoni guides had "followed since they were young," camped near Mount Enterprise [Rusk]. |
| June 14 | 4–5 [9.6–12] | Same | Continued along the pathway [southern Panola]. |
| June 15 | 5–6 [12–14.4] | Same | Continued along the pathway and camped a short distance north of Beckville; the Nasoni guide who had left the party returned [Panola]. |
| June 16 | 4 [9.6] | Same | Crossed a large river (probably the Sabine), which Joutel described as wide as the Cenis (Trinity) River, and continued their march; camped about eight miles south of Marshall [Harrison]. |
| June 17 | 3 [7.2] | Same | One man became ill; started at noon; followed a poor trail; camped near present-day Marshall [Harrison]. |
| June 18 | 5 [12] | Same | Crossed a deep river, probably Cypress Creek or Bayou near present-day Jefferson [Marion]. |
| June 19 | 5 (est.) [12] | Same | Crossed a large stream [Cass]. |
| June 20 | 4–5 [9.6–12] | NE | Continued through a swampy area and camped six to eight miles west of Atlanta [Cass]. |
| June 21 | 3 [7.2] | NNE (est.) | Continued along the way; crossed a river (probably the Sulphur River) [Bowie]. |

| June 22 | 5–6 [12–14.4] | Same | Continued along the route and camped six to eight miles west of Texarkana [Bowie]. |
| June 23 | 4–5 [9.6–12] | Same | Entered the Nasoni (Assoni) village on a branch of slough of the Red River, near the present-day location of McKinney Bayou, about one and a half leagues south of the Red River, northwest of Texarkana [Bowie]. |

From June 13 through June 23, Joutel traveled about fifty leagues or 120 miles from the Nasoni village in northern Nacogdoches County to the upper Nasoni village near the Red River, several miles west of the Great Bend. The straight-line measured distance between the two points is approximately 114 miles, according to USGS *Palestine*, NH15-1; USGS *Tyler*, NI15-10; and USGS *Texarkana*, NI15-7. Douay estimated the distance to be forty leagues and the direction to be north-northeast.

Joutel's party remained in the Nasoni village until June 30, when the French party left with guides to visit the Cahaynohoua (Cahinno) village near the Ouachita River on their way to visit the Cappa (Quapaw) near the junction of the Arkansas and Mississippi rivers.

| Date | Distance in French leagues [Miles] | Direction | Summary of Movement [County] |
| --- | --- | --- | --- |
| June 30 | 3.5 [8.4] | ESE | Moved one and a half leagues from the Nasoni village to the Red River, which Joutel described as wide as the Seine at Rouen; crossed the river with a canoe; and then moved two leagues eastward downstream and camped at the Cadodaquis village near Ogden [Little River, Ark.]. |
| July 1 | ——— | ——— | Waited on the Cahaynohoua guides who |

| Date | French leagues [Miles] | Distance in Direction | Summary of Movement [County] |
|------|------------------------|-----------------------|------------------------------|
| | | | were visiting the Cadodaquis and said they had visited the Cappa on the Mississippi [Little River, Ark.]. |
| July 2 | 4–5 [9.6–12] | NE | Continued along the north bank of the Red River near the Great Bend, camped on the right bank of the Little River near its junction with the Red River a few miles west of Fulton [Little River, Ark.]. |
| July 3 | 3 (est.) [7.2] | Same | Crossed the Little River with difficulty on a raft and camped near Sheppard [Hempstead]. |
| July 4 | 5–6 [12–14.4] | Same | Continued along the pathway with guides to a camp six to eight miles east of Hope [near the Nevada-Hempstead county line]. |
| July 5 | 5–6 [12–14.4] | Same | Crossed a stream and continued along the "common path," probably along the left bank of Terre Rouge Creek [Nevada]. |
| July 6 | 5–6 (est.) [12–14.4] | Same | Forded a river (probably the Little Missouri River) at 2 P.M.; crossed a smaller stream to meet a native reception party that escorted Jouel to the Cahaynohoua village a few miles west of Tate Bluff and the Ouachita River, about fifteen to twenty miles north-northwest of present-day Camden [Ouachita]. |

From June 30 to July 6, Joutel recorded that his party traveled approximately twenty-nine and a half leagues or 70.8 miles from the Nasoni village near the Red River northwest of Texarkana to the Cahaynohoua village near the Ouachita River, fifteen to twenty miles north of Camden. The measured distance is sixty-six miles, according to USGS *Texarkana*, NI15-7, and USGS *El Dorado*, NI15-8. Douay estimated the distance to be twenty-five leagues and the direction to be east-northeast.

Joutel's party remained in the Cahaynohoua village meeting leaders, exchanging gifts, and securing guides until July 11, when the French set out to visit the Cappas near the junction of the Arkansas and Mississippi rivers.

| Date | Distance in French leagues [Miles] | Direction | Summary of Movement [County] |
|------|------|------|------|
| July 11 | 5–6 [12–14.4] | E by N | Left the village with new guides, waded across a wide river (Ouachita River) about one and a half leagues east of the village and continued; a Tanico village was reported one day's travel downstream (perhaps near Camden); camped near Holly Springs [Ouachita]. |
| July 12 | 4 [9.6] | E | Continued along the route [near the corner of Dallas, Calhoun, and Ouachita]. |
| July 13 | 4.5 [10.8] | Same | Followed a winding route; camped a few miles south of Fordyce. |
| July 14 | 2 [4.8] | Same | Halted to hunt bison across a small river (probably Moro Creek) [Cleveland]. |
| July 15 | ——— | ——— | Remained at camp to smoke meat. |
| July 16 | 5 [12] | ——— | Continued along the winding route; camped near Orlando [Cleveland]. |
| July 17 | 5–6 [12–14.4] | E by S | Followed a winding way to "every point of the compass," perhaps moved |

| Date | French leagues [Miles] | Distance in Direction | Summary of Movement [County] |
|---|---|---|---|
| | | | lower in latitude to camp a few miles north of Warren [northern Bradley]. |
| July 18 | 3 [7.2] | Same | Waded with water waist-high across a broad river (probably the Saline River) and stopped to hunt bison; Indian guides visited the nearby Tanico village and returned to camp [Drew]. |
| July 19 | 5 [12] | ——— | Moved through heavy woods, camped near Montonger [Drew]. |
| July 20 | 5–6 [12–14.4] | NE | Crossed a large open plain [near the Drew–Lincoln county line]. |
| July 21 | 3 [7.2] | NE | Rain caused a late start; continued across the plain [Lincoln]. |
| July 22 | 2.5 [6] | ——— | Crossed a stream (perhaps Bayou Bartholomew) on a raft; saw alligators [Lincoln]. |
| July 23 | 5–6 [12–14.4] | ENE | Continued past Dumas, camped near Pea Ridge and the Arkansas River [Desha]. |
| July 24 | 5–6 (est.) [12–14.4] | ——— | Moved about three leagues to a river (Arkansas River) and downstream more than a league; crossed the river to reach a French post and village called Otsoté about five to six leagues northwest of the mouth of the Arkansas [Arkansas]. |

Joutel recorded traveling approximately fifty-nine leagues or 141.6 miles from the Cahaynohoua village on July 11 to the Arkansas River on July 24. Douay estimated the distance to be about sixty leagues and the direction to be east-northeast. According to USGS *El Dorado*, NI15-8, and USGS *Greenwood*, NI15-9, the direct line measurement between the two points is 105 miles. The party remained in the Otsoté village for two days (July 25 and 26) and then proceeded downriver on the Arkansas with guides on July 27.

| Date | Distance in French leagues [Miles] | Direction | Summary of Movement [County] |
|---|---|---|---|
| July 27 | 5–6 [12–14.4] | Downriver on Arkansas | Moved by dugout canoe to a second village, Thoriman, about the distance of one or two gunshots from the Mississippi River [Arkansas]. |
| July 28 | ——— | ——— | Continued meetings. |
| July 29 | 2 [4.8] | Upriver on Mississippi | Punted upriver on the Mississippi to the third village, Tongigua, on the east side of the Mississippi River a few miles northwest of Rosedale, Mississippi [Bolivar County, Miss.]. |
| July 30 | 8 [19.2] | Upriver on Mississippi | Punted upriver to the fourth village, Cappa, on the west side of the Mississippi southeast of Deerfield [Arkansas County, Ark.]. |

Joutel's party met with the Cappa until August 2, when Joutel and his party departed with guides upriver to winter at Fort Saint Louis on the Illinois River. The next spring they visited French officials in Canada and returned to France.

# Translator Notes

This translation attempts to be as true as possible to Joutel's very words. In places, it has been necessary to say in so many words what Joutel is saying or appears to be saying. We have not been true to Joutel's punctuation, as his nineteenth-century editor, Pierre Margry, was not. We have liberally reconstructed sentences and created new sentences, freely designated phrases as parenthetical and subdivided clauses with semicolons.

As clear and descriptive as Joutel's account is, there are areas where clarification is required. The implied noun, for instance, has been frequently substituted for the pronoun, or the word "thing" sometimes, where it aids the reader to recall the reference. Extraneous or repetitive phrases like "sort of," "that is to say," "the said," "the one named" often have been deleted. We also have deleted redundant sentences such as: "In short, the day was occupied with what I have mentioned."

Joutel switches into the present tense in descriptive passages denoting an ongoing condition. We have done the same. The soil "is" good and very fine corn "grows" there. The Indians "paint" their faces. We have occasionally changed the imperfect tense to the past conditional. Where Joutel uses the verb "to be" to reinforce an earlier verb, we may repeat that verb.

Joutel's inconsistencies in spellings of names have been made consistent. Where we know something to be other than how he identifies it, for instance, "ox (*boeuf*)/buffalo," "walnut/pecan," "eagle/vulture," "reed/cane," we have correctly identified it. *Sauvages* ("savages") we call "Indians" or "natives." The adjective *belle* is occasionally taken for its less common meaning of "large" or "lofty." Certain French terms we have kept in the text, italicizing them, either because we cannot translate them or, more often, because the French term works best, for instance, *sagamité* ("cornmeal porridge"). Most place names remain in French. Nautical directions are literally translated followed by the common English term in brackets.

René-Robert Cavelier, Sieur de La Salle, is variously referred to as the "Sieur de La Salle," "La Salle," or "the gentleman." Other named persons appear sometimes with the surname preceded by the title, sometimes without the title. La Salle's brother, Jean Cavelier, is usually referred to as "the Abbé."

Brackets occur often and are generally used when Joutel's words need elaboration. They are used to identify places, people, and dates; or to define terms; or to provide further explanation. They also are used to correct clear errors. When we have completed a thought, we have bracketed it in some cases unless it is obvious that it qualifies for the "in so many words" approach. For the most part, we do not bracket noun/pronoun substitutions or corrections of subject/verb agreement.

Although this is a translation of Pierre Margry's 1878 printed edition of Joutel's journal, we studied the transcription copy of the original journal held in

328 the Library of Congress, concentrating on the places where the word, phrase, or situation in Margry raised a question. We did find discrepancies and where the original version makes more sense, we have made the substitution and noted it.

Margry's editorial flourishes are evident in Chapter X, the most dramatic chapter. He has added transitional phrases such as "that night, L'Archevêque recounted" and "as for Duhaut," and inserted phrases such as "two days" and "to our enemies." He has embellished a few passages with feelings of abandonment, sadness, resentment, or fear. For instance, the sentence "All this passed through their minds again" has become "These old grievances rose in their hearts." Whole passages have been repositioned within the text, most notably the ones concerning the Indians' reaction when they notice that members of the party are missing. Margry's edits do, however, largely enhance and clarify what stands as a riveting and well-executed account.

# Index

(Illustrations are indicated by bold-faced page numbers)